PREVIOUS VOLUMES OF THE SURVEY OF LONDON

Norwood Cemetery and St. Luke's Church, c. 1840

SURVEY OF LONDON

GENERAL EDITOR: F. H. W. SHEPPARD

VOLUME XXVI

The Parish of
St. Mary Lambeth

Part Two
Southern Area

THE ATHLONE PRESS

UNIVERSITY OF LONDON

Published for the London County Council

1956

Published by
THE ATHLONE PRESS
UNIVERSITY OF LONDON
at 2 Gower Street, London, w.c.1

Distributed by Constable & Co. Ltd.
12 Orange Street, London, w.c.2

U.S.A.
John de Graff Inc.
31 East 10th Street,
New York, 3

Printed in Great Britain by
WESTERN PRINTING SERVICES LTD
BRISTOL

Preface

IN the last quarter of the 19th century London was expanding with unprecedented speed, and many buildings of great architectural interest were destroyed to make way for street after street of new surburban houses. In 1894 the public conscience was stirred by the demolition of the Old Palace of Bromley, a Jacobean house in Poplar whose site was later used for the erection of a school. As a result of this incident a voluntary committee, known as the Committee for the Survey of the Memorials of Greater London, was formed to compile a register or survey of whatever was still left of architectural interest in the eastern districts of London. In 1897 the London County Council agreed to print the first volume of the Survey which was published in 1900. Subsequently a formal agreement was made with the London Survey Committee by which the Committee and the Council prepared alternate volumes and the Council printed them all. The area to be covered was enlarged to include the whole of the administrative County of London.

Twenty-four volumes of the Survey were published between 1900 and 1952, each volume dealing with all or part of a parish; independently of the Council the Survey Committee also published a number of monographs dealing with individual buildings of architectural importance. After the publication in 1952 of the fourth and last volume dealing with the parish of St. Pancras the Survey Committee reluctantly decided that it could not undertake to prepare any more parish volumes, and the Council therefore decided to complete the Survey alone. The management of the undertaking was placed in the care of the Architectural and Historical Buildings Sub-Committee of the Town Planning Committee, and a General Editor was appointed in 1954. The thanks of the Council are due to Mr. J. H. MacDonnell, Mr. Ian L. Phillips, Mr. T. F. Reddaway, M.A., F.S.A., and Mr. John Summerson, C.B.E., F.S.A., who as co-opted members have provided the Sub-Committee with their expert knowledge.

This new phase of the Survey's development has presented the Council with a useful opportunity to take stock of the present position of London's architectural inheritance. During the war many buildings of great interest were damaged or destroyed, and the rebuilding schemes which are proceeding in many parts of the County threaten many more. The completion of the Survey, whose main purpose is to record the ancient fabric of London, is therefore a matter of great urgency. At the same time the Council has decided that the Survey must take serious note of 19th century buildings, to which many students of the history of architecture have paid increasing attention in recent years; and this decision has meant a considerable enlargement of the scope of the Survey, particularly in the outer areas of London such as southern Lambeth.

The problem facing the Council is therefore how best to make use of its necessarily limited resources for historical and architectural research. It has decided that while the publication of the Survey should continue with all possible speed, the recording of threatened buildings in those parts of the County which have not yet been covered must be undertaken while there is still time. The material assembled in this way will be incorporated in future volumes.

In order that as much information as possible may be included in the Survey, the format of the volumes has been modified to prevent their becoming unduly expensive or unwieldy. Most of the text has been set in double columns, and buildings of secondary importance have been illustrated with smaller photographs than have hitherto been used. An introduction prefixed to each future volume will provide a general view of the historical development and architectural wealth of the area under consideration.

The present volume completes the Survey of the parish of Lambeth. Relatively little building took place in the area before about 1800, and the volume is therefore largely concerned with various aspects of surburban expansion in the 19th century. The important part played in this process by the Manors, particularly those of Kennington, Vauxhall and Lambeth, has been emphasized.

The Council is much indebted to the Secretary of the Duchy of Cornwall for kindly permitting members of the Council's staff to examine the exceptionally interesting records of the Duchy relating to the Manor of Kennington; much valuable help has also been received from members of the Duchy Office staff. The Church Commissioners granted similar facilities for the study of their voluminous records, many of which relate to the Manors of Vauxhall and Lambeth. The Dean and Chapter of Canterbury, the British Transport Commission and the Royal Institute of British Architects kindly allowed the Council's officers access to their records. Much use has also been made of the Inclosure Award, Rate Books, Vestry Minutes and deeds in the possession of the Lambeth Borough Council, and of the large collection of records in the Minet Public Library. To all these bodies, and to the clergy and ministers of churches and chapels, and the owners or custodians of property deeds, the Council tenders its grateful acknowledgment.

This volume has been prepared under the general editorship of Mr. F. H. W. Sheppard, M.A., Ph.D., who has received much assistance from Mrs. Marie P. G. Draper, B.A., and Miss P. M. Barnes, B.A., of the Clerk's Department, and from the officers of the Athlone Press of the University of London, to whom the publication of the Survey has been entrusted. Valuable contributions on the architectural aspects of the volume have been received from Messrs. W. A. Eden, M.A., F.S.A., F.R.I.B.A., W. Ison, F.S.A., and K. S. Mills, A.R.I.B.A., A.M.P.T.I., of the Architect's Department; many of the photographs are the work of the Photographic Unit of the Architect's Department.

County Hall,   RICHARD EDMONDS
London   Chairman of the Town Planning Committee.

Contents

PLATES *and* INDEX MAP *at end*

EDITORIAL NOTE

The numbers in the margins of Chapters I to VII
correspond with the numbers on the Index Map
in the pocket of the end board, and serve to
identify the position of individual buildings

List of Plates

(Unless otherwise stated all the Plates are photographs whose copyright belongs to the London County Council)

List of Figures in the Text

General Introduction

THE ancient parish of Lambeth was nearly six miles long from north to south, while its average width from east to west was only about one mile. It stretched from the River Thames opposite the Temple gardens to the wooded heights bordering the great parish of Croydon. The earliest development in the parish took place to the north of Kennington Lane, and this area has already been described in volume XXIII of the *Survey of London*. The present volume describes the remainder of the parish, and includes part of Kennington and Vauxhall, as well as South Lambeth, Stockwell, Brixton, Denmark Hill, Herne Hill, Tulse Hill and West Norwood.

The expansion of London south of the Thames did not begin in earnest until the second half of the 18th century, and in Lambeth south of Kennington Common (now Park) there were few buildings before about 1800. In 1801 the population of the whole ancient parish was 27,985; in 1901 that of the Metropolitan Borough of Lambeth, whose boundaries differed from those of the ancient parish only in relatively small degree, was 301,895.[1] The development of the area under review was therefore largely concentrated within the span of a single century. Owing to the great length of the parish from north to south many of the rapidly changing phases of London's expansion are illustrated in Lambeth. Although few of its buildings are of great architectural distinction, the area does contain many churches, schools, institutions and domestic buildings which are of considerable interest to the student of 19th century architecture.

Geographically Lambeth falls into three parts: the northern area close to the river (most of which has already been dealt with in volume XXIII), a flat central plain comprising South Lambeth, Stockwell and part of Brixton, and the rising ground to the south, where Herne Hill, Brixton Hill, Tulse Hill, Knight's Hill and Gipsy Hill provide a pleasant contrast with the level expanse of the Thames basin. Down the length of the parish ran the River Effra (also known in its northern reaches as Vauxhall Creek) whose tributaries rose in Norwood and joined together to flow beside Croxted Road and Brixton Road, part of which was sometimes called the Washway, as far as Kennington. There it divided to the west of the Oval and ran in two separate streams into the Thames.

The land upon which the buildings of modern Lambeth stand formerly comprised ten manors, whose Lords, acting either individually or through the manorial courts, could even in the 19th century play an important part in controlling the tenure and use of the land. The manors are therefore the natural starting-point for a survey of the fabric of the area. The three most important manors were those of Lambeth, Kennington and Vauxhall. Except during the Commonwealth period, none of these has been in private hands since the early Middle Ages, and their long unbroken continuity of administration has probably been the cause of the safe preservation of the records from which so much of the information contained in this volume has been drawn.

Of these three manors, that of Lambeth was much the largest in area. It stretched from the timber-yards bordering the Thames in the north to the Vicar's Oak at Sydenham in the south, and contained 1,474 acres.[2] The manor became the property of the Archbishop of Canterbury in 1197,[3] and it remained (except during the Commonwealth) in the hands of his successors until its administration was taken over by the Ecclesiastical (now Church) Commissioners in 1862. In 1806 an Inclosure Act[4] was obtained, and the award of 1810 provided *inter alia* for the inclosure of Rush Common and Norwood Common.

Kennington Manor consisted of a large area on either side of Kennington Lane, and several detached portions to the north in Lambeth Marsh. The latter and all of the main parcel on the north side of Kennington Lane have already been described in volume XXIII of the *Survey of London*; the rest of the southern piece falls within the area covered by the present volume. In 1337 Edward III granted the Manors of Kennington and Vauxhall to Edward, Earl of Chester and Duke of Cornwall, commonly known as the Black Prince, to be held by him and his heirs, eldest sons of the Kings of England and Dukes of Cornwall; the grant provided that if any such duke should die without a son to whom the duchy might descend, the Manors should revert to the King until a son should be born who was heir-apparent to the realm.[5] Except during the Commonwealth, this grant has remained operative ever since, and the Manor of Kennington is administered with other estates belonging to the Duchy of Cornwall.

Until the close of the 13th century the area now known as Vauxhall seems to have been part of a large manor called South Lambeth Manor. In 1293 the latter and the Manor of "la Sale Faukes" came into the hands of Edward I.[6] No further mention has been found of South Lambeth Manor, which seems to have been divided into two parts known as Vauxhall and Stockwell Manors. In 1337 Edward III granted the former to the Black Prince, who in 1362 granted it to the Prior and Convent of Christ Church, Canterbury.[7] After the Dissolution Vauxhall Manor was granted to the Dean and Chapter of Canterbury; its administration was taken over by the Ecclesiastical Commissioners in 1862.[8] The core of the manor lay between Kennington and Stockwell in the areas loosely known as Vauxhall and South Lambeth, but there were large pieces of copyhold and common land in Streatham and Mitcham.

The other part of South Lambeth Manor, Stockwell, seems to have acquired manorial status at the end of the 13th century, but a connection with Vauxhall Manor was retained until as late as the early 19th century.[9] Since the early 14th century Stockwell Manor has been in private hands except for a short period in the 16th century when it was held by the Crown.[10] The manor lay in Stockwell and Brixton, and stretched south along the west side of Brixton Hill.

There were also six lesser manors, three of which appear to have had tenuous connections with Lambeth Manor. One-third of the Manor of Milkwell, which lay in Lambeth and Camberwell, was subject to a quit-rent of 6s. 8d. per annum payable to Lambeth Manor;[11] the small Manor of Heathrow or Knight's in Brixton was subject to a similar rent of 12d.,[12] while Levehurst Manor on the borders of Lambeth and Streatham owed 10s.[13] A fourth, Lambeth Wick Manor, was from the end of the 12th century owned by the Archbishops of Canterbury, who between 1480 and the beginning of the 19th century leased it for short terms.[14] Only two of these so-called manors in the area under review seem to have had no connection with Lambeth Manor—Bodley, Upgrove and Scarlettes, which occupied the area now called Tulse Hill and belonged to the Hospital of St. Thomas the Martyr in Southwark from the 14th century until the Dissolution;[15] and Leigham Court, the bulk of which lay in Streatham and was alleged to have been part of the ancient demesne of the Crown.[16]

Thus of the ten manors in Lambeth, four (Lambeth, Lambeth Wick, Kennington and Vauxhall) were held by Lords acting as custodians for their successors, and managed by courts which were still active enough to exercise a very important influence over 18th and 19th century building development. In manors of this type Acts of Parliament authorizing the Lord to adapt the ancient customs to the needs of developers were frequently obtained. In Stockwell and Leigham Court Manors it is doubtful if courts were held as late as the 19th century; in the Manors of Milkwell, Levehurst, Heathrow and Bodley, Upgrove and Scarlettes, courts may never have been held at any date, the Lords (or more accurately owners) either farming them themselves or leasing them.

But despite the wide variety of meaning which the term "manor" could imply, particularly in the 18th and 19th centuries, the manors still exercised an exceedingly important influence on the development of their areas. In carefully managed manors like Kennington or Lambeth the length of the leases or the licences to demise granted by the Lord or the scale of fines payable upon the admittance of a new copyholder, affected the type of buildings erected; while in the case of a small manor where no courts were held the enterprise or indifference of the owner, his financial position and even his testamentary dispositions could all affect the character of development.

Apart from the Turnpike Trusts the normal machinery of public administration played little part in the development of Lambeth or many other parts of London until the second half of the 19th century. The Open Vestry of Lambeth obtained a Local Act in 1810,[17] and it adopted Sturges Bourne's Act for poor law purposes between 1819 and 1827.[18] In the first half of the century the lighting of the parish was managed by nine separate local Trusts, while the road from Herne Hill to the Half Moon at Dulwich was lit by private subscription of the inhabitants.[19] In the second half of the 19th century, when the Metropolitan Board of Works and the Vestry began to control building development, much of the new character of the district had already been determined by other factors to which attention must now be turned.

ROADS AND RAILWAYS

In South London during the first half of the 19th century the course of the parish and Turnpike roads was often the deciding factor in determining where and when new houses should be built; in the second half of the century this rôle was to a great extent taken over by the railways.

In the area under review the two main arteries of communication were the road now known as Kennington Park Road and Clapham Road, and the road now known as Brixton Road and Brixton Hill (fig. 1). The former was part of Stane Street, which ran from the East Gate of Chichester through Pulborough, Dorking and Tooting to London. The date of its construction is uncertain, but it is likely that it was in use in A.D. 70. No trace of the Roman surface has been found in Lambeth, but there can be little doubt that it ran along Kennington Park Road and Clapham Road.[20]

Brixton Road and Brixton Hill may also have been part of a Roman road. Recent

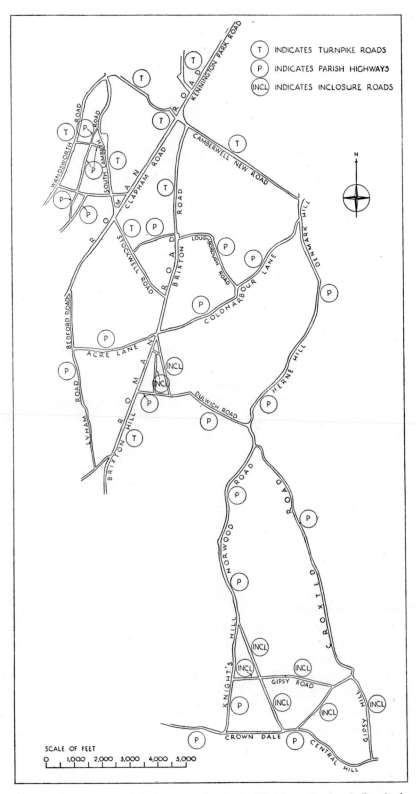

Fig. 1. Principal roads in southern Lambeth. Wandsworth, South Lambeth, Clapham, Stockwell, Kennington Park and Brixton Roads and Brixton Hill were all parish highways before being placed under the authority of Turnpike Trustees

research has shown that a Roman road ran from Brighton or Portslade through the Weald to the Caterham Valley gap, and then on to Croydon and Streatham, whence it either went straight on to Stane Street, or followed the modern Brixton Hill and Brixton Road to form a junction at or near Kennington Park.[21] Traces of this road have been found in Sussex and Surrey, and in their *History of Surrey* (1814) Manning and Bray thought that "it took its course by *Old Croydon* and the West side of *Broad Green*, where it is still visible. . . ."[22] From Croydon it probably continued up London Road to Streatham, a name suggesting the existence of a Roman road.[23] From there its course can only be conjectured, but Brixton Hill, which was formerly known as Brixton Causeway, and Brixton Road may well have been the northern continuation of this road.

In 1717 an Act of Parliament[24] set up Turnpike Trustees for the roads from the Stones End in Blackman Street, Southwark, to East Grinstead, Sutton and Kingston. The East Grinstead road comprised what is now Kennington Park Road, Brixton Road and Brixton Hill, and ran on through Streatham and Croydon; the Sutton and Kingston roads comprised Clapham Road and Wandsworth Road respectively. The Trustees were also responsible for a branch road from Vauxhall to Brixton, now South Lambeth Road and Stockwell Road.[25] In 1751 the Trustees were authorized to make a new road (now Kennington Road) joining Kennington Common with the south end of the road made by the Commissioners for building Westminster Bridge.[26] In 1786 these Trustees and the Trustees for the Southwark to Highgate (Sussex) roads became known as the Trustees of the Surrey New Roads.[27] Finally the system of Turnpike roads in the southern part of Lambeth was rounded off in 1818 by the formation of Harleyford Road, Harleyford Street and Camberwell New Road,[28] which were intended as approach roads to Vauxhall Bridge, opened in 1816.

Besides the great Turnpike roads there were also a number of ancient and often winding country lanes, which were repaired by the parish Surveyors of the Highways. Roque's Map of the Environs of London (1741–5) shows, amongst others, Coldharbour Lane (called Camberwell Lane) connecting Camberwell and Brixton, while Acre Lane (whose western extremity is now called Clapham Park Road) led on to Clapham. "The Back Road" ran along what is now Bedford Road and Lyham Road, forming a short-cut between Clapham and the top of Brixton Hill. Water Lane has been straightened at the west end and is now called Brixton Water Lane and Dulwich Road. Camberwell and Dulwich were connected by what are now Denmark Hill and Herne Hill. To the south ran "Crocksed" or "Crocksted" Lane, which eventually split into a number of tracks in Norwood, and "Night's Hill Lane", which followed the winding course of what is now Norwood Road and Knight's Hill. The only road running east and west in the south part of the parish was provided by what are now Streatham Common North, Crown Lane, Crown Dale, Central Hill and Westow Hill. Here and there, at Brixton or along the west side of Norwood Common, groups of cottages or an occasional farm stood beside these old roads. Often there was a tavern, but of this humble and rural type of building there is now no trace save the memory preserved by the name of an old inn, such as the Horns at Kennington.

Apart from the Turnpike roads and the ancient parish highways, almost all the roads of modern Lambeth were made in the 19th century. The first important extension of the

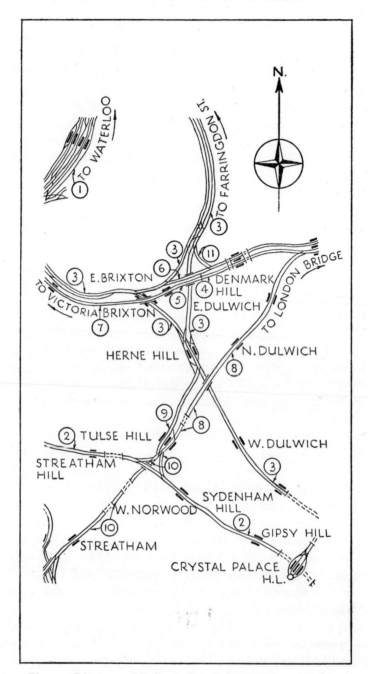

Fig. 2. Diagram of Railway Development (not to scale)

1. London and South Western 1848
2. West End of London and Crystal Palace 1856
3. London Chatham and Dover 1862–3
4. London Brighton and South Coast 1866
5. London Brighton and South Coast 1866
6. London Chatham and Dover 1866
7. London Chatham and Dover 1867
8. London Brighton and South Coast 1868
9. London Chatham and Dover 1869
10. London Brighton and South Coast 1871
11. Crystal Palace and South London 1872

system was made in 1810 when the Lambeth Manor Inclosure Commissioners provided for a number of new roads in the southern part of the parish. The purpose of most of these roads was to supply access to the new inclosures on Rush Common and Norwood Common. They included what are now Effra Road and St. Matthew's Road, Brixton, and Norwood High Street, Elder Road, Chapel Road, Gipsy Road, Salter's Hill, and Gipsy Hill. The occupiers of land and houses on the old Rush Common and Norwood Common were made responsible for the maintenance of these new roads; they were to form themselves into two distinct committees, appoint officials and meet the cost of the necessary work by levying a rate upon themselves not exceeding one shilling in the pound, and by collecting tolls from the users of the roads. In 1823 all these roads were taken over by the parish Surveyors of the Highways.[29]

Almost all the other roads of modern Lambeth were in the first place estate roads whose original purpose was to facilitate the development of the area through which they ran. After the death of Lord Thurlow in 1806, his Trustees obtained an Act of Parliament[30] permitting them, *inter alia*, to grant long leases on parts of his large estates in Lambeth and Streatham, and to build certain roads which included those now known as Palace Road and Canterbury Grove. A few years later Dr. Edwards, the owner of Tulse Hill Farm, built the roads now known as Tulse Hill and Upper Tulse Hill. Very gradually these estate roads provided communication across the fields which had been left untouched by the early ribbon-development along the old highways; ultimately the parish took them over, and the complicated street-system of modern Lambeth emerged.[31]

In the second half of the 19th century the railways played the decisive part in determining the type of development which overwhelmingly preponderates in the area today. In the first half of the century large houses, often with a coach-house attached, were built along the Turnpike and parish roads; many of these houses can still be seen in Brixton and Clapham Roads. This type of development continued along some of the earlier estate roads like Tulse Hill and Upper Tulse Hill. But the railways enabled a less prosperous and far more numerous section of the population to live in much greater comfort in the suburbs and travel to and from their work.

The first railway in the southern part of Lambeth (apart from a short piece of the Waterloo extension of the London and South Western Railway which was authorized in 1845, see fig. 2, no. 1) was the West End of London and Crystal Palace Railway, which was authorized in 1853 and opened in 1856[32] (fig. 2, no. 2). It ran from Battersea through Clapham, West Norwood and Gipsy Hill to the Crystal Palace, and continued on to a junction with the London, Brighton and South Coast Railway north of Norwood Junction. Next, and far more important, came the London, Chatham and Dover Railway, a late-comer, which started in the provinces as the East Kent Railway and shouldered its way into London through the territory of the South Eastern and the London, Brighton and South Coast Railways. In 1860 the London, Chatham and Dover Company's trains first reached Victoria by using lines owned by the Mid-Kent, West End of London and Crystal Palace, and Victoria Station and Pimlico Railways.[33] But in the same year the famous "Metropolitan Extensions" Act[34] granted the London, Chatham and Dover Company greatly improved access to London. From Penge Junction a line ran through Herne Hill to Farringdon Street, with a junction at Smithfield with the Metropolitan;

another line branched off from Herne Hill to the Victoria Station and Pimlico line at Battersea; finally a spur from Brixton to Loughborough Junction connected these two arms and completed a triangle of lines which formed the foundation of the complicated maze of railways in the area (fig. 2, no. 3).

By 1863 all the lines authorized by the Metropolitan Extensions Act had been opened.[35] In the same year a Select Committee of the House of Lords published a report on Metropolitan Railway Communication. The opening of the Metropolitan Railway between Edgware Road and Farringdon Street had just inaugurated a new era in London transport, and the report therefore stated that it was not desirable to bring any more main-line termini any further into London, that in the construction of any new railways in London, subways, tunnels or covered ways were to be preferred, and that girdle railways were needed to connect the existing main-line termini.[36]

With this report in mind, Parliament rejected several schemes for more lines in Lambeth. A most complicated arrangement was eventually approved in the sessions of 1863 and 1864, whereby Victoria and London Bridge were connected by direct lines above ground, the cost and the marshy character of part of the area presumably making covered ways impracticable. The Lambeth portions of these lines were built conjointly by the London, Brighton and South Coast and the London, Chatham and Dover Companies[37] (fig. 2, nos. 4–7). All these lines were opened by 1867, though not without mishap, for in 1864 nineteen newly-completed arches at Brixton collapsed when the centering was removed.[38] They also involved the construction of two high bridges over the Herne Hill to Brixton and Herne Hill to Loughborough Junction arms of the Metropolitan Extension, the latter having only been completed in 1863. In 1872 another spur, built by the Crystal Palace and South London Junction Railway and involving the erection of three iron bridges and the demolition of a number of houses in Flaxman Road, joined Loughborough Junction with the line to Peckham[39] (fig. 2, no. 11).

Apart from the widening of existing tracks, only two more lines were built in the southern part of Lambeth. The London, Chatham and Dover Company built a line from Herne Hill to Tulse Hill which was opened in 1869 and used by the London and South Western Company for a service between Wimbledon and Ludgate Hill[40] (fig. 2, no. 9). The London, Brighton and South Coast Company built a line from Peckham to Streatham, with spurs to the old West End of London and Crystal Palace Railway; the northern part of this line was opened in 1868, and the remainder in 1871[41] (fig. 2, nos. 8 and 10).

The 1860s saw the railways take their modern course through Lambeth; horse-drawn trams soon provided another means of travel. In 1861 G. F. Train opened a line from the south end of Westminster Bridge to Kennington Park, and within a few months his trams were carrying over half a million passengers a month. Legal difficulties ensued, however, and the line was closed soon afterwards.[42] By 1870, however, trams were running down Westminster Bridge Road and Kennington Road to the junction of Brixton Hill and Brixton Water Lane; another route ran down Clapham Road. Within twenty years most of the main roads of the area were served by trams,[43] and this tremendous expansion was matched by the development of buses, whose numbers nearly trebled in the whole of London between 1871 and 1898.[44]

The last stage in the growth of suburban transport in Lambeth was reached with the opening of the City and South London Railway in 1890. This was the first tube railway in London, and ran from King William Street to Stockwell. It was electrically operated, with twin tunnels never less than forty-five feet below ground level. As usual with a new form of suburban transport, the line attracted a constantly increasing number of passengers, and the King William Street terminus was incorporated into the Bank Station; at the south end, the line was extended to Clapham Common. In 1922 the tunnels were enlarged and the line was subsequently absorbed into the Northern tube line, which ultimately reached out above ground to Morden.[45]

With these new means of travel the development of Lambeth, and of many other parts of London, was jolted on to a new course in the second half of the 19th century, and undistinguished speculation provided thousands of homes for families which could never have afforded the more spacious suburban houses of the pre-railway age.

THE PATTERN OF DEVELOPMENT

Apart from a thin line of buildings along the riverside there was little development in Lambeth until the middle of the 18th century. The opening of Westminster Bridge in 1750, the authorization of Kennington Road in 1751, and the building of Blackfriars Bridge and its approach roads between 1760 and 1769 provided easy access to Kennington from Westminster and the City. In 1776 William Clayton, the lessee of the Kennington Manor demesnes, obtained an Act of Parliament[46] enabling him to grant building leases, and in 1791 the Council of the Duchy of Cornwall decided that copyholders might be granted licences to demise their property for 99 years.[47] In the eastern part of the Manor houses soon began to spring up in considerable numbers. West of Kennington Road development did not make much progress until the end of the 18th century; the area remained relatively inaccessible from London and Westminster until the opening of Vauxhall Bridge in 1816, and the building of Harleyford Road and Camberwell New Road in 1818.

Vauxhall and South Lambeth were also too remote to be much affected by the opening of Westminster and Blackfriars Bridges and their approach roads. The existing roads were considered adequate, and no new ones were authorized until the early 19th century. Moreover the different types of land tenure which persisted for centuries in the Manor of Vauxhall, the small fields and the impossibility of obtaining enough contiguous land to make development worth while, all hindered the making of side roads and the building of houses. With London so near, market gardening and dairy farming were very profitable, so that little housing development took place before the opening of Vauxhall Bridge in 1816. The opening in 1848 of the London and South Western Railway Company's extension from Nine Elms to Waterloo was largely responsible for the industrialization of much of the neighbourhood. Many of the surviving buildings of architectural interest were erected in the brief period between 1816 and 1848.

South of Kennington Common (now Park) there was little building in Lambeth before the 19th century. A large proportion of this area formed part of the Archbishop's Manor of Lambeth, whose development was greatly influenced by a number of Acts of Parliament. The Inclosure Act of 1806[4] resulted in the inclosure of Rush Common and Norwood Common and the formation of a number of roads. In the following year the Archbishop was authorized to grant 99-year leases in LambethWick Manor and parts of Lambeth Manor.[48] In 1824 this power was extended to a large area in Norwood.[49] More important still was the statutory authority obtained in 1825 for the Archbishop to grant his copyhold tenants licences to demise their property for 99 years.[50]

The application of these powers produced a spate of building, particularly in the Brixton area, which was affected by the opening of Vauxhall Bridge. Most of this early development took the form of undistinguished houses standing alongside the existing main roads like Brixton Road and Camberwell New Road. By the middle of the century ribbon development had stretched long fingers into most of the accessible parts of the Manor. Only in the northerly parts had the more laborious and expensive process of making side roads begun; Lorn Road, for instance, was formed about 1840, and Loughborough Park, which was in the Manor of Lambeth Wick, between 1844 and 1857.

Simultaneously another type of development was proceeding in several of the smaller manors where courts had never been held or had not been held for many years. Here there were no traditional manorial customs which could only be overridden by statutory authority, so that unless the private circumstances of the owner were unusual, no special Act of Parliament was necessary for development. In 1783, Samuel Sanders, a wealthy timber merchant, purchased that part of the Manor of Milkwell which occupied the areas now known as Denmark Hill and Herne Hill,[51] and shortly afterwards he began to grant long leases of large plots with frontages to the existing road. By 1843 an almost continuous line of houses stretched along the west side of the roads now known as Denmark Hill and Herne Hill. In the neighbouring districts of Tulse Hill and Brockwell Park, which formed part of the Manor of Bodley, Upgrove and Scarlettes, Dr. Thomas Edwards built two roads, now Tulse Hill and Upper Tulse Hill, in 1820–1,[52] and also began to grant long leases; while his wealthy neighbour John Blades, after toying with similar schemes, only lived long enough to build two large and a pair of semi-detached houses.

This type of development differed fundamentally from that which predominated in Kennington and Vauxhall. The houses were nearly all detached or semi-detached, and their relatively large front and back gardens provided a quasi-rural atmosphere which is completely absent from the terrace houses of 18th and early 19th century London streets. Perhaps because the ground landlords had a more personal interest in their property, better results were achieved at Denmark Hill, Herne Hill and Tulse Hill than by the haphazard development along Brixton Road.

Many of the inhabitants of these new residential areas were successful London business men. Two of the first inhabitants of houses built at Denmark Hill in the 1780s have been identified as a linen-draper from Southwark and a merchant from Budge Row, Cannon Street. The history of John Ruskin's family illustrates the first prosperous phase of the 19th century migration to the new suburbs. Until 1823 John Ruskin's father, a wine-merchant, lived in a terrace house in Hunter Street near Brunswick Square; his office was in Billiter Street in the City, and every summer the family moved for a few weeks to lodgings in Hampstead or Dulwich.[53] In 1823 he took a three-storey semi-detached house (with garrets and basement) at Herne Hill, whose previous occupant had been a linen-draper in Cheapside.[54] He continued to attend his office daily, returning to dine at Herne Hill at half-past four.[55] Of their neighbours the family saw almost nothing. "They were for the most part well-to-do London tradesmen of the better class" and often had "great cortège of footmen and glitter of plate, extensive pleasure grounds, costly hot-houses, and carriages driven by coachmen in wigs".[56] In 1842 his continued prosperity enabled Ruskin's father to take a larger and detached house at Denmark Hill where he lived until his death in 1864.[57] John Ruskin's loving descriptions of Herne Hill in his childhood go far to explain the attractions of suburban life. "The view from the ridge on both sides was, before railroads came, entirely lovely: westward at evening, almost sublime, over softly wreathing distances of domestic wood;—Thames herself not visible, nor any fields except immediately beneath; but the tops of twenty square miles of politely inhabited groves. On the other side, east and south, the Norwood hills, partly rough with furze, partly wooded with birch and oak, partly in pure green bramble copse, and rather steep pasture, rose with the promise of all the rustic loveliness of Surrey and Kent in them, and with so much of space and height in their sweep, as gave them some fellowship with hills of true hill-districts."[58]

Development similar to that on Denmark Hill, Herne Hill and Tulse Hill also took place in the small Manors of Heathrow and Levehurst. But in each of these cases the process was regulated by Trustees acting under Chancery supervision and in accordance with a private Act of Parliament. Robert Stone, the owner of Heathrow Manor, most of which lay on the east side of Effra Road and the north-east side of Dulwich Road, died in 1820 leaving so many debts that the whole estate was sold in the course of the next thirty-five years.[59] Levehurst Manor formed part of Lord Thurlow's very extensive estates. After his death in 1806 his Trustees obtained an Act[30] enabling them to develop the property, and Levehurst was sold in 1825. Here an attempt was made to lay out a large circus in a fine position on top of a steep hill, but the scheme petered out and Royal Circus remains as a memorial to an unsuccessful speculation.[60]

With the coming of railways, trams and buses, the pattern of suburban development changed. Except in certain parts of Norwood (Thurlow Park Road, Palace Road and near the Crystal Palace) where the undulating ground provided attractive sites, few large detached houses were built in Lambeth after about 1860, and the area became the scene of widespread routine speculative building. This process produced architecturally undistinguished results, but a few general points concerning its workings may be noted.

After an Act of 1841 had authorized Lords of Manors to enfranchise copyhold land upon receipt of a lump sum payment from the tenant,[61] the ancient manorial customs seldom proved obstacles to building. Although the Acts regulating building in London had applied to Lambeth since 1707,[62] there was probably little real supervision until the establishment of the Office of Metropolitan Buildings in 1844.[63] In 1855 the control of building was taken over by the Metropolitan Board of Works.[64]

Most of the building in the area was done by small local firms who seldom engaged to build more than ten houses at a time; their yards were usually within a mile of the sites.[65] There was, however, one firm in Lambeth which at the beginning of the 20th century was large enough to undertake big contracts all over the country. Higgs and Hill Ltd. began as two businesses in north London. At the beginning of the 19th century Thomas Hill, builder, was working in Islington. His grandsons, Rowland and Joseph Hill, married sisters, Matilda and Mary Ann Edmonds, and through a friendship which Mrs. Joseph Hill formed at school with Lettie Higgs, her husband met William Higgs, Lettie's father.[66] William Higgs had been apprenticed to his uncle, Joshua Higgs, of Davies Street, Berkeley Square, and after saving £50 he started his own business in Bishop's Bridge Road, Paddington, in 1845. Shortly afterwards he moved to Euston Road, and again in 1852 to Palace Road, Lambeth, where he secured many contracts for churches, schools and public buildings.[67] In 1867 the business was transferred to a large four-acre site in Lawn Lane, Vauxhall, and in 1874 the two firms were amalgamated as Hill, Higgs and Hill. The two Hill brothers came to live at Clapham, but Rowland retired in 1879, when the name of the firm was changed to Higgs and Hill. As well as many buildings in Lambeth (part of Spurgeon's Homes, part of Wyvil Primary School, the north and south blocks of County Hall, and the London Fire Brigade Headquarters on the Albert Embankment) Higgs and Hill obtained contracts for the erection of Peter Robinson's in Oxford Street, the Tate Gallery, the Royal Naval College, Dartmouth, etc.[66]

Many of the people who occupied the speculators' new houses were clerks, shopkeepers, skilled artisans and the rank and file of the commercial world. Some of them were migrants from the surrounding countryside, attracted to London by the hope of better wages and housing; others may have come from the inner districts of London, many of which had been invaded by the very poor class of people who had lost their homes through the building of railways and the widening of main streets. Throughout the new suburbs people were constantly on the move. "Southwark is moving to Walworth, Walworth to North Brixton and Stockwell, while the servant-keepers of outer South London go to Croydon and other places."[68] As early as 1848 commerce was invading a residential area of Kennington, for in that year the occupier of a house in Kennington Park Road wrote to the Duchy of Cornwall to complain of the dust caused by his neighbour, whose trade was "shaker of mats, rugs, carpets, etc."—"at Breakfast I sometimes get nearly smothered".[69] Inconveniences of this kind gradually led to the wealthier inhabitants moving further out of London; in 1871 John Ruskin gave up his house at Denmark Hill, which was later used as a hotel.[57] The leap-frog of suburban expansion had, in fact, begun in Lambeth long before the completion of the development of the area.

Many suburban householders had little capital, but were able to buy their houses through a building society. In the first half of the century a number of terminating building societies had been formed, which built houses for their members out of the capital accumulated by weekly subscriptions; when all the houses had been built and the advances paid off, the societies dissolved. The activities of these societies were supplemented by those of the land societies, whose original purpose was to buy land for distribution amongst their members, who would thus acquire a Parliamentary vote in counties. By the 1860s this political aim had been largely abandoned in favour of house ownership, while by about the same time many of the terminating building societies had been superseded by permanent societies, which borrowed from one class and lent to another. By 1870 there were 2,000 building societies in England and Wales, with a total membership of 800,000.[70] In 1874 the movement was regulated by an Act which remained the societies' basic code for many years.[71]

In the second half of the 19th century there were fourteen societies with names suggesting that Lambeth was the main scene of their activities. Of these the present Lambeth Building Society, found in 1852, is the sole survivor.[72] It is impossible to assess the extent or distribution of these societies' mortgages, but their work, and that of many other societies outside the parish, in the provision of money for the purchase of small houses made possible the tremendous suburban expansion of this period. Most of their advances were made to middle-class borrowers, and nearly five-sixths of their loans were for amounts of less than £300.[70]

The land societies do not appear to have bought large estates in Lambeth. A small estate on the north-east side of Dulwich Road was bought by the Westminster Freehold Land Society in 1855;[73] there were probably others. The area under review was too far from the middle of London for the semi-philanthropic housing bodies to buy land, and the Peabody Trustees' estate at Rosendale Road, where the earliest buildings were erected in 1901, provides the only example of this type of development.

Lambeth does, however, contain an early instance of the work of a land company, many of which were founded in the late 1860s after the constitution of joint stock companies with limited liability.[70] The purpose of these companies, of which the Artisans', Labourers' and General Dwellings Company, Ltd. was the most important, was to provide houses within the purchasing power of working men. In 1868 a 99-year lease of twenty-four acres was taken on behalf of the Suburban Village and General Dwellings Company.[74] The land lay beside the recently-opened eastern arm of the Metropolitan Extension of the London, Chatham and Dover Railway Company, and the rapid development of Milkwood Road, its main street, was greatly helped by the cheap fares for workmen which the Railway Company was compelled to provide.[75] The popularity of these cheap fares was, indeed, a most important factor in the development of working-class suburbs in the latter part of the century. By 1911 workmen's fares accounted for over twenty-five per cent of the entire passenger traffic on the South Eastern and Chatham Company's lines.[76]

The population of Lambeth reached its peak at the census of 1901, and with the virtual completion of the fabric of the area, later developments do not come within the scope of this volume.

THE FABRIC

In the area under review, a typical 19th century London suburb, the churches, chapels, schools and public buildings stand out in high relief against the general background of mediocrity created by the domestic buildings. There are, of course, several late Georgian terraces and houses of real merit, but in the main this is a fair generalization.

First among the churches are the four Greek Revival buildings erected between 1819 and 1825, known as the "Waterloo" churches and dedicated to the four evangelists, Matthew, Mark, Luke and John (Plates 2–12). These resulted from a resolution passed in 1819 by the Lambeth Vestry,[77] which appointed a committee to negotiate with the Church Building Commissioners for the provision of four churches in the parish, the cost being met by a grant from the Commissioners, by private subscriptions and by a church rate levied until 1850.[78] By far the finest of these churches is St. Matthew's, Brixton, consecrated in 1824, a noble Doric design by C. F. Porden. St. Mark's, Kennington, consecrated in 1824 and designed by D. R. Roper (also attributed to A. B. Clayton), is a far less satisfactory building, while St. Luke's, Norwood, designed by Francis Bedford and consecrated in 1825, is chiefly remarkable for the superb siting of its elegant portico and steeple. The fourth church, St. John's, Waterloo Road, also designed by Bedford and consecrated in 1824, is described and illustrated in volume XXIII of the *Survey of London*. The Brixton, Kennington and Norwood churches stand in open churchyards at important road junctions, but the demand for correct orientation prevented those at Brixton and Kennington from being sited for the maximum architectural effect. At Norwood, however, where a clause in the Inclosure Act of 1806 restricted the use of the site and caused the church to be built on a north to south axis, the portico and steeple command the attention they deserve.

The mid-19th century churches show a change in taste together with a decline in architectural quality, sometimes compensated by the part they play in providing a focal centre to a well laid-out residential area. Cases in point are St. Michael's, Stockwell Park Road (1841), an emaciated Gothic building of brick, reflecting the taste and parsimony of the Commissioners at that time (Plate 14a); St. Barnabas', Guildford Road (1850), a nondescript Gothic design in the increasingly popular ragstone; and St. John's, Angell Town (1853), a Gothic church of excellent form but poor detail, designed by Benjamin Ferrey (Plate 16).

Christ Church, Brixton Road (Plate 17), St. Anne's, South Lambeth Road (Plate 13c and d), and St. Matthew's, Denmark Hill (Plate 14b), superseded proprietary chapels, while St. Andrew's, Stockwell Green (Plate 13a and b), is actually a once charming late 18th century chapel recast in a sour Romanesque style.

The late Victorian churches are far more impressive. St. John the Divine, Vassall Road (Plates 18, 19), is outstanding, a Gothic masterpiece of G. E. Street, consecrated in 1874 and gutted during the war of 1939–45. All Saints', Rosendale Road (1888–91), is an unfinished but highly dramatic Gothic church by G. H. Fellowes Prynne (Plate 21), who also completed St. Peter's, Leigham Court Road (1870–7, Plate 20). Christ Church, Brixton Road (1898–1902), is an eclectic Byzantine design by that wayward original, Beresford Pite (Plate 17).

The Roman Catholic churches came later than those of the Establishment. First in date and architectural importance is the unfinished church of Corpus Christi, Trent Road (Plates 22, 23), first used in 1887, the torso of a sensitive and highly complex Gothic design by J. F. Bentley. St. Anne's, Kennington Lane (Plate 24), opened in 1903, is a Gothic hall church of noble simplicity, designed by F. A. Walters. Four small churches of no architectural distinction, known as Ellis churches after a generous benefactor, were built in the area during the first decade of this century, probably to the design of F. W. Tasker. They are St. Philip and St. James, Poplar Walk; St. Helen's, Robsart Street (now closed); St. Matthew's, Norwood High Street; and St. Francis of Sales and St. Gertrude, Larkhall Lane.

The earlier chapels of the Nonconformist sects adhere to the precedent of the 18th century preaching-box, but their later churches incline to the style and form of the Establishment's buildings. The earlier style is well represented by Trinity Congregational Church in St. Matthew's Road (Plate 25a), with its pleasant brick front of almost domestic character, but Trinity Presbyterian Church in Clapham Road (Plate 26b), designed in 1862 by Habershon and Pite, commands attention by its pompous Roman portico. The later type is represented by Roupell Park Methodist Church (Plate 27b), a Gothic ragstone building designed in 1879 by Charles Bell, the steeple of which is a conspicuous landmark in the neighbourhood.

The schools in the area belong to two distinct groups—those sponsored by religious societies, such as the National Society, and those built after 1870 by the London School Board, the buildings of each group clearly reflecting their origin. Befitting their parochial and denominational origin, the church schools are much smaller and architecturally more varied than those of the School Board, which was under a statutory obligation to provide an universal elementary education. Buildings of both types are fairly evenly distributed throughout that part of the borough lying north of Brockwell Park and Tulse Hill, and there is a further group of three School Board and two denominational schools in the extreme south. But in the predominantly middle-class area comprising Tulse Hill and West Dulwich there was, before 1904, only one school built by the Board and none by the denominational societies, the needs for primary education evidently being met by schools and kindergartens privately conducted in houses.

Two interesting early 19th century school buildings survive in the area. St. Mark's Primary School in Harleyford Road (Plate 34a), designed by J. Bailey and erected in 1824–5, is a Regency Greek building of modest size containing two parallel class-rooms, one for boys and one for girls, linked in front by houses for the master and mistress. Although altered internally and extended, the building still provides a clear example of the design of voluntary schools in the early 19th century. The same basic plan was used for the much more imposing school in Kennington Lane (Plate 33b), managed by the Society of Licensed Victuallers, a building now serving other purposes and known as Imperial Court. This school was erected in 1836 to the design of Henry Rose and cost some £14,000 as against the modest £2,500 (including furnishings) expended on St. Mark's School.

St. Mark's belongs to a time when only an eccentric would have departed from the conventional classical mode of architectural expression then prevailing. Within ten years, however, sentiment was changing, the Commissioners' churches were becoming Gothic and Pugin was soon to publish his influential *Contrasts*, making it clear that Gothic, preferably of the 13th and 14th centuries, was the only style of architecture compatible with true Christianity. Henceforth all church schools in the area affected some form of Gothic or picturesque expression.

Although some of the later voluntary schools, such as St. John's, Warham Street, and St. Andrew's, Lingham Street, show the influence of the Board's schools, these last are easily recognized as a type. They fall into two groups according to whether the architect was E. R. Robson or T. J. Bailey, and almost all have class-room blocks of three lofty storeys, usually flanked by cupola-crowned stair towers and linked by cloak-rooms contained in five normal storeys. The materials generally are brick, yellow stock with red dressings, and terracotta, the windows of highly complicated design being of wood. The architectural expression is that which at the time was so inappropriately called "Queen Anne", and which is in fact a hybrid of 17th and early 18th century vernacular strains. Kennington Manor School (Plate 35b), designed by Bailey and opened in 1897, is a typical example of the Board's later work. Robson, who was architect to the Board from 1871 to 1885, devoted great care to the design of the many schools for which he was responsible, but the Board was not popular in Lambeth[79] and none of Robson's experimental schools were built in the area.

The provision of public libraries was also strongly opposed by the Lambeth ratepayers, and in 1875, when an attempt was made to obtain approval for the adoption of the Libraries Act "every person who attempted to speak in favour of the adoption of the Act was literally howled down".[80] The Act was eventually adopted in 1886, and seven libraries were built in the area under review between 1888 and 1906. Four of them—Knight's Hill, Kennington Lane (Plate 38b), Brixton and South Lambeth Road—were designed by Sidney R. J. Smith, the architect of the Tate Gallery. Architecturally, they are florid "Renaissance" creations of red brick dressed with stone.

In the second half of the 19th century Lambeth became the home of several philanthropic institutions, some removing there from the overcrowded districts of Central London. The Jewish Orphanage (Plate 32a) at Norwood (formerly the Jews' Hospital and Orphan Asylum) was originally in Mile End Road, while St. Saviour's Almshouses, the first of which was built in 1862 in Hamilton Road, had been established in Southwark since the 16th century. But as the character of Lambeth in its turn changed, other institutions moved out; the children of Spurgeon's Homes (Plate 32b), founded in 1867, left the area during the war of 1939–45 to remain at Birchington in Kent. Stockwell Training College, deriving from the Borough Road Training College, came from Southwark to Stockwell Road in 1861 and moved to its present home in Bromley in 1935. Trinity Homes (formerly Asylum), Acre Lane, founded in 1822, has stayed on its original site (Plate 31a).

An indication of the growth of Lambeth may be obtained by comparing the old Vestry Hall (Plate 36a) of 1853 (now the offices of the Church of England Children's Society) and the Town Hall of 1908, designed by Septimus Warwick and H. Austen Hall (Plate 36b). The first is a small building, modestly classical in a belated Georgian manner, while the latter is large and imposing, an opulent Edwardian Baroque building that dominates the neighbourhood with its tall tower, the very embodiment of civic pride and pomp.

The domestic architecture of the area follows the pattern of other London suburbs where development accelerated during the 19th century. In Kennington there are several late Georgian terraces of excellent design and good building (Plate 50a, fig. 12), while the development of Clapham Road is particularly instructive, where the short terraces are at first interspersed with, and then succeeded by paired houses and small villas, with an occasional large house of quality such as Nos. 171 and 173 (Plate 55a) and No. 369. Brixton Road follows something of the same varied pattern (Plates 49a, 55c), but the cheap uniformity of the Camberwell New Road terraces represents the low ebb of Georgian street architecture, the bright relief of Clifton Cottage (Plate 55d) only serving to emphasize the drabness of the rest. The new demand for detached or at least semi-detached houses is everywhere apparent, and Nos. 205 and 207 Brixton Road (Plate 55b), erected in 1823, two individually-fronted houses actually adjoining, illustrate the lengths to which builders would go to satisfy the desire for this type of house.

Two estates at least were developed on well-defined lines. The Stockwell Park area of about 1840 represents the survival of the Regency *rus in urbe* with its crescent of mixed Greek and Gothic houses embowered by trees (Plates 56, 57). Angell Town around 1850, on the other hand, shows in its large and fairly uniform houses the heavy hand of Victorianism. Angell Terrace in Brixton Road (1855), and Albert Square (1846) off the west side of Clapham Road, seem like outposts of the stucco empire of Bayswater (Plates 49b, 50d).

Some of the finest individual houses in the area were those built for upper middle-class occupation at Denmark Hill and Herne Hill during the first period of suburban expansion. One of them, No. 154 Denmark Hill, designed by William Blackburn and built about 1785, was before mutilation perhaps the most distinguished house in the area (Plates 52, 53). The smaller houses that lined Upper Tulse Hill, mostly built during the second quarter of the 19th century, are fast disappearing with the extensive redevelopment which is changing the character of the neighbourhood (Plates 60b, 61). Other interesting houses are No. 30 Wandsworth Road (fig. 27); No. 274 South Lambeth Road (fig. 26); and No. 363 Kennington Lane (fig. 8). No. 30 Wandsworth Road, erected in 1758, is a handsome mid-Georgian mansion now surrounded by industrial squalor. No. 363 Kennington Lane, probably built in 1824, is a small house of unusual distinction and originality, attributed to Soane's disciple J. M. Gandy. Mention must also be made of No. 87 South Lambeth Road (Plate 42), where an unusually attractive group of industrial buildings was erected about 1810 for Beaufoy's vinegar manufactory. It is worth noting that a large house was built here for the proprietor at a time when many merchants and manufacturers chose to live in the suburbs at some distance from their work.

Brockwell Hall (Plates 66, 67) is the solitary reminder of the gentlemen's country seats which once graced the area. Caron House, a typical Jacobean mansion, was demolished in the late 17th century (Plate 44a); the fine classical house at Knight's Hill, designed by Henry Holland for Lord Thurlow, went in 1810 (Plate 44c), and Loughborough House in 1854. Brockwell Hall was designed by D. R. Roper and built between 1811 and 1813 for John Blades, a wealthy glass-manufacturer. Its survival is due to the surrounding lands having been acquired for a public park.

The only public park in the area before 1885 was Kennington Park, which had formed part of Kennington Common until the Inclosure Act of 1852. In 1889 William Minet presented the London County Council with the fourteen and a half acres of land known as Myatt's Fields, for use as an open space. Between 1890 and 1911, Brockwell, Vauxhall, Ruskin and Norwood Parks, containing in all some 214 acres, were opened to the public, in some cases part of the purchase money being contributed by private subscriptions.

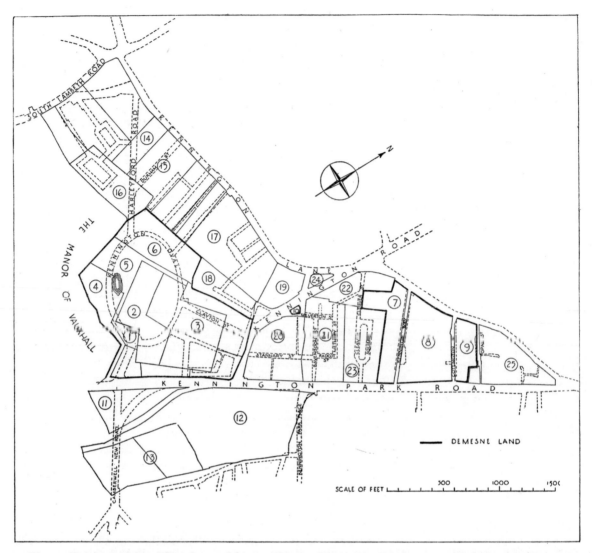

Fig. 3. Key map of part of Kennington Manor. This map is based on Hodskinson and Middleton's survey of the Manor in 1785; the broken lines show the modern street plan. The names of the owners or lessees in 1785 are given below, against the numbers of the plots ringed in the map

Demesne	*Common Land*	*Copyhold*	
1–9. William Clayton	11 and 12.	13.	Joseph Nainby
10. Roadside waste treated as demesne		14–19.	Sir Joseph Mawbey
		20.	Elizabeth Crooke
		21.	Sir William East
		22 and 23.	Mary Cleaver
		24.	Trustees of Surrey New Roads
		25 (part of)	George Rogers, Elisha Biscoe, Mary Frye

CHAPTER I

Kennington

THE whole of the part of Kennington which falls within the scope of the present volume is a section of the Duke of Cornwall's Manor of Kennington. Much of the early history of the Manor has been traced in Volume XXIII of the *Survey of London*, and it is only necessary here to consider in detail the development of the roughly triangular section of the Manor, bounded by Kennington Lane, the line of Vauxhall Creek (also known as the River Effra), Kennington Common and Kennington Park Road, which is shown on the key map in fig. 3. Material for the history of the Manor is extensive. An incomplete survey made in 1554[1] deals primarily with copyhold land. Other surveys were made in 1615 by John Norden,[2] in 1636 by Sir Charles Harbord dealing only with the demesnes,[3] in 1649[4] and 1652[5] by order of Parliament, and by John Hodskinson and John Middleton in 1785–6.[6] Of these surveys, Norden's, Harbord's, and Hodskinson and Middleton's (the last two accompanied by maps which are reproduced in *Survey of London*, Vol. XXIII, Plates 1 and 2) are the most useful and are constantly referred to in the following text. The enrolments in the Manor court and the correspondence between the officers of the Duchy of Cornwall and tenants of the Manor preserved at the Duchy Office in Buckingham Gate are invaluable for the detailed history of development, and many of these sources of information have been gathered together in E. R. L. Clowes' excellent though unpublished *History of the Manor of Kennington*.[7]

The part of the Manor covered by this volume falls naturally into two sections, south-western and north-eastern, divided by Kennington Road. In 1636 there were few buildings on either section. A single house stood on copyhold land in the south-western section near the site of the present Windmill public house. In the north-eastern section a house called the Buckshorns stood in Kennington Park Road, and there were a few buildings scattered along Kennington Lane. The general impression of the Manor at this date is of an area of meadow and pasture chequered by drainage channels. Kennington Lane, which bounds the part of the Manor under consideration, follows much the same line today as it followed in 1636. At that date, the section of the Lane between South Lambeth and Kennington Roads was known as the Kingston Road and the section leading into Newington Butts as the "Sohowe"; later these were known as Upper and Lower Kennington Lane respectively. The names "Upper" and "Lower" were abolished and the houses renumbered in 1936.[8]

Between 1636 and the publication of Rocque's map in 1745,[9] the appearance of the Manor had changed little; Ketleby's Rents had been built at the junction of Kennington Lane and Newington Butts, and a few houses lay thinly scattered along Kennington Lane. Within twenty years, however, the Manor began to assume its modern pattern. The opening of Westminster Bridge in 1750[10] and the building of Kennington Road under an Act of 1751,[11] brought an increasing volume of traffic through the Manor, and gave easy access to the cities of London and Westminster. The building of Blackfriars Bridge and its approach roads between 1760 and 1769[12] made Kennington even more accessible and desirable as a place for country residence; and in the last quarter of the century the ancient manorial customs of both the demesne and the copyhold lands were modified to meet the requirements of building development.

Under the charter granted by Edward III in 1337 the lands of the Duchy of Cornwall were to be held by Edward the Black Prince and his heirs, the eldest sons of the Kings of England, and in default of such heirs they were to revert to the Crown until a son should be born who was heir apparent to the realm. The lands of the Duchy were therefore sometimes vested in the Sovereign and at other times in the Duke of Cornwall, and consequently their tenure being somewhat insecure, little encouragement was given to tenants to improve their property. In 1622 however, an Act of Parliament[13] permitted the Duchy to grant leases for a maximum of three lives, or for 31 years. In 1776 William Clayton, lessee of the demesne lands of Kennington Manor, obtained a private Act[14] enabling him to grant building leases and in the following year he obtained a new lease from the Duchy for a long term of 99 years dependent on three lives.[15] As regards the copyhold lands the Prince's Council of the Duchy decided in 1791 that copyholders might be granted licence to demise their property for 99 years instead of the more usual 31 or 61 years.[16]

In the north-eastern section of the Manor described in this volume these more flexible arrangements resulted in the development of the relatively small parts of the demesne in the decade after 1777. The Cleaver, East and Crooke copyhold estates, containing nearly half of this section of the Manor, were also developed at this time, and when Hodskinson and Middleton produced their survey Opal Street (then Pleasant Row), Cottington Street (Mansion House Row) and Kennings Way (White Hart Row) had been laid out, and part of Stannary Street (Kennington Place) ran north eastwards from Kennington Road; along each of these roads were groups of houses. Almost continuous lines of houses stretched along Kennington Lane and Kennington Park Road, which Elmes later described as "those merchant's and sugar-baker's boxes which crowd the sides of Clapham Road and Kennington Common".[17] By the time that Horwood's map was published in 1799, the modern pattern of this part of Kennington had been set, except for alterations on the East estate some sixty years later.

The south-western section between Kennington Road and South Lambeth Road was developed more slowly than the other. Nearly all of it was low-lying and in constant danger of flooding from the tidal creek, and there was no ready access from the main roads. Hodskinson and Middleton's survey shows only a few houses along Kennington Lane and South Lambeth Road, and a group of buildings at the junction of Kennington and Kennington Park Roads; the rest of the area was set out as nursery ground and pasture, with one or two buildings attached to the various holdings. An agreement of 1789 between William Clayton and Isaac Bates and a number of associates for the development of the demesne lands in this area initiated building,[18] and produced the laying-out of the Oval and its communicating roads. The financial difficulties of Sir Joseph Mawbey, who held a considerable proportion of the copyholds in this area, led to

his granting a number of building leases at the end of the 18th and the beginning of the 19th centuries along the main road frontages of his property. The Mawbey property away from Kennington Lane and Kennington Road was not developed until the building of Harleyford Road under an Act of 1818,[19] when the pattern of the area was finally established.

By 1834, when the lease of the demesne lapsed on the death of Sir William Clayton and the Mawbey estate had been broken up, there was little room for further development, except on small pieces of land later used for the Vestry Hall and the houses at Kennington Cross. Soon Kennington ceased to be a semi-rural suburb and the value of the property in the area began to decrease. In 1856 Thomas Farmer wished to enfranchise his property, part of the former Crooke estate, and the Steward of the Manor admitted that "it cannot be denied that the Rentals of such a class of Property . . . are very uncertain and precarious". The Duchy was not, however, prepared to concede that decreased rentals should be taken into account when assessing the Lord's fine for enfranchisement, lest the future value of the estate might be disparaged.[20]

At the end of the 18th century, and for some considerable time afterwards, the Duchy of Cornwall did not exercise any close control over the standard of building which, being left to the discretion of the builder, was very mixed. The negotiations with Farmer are an indication of the changed attitude of the Duchy towards the Kennington estates during the second half of the 19th century. After 1850 a period of redevelopment began in the Manor, and the influence exerted by the Duchy was more rigid and direct than before. When the Lambeth Vestry wished to add another storey to the Vestry Hall, the Duchy would neither grant permission nor sell the land, as "an unsightly structure may take the place of the present edifice . . . and diminish the value of the Houses in the neighbourhood".[21] The same control was exercised in 1887 when Sir Gilbert East applied for a licence to demise the sites of Nos. 140–162 Kennington Park Road for rebuilding. The Duchy declined to grant a licence until plans for rebuilding had been submitted, and remained adamant despite East's complaint that no builder would incur the expense of preparing plans without the promise of a licence.[22] The houses were not rebuilt.

The Duchy was not always restrictive in its influence. Redevelopment of the former Cleaver copyhold estate received its encouragement,[23] and on the demesne lands the practice of granting a lease determinable on one or more lives was abandoned in favour of a definite term of years, as an encouragement to improvement. The increasing power of the Vestries and the Metropolitan Board of Works over the formation of roads and the enforcement of building lines also affected the character of the area, notably on the East estate. In 1913–15 the Duchy itself carried out the redevelopment of the land (outside the area covered by this volume) in the angle between Kennington Lane and Sancroft Street,

and achieved, in Courtenay Square at least, a standard of urban design that recalls the best work of the 18th century. The architects were the late Stanley Davenport Adshead, the first occupant of the Lever Chair of Civic Design in the University of Liverpool, and Stanley C. Ramsey.[a]

Since the abolition of copyhold tenure, the power of the Duchy has been supplemented by the increasing powers granted to Borough and County Councils for clearance, rehousing and town planning. A considerable amount of rehousing has already taken place in Kennington, and the blocks of flats on the north-east and south-west borders of the Oval have replaced the old houses.

THE DEMESNE LANDS

Most of the demesne lands in the part of Kennington Manor under consideration in this volume lay together in the south-western section of the Manor, and were bounded on the south-east by Kennington Park Road, and on the south by the Manor of Vauxhall. There were five closes, the Gallows Field, the Great Meadow, the Eight Acres, the Sluice Field, which took its name from a sluice on Vauxhall Creek approximately at the junction of Harleyford Road and the Oval, and the Little Field; together these were known as the Forty Acres. To the north-east lay the Six Acres, the Three Acres, the Three Acres pasture and the Two Acres, all of which lay between Kennington Lane and Kennington Park Road. These closes were all subsequently subdivided, probably during the Clayton leases of the demesne.

The Clayton family and particularly Sir William, the last Clayton to hold a lease of the demesne, had an important influence on the development of the Manor. Under the Act of 1622[13] leases of the Duchy lands could be granted for a maximum of three lives, or for 31 years. Several leases of the demesne followed; that granted to Lord Moore in May 1661 was assigned to Robert Clayton (later Lord Mayor of London and President of St. Thomas' Hospital) and John Morrice. In 1670 a new lease in reversion was granted to Clayton and Morrice, and from that time until the death of Sir William Clayton in 1834, the Clayton family retained their interest in the demesne.[24]

In 1776 William Clayton, realising that the value of his leaseholds in Kennington was rising rapidly, obtained an Act of Parliament to enable him to grant building leases. He believed "that many Persons would be willing to enter into Contracts . . . for the Purposes of building, or Improvement . . . and that if such Leases could be granted, the Estate would be considerably increased in the future Value and annual Rents thereof".[14] In the following year he obtained through Sambrook Freeman, a Trustee of his marriage settlement, a new long lease for 99 years instead of 31 years, determinable on three lives,[15] to encourage development. In fact, development did not follow immediately, but it was well under way in the north-eastern section of the demesne by 1785.

The development of the demesne land in the south-western section of the Manor dates from articles of agreement made on July 1, 1789 between William Clayton, and John Harwood, plasterer, of Lambeth, Thomas Dickinson, plasterer, of St. John, Westminster, Isaac Bates, brickmaker, of Kennington, and Richard Wooding, surveyor, of Bouverie Street, London. In the agreement Clayton covenanted to make subleases to the other parties when they had built houses "not to be less in number than one hundred and ten".[18] There was an attempt to provide an attractive layout of the area (Plate 40b), for the roadway round the Oval was laid out at this time, together with the roads linking it to

<hr>

[a] See the illustrated account by Patrick Abercrombie in *The Architects' and Builders' Journal*, 29th December 1915.

Kennington Park and Kennington Roads, and in 1790 the lease of the Oval was granted to a market gardener (see below); the whole must have provided a pleasant retreat from the traffic along Kennington Park Road. The leases covenanted for were executed on March 1, 1797,[18] although the development of the demesne, as Horwood's map of 1799 shows, was still far from complete. The house which was later adapted for St. Mark's Vicarage was then standing, but even in 1824 there was vacant land on which St. Mark's School could be built. It was not until 1845 that the Oval was taken over for cricket, and the modern pattern of the demesne lands set.

[1] THE OVAL

Fig. 3, plots 1–6

In 1615, when Norden made his survey of the Manor, the site of the Oval was part of five closes containing 38 acres, bounded by the Common, the common watercourse (Vauxhall Creek), and the lands of John Groome, Edward Carpenter and William Cockerham; these closes were in lease to Richard Salter and occupied by John Hubbard.[7] By 1636 the tenement was held by Mrs. Marie Coxe, widow,[3] and in 1649 by George Coxe;[4] from about this date the five closes seem to have been known collectively as the Forty Acres. In 1667 John Morrice and Robert Clayton, the lessees of a considerable part of the Manor,[24] appear to have erected a brick wall on the Forty Acres for growing fruit.[25] The area remained in lease for horticultural purposes, for William Malcolm, who had a sub-lease dating from 1758 of the part of the demesne now crossed by Clayton Street and Bowling Green Street, was required to provide in addition to a money rent "one hundred of Asparagus in the Month of *January* in every Year".[14] In 1785 the area of the five closes had been divided into three tenements, one occupied by Malcolm, another by Thomas Ellis, landlord of the Horns, and others, and a third by James and George Mitchelson;[6] this last included the greater part of the site of the Oval. The Mitchelsons' tenement is described as six fields of meadow, pasture and nursery ground, together with an old brick dwelling house, barn, stable, seed shop and sheds.[6] In 1790, after the laying-out of the Oval roadway, the tenements were redivided. The Mitchelsons' tenement now included only the area within the

Oval, mostly taken from their old holding, but it also included part of Malcolm's, and a new lease was granted for 64½ years. This lease was later assigned to John Archer, and after his death it was put up to auction in 1826 and purchased by the Rev. William Otter, minister of St. Mark's and later Bishop of Chichester.[16] The Clayton interest having lapsed in 1834, Otter was granted a head lease of the property, described as nursery or garden ground, by the Duchy on January 8, 1835, for 99 years determinable on one life,[27] which was later extended to three lives.[28]

Otter's purpose in buying the lease of the Oval was to provide a site for the minister's house and, by building over the remainder, an endowment for the living; this appears to have been the first building project at the Oval. When the subject was laid before the Prince's Council of the Duchy, one of its members, Lord Bexley, produced a "General Idea of Improvement". He proposed to "Inclose an Oval of an Acre or an Acre and a half in the Centre, and plant it with Lime Trees, to form an open Grove, with Gravel Walks round and across it, under the Trees". Apart from a roadway to the grove, the remainder was to be divided into 21 lots, one for the minister's house and the remainder for cottage villas, which were to be of "a general similarity, tho' not exact uniformity of appearance".[26] With the lapse of negotiations over the minister's house, the plan was, however, forgotten.

Otter found the nursery ground unprofitable and converted it into a market garden, but in 1836 he petitioned the Duchy for a building lease because "the market gardens in the immediate vicinity of London have gradually declined in value".[29] The Duchy was prepared to accede to this request despite the advice of the surveyor, James Bailey, that the value of the surrounding property would be greatly decreased, as the Oval afforded "not only the advantage of a large, open space, for the free circulation of air; but, also, a pleasant and agreeable object . . . to look upon".[29] A building plan made by Bailey at this date is preserved in the Duchy office; it shows a road running across the Oval from south-east to north-west, flanked by six pairs of houses, with other pairs facing outwards around the Oval roadway. Negotiations with Otter until his death in 1840, and thereafter with his Trustees, were continued. Another building plan (Plate 40a) was suggested, with a similar arrangement to Bailey's first plan, but with more pairs of houses, this time arranged about a road running north-east to south-west. However, the Duchy's terms were considered too high, and the Otter Trustees looked for another way of using the land. The last building proposal for the Oval was in 1851, when the Duchy proposed to promote a Bill in Parliament for building two crescents there; but at the instigation of the Prince Consort the plan was dropped and the Oval remained an open space.[30]

The Otter Trustees were at last successful in their search for a new use for the land; in March 1845 they reported that they were "desirous of letting it to a Gentleman who proposes to convert it into a Subscription Cricket Ground".[31] The new lessee was William Houghton of Brixton Hill, President of the Montpelier Club. The Club was formed about 1840 and played on the grounds of the Bee Hive Tavern at Walworth; these were, however, required for building in 1844. Soon afterwards the Treasurer, W. Baker, and William Ward, M.P. (who had already helped to preserve Lord's Cricket Ground from being built over) entered into negotiations with the Otter Trustees, nominating William Houghton as lessee.[32] The first cricket match appears to have been played in May 1845.[33] Considerable preparations had been necessary, for the Oval was "in a most ruinous condition and from the effluvium arising from decayed vegetables a nuisance and a source of ill-health".[31] In the spring of 1845, ten thousand turves from Tooting Common were laid.[34] Trees still studded the ground and in 1847 permission was given for some of them to be cut down.[31]

The Montpelier Club did not flourish at the Oval,[35] for Houghton's interest in it waned once he became lessee. Meanwhile, the Surrey Club (later the Surrey County Cricket Club) had been founded in the autumn of 1844 at a meeting held at the Horns Tavern.[34] While the Montpelier Club declined, the Surrey Club grew in strength, and has played at the Oval ever since its foundation, at first sharing the ground, and later becoming its sole lessee.

Although the cricket ground was immediately popular, Houghton got into financial difficulties, and attempted to solve them by introducing other attractions. After many protests that the sale of liquors would be his only source of profit, the Duchy gave permission, subject to annual review, for one of the buildings to be used as a licensed house, the precursor of the Surrey Tavern. Permission to apply for the licence was withdrawn in 1853, after complaints of rowdyism,[31] and it was only after Houghton had ceased to be lessee that the Tavern was established as a permanent feature of the ground. Houghton also attempted to provide other sport, and in 1851 he was allowed to introduce "Pedestrianism and Coursing". The pedestrianism involved a walking match of 1,000 miles in 1,000 hours. After the owners of neighbouring premises had objected, the Duchy's permission was withdrawn, despite Houghton's assurance that no disturbance had been caused, and that the public had not been "admitted on Sundays, and the Pedestrian on those days always walked in dark clothes".[31] The Duchy also declined to allow an exhibition of poultry on New Year's Day 1853, although 900 pens had been entered and the exhibition had distinguished patrons;[31] it was removed to a bazaar in Baker Street.[36] William Houghton's difficulties were such that in 1854 he assigned the lease to his brother George in settlement of a debt;[36] and in the following year a new lease was granted to the Surrey Club by the Otter Trustees.[37] William Houghton became bankrupt, and his last connection with the Oval was in 1855, when he wrote to the Duchy asking that an appointment might be granted to him as recompense for the treatment he had received. The application was refused.[36]

For the first few years the Surrey Club used the market-garden buildings for their pavilion and offices, and one of them was altered at a cost of £3,000 for use as a public house.[34] The painting shown on Plate 41a gives some idea of the Oval at this period. In 1858 the Club requested the Duchy's permission to erect a new pavilion; this was originally intended to stand opposite the end of Clayton Street, but the residents protested and the pavilion was built at the south-east end of the ground.[36] In 1874 the Otter Trustees put the remainder of the leasehold interest up to auction and it was bought by the Surrey Club for £2,800.[38] In order to raise the purchase money, the Club was granted a lease for a definite term of thirty-one years. The lease, dated May 3, 1875, outlined the purposes for which the Oval was then being used, for it laid down "that no game of sport other than the games of Cricket, Baseball, Football, Tennis, Fives and Racquets and Amateur Athletic Sports shall be played".[39]

Many improvements have been made at the Oval since the first pavilion was built. In 1876 the Club obtained permission to build a roller-skating rink, in the hope that the profits therefrom "would enable them still further to extend their operations" in the furtherance of cricket, "as well as to enlarge their sphere of utility as purveyors of athletic amusements for South London".[38] An asphalt rink was laid out, but no buildings were erected, and the rink was afterwards converted for use as practice wickets.[40] The Tavern was rebuilt in 1877–8 at a cost of £4,000[38] and in 1880 the circle of banks round the ground was completed by using the earth excavated when Vauxhall Creek was being inclosed.[41] The present pavilion (Plate 41b) and Tavern were designed by Thomas Muirhead of Manchester, the architect of the pavilion at Old Trafford, and built in 1895–7 by Messrs. Foster and Dicksee of London and Rugby.[42] Later improvements include the erection of the Hobbs Gates in 1934, to commemorate the connection of (Sir) Jack Hobbs with the Surrey County Cricket Club. During the war of 1939–45 the Oval suffered both from bombing and from neglect. It was used as a searchlight site and subsequently set out, though never used, as a prisoner-of-war camp. In 1945, after de-requisitioning, 40,000 turves from Gravesend were laid, and cricket was resumed at the beginning of the season of 1946.

The Surrey Tavern, which is dated "1897" over the entrance to the public bar, is designed in a freely conceived Jacobean style. It is of three storeys with attics, has an asymmetrical plan, and is built of red brick with stone dressings.

The Hobbs Gates adjoin the Surrey Tavern. The inscription "THE HOBBS GATES IN HONOUR OF A GREAT SURREY & ENGLAND CRICKETER" in the wrought ironwork over the gates, is surmounted by ornament composed of the entwined initials of the Surrey County Cricket Club in cursive lettering. The simply detailed gates are set between brick piers capped by stone vases. Each of the curving brick screen walls at the sides contains two doorways. The architect was Louis de Soissons.

[2] ST. MARK'S VICARAGE

Fig. 3, plot 1

After the building of St. Mark's Church, it was thought necessary to provide a parsonage close to both the church and to the centre of the parish. Surplus pew-rents were set aside for providing the house, and the incumbent, the Rev. William Otter, purchased the sub-lease of the Oval in 1826 (see page 22). The Oval contains approximately nine acres, a more than adequate space for the building of one house, but it was intended that the remainder should be built over "whereby the immediate revenue of the Duchy might be increased and a permanent income provided for the parochial minister".[26] Application was made to the head lessee, Sir William Clayton, for a building sub-lease, but he suggested that the better course would be for him to surrender all his interest in the Oval to the Duchy of Cornwall as Lord of the Manor, so that the freehold could be granted. The Duchy was prepared to sell for building a parsonage and suggested that a plot 150 feet deep with a 40-foot frontage to the south-west along the Oval roadway would be sufficient.[26] The scheme appears to have lapsed.

In 1832, the next incumbent, the Rev. Charlton Lane, together with Dr. D'Oyly, rector of Lambeth, proposed that if a new house was not built, the freehold of No. 25 The Oval, occupied by Thomas Procter, might be granted to them. Counsel advised that the Duchy had no power to sell land for providing ministers' houses, and negotiations for a lease were therefore undertaken.[26] The head lease of the house and garden was in the hands of the Clayton family. By the agreement of 1789 (see page 21) Richard Wooding had a sub-lease dated March 1, 1797;[43] Thomas Procter was his tenant. The house itself was built in 1794–5.[44] After Wooding's death in 1808,[45] his property was vested in Trustees, who in December 1835 assigned their sub-lease of this and other property to Dr. D'Oyly, the Rev. Charlton Lane, and William Reeves of Kennington Green for £215 regardless of the fact that the Clayton interest had lapsed in 1834.[43] When it was realised that the Clayton interest had ended, further money had to be laid out in obtaining a head lease from the Duchy, but on this occasion only the house and garden were included and were described as "All that brick messuage or dwellinghouse, out offices, Coach house and Stables with rooms over the same, yards, pleasure ground, Kitchen Garden and . . . appurtenances".[43] The lease was dated May 13, 1836, and was granted for an immediate payment of £340, and an annual rent of £10 10s. It was for 99 years, determinable on one life; two further lives were added in 1837.[43] Thomas Procter was only ejected from the house after a lawsuit, and Mr. Lane was eventually installed in June 1837.[26]

The lease from the Duchy was unsatisfactory. The incumbent was required to pay the ground rent, and although he had no security of tenure he found it necessary to make improvements, such as covering in a stretch of Vauxhall Creek, which bounded the property on one side, at a cost of £332 (fig. 4).[26] In 1851 Mr. Lane suggested that he should be given a lease of the house

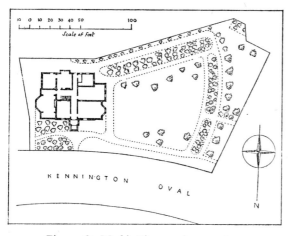

Fig. 4. St. Mark's Vicarage, lay-out plan

for a definite term of years together with a building lease of 150 feet of the Oval frontage and the freehold of a portion of Kennington Common, where a house to be permanently attached to the living could be built. It was suggested that two pairs of semi-detached cottages should be built on the Oval frontage, and for this the Duchy was prepared to grant a lease.[26] The project lapsed because Mr. Lane was concerned in promoting the inclosure of Kennington Common (see page 33) and did not wish to be accused of furthering the inclosure for his own purposes.[46]

In 1863 Mr. Lane again approached the Duchy to request them to sell the freehold of the house and part of the garden, which were to be permanently attached to the living; at the same time he offered to surrender a portion on the north-west boundary of the garden, with 110 feet of frontage to the Oval. The Duchy was now empowered to sell demesne for such a purpose, and proposed a price of £439. While

negotiations were still in progress a new incumbent, the Rev. Mr. Lloyd, was appointed. He wished to retain the whole of the property, and to make extensive alterations to the house.[26] Eventually the whole property was sold on August 1, 1865, for £989,[43] advanced by the Governors of Queen Anne's Bounty.[26]

The vicarage is a large house of three storeys and a basement. The original building has been considerably added to and altered, its exterior walls now being generally finished in stucco with decorative detail of Gothic derivation. The gabled entrance porch is placed centrally in the front facing the Oval, and the windows generally have chamfered reveals and heads.

Another house which formerly faced the Oval is illustrated in *Small Houses of the Late Georgian Period 1750–1820*, by Stanley C. Ramsey. It was demolished before 1919.

ST. MARK'S C.E. PRIMARY SCHOOL, [3] HARLEYFORD ROAD

Fig. 3, plot 6

An address to the parishioners of Lambeth in 1817 announced that "Considerable pains have been taken to ascertain the state of the Poor, as to Education, in the parish of Lambeth; and the result indisputably proves the necessity of establishing Schools upon the British system".[47] By 1823, a school for boys was being held in premises at Nine Elms, and subscriptions were being raised for a girls' school, the two to be linked as the "Kennington and South Lambeth National Schools". Kennington was chosen as the area to be served by the new school, because of the urgent need for educational facilities there. The projected linking of the Nine Elms and Kennington schools was, however, abandoned, and the new premises at Kennington provided for both boys and girls.

It was not easy to obtain a lease to build schools, for it was felt that the value of adjacent property would be lowered by such development. After protracted negotiations, which involved land at the junction of Kennington Lane and Kennington Road among other places, the site in Harleyford Road was obtained. The head-lease was in the hands of the Clayton family, and in 1824 the sub-tenant, Jemima Watts of Prince's Place, Kennington, leased the site to the "Trustees of the Kennington Subscription Schools for poor male and Female children"—the Rev. George

D'Oyly, rector of Lambeth, the Rev. William Otter, minister of St. Mark's, Thomas Lett of Commercial Road, John Kershaw of Walcot Terrace, and Richard Cannon of Upper Kennington Lane.[48]

The Trustees covenanted to spend £600 or more in erecting "one or more good and substantial building or buildings . . . for a school room or . . . rooms for the education of poor children".[48] The site was not an entirely suitable one, for it was liable to flooding from Vauxhall Creek, and the ground had to be inclosed and raised before building could begin, thereby adding considerably to the cost. The designs for both the schoolrooms and the houses for the Master and Mistress were made by J. Bailey of Buxton Place, Lambeth. Messrs. Pledge, Chart and Mason contracted to build the schoolrooms for £810, and the boys' school was opened in the girls' premises, since their own were not yet completed, on December 6, 1824. The girls' school was opened in March of the following year. By June 1825, 180 boys and 120 girls, all over the age of six, had been admitted.[49] The houses for the Master and Mistress were built in 1825 by James Hendrey, who contracted for a cost of £575 (Plate 34a, fig. 5). The first Master, Isaac Hitchen and the first Mistress, Rebecca Marchant, were employed at salaries of £80 and £50 per annum respectively.

School was held from nine to four in the winter, and nine to five in summer, with two hours' break at mid-day. In addition to Mr. Hitchen and Miss Marchant, two monitors assisted with the teaching, and from 1835 onwards they were paid 6d. per week. There were also two teachers of the top classes who received 3d. per week, and other teachers who received 2d. Except on Wednesdays and Saturdays, the girls spent each afternoon in doing needlework for the families of the district. The profits of this work were set aside for "providing a portion of the deserving Girls with Cloaks, Bonnets, Frocks, Tippets and Sleeves, in which they appear at Church on Sundays". The children were required to attend church twice on Sundays, and to keep their specially provided clothes at the school during the rest of the week. In 1828 parents were invited to contribute 1d. a week towards a fund for supplying shoes to the children of the schools.

The cost of preparing the site and of building and furnishing the schools was £2,581 16s. 10d.,

a considerably larger sum than had been anticipated. A gift of £100 from King William IV, private benefactions and gifts from the Trustees of Archbishop Tenison's and other schools of the parish, in part balanced the outlay. The Lambeth Vestry gave £134 6s. 3d. towards the cost of the houses;[49] this money represented part of the compensation paid for the abolition of common rights over the site of St. Mark's Church and burial ground, which had formerly been part of Kennington Common (see page 32). Nevertheless, considerable debts were outstanding, and about £20 a month were required to maintain the schools after their completion. Regular subscriptions and the preaching of sermons both in St. Mark's Church and South Lambeth Chapel aided the Trustees. The finances were not assisted by the increasing inefficiency, due to old age, of the Treasurer, Richard Cannon.[50] In 1835 a weekly payment of 1d. a child was introduced to offset some of the costs of maintenance. As well as augmenting the funds, the scheme had another result, for it was reported "that no Children were withdrawn from the Schools by their parents in consequence of the Introduction of the Pay System . . . and that since its commencement the daily attendance of the Children has been more regular than it was when the Instruction was given gratuitously".

On the determination of the Clayton lease of the demesne in 1834, the Duchy of Cornwall granted the Trustees, by deed dated October 11, 1835, a lease of the site of the schools for 99 years, determinable on the life of the Princess Alexandrina Victoria;[51] two more lives were added in 1839.[50] But in 1857 the Trustees were again in financial difficulties, and applied to the Duchy to exchange their uncertain tenure for a lease for a specific term of years, as a guarantee for the raising of funds.[50] This request was not granted; instead, the property was enfranchised and sold to the Trustees on November 5, 1860, for £450.[52] A small portion of the north-east boundary was surrendered at the same time, but was purchased in 1861 for £250.[50]

From time to time there have been alterations to the fabric of the building. In 1840 the heating and ventilation were improved, the latter being affected by the slated roof which was said to "attract and retain the heat of the Sun, and convey it in a very strong degree to the parts beneath, so that in hot weather the Rooms . . .

were at times scarcely supportable". The boys' schoolroom was enlarged in 1849, and other alterations have been made since. When the London County Council succeeded the School Board for London, it required many alterations before granting recognition as a non-provided school. It even recommended to the Managers that because of the extensive changes needed, the premises should be entirely rebuilt.[53] The Council's recommendation was not, however, adopted, and the premises still continue in use as a school. It is one of the oldest church schools still being used in London.

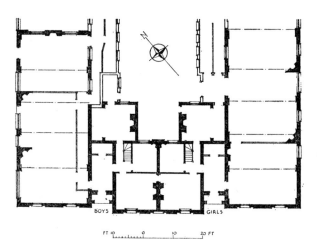

Fig. 5. St. Mark's Primary School, Harleyford Road, ground-floor plan.   Later additions at the back not shown

The school is a modest little building in the Regency manner. The two-storeyed dwelling-house, of three bays crowned with a simple cornice and pedimented blocking course, is flanked by single-storeyed pedimented class-rooms, one for boys and the other for girls, extending back from the frontage. The ground floor of the centre block is arcaded and divided from the first floor by a stucco string-course which forms the sills of the square-headed first-floor windows. The classroom blocks are linked to the centre block by means of stucco recessed entrance porches. The pedimented blocking course bears the inscription "KEN-NINGTON SCHOOLS" and the date, 1824, is inscribed on the frieze below.

Nos. 155 AND 157 KENNINGTON LANE   [4]
Formerly Nos. 155 and 157 Lower Kennington Lane
Fig. 3, plot 7

This pair of houses was probably built shortly after William Clayton obtained his building Act in 1776; both houses were certainly standing in 1780. It is not known who built them, but a sub-lease for adjacent property indicates that part, at least, of this area of the demesne was in lease to a Mr. Tegetmeyin,[54] or Tegetmeyer,[55] whose executors had the custody of the property in 1789. Tegetmeyer may therefore have been responsible for the erection of houses on this part of the demesne. James Bailey, who acted as local surveyor to the Duchy of Cornwall, lived at No. 155 for some years before 1792.[55]

These houses form a three-storey pair with simple fronts of plum brick, the windows having gauged flat arches of red brick. Their architectural interest centres in the two very fine wood doorcases (Plate 69a and b), which have similar key-ornamented architraves; though differing in detail the doorcases are complementary.

Nos. 137–145 (odd) KENNINGTON LANE   [5]
Formerly Nos. 137–145 Lower Kennington Lane; Nos. 137–143 were originally Nos. 43–46 (consec.) Guildford Place
Fig. 3, plot 8

These houses formed part of a row built on this piece of the demesne about 1785–6. They are not listed in the text of Hodskinson and Middleton's survey but are shown on the map of 1785; they first appear in the Land Tax records in 1787.[55]

No. 139, and the pair Nos. 141 and 143 which are set forward, are three-storey houses of plum brick with gauged flat arches of red brick to the windows. Each has an arched doorway emphasized with vermiculated blocks and a triple keystone. No. 137 was probably once of the same character, but has been unsympathetically re-fronted. No. 145, which is set forward from Nos. 141 and 143, is of the same height and has an original shallow-bowed shop-front with a dentil cornice over the fascia.

VAUXHALL BAPTIST CHURCH, COTTINGTON STREET   [6]
Fig. 3, plot 8

This building was erected in 1883, the foundation stone being laid by Alderman Sir William

McArthur, K.C.M.G., M.P., on July 9. The architect was G. L. Wade and the builder B. E. Nightingale. The church is an uninteresting stock brick building with red brick dressings; three large round-headed windows overlook the street.

[7] Nos. 86–92 (even) and 96 Kennington Park Road

> Formerly Nos. 12–15 (consec.) and 17 Clayton Place
> Fig. 3, plot 8

These houses were built between 1784 and 1787. They are not mentioned in Hodskinson and Middleton's text but are shown on their accompanying map, and were probably in course of erection while the survey was being prepared. Part of Clayton Place appears in the Land Tax records in 1786 and all of it in 1787.[55] It is not known who was responsible for building the houses. Thomas Holloway had the lease of the site of St. James' Chapel in 1796 (see below); he may have had the whole of the Kennington Park Road frontage of this section of the demesne on lease and undertaken its development.

Nos. 86 and 88 are a pair of tall plain terrace-houses of four storeys with semi-basements. The fronts are ornamented by cast-iron balconies and window guards on the first floor and by neat round-headed entrances with vermiculated voussoirs. The entrances adjoin and each has a triple keystone, fluted and vermiculated. Each house has a square boundary pier of brick with a stone capping. There is an elliptical patera beneath the cornice on each face of the piers.

Nos. 90 and 92 are a pair of three-storey houses, their stock brick fronts being united by the imposts of the arched ground-floor windows and doorways, and by the continued sill-band below the first-floor windows. The fronts are finished with a cornice and blocking course. The doorway of No. 90 has a reeded surround, while that of No. 92 has fluted pilasters with key ornamentation beneath its hood.

No. 96 is of the same height and finished with a cornice. Its ground-floor windows are recessed in round arches linked by an impost band, and there are two-storey wings which are slightly set back from the two-window wide centre portion. The northerly wing contains a reeded round-headed doorway.

St. James' Chapel, Kennington Park Road

> Fig. 3, plot 8

A chapel appears to have been built on the vacant site between the present Nos. 78 and 80, Kennington Park Road about 1796. In September of that year Thomas Holloway granted a sub-lease of the site to the Rev. David Bradberry.[56] The building is shown on Horwood's map of 1819 as the Kennington Meeting and Allen described it in 1826 as "a chapel for the use of the Independents . . . plainly fitted up with galleries round three sides, and an organ; and . . . capable of accommodating about five hundred persons".[57] Probably in the 1840s it was taken over for an Anglican proprietary chapel dedicated to St. James. The funds of the chapel subsequently declined and in 1863 were reported to be "in rather a drooping condition".[58] The sub-lease was put up for sale in 1873 after an action for ejectment, and was purchased by the minister, the Rev. Samuel Bache Harris. The lease was surrendered and the site purchased in 1874, and after alterations to the building, the chapel had a district assigned to it from St. Mark's in 1875. It remained a district chapelry until 1921 when it was united with St. Mary the Less; the site was sold to the Navy, Army and Air Force Institutes in 1923. The proceeds of the sale were given for the building of St. Anselm's Church, Kennington Road, which also received some of the church furniture.[56] The building was pulled down and the site used for an office building with an entrance to the N.A.A.F.I. premises between Kennings Way and Cottington Street.

Salvation Army Barracks, Kennington [8] Lane

> Fig. 3, plot 9

The former Carlisle Chapel (Congregational), which is now occupied by the Salvation Army, has a poorly designed front of stucco, finished with a pediment. The ground storey contains a round-headed window flanked by doorways, and there are three round-headed windows on the upper floor.

[9] THE CHURCH OF ENGLAND CHILDREN'S
SOCIETY HEADQUARTERS, KENNINGTON
ROAD

Formerly the Vestry Hall
Fig. 3, plot 10

The history of the site on which the Church of
England Children's Society building stands is
obscure. Harbord's map of 1636 suggests that it
was then part of a copyhold tenement which lay
on the west side of the old track from Kennington
Cross to the Common; this track followed the
line of Windmill Row across the present Kennington Road, turned at right angles south-west-
wards down Milverton Street and thence crossed
Kennington Road again to the north-west side
of Kennington Green (fig. 6). In 1615 the
extent of this copyhold, held by Edward Carpenter, was estimated at approximately 14 acres; by
1785 it had come into the hands of Sir Joseph
Mawbey. When Kennington Road was made
from Westminster Bridge Road to Kennington
Common, the old track shown on Harbord's map
appears to have been straightened, and compari-
son of Harbord's map with that of Hodskinson
and Middleton suggests that a triangular portion,
the site of the Society's building, had been detached from Mawbey's copyhold by the straight-
ening of the track. In 1785 the site is shown as a
pond. However, the extent of Mawbey's copyhold was estimated as 14ac. 3r. 16p. and the
description indicates that the pond was not included in it. When development was contem-
plated, the site was considered to be roadside
waste, and was treated as demesne land of Kennington Manor. Whether time and the useless-
ness of the site had obliterated the memory of
copyhold tenure, or whether Harbord's map is
inaccurate, it is impossible to say.

This triangular site was one of the last parts of
Kennington to be developed, probably because of
its dampness. In 1851 it was reported that the
surveyors of the parish highways "used it as a
place of deposit for materials and for Road
Scraping of which . . . there is a considerable
accumulation now upon the Ground";[59] this
may have been the reason for the disappearance
of the pond. In January 1851 the Rev. W. Leask
of the Esher Street Congregation enquired
whether a lease could be granted to him to use
the land "as a site for a chapel in connection with
the Congregational Body . . . our chapel . . .

being too small".[59] Nothing seems to have come
of this proposal, and instead Mr. C. J. Beckham
was accepted as tenant from Lady Day 1851 at
a rent of £30 per annum, to carry on a business

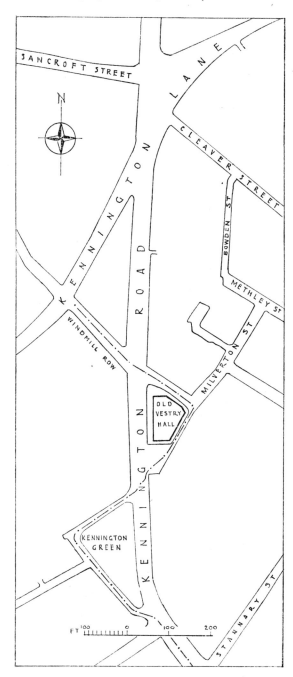

Fig. 6. Kennington Road, lay-out plan. The broken line
shows the course of the old road

as a summer-house- and chair-maker. Beckham found that the surveyors of the highways were loath to give up the ground, and the matter was taken up with the Vestry Clerk by the Duchy of Cornwall.[59]

In April 1849 the Lambeth Vestry had informed Members of Parliament for the neighbourhood that the old vestry hall in Church Street (built in 1809) was inadequate for the business of the parish, and that they wished a Bill to be promoted in Parliament to enable them to build a new hall.[60] The Vestries Act of 1850[61] gave vestries power, with the assent of the Poor Law Commissioners, to erect suitable buildings for their meetings, and after a three-day poll of the ratepayers it was decided that the Act should be put in force in Lambeth.[62] The Vestry then enquired whether the Duchy would "let the Parish have the ground with power to enclose and plant or to erect a public building thereon".[59] Negotiations for a lease were begun, but a number of vestrymen opposed the whole scheme on grounds of extravagance; when a vote was taken some of them declined "to come out of the room", while others appear to have voted twice.[63] Eventually another poll lasting four days agreed to the proposal.[62] By a lease dated June 16, 1852, the Duchy of Cornwall demised the site to the churchwardens and overseers of the parish for 99 years at an annual rent of £10, on condition that the lessees should "before the eleventh day of June one thousand eight hundred and fifty four improve the said demised premises by the erection thereon at a Cost of not less than two thousand five hundred pounds . . . of a substantial one story building [i.e. ground floor and one storey over] to be used as a Vestry Hall for the Parish of Saint Mary Lambeth".[64] Beckham was given notice to vacate the land,[59] and the Vestry borrowed £4,800 on the security of the Poor Rate for the new building.[65] The architects were Messrs. Willshire and Parris[66] and the work was carried out by William Higgs[67] (Plate 36a). The dampness of the area seems to have re-asserted itself, for the basement was flooded before the first meeting[68] on September 29, 1853.[62]

Within a few years the Vestry found the new hall too small for its purpose, and in 1856 applied to the Duchy of Cornwall for permission to add further accommodation. Permission was, however, refused because of the strict conditions laid down in the lease. The Vestry were not easily

dissuaded, and in 1860 enquired whether they could purchase the reversionary interest. Although it was not the Duchy's practice to sell demesne, it was prepared to consider a sale if a covenant could be inserted to prevent the building being raised above one storey, and so safeguard the value of the adjoining property. Plans were prepared for alterations, but the scheme lapsed. In 1881 and 1882 there were other applications to extend the accommodation, and in 1886 a request was made to purchase the freehold of the property; the price was estimated at £2,860. A dispute between the churchwardens and overseers of the parish, and the Vestry "as to the right of holding this property" arose, and the offer was eventually declined. Finally in 1892 more plans for extending the building to three storeys above ground level were prepared, but the Duchy still declined to relax the terms of the lease.[59]

With the setting up of Borough Councils in 1899 the 120 members of the Vestry were replaced by a Mayor, ten Aldermen and sixty Councillors. The new powers vested in the Borough Council made the problem of accommodation acute, and it became obvious that no amount of rebuilding would fit the Vestry Hall for the new functions of the Council. A new Town Hall was built at Brixton (see page 100), and the last meeting of the Council at Kennington was held on April 2, 1908.[69] The Borough Council suggested that the Duchy might purchase the remainder of the lease, but this offer was declined, and the lease was assigned to the Waifs and Strays for £2,600.[70]

The Church of England Children's Society, known as the Waifs and Strays until 1946, had early connections with South Lambeth. Prebendary Edward Rudolf, Superintendent of the Sunday Schools at St. Anne's, South Lambeth, and his brother Robert, were dismayed at the plight of poor children. At their instigation a meeting was held in 1881 at Mark Beaufoy's house in South Lambeth Road to establish a society within the Church of England[71] "To rescue and care for children who are orphaned, homeless, cruelly treated or in moral danger, and to relieve over-burdened homes".[72] The Archbishop of Canterbury consented to become President, and the first home was opened within the year at 8 Stamford Villas, East Dulwich.[71] The Society has had a considerable influence on modern legislation for the welfare of children. It still has its headquarters in the old Vestry

Hall, to which it moved after alterations[59] in 1909.

The building has an asymmetrical plan due to the limitations of its triangular site. The exterior, Classical in design and rather pompous in expression, is of two storeys and is built of grey brick ornamented with stone and stucco. The Kennington Road front is dominated by the centrally placed portico, tetrastyle and of the Roman Doric order, set slightly forward from the general building face. The outer columns are paired with antae and the entablature is surmounted by a triangular pediment. The middle bay contains the main entrance, framed by a doorcase formed by rusticated pilasters and quoins and a pedimented entablature. Each flanking wing has three widely-spaced windows to the ground- and first-floors, the former being round-headed and the latter segmental-headed. All are recessed with marginal surrounds and the middle window on each floor is flanked by paired pilasters. The ground-floor arches have moulded imposts and archivolts, with keystones rising to the continued entablature below the first-floor windows. These latter have keystones rising to the crowning modillioned cornice, above which is a blocking-course parapet.

COMMON LAND

KENNINGTON COMMON

Fig. 3, plots 11 and 12

The common land in Kennington lay on the south-eastern border of the Manor, and is now covered by St. Mark's Church and burial ground, the triangle of land between Brixton and Kennington Park Roads, and a large part of Kennington Park. The Common was bounded on the south-west by Vauxhall Creek and was marshy; Hodskinson and Middleton's survey shows a pond near the south-east corner, and a ditch on the north-east and east sides.[6] Cattle belonging to the tenants of the Manor were grazed there, provided that they were clearly marked, and in 1660 it is recorded that 2d. was to be paid to the "common keeper" for every horse or mare and 1d. for every head of kine set to pasture there.[73] The animals were probably driven to pasture from the riverside parts of the Manor along the track which became Kennington Road. Fines for making cartways across the Common are recorded frequently in the court rolls; in some cases the carts were said to be carrying bricks.

In the 18th and 19th centuries Kennington Common gained an evil reputation. Part of it, including the site of the church and burial ground (plot 11) and the triangle of land between Brixton and Kennington Park Roads, was used as a place of execution and known as Gallows Common. Several Jacobites were executed here after the rising of 1745, and in 1866 when the removal of Temple Bar from Fleet Street was being considered, there was a suggestion that it should be re-erected in the Park to commemorate their execution.[74] Crowds came to the Common not only to witness executions, but also to hear itinerant preachers "arguing upon their different religions",[46] and to see the cricket matches so profitable to the landlord of the Horns Tavern.

In 1801 the Grand Surrey Canal Company approached the Duchy of Cornwall with a request to purchase Gallows Common for the construction of a canal basin there. Similar proposals were made in 1807 and 1817 but they all failed.[75]

A part of the Common was surrendered for the formation of Camberwell New Road and another for St. Mark's Church and burial ground (see below). Rights of common were extinguished over the surrendered portions and the remainder was inclosed with posts and rails.[49] After the Reform Act of 1832 candidates for the Parliamentary Borough of Lambeth were nominated on the Common and some twenty thousand Chartists gathered there in 1848 before the presentation of the National Petition to Parliament.[76]

The Common was converted into a Park by the Kennington Common Inclosure Act of 1852, which extinguished all rights of common.[77]

ST. MARK'S CHURCH   [10]

Fig. 3, plot 11

St. Mark's was the second of the four "Waterloo" churches to be built in Lambeth under the Act of 1818 for providing additional churches in populous areas.[78] From the funds available to them the Commissioners for Building New Churches appointed under the Act granted £64,000 for the four Lambeth churches.[79] Considerable financial restrictions were therefore imposed on the designing and building of the churches.

The site chosen for the church at Kennington was part of Gallows Common; the Duchy of Cornwall was approached to convey the site, but it had no power to sell common land.[80] The only solution to the dilemma was to obtain an Act of Parliament empowering the Duchy to convey and the Commissioners to acquire common land of Kennington Manor. The negotiations were necessarily protracted, and in June 1823 the Lambeth Vestry expressed its desire "to avoid the unpleasant circumstance of finding the consecration of the church delayed after its completion from the want of power to convey the site".[80] The Vestry's fears were almost realized; the Act of Parliament did not receive the Royal Assent until June 24, 1824,[81] six days before the church's consecration.

Common rights over the church site and burial ground were extinguished, and £484 6s. 3d. was paid as compensation to the Lambeth Vestry, which was presumably acting on behalf of the tenants of Kennington Manor. Part of this money was given to the Trustees of the Kennington Schools and part was used for fencing, marking and draining the rest of the Common and "for the erection of further Lamp Posts or Pillars in Saint Mark's Church Yard and otherwise improving the said Common".[49]

The architect appointed for the church was D. R. Roper.[80] It has been suggested that A. B. Clayton "ghosted" for Roper,[82] but this cannot easily be proved; Roper certainly dealt with the Church Building Commissioners in all matters concerning the church. The contractors were Messrs. Moore, Grimsdell and Davis.[83] The design was for a building of "The Grecian Doric Order. . . . With Portico, and Tower, terminated with a Cupola of the Grecian Ionic Order".[80] Roper estimated the cost at £15,248, the lowest figures "consistent with the Stability and Character of the Building".[80] Of the final cost of £16,093 4s. 3d., the parish of Lambeth raised £8,442 2s. 6d. and the rest was paid by the Commissioners.[80] The first stone was laid on July 1, 1822, and the church was consecrated on June 30, 1824, both ceremonies being performed by the Archbishop of Canterbury[84] (Plates 2, 4a, 11a).

The church had accommodation for over two thousand persons. 1,082 of the sittings were rented, and under a deed of February 13, 1827[80] the surplus of the pew rents after paying the minister's stipend was set aside for providing a parsonage house. The first incumbent was the Rev. William Otter, later Bishop of Chichester.

Correctly orientated and sited within an extensive churchyard, St. Mark's has a direct and well-articulated plan on conventional lines. The body of the church forms an oblong with splayed angles, its major axis running east–west. An extension at the west end, fronted by the portico, contains an octangular vestibule placed centrally and forming the base of the steeple, flanked by staircases that lead to the gallery extending round three sides of the interior. A shallow eastern extension forms a recessed setting for the altar.

The plan is well expressed in elevations of Grecian design with a distinct Regency flavour, built in grey brick with dressings generally of Bath stone. Steps bounded by plain pedestals rise to the portico, which is wholly of Portland stone. In elevation this portico is tetrastyle in antis, but since the ends are open the antae have the form and function of square piers. The deep entablature, appropriately adorned with triglyphs, is surmounted by an ill-proportioned pediment.

Each side of the building presents a brick face divided into five equal bays by stone pilasters. Appropriately spaced within these bays are two tiers of windows, segmental-headed and without architraves, the lower tier being of squat proportion. The splayed angle walls form a further windowless bay at each end, and the return face of the portico includes a stone-faced bay containing a doorway with a window over.

The steeple, which is placed centrally behind the portico but free of the roof over the body of the church, is a curious design savouring of the ill-assorted flavours of Soane and Smirke. The square first stage has four identical faces, each with a louvred segmental-headed opening framed by wide antae and a simple entablature. At each corner is a tall pedestal-like pier crowned by an elaborate anthemion ornament. From an octangular pedestal, each cardinal face containing a clock dial flanked by stele, rises the extremely attenuated lantern. Circular in plan, its eight Ionic columns support an entablature and a hemispherical dome of stone, surmounted by a cross. A tall pedestal is introduced into each intercolumniation.

St. Mark's was a typical Commissioners' church in the arrangement and decoration of its interior. The gallery extends round three sides and over all there is a single-span ceiling, here with a shallow coved surround. Doric columns of cast-iron support the gallery, its front being appropriately adorned with a simple entablature. The walls behind the gallery are divided into bays by pilasters with moulded capitals, supporting an entablature having a frieze relief of anthemion ornament with paired sphinxes over the pilasters. The altar recess is handsomely framed by paired Ionic columns. Further plaster enrichments, including the festoon and cherub-head motifs over the windows, were introduced during the 1901 restoration.

The interior has, in fact, undergone extensive restoration twice, each time at the hand of an architect who was completely out of sympathy with his predecessor. In the 1870s, when the original pews were replaced by the present seating and choir-stalls, and the organ was removed from the west gallery to the east end, the mode was fiercely Gothic, while in 1901 it was revived Wren. The church was severely damaged by enemy action in September 1940; after partial restoration it was re-dedicated on April 9, 1949. In 1898 the fine late 19th century carved oak pulpit was brought from the demolished City church of St. Michael's, Wood Street.[85] The brass lectern was presented in the same year by Charlotte Darlington and was restored in 1949. In 1899 the font, which was originally erected in 1844, was removed to the west end. In 1903 eight tubular bells were given by the vicar, John Darlington. The communion rails were presented in 1905, and the oak screen in the gallery in 1919. The oak screen in the chapel in the south aisle was given by Emily Sophia Kinchin in 1935. The stained-glass window on the south side of the church was given in memory of John Arnoldi Cotton and his wife; it was designed by W. T. C. Shapland and made in 1952 by Barton, Kinder and Alderson; the subject is St. John baptising Our Lord. A stone set in the south wall is crudely carved "W.H. 12 Aug 1769".

[11] KENNINGTON PARK

Fig. 3, plots 11, 12 and 13

With the rapid development of the surrounding area in the first half of the 19th century, Kennington Common lost its ancient agricultural purpose and became a mere dumping ground for rubbish. In 1849 an observer stated that "The stunted herbage is trodden and soiled by a troop of cows belonging to a neighbouring milkman. A kind of pond near one corner, and a deep ditch opposite South Place, are the cemeteries of all the dead puppies and kittens of the vicinity." The vitriol factory on the east side gave off a constant stream of sulphurous vapour, and the ditches presented "an accumulation of black offensive muddy liquid, receiving constant contributions from numerous unmentionable conveniences attached to a line of low cottage erections".[86]

In 1841 there was an unsuccessful proposal to form a park in the area between Doddington Grove and Wyndham Street a little to the east of the Common. Ten years later the Rev. Charlton Lane, minister of St. Mark's Church, perhaps alarmed by the vast Chartist gathering in 1848, led a deputation to the First Commissioner of Works and the Duchy of Cornwall requesting that the Common should be made a Park. A local committee was set up to raise £1,000 of the estimated cost of £3,650, and a Bill was promoted in Parliament,[46] which became law in 1852.

The Kennington Common Inclosure Act vested the Common in the Commissioners of Her Majesty's Works and Public Buildings, "freed and discharged from all Rights of Common and all other Rights whatsoever". It also gave the Commissioners power to inclose, drain and plant the Common, and to divert Brixton Road and move the toll-gate and house.[77] Iron railings were immediately erected round the Common by Messrs. H. and M. D. Grissell, and the levelling and planting of the ground was completed by March 1854.[46] Prince Consort Lodge was also re-erected there by William Higgs (see page 36).

Before 1852 the junction of Brixton and Kennington Park Roads stood some 550 feet from St. Mark's Church, and a toll-gate controlling both roads stood near Magee Street (Plate 37b). The first draft of the Act of 1852 proposed a junction some 200 feet from the church, leaving more common land to the north-east of the junction. The Trustees of the Surrey New Roads and a number of local inhabitants objected, and as a compromise the junction was made in its present position some 300 feet from the church; the work of diverting Brixton Road was carried

D

out by Robert Neal at a cost of £746. The position of the toll-gate and house had also to be changed. The old house was sold for £33 and William Higgs built a new one at the reconstructed junction for £199; he also moved the toll-gate to its new position.[46] The house and gate were finally taken down in 1865.

A triangular piece of ground containing about three-quarters of an acre in front of South Place, now Kennington Park Place, was not fenced in after the Act of 1852 because it was not part of the Common. The inhabitants of South Place protested that if the land were left unfenced it would be used by the undesirables who had hitherto given the Common a bad name. The triangle of land had been included in the area to be purchased for the Park, but the owner, Captain Faunce de Laune, objected to its being incorporated in the Park. In 1864 the inhabitants of South Place obtained a leasehold interest and fenced the land at their own expense. Captain de Laune's successor, another de Laune, offered the land to the Commissioners in 1884 for £3,000, but his offer was declined. The inhabitants' lease lapsed in 1886 and de Laune erected a notice-board offering to let the land as a nursery ground.[46]

At this point the impact of wider considerations provided a solution of the problem. Before 1888 several other London parks as well as Kennington Park had been maintained by the Office of Works, although not Crown property. For some years Members of Parliament sitting for provincial constituencies had objected to this practice, on the ground that provincial parks had to be maintained out of local and not central government funds. The vote for the London parks was defeated in 1887, and in the same year the London Parks and Works Act transferred Victoria, Battersea and Kennington Parks, among other properties, to the Metropolitan Board of Works;[87] the Board immediately purchased de Laune's land for £2,000.[88] The London County Council took over the Park in 1889.

In 1920 the Kennington Park Extension Committee was formed to raise subscriptions for the purchase of six acres of land[89] adjoining the south-east corner of the Park.[90] These six acres were part of a croft of land and natural pasture containing eight acres, known as Shotesgrove in Hazards Marsh (fig. 3, plot 13) which lay near Hazards Bridge over Vauxhall Creek.[2] The formation of Camberwell New Road had divided Shotesgrove, leaving some six acres on the north-east side of the road. By 1920 four of the six acres were covered by houses whose leases were due to expire between 1921 and 1924, and the remaining two acres were taken up by a private road and a playground used by the schools of the district. With contributions from the Lambeth and Southwark Borough Councils and from other bodies the Committee raised £15,101 and the balance of £23,256 was contributed by the London County Council; the purchase of the land was completed in December 1921.[89] The six acres are now occupied by a flower garden, swimming pool and children's playground.

At the suggestion of the Master of Bolton Street school, a gymnasium was erected in the Park in 1861 opposite the church of St. Agnes.[46] In 1862 Felix Slade presented a drinking fountain; the steps and the bowl were of granite and were surmounted by a bronze vase upon which Jacob, Rebecca, Hagar and Ishmael were represented in low relief. The fountain was designed by Charles H. Driver; the bronze work was executed by Messrs. Elkington and the mason's work by Thomas Earp.[91] The bronze vase has now been removed, and the bowl is used as a jardinière. Another fountain, representing "The Pilgrimage of Life" was modelled by George Tinworth and was given by Sir Henry Doulton in 1869.[46]

PRINCE CONSORT'S MODEL LODGE, KEN- [12]
NINGTON PARK

Fig. 3, plot 12

This building was originally erected by the Society for Improving the Condition of the Labouring Classes as part of the Great Exhibition of 1851. The Society was established in 1844 with the Prince Consort as its President; its Honorary Architect, Henry Roberts, was a pioneer in the improvement of working-class housing. Through the influence of the Prince Consort a site at the Knightsbridge Cavalry Barrack-yard adjoining the Great Exhibition was obtained, and model houses for four families were erected there.[92] The houses (Plate 73a, fig. 7) were designed by Henry Roberts, and embodied a number of novel ideas. Each flat had a living-room, three bedrooms (each with separate access) and a scullery fitted with a sink, plate-rack, coal-bin, dust-shaft and meat-safe; there was also a water-closet.[93] The living-room had a cupboard

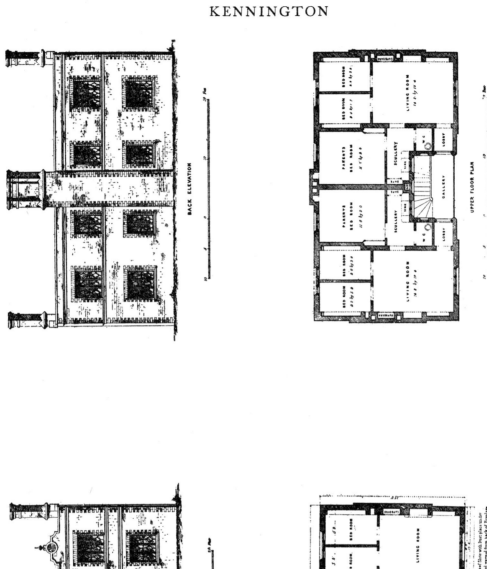

Fig. 7. Prince Consort's Model Lodge, 1851–2. Henry Roberts, architect

heated by warm air from the fireplace.[93] The most prominent feature of the design was the covered central staircase in the front, which gave access to the two upper flats. The construction of the houses was equally unusual. Hollow bricks were used, whereby it was claimed that "dryness, warmth, durability, security from fire, and deadening of sound, are obtained, as well as economy of construction to the extent, as compared with the cost of common brickwork, of at least 25 per cent".[94] No timber was used for either the first floor or the roof, which were formed with flat arches of hollow brickwork, rising from eight to nine inches, set in cement, and tied by wrought-iron rods connected with cast-iron springers, which rested on the external walls and bound the whole structure together. Concrete was used for levelling off the arches. The internal face of the walls was so smooth that plastering was unnecessary.[94] The total cost of the four dwellings was £458 14s. 7d.[93] The design was subsequently used in a number of places, notably in Cowley Gardens, Stepney, in Fenelon Place, Kensington and in Hertford, but the use of hollow bricks, despite its advantages, was never very widespread.[93]

After the Great Exhibition had closed, the houses were re-erected in 1852 by William Higgs on their present site for £557. The projecting porch at the back, which does not form part of the original design, was probably added at this time. The houses were to be used as homes for two attendants and "as a Museum for Articles relating to Cottage economy to which the public may be admitted".[46] When the outside staircase was enclosed in 1898,[46] part of the ground-floor set of rooms was used as store-rooms and offices, and the remainder, together with the upper rooms, was inhabited by the Superintendent of the Park.[95]

THE COPYHOLD LANDS

The copyhold lands in this area of Kennington fall naturally into two sections, divided by Kennington Road. In the south-western section along Kennington Lane between Kennington Road and South Lambeth Road there were several copyholds, among them the Coachfield or Stonebridge Close, the "Hornehalfeacre" and the Oatfield. In 1615 they were split among a number of copyholders but by 1785 the closes had been grouped into two large estates, belonging to James Bradshaw Peirson and Sir Joseph Mawbey, and a single copyhold in the hands of Edward Dawson. Of these three estates, only that belonging to Sir Joseph Mawbey has any building of historical or architectural interest upon it. Development in this section of the Manor was orientated upon Kennington Lane. Most of the copyholds were bounded by the Lane, and side roads were laid out to give ready access to it. The shape of the holdings, with their narrow frontages to the Lane and considerable depth, was probably responsible for the pattern of this development; only on the largest of the Mawbey copyholds (fig. 3, plots 17, 18 and 19) was the area large enough to permit a more ambitious plan.

In the north-eastern section of the Manor between Kennington Road and Newington Butts lay a number of copyholds which were divided between several persons in 1615 and, unlike the south-western section, remained so. Among these was Broadgates and the closely packed collection of copyholds at the junction of Kennington Lane and Newington Butts. In this section of the Manor there was no problem of access, for nearly every estate had frontages to both Kennington Park Road and either Kennington Road or Kennington Lane. Here estates had to be developed to make use both of the main road frontages and the intervening land. Contrasting results were achieved in Cleaver Square and the network of roads on the adjoining East estate.

THE MAWBEY ESTATE

The Mawbey copyhold estate was the largest in this part of the Manor of Kennington, being some 28 acres in extent. Sir Joseph Mawbey, senior, who held the estate in 1785, was born in Ravenstone, Leicestershire, in 1730, the son of John Mawbey and Martha Pratt. When still a child he was brought to Surrey by his maternal uncle, Joseph Pratt, a distiller at Vauxhall. It was originally intended that Mawbey should be trained for the Anglican ministry, but in default of male issue to Joseph Pratt he was taken into the distillery business.[96] When his uncle died in 1754 the business was divided between Mawbey and his cousin, Richard Pratt, son of one of Joseph Pratt's brothers.[97] After Richard Pratt's death in 1756,[98] Joseph Mawbey set himself up as a landed proprietor, buying the Manor of Botleys in Chertsey in 1765 (where he lived for most of the remainder of his life),[96] as well as other property, including some in other parts of Lambeth. He was at various periods Sheriff of Surrey, Chairman of the Quarter Sessions, and Member of Parliament first for Southwark and then for Surrey. Mawbey was created a baronet in 1765, and after his death in 1798 was succeeded by the second and last baronet, another Sir Joseph.[96]

Mawbey's property in Kennington was inherited from Joseph Pratt. Pratt held a considerable amount of land in the Manor which, on his death in 1754, was divided between Joseph Mawbey and Richard Pratt. Joseph Mawbey was granted land in Vauxhall and, in addition, a house and garden ground in Kennington Lane then occupied by Richard Pratt, together with a half share of the furniture and household goods;[97] the house stood on the site of Imperial Court.[99] The greater part of the estate was bequeathed to Richard Pratt. On the death of Richard in 1756, his daughter Elizabeth inherited the Kennington property.[98] Elizabeth Pratt married Joseph Mawbey in 1760 and under their marriage settlement Sir Joseph was subsequently admitted to her property in 1767,[100] thus reuniting the Pratt estate.

Towards the end of his life Sir Joseph granted some building leases of his Kennington property, perhaps because he was in financial difficulties. After his death in 1798[101] it was discovered that his debts, which amounted to about £45,000, could not be settled without selling property. His freehold lands in South Lambeth were put up to auction in 1800, but the proceeds were insufficient to pay the debtors. After proceedings in Chancery the Mawbey family obtained an Act of Parliament in 1805 to permit them to sell more property.[102] The greater part of the land sold under this Act was outside the Manor, but parts of the largest of the Mawbey copyholds (fig. 3, plots 17, 18 and 19) were sold in 1806. The rest of the Mawbey estate was vested in Trustees until Sir Joseph junior's death in 1817, when he too was found to be in debt.[103] The property was again vested in Trustees and gradually sold off, beginning in 1819.

No. 363 KENNINGTON LANE [13]

Formerly No. 173 Upper Kennington Lane, originally Eldon House or No. 3 Eldon Place
Fig. 3, plot 14

In 1615 the land on which this house and the church of St. Anne stand, together with houses in Harleyford Road, was owned partly by Garret Vanhey (or Vantry) and partly by James Allen.[2] In 1785, when it had come into the hands of Sir Joseph Mawbey, a house stood on the Kennington Lane frontage and its gardens ran southwards across the line of the present Harleyford Road.[6] The Trustees of Sir Joseph Mawbey, junior, sold the piece of copyhold in 1819 to Stephen Tayler of Dorset Place, Clapham Road for £1,570.[104] Tayler obtained a licence to demise his property in 1820 but it was not until January 1825 that he leased a portion of it, lying between Harleyford Road and Kennington Lane, to John Wright Snow of Kennington Lane. The lease was for 69 years from Lady Day 1824, and mentions three messuages "erected and built by the said John Wright Snow".[105] It therefore appears that Snow was responsible for pulling down the existing building and redeveloping the land in 1824. The row of houses was known as Eldon Place.

Mr. Summerson attributes the design of the house (fig. 8) to the architect J. M. Gandy (1771–1843). His evidence is primarily stylistic, and he describes the house as a striking example of Gandy's manner of decoration.[106] Gandy was for a short period in Sir John Soane's drawing office and Soane befriended him on several occasions. In the Exhibition of the Royal Academy in 1825, Gandy exhibited a picture of "Dwelling houses, &c. now building in Vauxhall Road, and other places".[107] Wandsworth Road was sometimes known as Vauxhall Road, and the houses there which Mr. Summerson attributed to Gandy have recently been demolished. Since No. 363 Kennington Lane was built in 1824 and there may well have been some delay between Gandy's picture being completed and being hung, the coincidence of dates may perhaps be held to give additional weight to the attribution.

No. 363 Kennington Lane consists of a semi-basement, three storeys, and an attic within the

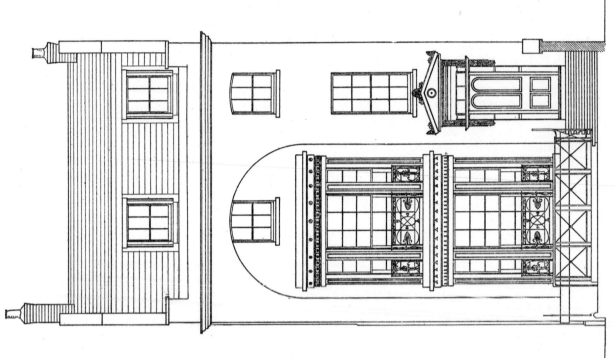

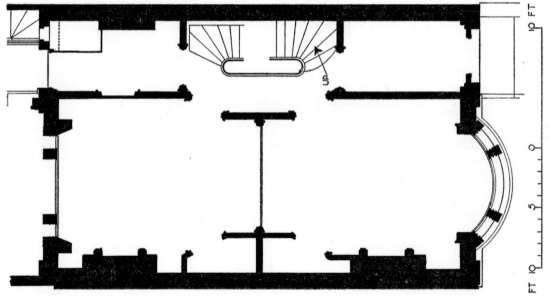

Fig. 8. No. 363 Kennington Lane, 1824, attributed to J. M. Gandy: ground-floor plan and front elevation

roof. The stucco-faced front is a design of marked originality, asymmetrical in composition and dominated by the large arch-headed recess which surrounds the shallow segmental bay of three-light windows—lighting the semi-basement, ground- and first-floors—and the small second-floor window. The mullions between the bay windows are grooved to form panels, and the ground- and first-floor windows have cast-iron guards of conventional wave and anthemion pattern. On the right of the arch-headed feature is the entrance doorway, with an elaborate pedimented hood borne on normal and inverted consoles, and above are two unornamented windows. The rear elevation is basically similar in composition to the front, but without a bay and finished in stock brick. The ingeniously planned interior contains a top-lit staircase of simple design but extremely elegant form. The principal rooms are adorned with plaster cornices and marble chimney-pieces in the Grecian taste, and the joinery is of unusual and interesting design.

Eldon Place and the land adjoining it, which was enfranchised in 1883, remained in the hands of the Tayler family until December 1891 when it was conveyed to Edward John Fooks of Lincoln's Inn in settlement of a mortgage. In the following January, Fooks conveyed the property to the Roman Catholic Diocese of Southwark, and a trust was formed to enable it to be used for a church, priests' residence, schools or cemetery.[105] No. 363, now known as St. Anne's House, was adapted for a priests' house, and a Mission with a district assigned to it from St. George's Cathedral district, was opened in 1892.[108]

[14] St. Anne's Roman Catholic Church and Primary and Secondary Schools

Fig. 3, plot 14

In 1900 the three houses adjoining No. 363 Kennington Lane were pulled down to make way for the new church designed by Frederick Arthur Walters. The foundation stone was laid on November 3, 1900, by Bishop (later Cardinal) Bourne.[109] The church was ready for use on January 31, 1903, and the opening ceremony was performed on October 25 of the same year. The tower, with the confraternity chapel and the parish room, was added in 1906–7 and the church, which seats 500 and cost £12,000 to complete, was consecrated on March 20, 1911.[110] The contractors were Messrs. Goddard and Sons of Farnham and Dorking[111] (Plate 24).

This fine church, by reason of site limitations, is built with its major axis running north to south, the entrance front to Kennington Lane facing north and the high altar being at the south end. The deeply recessed north porch leads to the wide nave of five arcaded bays, the first four opening to narrow processional aisles, that to the east being flanked by the tower and a chapel above which is the parish room. The southernmost bay of the nave, which opens to transepts of unequal length, is canted inwards to meet the chancel arch. The chancel is short and square-ended, and is flanked by chapels.

The design is an interesting and original conception, described in *The Builder*[111] as "Early English" in style, but having in fact much in common with the brick Gothic churches of the Baltic countries. The exterior, of dark red brick sparingly dressed with stone, derives most of its interest from the bold modelling of its forms. The gabled porch, its moulded arch dying into splayed jambs, has one-storey flanks each containing two small lancet windows, with a hipped lean-to roof rising to the gabled north wall of the nave. This is divided into three bays by offset buttresses, the outer ones forming a prolongation of the nave side walls. The lateral bays are quite plain but the middle one contains two tall lancet windows and a vesica-shaped opening over the central pier. The very fine tower has two tiers of tall lancet arches, the lower pair with acute gabled heads. The attenuated upper pair, which are repeated on each face, contain louvred openings and are set in shallow recessions with corbelled heads. Each face of the tower is flanked by tall flat buttresses with stone gable-heads, and the saddle-back roof produces a gable on the north and south faces, each containing three narrow lancets. The side elevations, being closely hemmed in by buildings, are of no great interest, but the south end wall presents a shallow arched recess flanked by buttresses and containing three lancet windows in its upper part. There is a gabled bellcote rising above the chancel-arch wall.

Inside, the moulded arches of the nave arcades die into chamfered piers, linked to the outer walls by buttresses that are penetrated by low arches to form the processional ways. There is no clerestory, but over the arcade runs a corbel-table of open arches. The nave is ceiled with a simple hammer-beam roof of pine, its trusses resting on simply carved stone corbels, and the pitch is continued by the lean-to roofs of the aisles. The white simplicity of the nave leads the eye to the elaborate polychromy of the stencilled decoration adorning the chancel arch, the sanctuary and its side chapels, which open to the chancel by two-bay arcades, these being surmounted by a clerestory of tall lancets. The carved canopy above the high altar, the organ case, and the rood-beam add their interest to the rich concentration of colour around the sanctuary.

Schools were built in Harleyford Road in 1892; they were extended in 1926 and 1932,[111] and occupy an unpretentious three-storey stock brick building, which stands behind the church.

[15] Nos. 48–68 (even) Harleyford Road

Formerly Nos. 4–1 (consec.) Clun Terrace and 20–14 (consec.) The Parade
Fig. 3, plots 14 and 15

This section of the Mawbey property was not developed until the Trustees of the Surrey New Roads had constructed the new road from Vauxhall to Camberwell under an Act of 1818.[19] Previously there had been no access to the Oval from Kennington Lane (see Plate 40b). The new road was named Harleyford Road to distinguish it from Harleyford Street which connected the Oval and Kennington Park Road. Harleyford, in Buckinghamshire, was the seat of the Clayton family, lessees of the demesne. Harleyford Road and Durham Street gave ready access to part of the Manor hitherto undeveloped, and building quickly followed.

Stephen Tayler, who had acquired property from the Mawbey Trustees in 1819, leased his ground fronting the south-west side of Harleyford Road to Samuel Burrows for 80 years from Christmas 1820.[112] Nos. 56–60 were built in 1821[44] and Nos. 48–54 in 1826. Nos. 62–66 were added about 1831.[44] The property was enfranchised in 1894.[112]

Nos. 48–54 form a plain three-storey terrace with basements. They are built in stock brick and above their cornice and blocking course is a panel reading "CLUN TERRACE 1826". No. 56, of the same height, abuts this terrace but is not part of its composition. Nos. 58 and 60,

a plain three-storey pair adjoining, have an elliptical tablet in the centre of the front wall at second-floor level reading "THE PARADE 1821".

Nos. 62–66 are three humble two-storey houses of stock brick, forming a group with the central house projecting slightly. Each house has a cornice and blocking course to the parapet and a sill-band to the first floor windows.

The site of No. 68 was divided between the copyhold granted to Stephen Tayler in 1819 and that leased by the Mawbey Trustees to William Henry Jackson, carpenter, of Church Street, Westminster, in December 1822[113]; the house appears to have been erected in 1822. Jackson's lease was for 61 years, in consideration of his expenses in building a house on the property. Although the "whole of the garden at the rear together with the scullery and Part of the Kitchen with parts of the rooms over" was on Tayler's copyhold,[114] the house seems to have been regarded as belonging to the Mawbey Trustees. In 1824 their interest was sold to John Woodcock, oilman, of Honey Lane Market, Cheapside.[115] The portion of the house on Tayler's copyhold was enfranchised with the rest of his property in 1894 and the remainder by Woodcock's descendants two years later.[114] The house came into the hands of one owner in 1899 by the purchase of both parts by Robert Briant of Kennington Park Road, auctioneer and surveyor.[113]

Nos. 40 and 42 Durham Street [16]

Formerly Nos. 11 and 12 Durham Street
Fig. 3, plot 15

The original wood shop-fronts of these houses still survive. The fronts have fascias with swept ends, and are flanked by narrow reeded pilasters. The private entrance to No. 42 is incorporated within the shop-front while No. 40 has a separate entrance with a small patterned fanlight. These houses and those opposite have recessed rectangular panels to the parapets over the first-floor windows similar to those at Nos. 76–82 Harleyford Road.

No. 337 Kennington Lane [17]

Formerly No. 143 Upper Kennington Lane
Fig. 3, plot 15

The land on which this house stands was part of a close of pasture owned in 1615 by Ralph Hanmer; Hanmer also held the Stonebridge Close which took its name from the stone Cox's Bridge over Vauxhall Creek in South Lambeth Road. From the close of pasture a slip of land had been taken which was known as the "Hornehalfeacre";[2] it is now covered by the buildings in Farnham Royal.

A house is shown on or near the site of No. 337 on Rocque's map of 1745, and a house is mentioned on the property in 1767.[100] It is not certain whether either of these can be identified with No. 337. Sir Joseph Mawbey obtained a general licence to demise his property in 1770,[116] and architectural evidence suggests that No. 337 was built under that licence. For some years before 1789 it was occupied by Thomas Fassett.[55] Fassett took over Sir Joseph Mawbey's distillery at Vauxhall in 1779–80[117] and it seems possible, though by no means certain, that he built himself a dwelling-house on another part of Mawbey's property at no great distance from the distillery. The house had extensive grounds which are now covered by the buildings in Durham Street and Kennington Grove.

No. 337 is a plain stock brick fronted house containing a basement, three storeys, and an attic within a mansard roof. The entrance is placed in a small single-storey wing on the east side, the doorcase being formed by panelled pilasters supporting consoles on which rests a dentilled open pediment.

[18] Nos. 70–82 (even) HARLEYFORD ROAD

Formerly Nos. 13–7 (consec.) The Parade
Fig. 3, plot 16

In 1615 the copyholder of the land on which these houses stand was Frances Froome, widow, and her holding was described as a close of meadow called Hales.[2] By 1785 it had changed its name, then being called the Oatfield, and was part of the property held by Sir Joseph Mawbey, senior.[6] Harleyford Road was cut diagonally across the southern end of the plot, and these houses were built on the south-west side of the road In 1821 the Trustees of Sir Joseph Mawbey, junior, obtained a licence to demise this property,[118] but the land was not developed at that date. In May 1828 their interest in the property was sold to William Foxton the younger, of the Exchequer Office, Somerset Place.[119] The houses appear to have been built between 1828 and 1831.[44] The property was enfranchised in 1879.[120]

Nos. 68–74 are mean two-storey houses, some with semi-basements. Nos. 76–82 are two-storey houses of broader frontage with round-arched entrances at the centre which set forward slightly. The windows over these entrances are blank. There are recessed rectangular panels in the parapets over each of the two first-floor windows and the blanks, and over each of the entrances. The group of four is unified by a sill-band on the first floor. The fronts of Nos. 76 and 78 have been rebuilt with Fletton bricks.

Nos. 43–55 (odd) HARLEYFORD ROAD [19]

Formerly Nos. 1–7 Slaney Place
Fig. 3, plot 16

This is a terrace of seven houses, built of stock brick, each containing a semi-basement, two storeys, and an attic within a mansard roof. Each front is two windows wide and they are combined to form a composed elevation in which a central feature, embracing three houses and crowned by a triangular pediment, is set slightly forward from wings, each of two houses. The ground storey, faced with coursed stucco, contains the doorways which have fluted quadrant reveals and patterned fanlights.

Nos. 231–245 (odd) KENNINGTON LANE [20]

Formerly Nos. 31–45 (odd) Upper Kennington Lane, originally Nos. 1–8 (consec.) Kennington Terrace
Fig. 3, plot 17

The ground on which these houses stand, together with the gasholder station, Imperial Court and other houses in Kennington Road, formed part of one large copyhold. In 1615 the copyholder was Edward Carpenter, whose property is described as a tenement in part newly-constructed (lying in Kennington Lane) together with an orchard and three closes of meadow and pasture.[2] On or near the site of Edward Carpenter's house was the residence of Richard Pratt, which in 1754 was inherited by (Sir) Joseph Mawbey. Imperial Court now covers the site.

On December 30, 1793, Sir Joseph Mawbey granted a lease of the site of Nos. 231–245 Kennington Lane to Thomas Cope[a] for 61 years from Michaelmas 1790.[121] This evidence, connected with that from other records of the Duchy of Cornwall[122] suggests that the houses were

a Possibly Thomas Corpe; see Index.

standing by 1793 and were probably built in 1791. However, the terrace does not appear in the Rate Books of this area in 1794. In 1795 the houses were said to be new built, and all eight appear in the Rate Book of 1796.[44]

These houses were sold by the Trustees of Sir Joseph Mawbey, junior, together with other adjacent property including No. 356 Kennington Road (see page 45), to Allen Williams, surgeon, of St. Saviour's, Southwark, in 1819.[121] The property remained in the hands of the Williams family until 1904 when it was sold in two lots by the Trustees of Catherine Williams. A number of the houses were acquired later by Hayward Bros., pickle manufacturers, for for extension of their premises.[123]

Benjamin Gompertz, F.R.S. (1779–1865), mathematician and actuary, lived at No. 231 from 1811 or 1812 to 1865. He collaborated with Francis Baily in the construction of tables for the mean places of the fixed stars; he was also actuary to his brother-in-law Sir Moses Montefiore and to Nathan Rothschild, founders of the Alliance Assurance Co., as well as a consultant actuary to the Government. His law of human mortality was a basis for many later actuarial developments.[96]

Nos. 231–245 form a plain three-storey terrace raised above semi-basements, with a slated, mansard-roofed attic storey. Nos. 237 and 239 and the end houses are a little higher than the others and are set forward slightly. The centre houses have Victorian cast-iron window guards on the first floor. Except where repaired, the façades are finished with dentilled cornice bands to the parapets.

[21] THE GASHOLDER STATION

Formerly the South London Waterworks
Fig. 3, plots 17 and 18

In 1805 an Act of Parliament was passed instituting the Company of Proprietors of the South London Waterworks for the purpose of supplying the parish of St. Giles, Camberwell, parts of the parish of St. Mary, Lambeth, and other places in Surrey with water. The Company was restricted to supplying those parts of Lambeth not already supplied by the Lambeth Waterworks on the South Bank, and was to obtain water from the Thames and Vauxhall Creek.[124] To the north of the Oval, the Company constructed an engine house, sluice house, offices, reservoirs and a canal (Plate 40b). Sir Joseph Mawbey, junior, one of the proprietors of the Company, sold the land to the Company in 1808.[125]

Water was first supplied in 1807, but in the same year the engine house and a wooden reservoir were destroyed by fire.[126] In 1822 two steam engines were in use, but because the site was low they proved inadequate and a new 45 h.p. engine was installed. Another was erected by the Thames at Cumberland Gardens,[127] on land belonging to the Dean and Chapter of Canterbury. Soon afterwards the removal of old London Bridge and the accumulation of rubbish in Vauxhall Creek affected the quantity and quality of the water supply. A tunnel was therefore laid which conveyed water from the bed of the Thames directly to the works,[126] and Vauxhall Creek was returned to the jurisdiction of the Commissioners of Sewers.[128] A new reservoir and filter bed were also constructed; they were so effective "as to render . . . [the water] transparent".[127]

In 1834 the name of the Company was changed to the Vauxhall Waterworks Company,[129] and it took over the area formerly supplied by the Lambeth Waterworks.[130] In 1845 the Company was amalgamated with the Southwark Company to form the Southwark and Vauxhall Water Company, and the works at Kennington were abandoned.[131] They were purchased with the site in 1847 by the Phoenix Gas Company.[126] The gasholders erected by this Company are decorated with phoenix devices; their proximity to the Oval has made them famous amongst cricketers.

NOS. 362–366 (even) KENNINGTON ROAD [22]

Fig. 3, plot 18

These houses were erected shortly after 1800. They form a dull three-storey terrace with semi-basements and attics. The plain round-headed entrances have artificial stone keystones of stock pattern modelled respectively with the heads of a smiling youth, a bearded man, and a woman. The keystone masks at Nos. 362 and 366, which are in semi-profile, are identical with those over the side wings of No. 274 South Lambeth Road. Similar keystones, salved from houses demolished in Pollard Row, Bethnal Green, are marked "COADE LAMBETH 1791".

[23] IMPERIAL COURT, KENNINGTON LANE
        Formerly the Licensed Victuallers' School
        Fig. 3, plot 19

In 1803 Sir Joseph Mawbey granted a lease of
Kennington House on the south side of Kennington Lane to seven Trustees acting on behalf of
the Friendly Society of Licensed Victuallers.
The lease, which was dated from Christmas 1802,
was for 21 years, and the rent was £100 a year.
The house (Plate 33a) had formerly been occupied
by Sir Joseph Mawbey and more recently by the
Abbé de Broglio. It had a frontage of 85 feet,
and contained a large number of rooms, including
a school-room, nursery, two kitchens and a
number of additions at the back.[132] A school
was opened there on January 10, 1803.[133]

In 1807 Kennington House was sold under
the terms of Sir Joseph Mawbey's Act of Parliament of 1805[102] to the Licensed Victuallers for
£1,080. The school was evidently successful, for
in 1819 the Society acquired the next two houses
on the north-east side of Kennington House from
Sir Joseph Mawbey's Trustees for £2,045.[132] In
1827 Elmes described the school as "an establishment more to be regarded for the benevolent
views of its patrons, than for the architectural
beauty of the building", and noted that money
from *The Morning Advertiser* supplemented the
funds of the Licensed Victuallers.[134] The two
houses were subject to leases of which several
years were still unexpired, and (perhaps owing to
lack of money) the Society granted new leases of
21 and 28 years' duration in 1831 and 1832.
Shortly afterwards it was decided to erect entirely
new buildings; these two leases were surrendered
and all three houses were demolished. The
Society was incorporated by Letters Patent in
1836 as "The Society of Licensed Victuallers".[132]

The foundation stone of the building now
known as Imperial Court was laid by the Prime
Minister, Lord Melbourne, on January 21, 1836.
An hermetically-sealed glass vase containing plans
of the building and specimens of coins of the
realm was placed in a cavity in the stone, and the
cavity was then covered with a brass plate with
the following inscription: "GULIELMO
QUARTO REGE.—The first stone of the
Licensed Victuallers' School, Established Anno
Domini MDCCCIII., for the Education,
Clothing and Maintenance of the Orphans and
other Destitute Children of Members of the
Friendly Society of Licensed Victuallers, was

laid by the Right Hon. William Lord Viscount
Melbourne, Prime Minister of England, in the
name of his Most Gracious Majesty King William
the Fourth, the Patron of the School, on Thurs-
day, the 21st day of January, MDCCCXXXVI.,
in the presence of the Officers of the Society."[135]
The building was designed by Henry Rose,[136]
the builders were Messrs. Webb, and the cost
was about £14,000.[137] (Plate 33b, fig. 9).

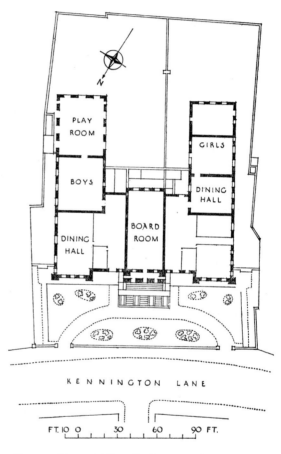

Fig. 9. Licensed Victuallers' School (now Imperial
Court), plan based on the Ordnance Survey map of 1870

The ambitious scale of these new buildings was
evidently justified, for by 1844 the number of
children admitted since the school's foundation
in 1803 had reached 995 of whom 112 were
actually in the school at that date. Of these 995,
248 had, on leaving, been apprenticed, 403 had
been sent to service, 200 had been taken by relations and friends, 22 had died in the school,

10 had been expelled for repeated misconduct, and 112 were still there. A further 30 pupils were admitted in 1844, bringing the number up to 142.[133]

The whole property was enfranchised in 1857.[133] In 1888 a house on the north-east side of the school (which had been enfranchised in 1866) was bought,[132] and a small new building was erected in 1890 on its site. In 1921 the school acquired new premises at Slough, Buckinghamshire, and the Kennington Lane property was bought shortly afterwards by the Navy, Army and Air Force Institutes and renamed Imperial Court.[132] The rear part of the building has since been very considerably altered and enlarged.

The present Imperial Court presents an imposing front which consists of a central feature and end pavilions, each of three bays, projecting boldly from wings, also of three bays. The lower stage of the front, containing the ground floor and mezzanine, is rusticated and of stucco, the centre and end pavilions being arcaded. The upper stage is of stock brick and contains two tiers of rectangular windows, those to the end pavilions having stucco dressings. The centre is adorned with a tetrastyle portico of Composite columns carrying a triangular pediment, its entablature being pitched slightly higher than that over the wings and end pavilions.

[24] Nos. 320–326 (even) KENNINGTON ROAD
Formerly Nos. 2–5 (consec.) Minerva Place
Fig. 3, plot 19

On August 3, 1793, Sir Joseph Mawbey granted a lease of land at Kennington Green "with the two new Erected Messuages . . . thereon" to John Adams, James Willis and Sarah Williams, widow of William Williams, for 61 years from Midsummer 1794.[103] The lease was granted in consideration of the expenses incurred by William Williams, coal merchant, before his death, and Adams and Willis thereafter, in erecting the two houses, Nos. 324A and 326. Two years later Mawbey granted a lease of property adjoining the site of Nos. 324A and 326 on the north, to John Ditcham, carpenter, of Church Street, Southwark, also for 61 years. Ditcham covenanted to build "three or more good and substantial Brick Messuages" on the land within five years.[103] Nos. 320 and 322 were built on this land. Both these pieces of property remained in the hands of the Mawbey family until 1819 when, together with

another piece of property fronting Kennington Road, they were sold to Henry Budd of Russell Square for £1,410.[103]

Nos. 324A and 326 are a pair of stock brick houses of three storeys and semi-basements. They share a thinly-moulded pediment with a lunette in its tympanum, and are united by a continuous sill-band on the first floor. The wood doorcases have open pediments resting on delicately foliated consoles above fluted pilasters with foliated (324A) and plain (326) caps. Each console is faced with a patera and each door is surmounted by a semi-circular fanlight of radiating pattern. The flutings of the door pilasters are stopped at the bottom by reeding.

Nos. 320 and 322 are a plain pair of the same height, with recessed round-headed ground-floor windows and doorways. Each doorway has a simple fanlight of radiating pattern.

Nos 346–356 (even) KENNINGTON ROAD [25]
Formerly Nos. 1–6 (consec.) Kennington Green
Fig. 3, plots 17 and 19

The conformation of this part of the Mawbey property was slightly altered when Kennington Road was cut through from Westminster Bridge Road to Kennington Common, under the Act of 1751 (fig. 6). The old path which ran between Kennington Cross and Kennington Common was straightened, leaving a triangle of land on the east side of the new road where the Church of England Children's Society building (formerly the Vestry Hall) now stands. The path had also made a right-angled detour round a pond; after the track had been straightened, the pond and the old pathway were left vacant on the west side of Kennington Road. The pond, known as Mawbey's pond, was connected by a ditch or sewer to Vauxhall Creek. In 1813 it was filled up and the area which it had covered, later known as Kennington Green, was inclosed with posts and rails.[138]

Sir Joseph Mawbey, junior, was admitted to the Mawbey property in 1800 after his father's death,[139] and the row of houses bordering the north-west side of the green was built soon afterwards (fig. 10). Nos. 346–352 were erected in 1804–5 and No. 354 in 1802–3.[44] In October 1806 these five houses were sold to Thomas Ward Blagrave, Henry Pilleau, John Austin, George Bye and Edmund White respectively,[140] to assist in the settlement of the debts of Sir

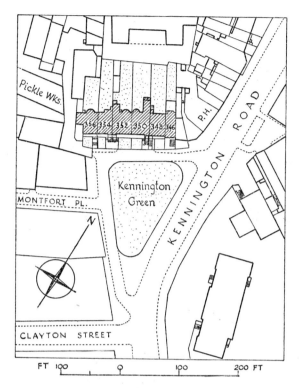

Fig. 10. Nos. 346–356 Kennington Road, lay-out plan

Joseph Mawbey, senior. The houses were enfranchised at various periods, the first, No. 350, in 1872.[141]

No. 356 formed part of plot 17 and was built on land leased by Mawbey in November 1802, to William Weston, for 61 years. The house was erected in 1802–3 and was sold by Mawbey in June 1819, together with other adjoining parts of his property (see page 42), to Allen Williams, surgeon, of St. Saviour's, Southwark.[121] In 1882 most of the garden of the house was made into a builders' yard,[122] and is now part of the premises of Messrs. C. T. Kent, Ltd., oiled-silk manufacturers.

Nos. 346–356 (figs. 11, 12a) form a continuous range of stock brick houses, grouped in pairs and lying at an angle to Kennington Road to face the small ornamental garden at Kennington Green. Although they are not all uniform in height, each house has three storeys well raised above a semi-basement, and (except at Nos. 346 and 348) an attic storey with lunette dormers in a slated mansard roof.

Nos. 350 and 352 provide in effect a central

feature of charming design, their united fronts forming a composition with six equally-spaced windows in each storey. The ground- and first-floor windows are set within shallow arched recesses, the former being arch-headed and the latter rectangular. Artificial stone (probably Coade) is used for the guilloche impost-bands and female-mask keystones to the ground-floor arcade (Plate 70e), and for the ram's-head impost-blocks and lunette rosettes of the first-floor arcade. A lattice-pattern balcony railing of cast-iron continues across the front at first-floor level; the second-floor windows are without ornament; and the front finishes with a simple entablature. A further arch extending on either side of the ground storey contains an entrance door, flanked by paired columns with slender fluted shafts and leaf capitals, carrying a transom originally enriched with compo ornaments. No. 350 still has its ornamental metal fanlight of radial design (Plate 68a).

No. 354 has a similar doorway to those last described, retaining its transom ornament of a vase flanked by guilloche bands with swagged lion-heads over the paired columns. The house front, however, is of different design with two windows in each storey. The ground-floor openings are ellipse-headed while those to the

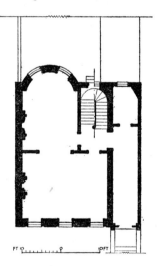

Fig. 11. No. 350 Kennington Road, ground-floor plan

first floor are rectangular and set in arched recesses with fan-ornamented lunettes of stucco. The entrance to No. 356 has a similar transom to No. 354, borne by a single substantial column on

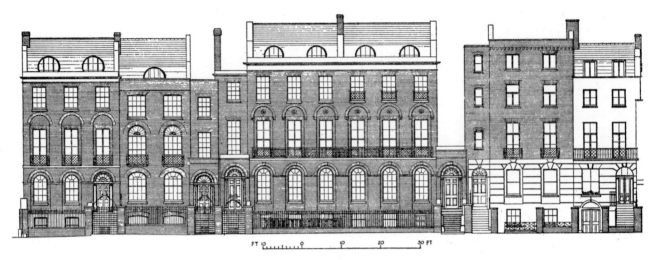

Fig. 12a. Nos. 346–356 Kennington Road, 1802–5

Fig. 12b. Nos. 146–156 Kennington Park Road, 1769–88

each side of the door. The first-floor windows of this pair have cast-iron window guards of lattice pattern with chamfered corners.

No. 346 has a rendered front and its entrance door is flanked by plain columns bearing a mutule transom. No. 348, the upper part of which has been altered, has an entrance doorway with a keystone similar to those at Nos. 350 and 352, the transom being smaller but similar in pattern to that at No. 354.

THE CROOKE ESTATE

The land on which the Horns Tavern and Nos. 176, 178 and 180 Kennington Park Road stand was formerly part of an estate of approximately five acres, bounded (at the present time) by Kennington Road, Kennington Park Road and the backs of houses on the south-west side of Ravensdon Street. In 1615 it was held jointly by Jane and Elizabeth Dalton and was described as pasture land.[2] Joseph Fortee was admitted to the copyhold in 1726 and in 1764 his heir surrendered it, among other property, to Thomas Parry of Lambeth.[142] Much of the development of the estate took place during the tenure of the Parry family. The estate was a compact one, lying at the junction of Kennington Park Road and the newly constructed Kennington Road, but unlike the adjacent Cleaver estate, it was not granted on a single lease for development. Instead, building leases were granted to a number of persons.

The land passed into the hands of the Crooke family on the marriage of Elizabeth Parry and John Crooke in 1776. Their heir, a second John Crooke, became involved in financial difficulties and in 1811 part of the estate, including the Horns and No. 180 Kennington Park Road, but excluding Nos. 176 and 178, was sold to Richard Farmer. Farmer was the owner of a vitriol factory on the site of St. Agnes' Church, St. Agnes Place.[143] No. 180 Kennington Park Road was sold by Farmer to Robert Cottle in 1822,[142] but Farmer retained other parts of the property in his hands for a considerable period.

[26] THE HORNS TAVERN, KENNINGTON PARK ROAD

Fig. 3, plot 20

A tavern appears to have been the first building erected upon this copyhold. The site chosen was bounded on the south-east by Kennington Park Road, which must have carried a considerable volume of traffic from an early date and a greater volume after it was made a turnpike road in 1717.[144] The turnpike stood in the roadway near Magee Street. To the south-west the site was bounded by a track-way or path connecting Kennington Lane and Kennington Common, which later became Kennington Road. The date of the building of the first tavern is not known. There was only one building on the copyhold when Joseph Fortee was admitted in 1726[142] and since a Coroner's Inquest was held at the Green Man and Horns in 1725,[7] it seems reasonable to assume that the tavern was the building noted in Fortee's admission. Rocque's map of 1745 also shows the tavern as the only building on the property.

The Manor court met at the Horns for a considerable period, but its records shed little light on the antiquity of the tavern. The earlier court rolls do not give the place of meeting of the court; later, in the 1720s it is stated to have met on a few occasions in Spring Garden House,[145] and in 1764 a special Court Baron was held "at the House of John Tyers, Esq., at Vauxhall".[146] The special mention of courts being held at Spring Gardens, which Tyers had in lease, and the absence of other mention of the places of meeting of the court suggest that to meet at Spring Gardens was not normal practice. The first

record of the court meeting at the Horns was on January 22, 1767,[100] when it was held "at the House of Thomas Ellis commonly called or known by the Name or Sign of the Green Man and Horns". Thereafter meetings were regularly held there with the exception of a few held at the Crown and Cushion in Lambeth Marsh. The Horns Tavern has experienced several changes of name which can be traced in the court rolls; it appears, at various times, as the Green Man and Horns, the Surrey Hotel and Tavern and finally the Horns.[147] Apart from being the place of meeting of the Manor court, the Horns was a focal point of activities in the neighbourhood, and must also have drawn much custom from the public meetings and executions which brought crowds to Kennington Common.

As well as the tavern itself, the landlord of the Horns had premises on the opposite side of Kennington Road, part of the demesne lands of the Manor. The earliest mention of the leasing of this property is in 1755 when Thomas Smith obtained a sub-lease of a building there, together with a garden.[14] By 1785 part of this leasehold was being used as a bowling green,[6] which gave its name to the present Bowling Green Street. Later, about 1820, another landlord, Mr. Bryant, turned the demesne leasehold into a tea-garden, but the land was soon surrendered for building.[7]

The tavern was a prosperous one, and in 1826 was said to provide "ample accommodation" for the cricketers frequenting Kennington Common, and to have "a large assembly-room attached to it".[148] During the next thirty years the prosperity of the tavern seems to have declined, and its landlord became bankrupt;[149] in 1856 it was reported as being closed.[20] But prosperity returned a few years later. The assembly hall (destroyed in the war of 1939–45), which was "occasionally appropriated for Horticultural and Floral exhibitions; and also used for the delivery of lectures, both scientific and amusive",[150] was clearly an asset to the landlord. The Horns has been rebuilt on at least one occasion, and still retains its importance as a landmark in Kennington.

NOS. 176–180 (even) KENNINGTON PARK ROAD [27]

Formerly Nos. 1 and 2 Kennington Row
Fig. 3, plot 20

These houses were built during the period that

Thomas Parry and his heirs held the property. In 1767 Thomas Parry obtained a licence to demise his copyhold, and the houses known as Kennington Row were built a few years later. The building leases were granted between 1769 and 1775.[142] Although the lease for No. 178 has not been found, the house was standing in 1780, when John Law was paying Land Tax for it.[55] The house was surrendered by John Crooke, junior, to George Pearson in 1811. Between 1824 and 1830 wings were added and a shop-front built across its front garden. The house has subsequently been divided into two, Nos. 176 and 178 Kennington Park Road. The building lease for No. 180 was granted on June 24, 1771, to James Spencer, for 60 years at an annual rent of £5.[142]

The house now Nos. 176–178 is uninteresting except for the well-designed shop-front with engaged Ionic columns supporting its fascia and dentilled cornice. No. 180, a refronted house of three storeys with a mansard attic behind its corniced parapet, retains a richly detailed entrance porch of wood. Doric-type columns and pilasters with fluted shafts support an entablature which has its architrave enriched with guttae, its frieze adorned with fluting between wreaths, and a mutule cornice. The porch ceiling has a key-ornamented panel.

[28] KENNINGTON MANOR SECONDARY SCHOOL, KENNINGTON ROAD

Fig. 3, plot 20

This school was built by the London School Board and opened on August 23, 1897. The architect was T. J. Bailey and the contractors were J. and M. Patrick of Rochester; their tender for a school for 894 children was for £17,308.[151] The school (Plate 35b, fig. 13) is a long three-storey building with the centre portion flanked by towers containing the staircases. The pedimented wings are joined to the centre by lower links of five storeys which have smaller windows. The southern wing was not built until 1900.

THE EAST ESTATE

In 1554 Thomas Gon (or Gan) held a close containing 11 acres known as "Brodegates" or Broadgates, another of three acres called the "Pightell" and a third containing eight acres, all lying on the south side of the road from Southwark to Kingston-on-Thames (Kennington Lane).[1] Gon's holding seems to have comprised most of the copyhold land lying between Newington Butts and Kennington Road. By 1615 his estate had been broken up. John Bardesley and his wife had acquired Broadgates, now three closes, and the rest of the property had been divided between Daniel Wynch and Elizabeth and Jane Dalton.[2] Later, Broadgates was itself subdivided, part being incorporated in the Cleaver estate and part coming into the hands of the East family. In 1785 Sir William East's copyhold, although said to have been formerly Broadgates, was estimated as only 6 ac. 35 p.[6] compared with 11 acres in 1554.

The East family was related by marriage to

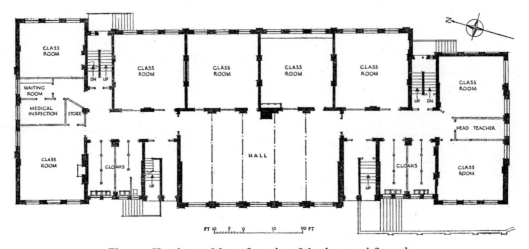

Fig. 13. Kennington Manor Secondary School, ground-floor plan

the Claytons, lessees of the demesne. The daughter of Sir William East, copyholder in 1785, married (Sir) William Clayton, the last lessee. The East family had other property in Lambeth, including the site of St. John's Church, Waterloo Road.[152] Part, at least, of the Kennington property remained in their hands until recent years.[153]

[29] METHLEY, RADCOT, RAVENSDON AND MILVERTON STREETS

Fig. 3, plot 21

Hodskinson and Middleton's survey of 1785 shows no development on the site of these streets,[6] but when Horwood's map of 1799 was published, Queen's Row, now Ravensdon Street, connected Kennington Park Road and Kennington Green, and some houses were standing on the south-west side of it. The ground between Queen's Row and Prince's, later Cleaver, Square appears to have been laid out as a garden. The laying out of Methley, Radcot, Ravensdon and Milverton Streets belongs, therefore, to the period of redevelopment in Kennington.

In 1868 Sir Gilbert East was admitted to the estate on the death of his father, and he obtained a licence to demise his property for a term not exceeding 65 years.[22] Sir Gilbert had already submitted a plan for developing the land between Queen's Row (Ravensdon Street) and Cleaver Square to the Metropolitan Board of Works. The old buildings in Queen's Row were to be pulled down and the road widened. In addition, three new roads, Methley, Radcot and Milverton Streets, were planned. Since the area had little access to the adjacent main roads, Sir Gilbert agreed with the adjoining copyholders to extend the new Methley Street and provide a route to Kennington Lane by what is now Bowden Street (fig. 14). To facilitate the passage of traffic from Kennington Road, Kennington Place, now Stannary Street, was extended to meet the new Radcot Street. A further proposal to rebuild the houses facing the north side of the Vestry Hall and widen the road there had to be delayed as Sir Gilbert's tenants were unwilling to sell their leases. As a temporary measure, the forecourts of the houses were taken back to give a roadway of 40 feet, on the understanding that rebuilding would be carried out when the leases fell in.[154] The houses were rebuilt a few years later.

The estate was designed by Alfred Lovejoy, architect and surveyor, of Cannon Street, E.C.[154]

E

The houses form terraces with simple elevations of grey brick and are generally of two storeys raised above semi-basements (Plate 49c). Something of a polychromatic effect is achieved by the linking of the sills and window heads with red

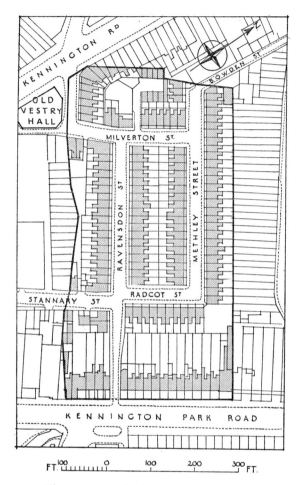

Fig. 14. Ravensdon Street area, lay-out plan

brick bands and by the alternating of red and blue brick in the arches over the windows and over the recessed entrance porches. The long terraces are articulated by the separate setting forward of the fronts of each of the houses, and Methley, Radcot and Ravensdon Streets are formalized in an easy manner by the addition of an extra storey to the centre groups of houses in each street.

The houses in the west corner of the estate near the old Vestry Hall, Kennington Road, were built a little later. They form no part of the uniform development of the rest of the estate.

[30] Nos. 140–170 (even) Kennington Park Road

Formerly Nos. 2–17 (consec.) Queen's Place
Fig. 3, plot 21

Sir William East obtained a licence to demise his property in 1769 and in 1785 Nos. 140–146 and 150–154 had already been built.[6] Nos. 148 and 156–162 had been added by 1788 and Nos. 164–170 shortly afterwards.[44] Sir Gilbert East was admitted to the estate in 1868 on the death of his father and in 1887 wished to rebuild Nos. 140–162, but this project was never carried out (see page 20).

Nos. 140–162 form a long regular three-storey terrace of which the centre houses, Nos. 148–152, are a storey higher. These houses are also defined by the cast-iron window guards at their first-floor windows. Nos. 140–146 have wood doorcases with full pediments carried on consoles, while the others have open pediments resting on simple pilasters. The whole terrace has a plain parapet from end to end, and is raised above a semi-basement storey (fig. 12b).

Nos. 164–170 form a similar three-storey terrace which has been much spoilt by refronting. Nos. 164 and 166 have pedimented doorcases with Doric-type engaged columns and patterned fanlights; the others have poor quality round-headed entrances with moulded archivolts and fluted pilasters.

THE CLEAVER ESTATE

In 1615 the Cleaver estate was owned partly by Daniel Wynch and partly by John Bardesley.[2] Mary Cleaver was admitted to the estate in 1743 on the death of her husband[155] and the property then consisted of one large field, known later as the White Bear Field,[156] and other land lying along Kennington Lane and Kennington Road, including the triangle at the junction of these two roads (see page 53). During Mary Cleaver's tenure of the estate, the triangle and other small pieces of land were sold to the Trustees of the Surrey New Roads for making the new Kennington Road,[157] and another small parcel in Kennington Lane was sold to William Allen, but the bulk of the property was leased at some date before 1783 to Thomas Ellis, victualler, of the Horns, Kennington Road.[158] Ellis was responsible for developing the greater part of the estate and he granted a number of building sub-leases to various persons, notably William Brooks and William Ingle. Development had advanced considerably by the time that Mary Ann Cleaver was admitted on her mother's death in 1797.[155]

Mary Ann Cleaver held the estate until September 1815, when she surrendered it to John Bowden, then of Fulham but later of Grosvenor Place, in exchange for an annuity of £200.[159] The later development of the property took place while it was in the hands of the Bowden family. Under a deed of 1853 the estate was divided between the Rev. Henry George Bowden and the Rev. Charles Bowden, both of Brompton Oratory. The Rev. C. Bowden acquired all the property north-east of a line drawn from Cleaver Street to Kennington Park Road, and the Rev. H. G. Bowden all the property to the south-west of that line.[23] The estate remained divided between various members of the family until 1906, when it was reunited in the hands of the Rev. H. G. Bowden, and was enfranchised in 1907.[157]

Nos. 309–341 (odd) Kennington Road   [31]

Formerly Nos. 18–2 (consec.) Marlborough Place
Fig. 3, plot 22

As far as can be judged No. 317 Kennington Road was the first building erected during Thomas Ellis' development of this section of the Cleaver property. The formation of Kennington Road had left the Cleaver estate with a long, straight frontage which invited building development. No. 317, then known as Marlborough House and at a later date as No. 14 Marlborough Place, first appears in the records in 1787. It was then occupied by William Edridge.[55] No building sub-lease for the house has been found, but that for an adjacent house indicates that the site was in lease to Edridge;[160] the initials "W E" on a tablet on the house further suggest that Edridge at least commissioned the house if he was not himself responsible for building it.

For a few years Marlborough House stood alone on this part of the Cleaver estate. Then under a series of building sub-leases granted by Ellis in 1790 and 1791 Nos. 299–315 and Nos. 319–343 were built. Nos. 299–305 were rebuilt in the latter part of the 19th century; they were formerly Nos. 2–5 (consec.) Brooks Place, a name probably derived from William Brooks, mason, of St. George, Bloomsbury, who was responsible for building most of the new houses.[161]

Sub-leases were also granted to John Ashley of Lambeth, bricklayer,[162] for one house, George Lovell of Red Lion Street, St. George the Martyr, Middlesex, for two houses,[163] and John Jeffkins Clarke of St. Giles in the Fields, plumber and glazier, for one house.[164]

In 1872 permission was given for No. 343 to be taken down and the site exchanged with Sir Gilbert East for another small piece of land. At the same time the Metropolitan Board of Works sanctioned the erection of shop-fronts to the remainder of the houses then standing.[23] According to Clowes' History of the Manor, No. 317 was for a period used as a "picture palace".[7]

Nos. 309–341, a long stock brick terrace of three-storey houses, mostly with attic storeys in slated mansard roofs, have been spoiled by the shops which were built across their front gardens in 1872. The front of No. 317 is five windows wide, the middle three windows being embraced by a slight forward break which is crowned by an open mutule pediment. The tympanum contains an elliptical tablet inscribed "W E MARLBOROUGH HOUSE" and is flanked by festoons joined by a ribboned knot at the top.

[32] No. 165 KENNINGTON LANE

Formerly No. 165 Lower Kennington Lane, originally No. 10 Kennington Cross

Fig. 3, plot 22

On Harbord's map of 1636 a house, described as the property of Sir Richard Manley, stood at the junction of Cleaver Street and Kennington Lane near the site of No. 165,[3] and a house and gardens are shown on approximately the same site on Rocque's map of 1745. In July 1773 George Matthews obtained a lease of land with a frontage of 77 feet to Kennington Lane for sixty years, but no description of the property at this date has survived.[165] Matthews is described in a rental of 1783 as a surveyor[158] and it seems possible that he was responsible for building the three houses, Nos. 165–169 (odd), which later stood on his leasehold. The houses were certainly standing in 1780, when Matthews was paying Land Tax for No. 165.[55] No. 167, which was for some years a police section-house, was demolished to make way for the Durning Free Library.

Although most of the Cleaver property passed into the hands of the Bowden family, Matthews' leasehold was an exception. In 1793 the three houses were sold to William Allen of Clifford's Inn[165] and this property was never reunited with the larger part of the Cleaver estate.

No. 165 has a rebuilt front but retains its original doorcase of wood, consisting of a rusticated architrave surround surmounted by a triangular pediment resting on consoles. The competence of the design suggests the craftsman's use of an 18th century pattern-book.

THE DURNING FREE PUBLIC LIBRARY [33]

Fig. 3, plot 22

This building and its site were provided by Miss J. Durning Smith at a cost of £10,000. The architect was Sidney R. J. Smith, and the builders were Messrs. Hall, Beddall and Co.[166] The library (Plate 38b) was opened on November 6, 1889, by Alderman Sir James Clarke Lawrence. It is a four-storey building designed in the North Italian Gothic manner favoured by late Victorians, and built in Fareham red bricks freely ornamented in stone and terracotta, the latter being made by Messrs. Stiff of Lambeth.[167] It has steeply pitched slate roofs and a tower surmounted by a lantern on the east side. The projecting single-storey arcaded entrance is approached from a raised terrace.

CLEAVER SQUARE [34]

Formerly Prince's Square

Fig. 3, plot 23

Cleaver Square had not been laid out when Hodskinson and Middleton's survey of the Manor was made,[6] but building began there soon afterwards. In 1789 Thomas Ellis, lessee of a large part of the Cleaver property, granted a building sub-lease to John and Thomas Corpe, carpenters, of Kennington, of land on the north-west side of the square (fig. 15).[156] This was followed in 1791 by a similar sub-lease of land on the north side of the square to William Brooks, mason,[168] and in 1792 Nos. 8 and 9 in the square, described as lately erected, were leased to William Ingle, builder, of St. Mary, Newington.[169] By the time that Mary Ann Cleaver was admitted to her mother's property in 1797 there were stated to be 36 houses in the square,[155] although the Rate Book evidence suggests that the number was nearer 40.[44] Ellis' Trustees continued the development of the square after his death, and in 1806 granted a lease of land on the south side to John Cartwright, bricklayer, of Kennington Cross.[170]

Of the development during the period of Ellis' lease some houses, Nos. 2–20 (consec.) and Nos. 34–41 (consec.), are still standing. No. 1 was also built about this time, but it forms part of a terrace in Cleaver Street, and was not part of the original layout of the square.

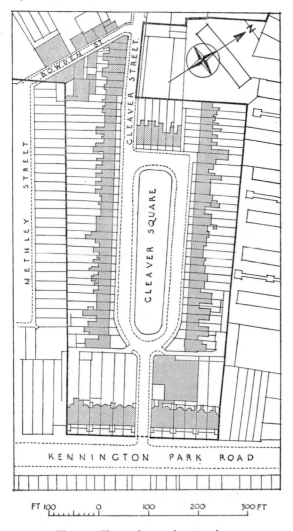

Fig. 15. Cleaver Square, lay-out plan

Between 1815 and 1824, when the Cleaver property had passed into the hands of the Bowden family, Nos. 42–46 (consec.) were built.[44] Henry Bowden was admitted tenant in 1844[171] and between this date and 1853 Nos. 21–33 (consec.) were added to the square and Nos. 49–61 (consec.) rebuilt to the designs of William Rogers of Palace Chambers, Old Lambeth.[172]

The houses surrounding Cleaver Square (Plate 46a) are mostly of three storeys with semi-basements and all are built of yellow stock brick. Nos. 34–41 form the most interesting terrace as the houses have suffered less refronting than the others. Generally there is little ornament, though there are a few simple door fanlights of radiating pattern; No. 7 has a plain wood doorcase with a pediment on fluted brackets. Nos. 26–33 and 21–25, which stand at the southeast ends of the long sides of the square, have the end houses in each terrace set forward slightly with stucco quoins at the corners. These two terraces have channelled or plain stuccowork to their ground storeys. The cornices and blocking courses to the parapets, the window architraves and the Soanic fret pilasters marking the party walls are also of stucco. All the house fronts have parapets except for the terrace, Nos. 56–61, which was rebuilt to the designs of William Rogers and has brick dentilled eaves. The red brick and terracotta fronted public house, the Prince of Wales (No. 48), was rebuilt in 1901.

Nos. 114–136 (even) Kennington Park Road [35]

Formerly Nos. 1–12 (consec.) Princes Place
Fig. 3, plot 23

At the time of Hodskinson and Middleton's survey of 1785 the Kennington Park Road frontage of the Cleaver estate had not been developed.[6] Princes Place was built in 1788, for on October 25 of that year, Ellis granted sub-leases of Nos. 1–6 and 9 Princes Place, now Nos. 114–124, and 130 Kennington Park Road, to James Hall of Southwark, painter,[173] John Sergeant of Bermondsey, bricklayer,[174] John Poynder of St. Mary at Hill, City of London, plumber,[175] George Britton of Bermondsey, paper stainer,[176] William Gates of Old Swan, Thames-side, mason,[177] John Dowley of Fish Street Hill, City of London, smith,[178] and William Ingle of Newington, builder,[179] respectively, in consideration of their expenditure in building the houses. The Rate Books show that all of Princes Place was built at this period[44] and it seems probable that the building work was carried out by Ingle, and that the other lessees were responsible for other work on the houses (Plate 50a, fig. 16). A tablet on No. 124, bearing the device of a phoenix, records that it was rebuilt in 1789, and suggests that the original house was burnt down almost immediately after its erection, and was quickly replaced. Part of the property seems to have been enfranchised in 1880, and the remainder in 1907.

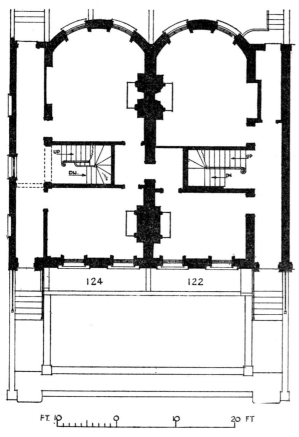

Fig. 16. Nos. 122–124 Kennington Park Road, ground-floor plan

In 1879 the City and Guilds Institute established an art school at Nos. 122 and 124, and built additional studio accommodation at the rear of these houses.[157] The Institute had been established by the City Corporation and certain of the Livery Companies in the previous year to encourage the application of science and the fine arts "to productive and technical industries especially and to commerce and industry generally".[180] The school was founded to provide further training for artists already working in the local industries, among them Doulton's pottery works on the Albert Embankment, and the first courses covered carving, modelling and architectural decoration.[181] In June 1880 it was reported

that "The success of the Technical Art Schools erected recently at Nos. 122 and 124 Kennington Park Road necessitates their immediate enlargement (almost before completion),"[157] and it was proposed to add further studio accommodation at the rear of adjoining houses, but this does not appear to have been done until 1936. Nos. 122 and 124 were bought by the Institute in 1926 and Nos. 118 and 120 in 1933.[182] The scope of the school's curriculum has increased to meet the developing needs of modern processes, but the school retains its original purpose in offering craftsmen an opportunity to develop their skills.

Nos. 114–124 and 126–136 (excluding No. 134, destroyed in the war of 1939–45) are two continuous ranges built in pairs, and are symmetrically grouped about the roadway leading to Cleaver Square. The pairs Nos. 122 and 124 (now the City and Guilds of London Art School), and 126 and 128, flank the roadway; each of these two pairs shares a pedimented attic storey with a lunette window; the other houses have attics in mansard roofs behind plain parapets. All have three main storeys and are linked by narrow entrance wings, which are generally of two storeys. The arched entrances have vermiculated voussoirs and triple keystones, and the ground-floor windows are recessed in round arches, linked by plain imposts. Nos. 122 and 124 had pediments added to the first-floor windows and jalousies fixed to the upper windows in the late 1920s. The doorways of some of the houses have neat fanlights of radiating pattern, and cast-iron scroll-ornamented railings inclosing the semi-basements.

KENNINGTON CROSS   [36]

Fig. 3, plot 24

The triangle of land bounded by Kennington Lane, Windmill Row and Kennington Road (fig. 6), formed part of the copyhold estate of Mary Cleaver. It had long been a detached piece of land, and is shown as such on Harbord's map of 1636.[3] In 1752 and 1754 the Trustees of the Surrey New Roads purchased some land from Mary Cleaver for the making of Kennington Road but they were never admitted to it in the Manor court. The triangle was not required for the road and was let "to various tenants who used it for gardens".[157]

In 1823 the triangle was considered as a site for St. Mark's Schools, but negotiations could not be brought to a satisfactory conclusion and it re-

Fig. 17. Nos. 75 and 77 Kennington Lane, paired doorcases

mained undeveloped. The land became increasingly valuable as vacant land in Kennington was taken up for building and in 1842 the Trustees applied to be admitted as copyholders so that they could sell their interest. Although their title could not be established by copy of court roll, it was conceded two years later by Henry Bowden, who had inherited the copyhold formerly held by Mary Cleaver. Meanwhile in 1842 it had been proposed "to build a Police Court for the Metropolitan Police District" on the site, but this was abandoned because of the opposition of the local residents. The interest in the land was said to have been sold by the Trustees in 1843 to Mr. Howard, a builder, but in 1845 a licence was granted to the Trustees to demise the property to Thomas Lee, builder, of Blackfriars Road; Lee had already started building on the land in September of the previous year.[157]

MINOR COPYHOLD ESTATES

[37] Nos. 57–61 and 67–87 (odd) Kennington Lane

Formerly Nos. 57–61 and 67–87 Lower Kennington Lane, originally Nos. 17–19 and 22–31 (consec.) Portsmouth Place

Fig. 3, plot 25

The land on which these houses stand was owned in 1615 by Robert Manchester. At that date there were four houses on the property, which had been built during Manchester's ownership.[2] When George Rogers was admitted to it in 1742 on the death of Thomas Rogers, the four houses were still standing.[183] In 1763 Rogers was granted a licence to demise his property at Kennington for 61 years from Michaelmas 1763[184] and these houses were built under that licence. It is not possible to be precise about the date of their erection, but they were certainly standing in 1780.[55]

Nos. 57–61, old buildings of two storeys with mansard roofs, are now somewhat altered and each has a shop-front. Nos. 67–77 form a stock brick two-storey terrace with a slate-roofed mansard attic storey. Except at No. 69, which has been mutilated by a shop-front, the houses have their entrances paired to share wood doorcases formed by pilasters supporting triglyphed entablatures (fig. 17). Nos. 79–83 are poor three-storey buildings and have original flush-framed double-hung sashes to their windows. Nos. 83A and 85 are mean two-storey houses wedged between the last terrace and No. 87. The latter has two storeys with a slate-roofed mansard attic; the centrally placed doorcase has an architrave-lining and a hood borne on consoles.

[38] Nos. 10–28 (even) Kennington Park Road

Formerly Nos. 5–14 (consec.) York Row
Fig. 3, plot 25

In 1615 the copyholder of the land on which these houses stand was Benjamin Kirwyn, whose tenement is described as a beautiful brick messuage, with another messuage adjoining and three acres of land. Kirwyn also held the adjoining five closes of demesne on lease, and Norden notes that an orchard on one of these was "excluded by a strong quick sett hedge from the reste which time may easilie wynn from the demeisnes . . . if the succedinge tenantes shoulde be of corrupt mindes".[2] Kirwyn himself does not seem to have been above sharp practice, for Harbord reported in 1636 that he had encroached upon the roadside waste, and that the boundaries between copyhold and demesne land at this point were not clearly defined.[3]

In 1629 Kirwyn's property was surrendered to Lawrence Whitaker, Steward of the Manor and a Member of Parliament.[5] In 1649 Whitaker's house, called the Buckshorns (probably to be identified with Kirwyn's beautiful messuage), was said to be on demesne land.[4] It was listed in particulars for the sale of Crown lands in Kennington in 1650[185] and was sold to a Mr. Graves.[5] A protest was made by Whitaker, and in 1652 those appointed to decide the matter reported that after inspecting Whitaker's copy of court roll and hearing the evidence of the homage at the Manor court, they had concluded that the Buckshorns and the smith's forge beside it were on copyhold land, but that a lean-to roofed "with Panntiles" and an old thatched shed adjoining the Buckshorns were built on demesne.[5] Whitaker's house seems to have stood between No. 26 Kennington Park Road and the Red Lion public house.

The part of Whitaker's copyhold on which these houses stood came into the hands of George Rogers in 1742.[183] He was given a licence to demise his property for 61 years from Michaelmas 1763.[184] It is not known exactly when these houses were built, but they were certainly standing in 1785.[6]

Nos. 10 and 12 are a plain pair of three-storey stock brick houses with semi-basements. No. 10 has a pedimented wing of full height over an alleyway at the side, which leads to the South London Plaster of Paris Works. Over the entrance to the alleyway is a life-size statue of a craftsman with a small bust at his feet. No. 12 has a doorcase with an open pediment borne on consoles. Several houses in the terrace Nos. 14–28, which is of the same height and materials, also have open pedimented doorcases. The terrace has suffered much from refronting and mutilation.

Nos. 45–55 (odd) Kennington Lane [39]

Formerly Nos. 45–55 Lower Kennington Lane, originally Nos. 1–6 (consec.) Portsmouth Place
Fig. 3, plot 25

In 1615 the copyholder of the land on which these houses were later built was Mary Lee, whose property was described as consisting of seven tenements.[2] In the succeeding century there was further development of the property, for when Daniel Merigeot, peruke-maker, was admitted in 1726, there were 19 houses along the Kennington Lane frontage.[186] Elisha Biscoe inherited the property in 1779,[187] when only 16 houses were recorded along Kennington Lane; these are described in Hodskinson and Middleton's survey as small and old.[6]

Nos. 45–55 were built during Biscoe's ownership of the copyhold. The Rate Books suggest that redevelopment took place in 1808–9.[44] Certainly, when Trustees were admitted on the death of Elisha Biscoe, the property listed included "Six Brick Dwelling Houses (called Portsmouth Place)".[188]

Nos. 45–55 are a symmetrical group of three-storey houses built in stock brick; several have been mutilated or altered and No. 55 has been rebuilt. Nos. 49 and 51 (fig. 18) project slightly and share a flat pediment beneath which is the inscription "PORTS✻MOUTH · PLACE". They are joined by plain bands at ground-floor window-head and first-floor sill levels, and the paired entrances are flanked by pilasters supporting an entablature, its frieze adorned with wreaths.

Nos. 1 and 3 Kennington Lane [40]

Formerly Nos. 1 and 3 Lower Kennington Lane, originally Nos. 1 and 2 Manifold Place
Fig. 3, plot 25

The land on which these houses stand was formerly part of a copyhold held in 1615 by Benjamin Kirwyn; neither at this date nor in 1636[3] were there any buildings on the property. Rocque's map of 1745 shows a group of buildings on the tongue of land between Kennington Park

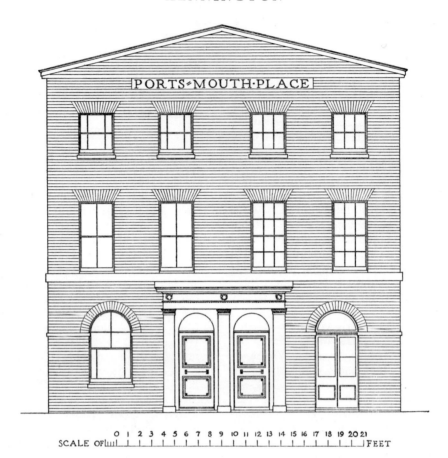

PORTS·MOUTH·PLACE

SCALE OF ‖‖‖‖ 0 1 2 3 4 5 6 7 8 9 10 11 12 13 14 15 16 17 18 19 20 21 FEET

Fig. 18. Nos. 49 and 51 Kennington Lane, probably 1808–9

Road and Kennington Lane, but as far as can be judged, the site of Nos. 1 and 3 Kennington Lane was undeveloped. Hodskinson and Middleton's survey describes the property, which was then in the tenure of Mary Frye, as an old dwelling-house, warehouse, sheds, etc., situated at Harrow Corner. The name Harrow Corner was derived from a public house, the Plough and Harrow, which stood on the adjoining copyhold and abutted directly on the site of No. 1 Kennington Lane.[6]

Horwood's map of 1813 shows that there were as yet no buildings where Nos. 1 and 3 now stand, and when John Vincent, spur-maker, was admitted to the property in October 1815, the description corresponds with that of Hodskinson and Middleton 30 years earlier.[189] Vincent paid

£400 for the property, but sold it two years later to Abraham Young, auctioneer, for £800. As well as the old dwelling-house, warehouse, etc., Young's admission records "new Erections and Buildings lately erected and built" on the copyhold.[190] The Rate Books do not provide completely satisfactory evidence that Nos. 1 and 3 were among the newly-built houses but Horwood's map of 1819 shows that Nos 1 and 3 were then standing, and it seems almost certain that the houses were built during Vincent's ownership.

These two houses share a curved frontage and have three storeys with attics. The fronts are faced with stucco and contain shop-fronts of austere design, having reeded wood frames with elliptical stops at the heads.

CHAPTER II

Vauxhall and South Lambeth

THE description of the development of this area is keyed to a plan (fig. 19) which is based on the map of Vauxhall Manor drawn by Thomas Hill in 1681.[1] The numbers in brackets in the text which follows refer to the plot numbers marked on the plan.

The map of 1681 shows the Manor bounded on the west by the Thames and the common sewer called Battersea ditch. The ditch was also the boundary between the parishes of Lambeth and Battersea, and the borough boundary follows its course. In 1584 it was the subject of a lawsuit brought by Elizabeth Roydon, who held the Manor of Battersea, against Laurence Palmer and others, owners and occupiers of land in Lambeth and Clapham.[2] The dispute concerned the responsibility for paying for the scouring of the ditch and the maintenance of two sluices. According to the evidence submitted in the case, the sewer drained lands in Battersea, Clapham and Lambeth, which were "drowned" if the sluices were not kept in good repair. On the north the Manor was separated from Kennington Manor by the northern arm of Vauxhall Creek (sometimes called the River Effra) which divided into two streams, just west of where the Oval now lies, before entering the Thames. The three main roads shown on the plan—Wandsworth Road, South Lambeth Road, and Clapham Road—are

all of considerable antiquity (see fig. 1); the bridges which carried them over Vauxhall Creek are also shown. At the junction of Wandsworth Road and South Lambeth Road, where the railway bridge now stands, was Cox's Bridge, sometimes called Vauxhall Bridge.[3] In 1340 the Abbot of Westminster was charged with the repair of "cokkesbrugge",[4] and in 1504 one of his successors was paying rent to the Prior and Convent of Christ Church, Canterbury, for a wharf which he held at "cokkes brugge".[5] At the beginning of the 17th century a dispute arose about the maintenance of the bridge, for by reason of the "enundacion and outrage of waters" it had become "prostrate and throwne downe" and the fallen stones were hindering the flow of water.[6] The Commissioners of Sewers judged that the responsibility for repair lay with the Crown and referred to land previously held by the Abbot of Westminster then in the hands of the King, but the surveyor appointed to examine the case could not find the land in question, even by "dilligent enquiery", and denied the Crown's liability. The bridge over Vauxhall Creek in Clapham Road is also shown on the map; it was called Merton Bridge and took its name from the Merton Road, i.e. Clapham Road. A lane is also shown marking the line of the present Lansdowne Way (Green Lane).

VAUXHALL MANOR

The area beside the Thames near the present Vauxhall Bridge known as "Vauxhall" seems originally to have been part of the extensive Manor of South Lambeth, which was held in the 13th century by the de Redvers family.[7] The name "Vauxhall" (Fauxhall) is derived from Falkes de Breauté, the second husband of Margaret, widow of Baldwin de Redvers.[8] According to an inquisition relating to the de Redvers' possessions taken in 1263,[9] the Manor of South Lambeth included lands at Streatham and Mitcham, but no mention is made of Vauxhall, though de Breauté's lands had reverted to the de Redvers

family after his death.[10] In 1293 South Lambeth Manor and the Manor of "la Sale Faukes" passed, probably by trickery, to Edward I.[11] Whilst the Manor of South Lambeth disappeared almost immediately afterwards, Vauxhall acquired a definite manorial status which there is no evidence that it possessed hitherto. Courts were held there from 1340 onwards[12] and in 1362 the Manor was granted by Edward the Black Prince to the Prior and Convent of Christ Church, Canterbury, to maintain a chantry in the Cathedral crypt.[13] From this date Vauxhall Manor included the areas now known as Vauxhall and South

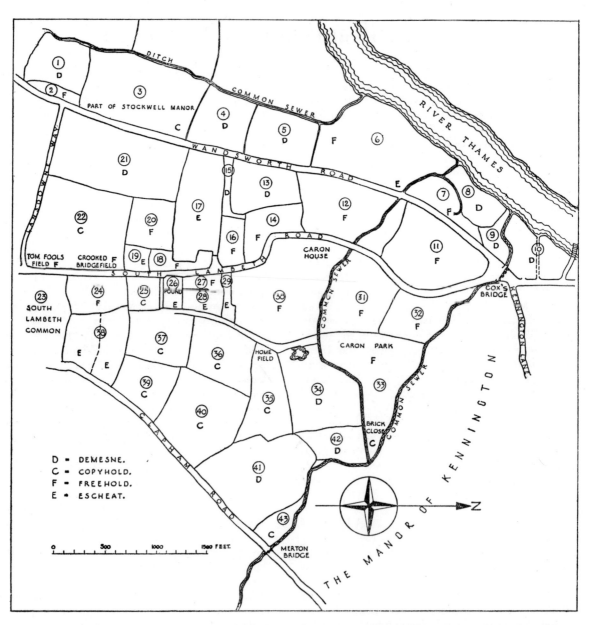

Fig. 19. Vauxhall Manor. The plots are referred to in the text by the numbers on this plan, which is based on a map of Vauxhall Manor drawn by Thomas Hill in 1681. Plot 3 consists of a detached portion of Stockwell Manor and a piece of copyhold of Vauxhall Manor

Lambeth, and (more significant) lands in Streatham and Mitcham.

A grant of land in Stockwell made by William de Redvers early in the 13th century,[14] and the fact that Isabel de Fortibus (who, as Baldwin de Redvers' sister, held South Lambeth Manor) died at Stockwell in 1293,[11] both suggest that at this date Stockwell was also part of South Lambeth Manor, but there is evidence that about 1294 Stockwell also became a separate manor (see page 81).

The conclusion which may be tentatively drawn from the fragmentary evidence is that until the end of the 13th century the de Redvers' Manor of South Lambeth included the areas now known as Vauxhall and Stockwell as well as certain lands in Streatham and Mitcham; that it was split up soon after it came into the hands of the King in 1293—hence its disappearance as a Manor—and that the Manors of Vauxhall (which included lands in Streatham and Mitcham) and Stockwell took its place. The term "South Lambeth" has survived as a vague geographical expression denoting the area on either side of South Lambeth Road; this district was part of Vauxhall Manor. The lands belonging to the Manor in Streatham and Mitcham do not fall within the scope of this volume.

Vauxhall Manor was transferred after the Dissolution to the Dean and Chapter of Christ Church, Canterbury,[15] but some lands in Lambeth Marsh, originally belonging to the Manor, were granted to the Archbishop of Canterbury[16] and absorbed into the demesne lands of Lambeth Manor.[17] Most of the demesne lands of Vauxhall were sold off at the beginning of the 19th century but the copyhold lands remained part of the capitular estates until vested in the Ecclesiastical Commissioners in 1862.[18] No trace has been found of a sale of the Manor during the Commonwealth period, but from 1651–2 John Adrian, and from 1653–9 Henry Hampson, appear in the court rolls as Lords of the Manor.[19]

Manorial administration is not a matter of primary concern in a work of this nature, but one or two points of general interest emerge from the records consulted. When Vauxhall was still part of South Lambeth Manor the freeholders had to perform certain services. They had to plough twice a year, provide two oxen for one day in the autumn to carry the Lord's hay, and to provide two boon-days at which all their tenants were to attend, and carry the Lord's hay one day in the year.[9] For all except the last service they were provided with their estovers (food and drink). These services were eventually commuted. In the 16th century freeholders still owed suit of court, and paid heriots and reliefs when they fell due.[5] Copyhold tenure was by Borough English, i.e. the youngest son inherited, and if there were no sons, the property was divided among the daughters. The fine series of manorial accounts and rentals preserved in the Library of the Dean and Chapter include accounts for the repair of the barn, which had a mud wall and was thatched with reeds.[20] The office of bedell for both the Manors of Vauxhall and Walworth (which was also owned by the Dean and Chapter) was usually held by the same person, often a tenant.[21]

In Vauxhall, inclosure was well advanced by the beginning of the 16th century.[22] The Prior and Convent owned many manors scattered throughout south-east England which were administered by laymen on the spot, and were visited perhaps only once or twice a year by the Convent's officers. After inclosure the closes were leased, and the rents provided a regular income which was of more use to absentee landlords than the old services in kind.

THE DEMESNE LANDS

It is not known when the Prior and Convent began to let the demesnes of the Manor. A small piece of land between the Thames and the King's highway was demised in 1387,[23] but the earliest record of a lease of the whole Manor with all arable lands, feedings, pastures and rents, farms, fines, etc., occurs in 1449, when it was demised to Thomas del Rowe and Peter Pope, citizens of London, for twenty years at an annual rent of £20.[24] But even this rent was not enough to maintain the chantry which the Black Prince had founded, for in 1472 Thomas Bourchier, Archbishop of Canterbury, wrote to the King complaining that the Manor was scarcely worth £20, whereas the chantry expenses amounted to almost £40 a year. He suggested that application should be made to Rome for the Manor to be "delyu'yd unto the chantry prestes they to make it as good as they kan and fynde them self ther with and repayr ther place we beynge only bownd to fynde the seid chantry prestes bothe wex & brede and wyne and reparacion of vestmentes perteynyng to the Autyr nothyng reserving unto us of the seid maner of Fawkyshall".[25]

Though the Archbishop's attempt to shift this burden failed, there is evidence that the leasing of the whole Manor was discontinued about this time and that it was let more profitably in separate parcels.[22] After the Reformation, however, the demesne lands in South Lambeth were let in such a muddled fashion that they became the subject of a Chancery suit.[26] The successful plaintiff, Laurence Palmer, subsequently obtained a lease of all the demesnes in South Lambeth,[27] which continued to be let together until the beginning of the 19th century. In 1590, the date of Palmer's lease, they are described as Barrlands in South Lambeth Field (fig. 19, plot 21); a meadow near Our Lady's Acre in Clapham (plot 1); a meadow near "Faux well"[a] (plots 4 and 5); and a meadow on the south side of the highway (plots 13 and 15); these lands were all held by Sir John Leigh at the beginning of the 16th century;[5] two closes called Claylands (plots 34, 41 and 42), which were on lease to Peter Palmer in 1475;[32] a close and parcel of land at "Cockesbridge", a croft at Lambeth Cross and a meadow near the Thames (plots 8, 9 and 10). The lease also included Vauxhall Barn and the Court Lodge adjoining it. Apart from the fact that these buildings stood near the Thames, nothing is known about them after this date. Palmer covenanted to maintain the barn and to provide meat, drink and lodging for the officers of the Dean and Chapter and their servants, and stabling for their horses, for one day and one night twice a year. He was able to compound for this hospitality by payment of 40s. to the Dean and 20s. to the Receiver, Surveyor or Auditor, when they visited the Manor. In addition, Palmer was required to provide for the Steward when the latter held courts. These covenants were still included in leases made at the end of the 18th century[33] when the demesnes were in the tenure

of Sir Joseph Mawbey, senior, who first took a lease of them in 1767.[34] Mawbey died in 1798 (see page 37), and the property was put up for auction in 1800 to settle his debts.[35] Barrlands, also spelt Berelandes, Berlondes, Bearlands, etc. (plot 21), the seven acres (plot 1), the fourteen acres, then divided into two pieces called Rushy Mead (plot 4) and Vauxhall or Vauxwell Mead (plot 5), and the seven acres (plots 13 and 15), were assigned to John Suter and Mr. Phillips, who appear to have purchased the fee simple of these lands from the Dean and Chapter shortly afterwards.[36] The subsequent development of the land was consequently carried out by private individuals.

Claylands or Clayfields were also sold by the Dean and Chapter at this time. John Daniel of The Lawn purchased plots 34 and 42 in 1801, and sold a piece of land adjoining Carroun House and grounds to Sir Charles Blicke (see page 67) and another piece to John Fentiman, senior,[35] who also purchased plot 41.[36] According to Brayley,[37] Fentiman drained Claylands at his own expense, the land being very marshy, with stagnant pools, and built himself a "handsome mansion". This house stood south of the Oval opposite the end of Claylands Road,[38] which commemorates the name of the field on which it was built. Fentiman Road was laid out about 1838 (see page 67).

The remainder of the demesne land was also sold off by the Dean and Chapter before their estates came under the control of the Ecclesiastical Commissioners. Plots 8, 9 and the part of 10 on which the Cumberland Tea Gardens stood, are now occupied by the works of the South Eastern Gas Board.

METHODIST CHURCH, FENTIMAN ROAD   [41]
Fig. 19, plot 34

This church was erected in 1900–1 for the congregation of a chapel in Miles Street which was founded in 1854. The architects were George and Reginald P. Baines, and the builder was J. O. Richardson.[39] The church is a red brick building with Perpendicular stone tracery to the windows. It has a short battlemented tower, banded with stone, and a spirelet at the

---

[a] In a lease of 1510[28] this meadow was said to lie "next a well called Fauxwell". The spring was situated roughly at the point where the ditch or stream dividing the meadow met Wandsworth Road.[29] The well was still in use in 1856 when Dr. Young[30] said it was "noted for the purity of its water". In the Victoria and Albert Museum there is a water-colour of the steps leading to the well.[31]

south-west corner. There are projecting entrance lobbies in the middle of the Fentiman Road front and set splay-wise at the south-west corner of the tower. Renovations were carried out in 1954. The ancillary buildings are similarly designed and of the same materials as the church.

[42] CLAYLANDS CONGREGATIONAL CHURCH, CLAYLANDS ROAD

Fig. 19, plot 41

In 1836 John Fentiman granted a lease of a piece of land on the north side of Claylands Road[40] for the erection of a new chapel to accommodate the seceding part of the congregation of Holland Chapel under the ministry of Dr. John Styles (see page 118). The building was opened as a Congregational church on June 29, 1836, and Styles continued as minister until 1844.[41] The church is now disused. It is a plain stock brick building with a Classical pedimented front (Plate 25b). In the centre of the front there are three entrance

doors divided by stucco pilasters with a cornice and blocking course above. All the windows are round-arched with recessed rectangular panels beneath. The foundation stone at the south-west corner was laid by the Rev. John Styles, D.D., on January 1, 1836. The Sunday schools at the rear were built in 1899 by Messrs. Rice and Son, with W. E. Davis as architect.[39]

ASHMOLE PRIMARY SCHOOL, ASHMOLE [43] STREET

Fig. 19, plot 41

This school was built by the London School Board to accommodate 800 children and was opened on September 23, 1879. The architect was E. R. Robson and the contractors were Higgs and Hill, whose tender was for £7,667.[42] The school is a tall three-storey building built in yellow stock brick. It is approximately square in plan and has an entrance wing on the west side.

THE COMMONS

Most of the common land appurtenant to the Manor lay in Mitcham and Streatham; only about three and a half acres lay in South Lambeth (plot 23). In 1806 the Dean and Chapter requested John Middleton to survey the waste lands of Vauxhall Manor.[43] In his report he stated that inclosure would be opposed by "persons from London, who live in Genteel houses which front the commons"; and to avoid the consequent trouble and expense of obtaining an Act of Parliament he suggested that the Dean and Chapter should grant small pieces of the waste to such persons as would inclose and cultivate them. Only the consent of the Homage was necessary for this. Middleton also reported that the three and a half acres of South Lambeth Common, bounded by Lansdowne Way, Clapham Road and South Lambeth Road, had been inclosed with posts and rails by the subscriptions of people living near by, who alone kept cattle on the land, although as they were all inhabitants of Stockwell Manor they had no right to do so. He advised the removal of the posts and rails to prevent the "squatters" acquiring a claim to the land. His advice was followed, and in 1817 Edward Shewell of Stockwell was admitted as a copyhold tenant to the three and a half acres, on condition that

the land was cultivated and not built on except for the erection of a gardener's cottage.[44] In 1838 John Notley of Clapham Road, builder, was

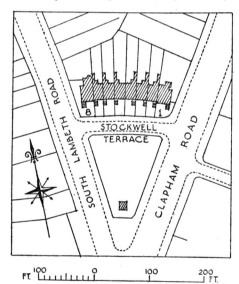

Fig. 20 Stockwell Terrace, lay-out plan

admitted as a tenant, and five years later he obtained the discharge of the building restrictions and covered the ground with houses.[45] The small triangle on which the clock-tower stands is the only part of the Common left open (fig. 20).

[44] Nos 1–8 (consec.) Stockwell Terrace

Formerly Stockwell Crescent
Fig. 19, plot 23

These houses (Plate 51d, fig. 21) were erected on the Common[46] shortly after 1843 by John Notley. They are raised above semi-basements, have three storeys and attics, and are built in yellow stock brick with stuccoed ground storeys and surrounds to the first-floor windows. The stucco-work is channelled except on the end houses where it is rusticated.

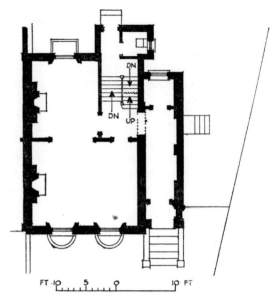

Fig. 21. No. 1 Stockwell Terrace, ground-floor plan

THE COPYHOLD LANDS

Most of the copyhold lands in the Manor consisted of small fields amalgamated into two holdings known as the 34 acres and 32 acres. At the beginning of the 16th century most of these small fields were held by Sir John Leigh.[5]

THE 34 ACRES

In 1672 William Hall, citizen and fishmonger of London, surrendered to the use of his will two third parts of four messuages and 34 acres, which he bequeathed to his sons, Richard and John.[47] They purchased the remaining third part from Thomas Cason in 1689[47] and the whole property was subsequently divided between their heirs. Richard Hall's share was sold in 1793 by Mary Cleaver, widow, and Mary Ann Cleaver, her daughter, to John Wilkinson of Woodford, Doctor of Physic.[48] It comprised the Pightle (plot 43) and the 14 acres (plots 25, 37 and 39), in the tenure of John Ismay. Wilkinson died in 1818 and left one moiety of his estate to his nephew, Joseph Wilkinson, and one moiety to another nephew, Josiah Williamson.[49] In 1843 an Act of Parliament vested Joseph Wilkinson's moiety in trustees and empowered them to join with the owners of Josiah Williamson's moiety to grant building leases for the development of the estate.[50] Hanover Gardens was built on the Pightle, and Albert Square, Aldebert Terrace (formerly Williamson Street), Wilkinson Street and St. Stephen's Terrace were built on the 14 acres in the late 1840s and early 1850s. Most of the houses were the work of local builders[51] including John Snell who also erected houses on the 12 acres (see page 63).

Albert Square   [45]

Fig. 19, plots 37 and 39

The houses in this square are interesting and vigorous examples of early Victorian architecture and share the distinction with Angell Terrace of being the only examples of their type in the area covered by this volume. The square is joined to Clapham Road by a broad tree-lined approach, and surrounded by substantial four-storey houses of Classical design (Plate 50d). These are closely and symmetrically grouped, singly, in pairs, and in threes, and are given the appearance of being continuous terraces by the linking together of their single-storey entrances. The square was the work of a north London builder, John Glenn of Islington, who was granted a building lease of the land from September 29, 1846.[52]

[46] ST STEPHEN'S CHURCH, ST STEPHEN'S TERRACE

Fig. 19, plot 37

In 1857 the increasing number of inhabitants in this part of his parish prompted the Rev. Charles Kemble, incumbent of St. Michael's, Stockwell, to urge the need for a new church in this district. Two years later the copyholders conveyed their interest in the site of St. Stephen's Church and parsonage to the Ecclesiastical Commissioners, and the Dean and Chapter of Canterbury enfranchised the land.[53] The church (Plate 15c), which accommodated 1,200 persons, was designed by John Barnett,[54] and the contractor was George Myers[55] who was also responsible for the building of St. Barnabas'. It was consecrated by the Bishop of Winchester on April 23, 1861, and a district was assigned in the same year.[56] The spire was damaged by the cable of a drifting barrage balloon in 1940; it is to be rebuilt shortly.

St. Stephen's is a Decorated Gothic building with an exterior of Kentish ragstone dressed with Bath stone. The plan is T-shaped, with a wide aisleless nave and short transepts, the altar being placed in a shallow projection from the east end. The most prominent external feature is the steeple at the north-east corner. This is of three stages and each face is flanked by offset buttresses surmounted by tall octagonal corner pinnacles. From the centre of each face rises a gabled dormer containing a two-light louvred window. The dormers project from the belfry stage of the octagonal spire. Each of the nave windows is surmounted by a gable. Internally, the timber roofs, which are braced and of scissors construction, have exposed members and are carried on moulded corbels borne by short shafts. Over the altar is a distinctive Catherine-wheel window containing blue and green glass. The geometrically patterned glass of the five-light transept windows is also richly coloured. A deep organ gallery extends across the west end and is supported on slender cast-iron columns.

[47] St. Stephen's Church of England Primary School, Dorset Road, was erected in 1847; it was originally the church school of the parish of St. Michael, Stockwell, but the school was transferred to St. Stephen's parish in 1862. It now occupies several one- and two-storey buildings erected at different times.[57]

John Hall's portion of the 34 acres descended to John Wilkins, who died in 1778.[58] In 1806[59] it was purchased by James Humphrys and included the 12 acres (part of plot 22) and four acres on the west side of Wandsworth Road (part of plot 3). Humphrys died in 1861[60] and was probably the architect who partnered Isaac Clarke in the designing of St. Barnabas' Church, which stood on his land. It seems likely that he was also personally responsible for the well-planned layout of his estate.

LANSDOWNE GARDENS AND NEIGHBOURHOOD, ST. BARNABAS' CHURCH, GUILDFORD ROAD

Fig. 19, part of plot 22

On the 12 acres the pattern of development took the form of a circus at the centre, containing a garden, with roads radiating towards the cardinal points (fig. 22). The land was divided into small plots and developed under licences to demise granted between 1843 and 1850.[61] The houses [48] in the circus (Plate 51c) which, together with most of the others on the estate, were erected by John Snell of Dorset Street (now Road), builder, are simple well-proportioned two-storey villas with semi-basements. They are built of stock brick and most have projecting porches carried on Doric columns. In Hartington Road, however, the porches are recessed, the openings being flanked by antae with wreaths in the friezes above. In Lansdowne Way there are plain three-storey terrace houses. No. 45 Guildford Road is a [49] small cream-painted Gothic house with battlemented gable, angle buttresses and carved head stops to the labels (Plate 58a). The house was erected about 1844 under a lease granted to Humphry Joseph Lightly of the City of London.[61] The large vicarage adjoining the church of St. Barnabas was erected by John Snell[61] and also has Gothic detail.

While the estate was being developed a site was conveyed to the Church Building Commissioners for the erection of St. Barnabas, Guildford [50] Road. The first stone was laid on July 27, 1848, by Adolphus Frederick, Duke of Cambridge, and the fabric (excluding the bell-turret) was erected by George Myers at a cost of £4,800[62] to the designs of Isaac Clarke and James Humphrys.[63] The building provides accommodation for about 1,500 people; it was consecrated on June 24,

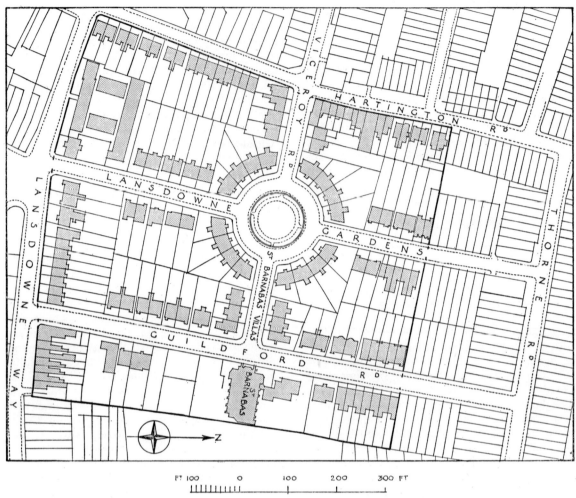

Fig. 22. Lansdowne Gardens area, lay-out plan

1850, by the Bishop of Winchester,[62] and a district was assigned in 1851.[63] Dr. Ralph Vaughan Williams, O.M., was at one time organist here.[64]

The church (Plate 51c, fig. 23) is placed axially on the road leading east from Lansdowne Gardens, and has a simple plan with a nave and aisles of six bays terminated by a shallow apse at the east end. The building is designed in the Early English Gothic style and externally faced with Kentish ragstone dressed with Bath stone. The nave is clerestoried and there is a slender bell-turret of octagonal plan against the south-west corner of the nave, which projects slightly beyond the aisles.

The interior is plain and dignified with tall two-light windows lighting the eastern apse. The graceful nave arcading, borne on alternate octagonal and circular stone columns with foliated capitals, supports a hammer-beam roof. The east window contains rich stained-glass portraying St. Barnabas and St. Paul.

The church was restored in 1948 and re-furnished with the organ from All Saints' Church, Allen Edwards Road, and the pulpit from St. Augustine's Church, Clapham Road[65] (see page 83). All Saints' Church was designed by Alfred Bedborough[66] and erected in 1876–8, but after being damaged during the war of 1939–45 it was pulled down and most of the parish combined

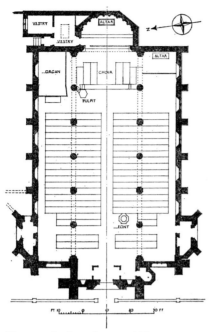

Fig. 23. St. Barnabas, Guildford Road, plan

with that of St. Barnabas. The mission church of St. Silas, Dawlish Street, which was designed by A. D. Gough[67] and erected in 1862,[68] has also been demolished after war damage.

THE 32 ACRES AND BRICK CLOSE

In 1663 Foulke Bignall was admitted as a copyhold tenant to a messuage and 36 acres in South Lambeth, which had previously belonged to Philip Pinchon[69] or Pincheon.[1] The 36 acres included four acres called Brick Close which Foulke's son, Robert, sold in 1680 to William Kempe of Chelsea, yeoman;[70] in 1865 this land was enfranchised and sold to William and Sarah Bell of Lawn Place.[71] The probable site of Brick Close is indicated on the key plan (plot 33); it was said to abut on Caron Park on the west in 1680[70] and on the east in 1822,[72] but evidence suggests that the earlier description is correct. The remaining 32 acres (plots 35, 36 and 40) were not split

until 1806 when they were purchased by John Fentiman, the elder, of Kennington.[73] He sold about one and a half acres to Robert Orford, John Bridges and Sir Charles Blicke. Orford's piece fronted the Clapham Road, Bridges' piece was part of Home Field and Blicke's adjoined this on the north.[74] Fentiman also purchased most of Claylands (part of the demesne of the Manor) which abutted on the 32 acres (see page 60). The copyhold estate covered the area between Meadow Road, Fentiman Road, Clapham Road and Wilkinson Street. When Fentiman died in 1820 his sons did not sell his property as directed in his will but divided it between them; John Fentiman, junior, took the remaining $30\frac{1}{2}$ acres of Vauxhall Manor copyhold; on his admittance in 1823 he was described as a brick merchant of Camberwell.[75] The estate was mortgaged and when John William Fentiman was admitted in 1857 it had dwindled to the land between Meadow Road, Fentiman Road, Palfrey Place and Dorset Road.[76] Dorset (formerly South Lambeth New) Road was probably laid out about 1806, when John Fentiman, senior, agreed that it should remain open for the use of the public for ever.[77] Both the Fentimans and Thomas Waite Marson, who held a mortgage on the estate,[75] granted building leases and the property was developed under these leases, chiefly by local builders.

Nos. 60–66 and 92–122 (even) Clapham Road

Formerly Nos. 16–13 (consec.) Dorset Terrace and Nos. 16–1 (consec.) New Dorset Place
Fig. 19, plot 40

These houses are examples of the original development on the Fentimans' copyhold estate, though their architectural poverty makes them otherwise unremarkable. Nos. 92–122 were [51] erected about 1824,[78] probably by Thomas Coope;[79] they form a plain three-storey terrace with attics. Shops have been built across the front gardens of Nos. 106–110. Nos. 60–66 were [52] erected a little later, in the 1830s,[78] and form a four-storey range with continuous cast-iron balcony railings on the first floor.

F

THE FREEHOLD LANDS

Most of the freehold land in Vauxhall Manor was held at the beginning of the 17th century by Noel de Caron, Lord of Schoonewale in Flanders, one of the most distinguished inhabitants of Lambeth. In 1581 Caron was elected to the States General of the United Provinces, where he proved himself a devoted follower of the Prince of Orange. He was consequently chosen to be one of the envoys sent to England for the negotiations between the States General and Elizabeth I in 1585. From this time he appears to have become an enthusiastic anglophile and lived chiefly in England. After the death of their agent to the English Court, the States General elected Caron as his successor in 1591.[80] He was often referred to as "Sir" Noel de Caron, but this was probably a translation of his Flemish title as he does not seem to have been granted an English knighthood.

Caron purchased his property in South Lambeth in two parts. In 1602 he bought a "greate howse" with a dairy-house and about 70 acres, from Thomas Hewytt (Hewett) of St. Andrew Undershaft.[81] The property had been sold in 1586 by William Henbury and Morgan Pope to a William Hewett, whose sons had mortgaged it and conveyed the reversion to the Queen after the death of the mortgagees. The reversion was subsequently granted by Letters Patent to Caron, who held the property "as of the Manor of East Greenwich", i.e. in socage.[82] In 1618 he added to his already considerable estate several pieces of land purchased from (Sir) William and Catherine Foster.[83] Catherine had inherited this property from her grandfather, Laurence Palmer,[84] who settled his estate on his son, Symon, and his heirs in 1592.[83] Caron also enjoyed the profits of the neighbouring Manor of Kennington.[85] He continued as ambassador until his death in December 1624,[86] and was buried in St. Mary's, Lambeth, in the following January.[87] The settlement of both his real and personal property took several years. His will[88] was imperfect and his kin began several lawsuits to recover his property.[89] The matter was referred to the Privy Council and in 1627 the Council politely informed the new ambassador of the States General that although all rights and privileges due to the quality of ambassador would be accorded to Caron's goods and estates, the lands he purchased in England were subject to the laws of the realm and that "none could inherit from an allien made dennizon (as Sir Noel Caron was) but the issue of his own boddy begotten".[90] Caron had apparently never married and it was not until 1632 that the Privy Council was advised that it was "honourable and just" for the lands of Noel de Caron to be sold and the proceeds distributed amongst his kin.[91] The lands which he purchased from Hewytt were apparently divided and sold but the lands purchased from the Fosters were escheated to the Lords of the Manor of Vauxhall, and were subsequently known as "The Vauxhall Escheat".

CARON HOUSE ESTATE

Perhaps on the site of the "greate howse" which he purchased from Hewytt, Caron erected a large mansion house (plot 30) which took several years to build.[92] Its grandeur may be judged from Plate 44a and from the little sketch which appears on the map of 1681, reproduced on Plate 123 of volume XXIII of the *Survey of London*. The large park which surrounded the mansion (fig. 19, plots 30, 31, 32 and part of 33) was well watered by Vauxhall Creek and studded with trees. During the Commonwealth period the house was owned and occupied by Alderman Francis Allen,[93] one of the Commissioners appointed to try Charles I,[94] and "a violent person against His Majesty".[95] In 1666 the house and park were granted by the King to the Lord Chancellor, Edward, Earl of Clarendon, for a yearly rent of 10 shillings.[96] Clarendon sold the estate in April 1667 to Sir Jeremy Whichcott (Whichcote) of Hendon,[97] who had been Solicitor-General to the Prince Elector Palatine,[98] Charles Lewis, son of Frederick V. In the following September a patent was issued constituting the Fleet Prison to be at Caron House and granting the office of warden to Sir Jeremy.[99] He died in 1677[100] and in that year his son, Sir Paul Whichcott, was said to be the owner of Caron House and park.[101] In 1683 the estate was leased by Sir Francis Pemberton, Benjamin Whichcott and Christopher Cratford of St. Giles in the Fields, to Thomas Grover, citizen and tallow-chandler of London, for one year at a peppercorn rent.[102] Sir Francis Pemberton was Lord Chief Justice of the King's Bench and had married Anne, the eldest daughter of Sir Jeremy; Benjamin Whichcott was Sir Jeremy's brother and Vice-Chancellor of Cambridge University until he was ejected at the Restoration.[103] Between 1683 and 1685[104] Caron House was pulled down, but its name survived and during the 19th century two houses stood on the estate, one called Carroun House and the other Caron Place (see below). There is no proof that either of these stood on the site of the old Caron House.

The history of the estate can be traced from 1685 through deeds preserved at the Minet Public Library and at Lambeth Town Hall. In 1725 it was purchased by Edward Lovibond of St. James, Clerkenwell, and remained in the possession of his family until 1797, when it was sold to (Sir) Charles Blicke[35] who probably had

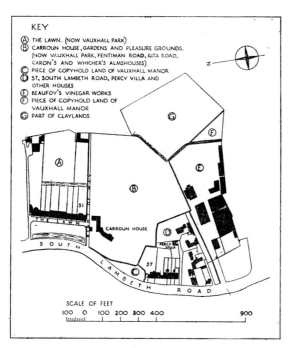

KEY
(A) THE LAWN. (NOW VAUXHALL PARK)
(B) CARROUN HOUSE, GARDENS AND PLEASURE GROUNDS.
(NOW VAUXHALL PARK, FENTIMAN ROAD, RITA ROAD.
CARON'S AND WHICHER'S ALMSHOUSES)
(C) PIECE OF COPYHOLD LAND OF VAUXHALL MANOR
(D) 57, SOUTH LAMBETH ROAD, PERCY VILLA AND
OTHER HOUSES
(E) BEAUFOY'S VINEGAR WORKS
(F) PIECE OF COPYHOLD LAND OF
VAUXHALL MANOR
(G) PART OF CLAYLANDS

SCALE OF FEET
100 0 100 200 300 400   900

Fig. 24. Plan of the estate of Sir Charles Blicke

Carroun House erected for his residence (see below). The plan of Blicke's estate reproduced here (fig. 24) is based on a plan of the estate drawn in 1838 and covers the area from Lawn Lane to the backs of houses in Heyford Avenue, and extends east to a line drawn from the rear of Vauxhall Park to the junction of Meadow and Fentiman Roads. From internal and external evidence there is no doubt that it describes the

land granted to Clarendon in 1666 with the exception of a piece of Claylands (see page 60) and two small pieces of copyhold of Vauxhall Manor to which Blicke was admitted tenant in 1806 (see page 65) and 1808.[105]

VAUXHALL PARK   [53]
Fig. 19, plots 31, 32 and part of 33

The land marked A on fig. 24 was let on two leases in 1791 by George Lovibond to James Gubbins and Philip Buckley, together with the eight houses which they had erected.[35] These were Nos. 1–8 (consec.) The Lawn, so-called from the extensive grass plot which lay before them, later Nos. 37–51 (odd) South Lambeth Road. Henry Fawcett, M.P., the blind Postmaster-General, lived at No. 51 from 1875 until his death in 1884.[106]

The large house shown on the land marked B on fig. 24 and called variously Carroun, Carron or Caron House, was occupied by Sir Charles Blicke. His heirs sold the house and grounds to William Evans in 1838 and it was subsequently occupied by John Cobeldick.[35] Fentiman Road was laid out on a line just south of the house in 1838, and the garden ground thus divided from the house by the road was sold by Evans to Henry Beaufoy.[107] Part of Rita Road now stands on this site. The part of the estate north of Fentiman Road which included The Lawn, and Carroun House and gardens, is now covered by Vauxhall Park.

A proposal was made in 1886 that roads should be formed across this part of the estate so that it could be developed for housing purposes,[108] but owing to the activity of Octavia Hill eight and a half acres were purchased for £43,500 from John Cobeldick by the Lambeth Vestry in 1889 for the formation of a park.[109] The purchase was made under powers granted by an Act of Parliament passed in 1888.[110] The London County Council and the Charity Commissioners contributed towards the purchase price,[111] and Mark Beaufoy, who was at that time M.P. for Kennington, also made a contribution.[112] The cost of forming the park was borne by the Kyrle Society whose landscape gardener, Fanny R. Wilkinson, designed the layout.[112] C. Harrison Townsend designed the entrance gates and railings.[35] The Society's Treasurer, Octavia Hill, was present at the opening ceremony on July 7, 1890, which was performed by Albert Edward, Prince of Wales.[113]

On the site of Henry Fawcett's house, which was pulled down for the formation of the park, stands an artificial stone statue to his memory (Plate 71b). It was modelled by George Tinworth and made at Doulton's manufactory, and was unveiled on June 7, 1893.[114] The statue stands on a pedestal which has panels representing Justice, Good and Bad News, Sympathy, Courage, Truth, India and the Post Office. The slightly raised terrace running northward from the statue follows the same line as the paved way in front of The Lawn.

[54] CARON'S ALSMHOUSES, FENTIMAN ROAD
      Fig. 19, plot 33

In 1618[115] Noel de Caron founded an almshouse on land belonging to him on the west side of the Kingston (now Wandsworth) Road (part of plot 7). The almshouse was a long, low, two-storeyed range (Plate 30a) containing seven separate apartments, and housed seven women aged over 60. In his will Caron stipulated that whoever occupied his house in South Lambeth should pay an annual rent of £28, from which a pension of twenty shillings was to be paid quarterly to each almswoman.[88] This proved an unsatisfactory arrangement, and in 1677 Sir Paul Whichcott, the owner of Caron House, was ordered by the Court of Chancery to pay the arrears which had accrued.[101] The charity was further endowed in 1773 by the Countess of Gower, in 1783 by Hayes Fortee and in 1867 under the will of Robert Forest.[101] The owner of Caron House, and later the owner of the site, continued to nominate the women for vacancies in the almshouse. By 1853 the building had become "uncomfortable and unsuitable" for aged persons, and an offer of £1,500 was made for the site by Price's Patent Candle Company.[116] A petition was presented to the Court of Chancery and permission was granted for the Company to purchase the site on condition that the £1,500 was appropriated for the erection of new premises on a piece of land belonging to the Caron House estate then owned by William Evans. The new almshouses (Plate 30b) were erected on the north side of Fentiman Road in 1854. Under a scheme promulgated in 1893 the charities of the Countess of Gower, Hayes Fortee and Robert Forest were combined with Caron's and vested in the Official Trustee.[101] They are now administered under the United Charities of Lambeth Scheme (1924),

and the almswomen are elected by the Trustees.[117] The site of the old almshouse, which measured about 105 by 47 feet, was sold to the Phoenix Gas Light and Coke Company in 1865, and is now incorporated with the works of the South-Eastern Gas Board.[116] The present almshouses are designed in Tudor style and built in a rich red brick with stone dressings. Tablets recording the benefactions of Caron and Evans, together with their coats of arms, are set in the gable over the centre house, which has a stone hood over its entrance.

WHICHER'S AND KIFFORD'S ALMSHOUSES, [55]
STANLEY CLOSE, FENTIMAN ROAD
      Fig. 19, plot 33

These two almshouses were both founded in Westminster at the end of the 17th century, and were moved to Lambeth shortly after 1855.[35] By his will dated November 17, 1680, George Whicher left £1,500 for the purchase of land and the erection of an almshouse for six old men who were to be maintained from the residue of the money. The almsmen were to be nominated by Whicher's executors during their lives, and then by the Deans of Westminster and the Chapel Royal.[118] An almshouse was built in Little Chapel Street (now Caxton Street).

By her will dated December 30, 1698, Judith Kifford left £300 for the foundation of an almshouse for two "decayed virtuous poor gentlewomen" who were to be nominated by her executors and the survivor of them, and then by the executors of such survivor.[118] Two houses were erected in Brewer's Green in 1705, on land belonging to the Dean and Chapter of Westminster. The charity was abandoned by Mrs. Kifford's representatives and in 1824 an Order of the Court of Chancery appointed the Dean and Chapter as Trustees.[119]

By 1853 Whicher's almshouses were unfit for habitation and the Westminster Improvement Act[120] empowered the Dean and Chapter to sell both sets of almshouses to the Westminster Improvement Commissioners. The proceeds were to be applied to the purchase of a site and the erection of new houses which were to be conveyed to the Dean and Chapter, in accordance with a scheme to be sanctioned by the Court of Chancery. In 1855, William Evans sold a strip of land on the west side of Caron's almshouses to the Dean and Chapter;[35] two houses designed by

Messrs. Hunt and Stephenson were erected there shortly afterwards,[119] one for each charity. They form a two-storey terrace designed in Tudor style. Their gables have ornamental wooden bargeboards with pendant finials.

[56] Nos. 57 AND 59 SOUTH LAMBETH ROAD

Formerly Nos. 13 and 14 South Lambeth Road
Fig. 19, plot 30

In 1768, when the Caron House estate was still owned by the Lovibond family, a lease of four and a quarter acres was granted to William Blackwell, a gardener, for 99 years. He was given licence to build on the land but also covenanted to maintain the garden ground in a "Husbandlike and Gardenerlike manner" and to keep about 200 standard fruit trees on the ground "in good heart" and to replace them as they decayed. This policy of making the best of both worlds led to the erection of Nos. 57–67 (odd), formerly Nos. 13–18 (consec.) South Lambeth Road, by William Burrows, plasterer, who had a sub-lease from Blackwell.[35] No. 57 is a plain stock brick terrace house of three storeys with an attic (fig. 25). The doorway has a patterned fanlight and there are keystones with modelled heads, probably in Coade's artificial stone, over the ground-floor round-headed arches (Plate 70a, b, c). The front of No. 59, a three-storey house with a narrower frontage, has no ornament. The carcase of the adjoining building (formerly part of No. 59) remains, though it has been refronted in recent years. Nos. 61–67 have been demolished. Most of the site marked D on fig. 24 is now occupied by William Bloore and Son, Ltd., timber merchants. The firm has occupied No. 57 South Lambeth Road since 1879,[121] but was established earlier in Bond Street[122] (now Bondway). The house marked Percy Villa on fig. 24 and now pulled down was the home of Lionel and Mary Brough,[122] the famous actor and actress.

[57] No. 87 SOUTH LAMBETH ROAD

Fig. 19, plot 30

The land marked E on fig. 24 is the site of Beaufoy's Vinegar Works. These formerly occupied a site on the south bank of the Thames which was needed for the formation of Waterloo Bridge.[123] In 1810 John Hanbury Beaufoy bought four acres of land from Sir Charles Blicke[35] and built a new manufactory and family residence (Caron Place) on the site (Plate 42); the architect is not known. The buildings have a distinguished quality which compares favourably with the later industrial buildings near by. The manufactory and offices are housed in substantial buildings of two and three storeys, built in stock brick with stone dressings, and grouped about a long yard. This yard was approached through a walled garden along a short private road, at the inner end of which stood two single-storey lodges. The south lodge was destroyed by bombing on October 12, 1940, but the surviving north lodge has a loggia with cast-iron columns, surmounted by the arms of the Beaufoy family. The iron gates illustrated on Plate 42a were removed from the Royal Exchange after the fire of 1838;[124] they are now preserved at the Beaufoy family's present home at Heyford in Oxfordshire. On the south side of the yard stands Caron Place, a plain building formerly inhabited by the Beaufoys, and now used as offices. Alongside is the shell of a two-storey building burnt out in an air-raid on May 10, 1941. The first floor of this building was formerly used as a ballroom, which was lit by stone-dressed Venetian windows on the north and east sides. The stock brick elevations are finished with a triglyphed frieze beneath a stone cornice and blocking course. The dominant building in the group is the vat house, which stands at the east end of the yard. It is surmounted by a wooden cupola which is raised above a wooden rusticated stage containing a clock. Before a fire damaged the building in 1916 the copper-covered cupola was supported by a solid square stage, pilastered at the corners, instead of by the present eight free-standing columns. The bell hanging in the cupola is cast with the inscription "THOMAS MEARS LONDON FOUNDER 1843". Another bell preserved on the premises but not hung is inscribed "HENRY BEAUFOY ESQ., 1833". The floor of the cooperage behind the yard is paved with mill stones formerly used in the manufactory. The premises are now owned by British Vinegars Ltd., and are used for blending, bottling and cooperage work.

THE BOND ESTATE

The history and disposition of the remainder of the freehold lands which Noel de Caron purchased from Thomas Hewytt are not so easily traced, but it is possible to sketch their descent by means

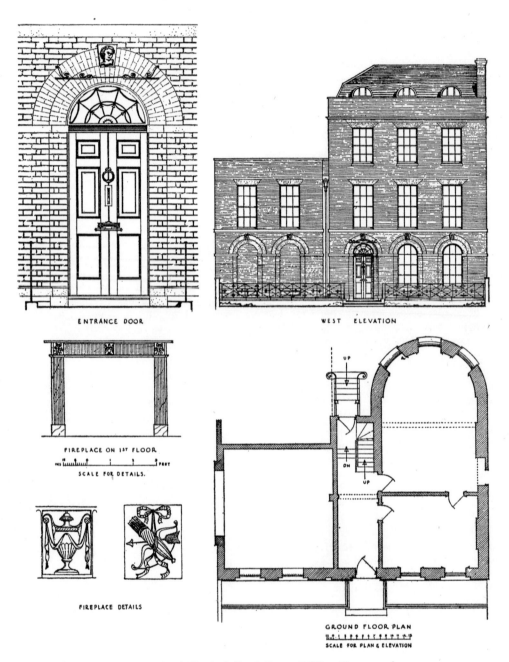

ENTRANCE DOOR

WEST ELEVATION

FIREPLACE ON 1ST FLOOR

SCALE FOR DETAILS.

FIREPLACE DETAILS

GROUND FLOOR PLAN

SCALE FOR PLAN & ELEVATION

Fig. 25. No. 57 South Lambeth Road. Lessee, William Burrows, plasterer

of the evidence of field names in a few surviving deeds. An idea of their disposition may be gained from the fact that the Bond estate, with which they nearly coincided, included plots 11, 12, 14, 20, 24 and part of 22 (fig. 19).

When Thomas Hill drew his map of Vauxhall Manor in 1681 most of this property was owned by John Plumer and William Freeman. Plumer sold 20 acres to Elias Ashmole in 1686[125] and Thomas Cooper purchased Freeman's lands in 1683.[126] Both estates became vested in Cooper's great grand-daughter Emma Miles[127] and in 1766 she sold them to John Bond of Crutched Friars, merchant, and Sarah his wife,[128] who were responsible for their development. In 1778 they obtained a building Act[128] and let the ground in small plots and the present Bondway, Miles Street, Parry Street and Wyvil Road were laid out to form a neat residential area. The houses erected under the building leases were provided with long gardens[129] and a proprietary chapel (now St. Anne's Church) was erected to meet the spiritual needs of the increased population. The subsequent incursions of the London and South Western Railway Company have completely altered the character of the neighbourhood.

[58] St. Anne's Church, South Lambeth Road

Fig. 19, plot 12

This church stands on the site of South Lambeth Chapel which was built in 1793 (Plate 13c). On January 9 of that year John and Sarah Bond granted a lease for 99 years of land fronting South Lambeth Road to certain local inhabitants, for the erection of a proprietary chapel.[130] The committee appointed to supervise its erection included John Dollond, the optician, Philip Buckley, James Gubbins and Sir Charles Blicke, who all had interests in the development of the vicinity.[131] The members of the committee decided to limit the cost of the chapel to £3,000, including the furniture and ornaments, and this sum was to be raised by issuing 60 shares at £50 each. Each share entitled the holder to four seats. Seats not allocated in this way (there was accommodation for about 600 persons and no seats were free) were let only to persons approved by the proprietors. For the governing of the chapel's affairs a committee of six was elected. The minister was chosen by the rector of St. Mary's,

Lambeth, but his salary of £40 a year was paid by the proprietors.[130]

After the building of the Nine Elms railway terminus and the works of the Phoenix Gas Company, most of the wealthy proprietors moved away from the district and the prosperity of the chapel declined.[132] The building was badly damaged by fire in 1856[133] and the committee tried to persuade the Ecclesiastical Commissioners to purchase the building for a parish church.[132] The Commissioners eventually bought the freehold interest of the chapel, and the building was consecrated as St. Anne's Church on February 3, 1869,[134] on the understanding that it would soon be altered and enlarged. The present church (Plate 13d) was erected in 1876 to the designs of R. Parkinson[135] and consecrated in the same year on December 19.[134] It was built in quasi-Romanesque style, in stock brick diapered with red brick, and with stone dressings. The body of the church is plain, with an apse at the east end. At the north-east corner stands an unfinished tower with a semi-circular stair projection. The entrance is at the base of the tower on the Miles Street frontage. As a result of war damage in 1941 the church has not been used for some years, but it is hoped that restoration will begin in 1956.

Wyvil Primary School, Wyvil Road   [59]

Fig. 19, plot 14

This school was built by the London School Board and opened on January 8, 1877. The architect was E. R. Robson. The contractors were Hill, Higgs, and Hill of South Lambeth Road, and their tender for a school for 828 children was for £7,782.[136] The building has been remodelled and extended. It has three storeys and is built of stock brick; the north and south elevations are symmetrically arranged and finished with gables, those on the south being flanked by short towers.

Tate Free Library, South Lambeth Road [60]

Fig. 19, plot 16

This building and its site were provided by (Sir) Henry Tate at a total cost of nearly £6,000. The architect was Sidney R. J. Smith, and the builder B. E. Nightingale. The library was opened by A. J. Mundella, M.P., in 1888.[137] It occupies a three-storey building built of red brick with Portland stone dressings, and is sited with its principal axis equiangular with Wilcox

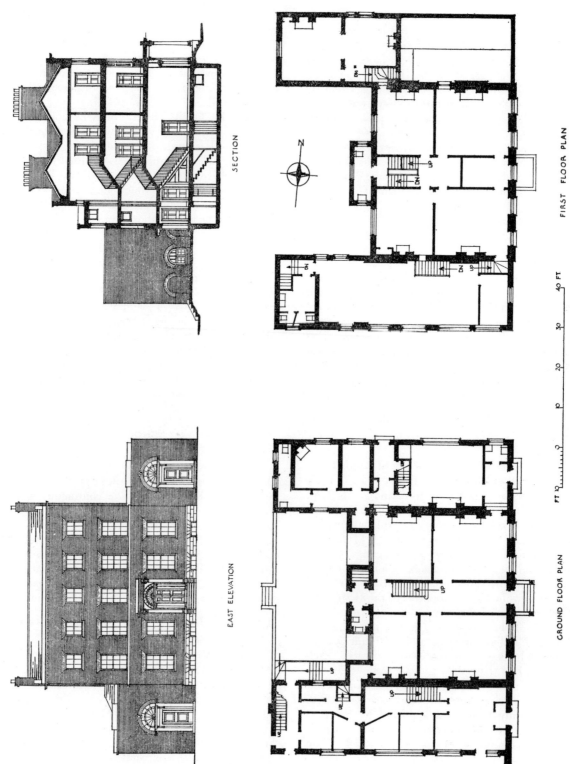

SECTION

EAST ELEVATION

FIRST FLOOR PLAN

GROUND FLOOR PLAN

FT 0   10   20   30   40 FT

Fig. 26. No. 274 South Lambeth Road, 1791–8. Lessee, William Burrows, plasterer

Road and South Lambeth Road. The semi-circular projecting porch at the road junction is supported by caryatides and telemones. A pedimented bay sets forward over the entrance and is flanked by two short towers each with a lantern termination. The building has single-storey wings and all the roofs are slated.

[61] Nos. 268–274 (even) SOUTH LAMBETH ROAD

Formerly Nos. 248–254 (even) South Lambeth Road
Fig. 19, plot 22

In 1791 Crooked Bridge Field was let by John and Sarah Bond on building lease to William Burrows of South Lambeth, plasterer,[138] who erected these houses on the site. No. 274, Beulah House, is a well-proportioned three-storey house with single-storey wings (fig. 26). The wings and central Ionic porch have been altered or rebuilt sympathetically. The modelled keystones to the arches in the wings are almost certainly of Coade's artificial stone (Plate 70 d and f); they are very similar to the keystones on Nos. 362–366 Kennington Road. The house was first leased in 1798 to Horatio Clagett.[138] From 1825 until his death in 1849[78] it was occupied by John Poynder, clerk and solicitor to Bridewell Hospital. He was the author of several theological tracts and "Literary Extracts from English and other Works, collected during Half a Century". He was also a stock-holder in the East India Company, and as a result of his passionate campaigning the practice of *suttee* was in 1829 declared to be punishable as culpable homicide.[103] In 1852 a lease of the house and premises, including a wash-house, laundry and drying ground in the rear, was obtained by Thomas Cook, William Hill and Henry M. Rogers, "scourers".[138] The premises are still used by Rogers and Cook, Ltd.

STOCKWELL BAPTIST CHURCH, SOUTH [62] LAMBETH ROAD

Fig. 19, plot 22

This church with its ancillary buildings also stands on part of Crooked Bridge Field.[139] It was founded and erected in 1866 by James Stiff, the pottery manufacturer, who had a factory in High Street, Lambeth.[140] The church is built of yellow stock brick and has an ill-proportioned front composed of a deep tetrastyle Corinthian portico with flanking pavilions pilastered at the corners. A dentilled pediment surmounts the portico, and the entablature is carried in a simplified form across the pavilions. The portico has a cement finish.

VAUXHALL ESCHEAT

Owing to the paucity of records for the period it is not clear why the lands which Noel de Caron purchased from the Fosters should have been escheated by the Lords of the Manor of Vauxhall, whereas his other property was not. From 1661[141] or earlier, the Dean and Chapter of Canterbury leased the escheated lands together under the name of "The Vauxhall Escheat" for terms of 21 years. At the end of the 18th century their lessee was Benjamin White, bookseller, of Fleet Street. After his death in 1794 his trustees were granted a new lease, and in 1810 they and the Dean and Chapter obtained an Act of Parliament enabling them to grant building leases of the Escheat and two acres of enclosed waste land which had been added to it.[142] The Act provided for building leases to be granted for 98 years, though the term of the trustees' lease was to remain at 21 years. A great deal of trouble had been caused by a similar arrangement in the Dean and Chapter's neighbouring Manor of Walworth, where the head lessees had granted building leases for longer terms than they themselves possessed.[143] A clause was therefore inserted in this Act permitting the renewal, every seven years, of the head lease for a term of 21 years without the validity of the building leases being affected. The head lease was to end, however, as the building leases fell in, and the property was to revert to the Dean and Chapter. The rents were to be divided, one half to go to the Dean and Chapter and one half to White's trustees. Probably owing to the smallness of the plots the trustees were unsuccessful in letting the estate, and in 1820 they asked, and received, permission to sell their interest. This was done in May 1821,[89] but even then building development did not follow immediately on all the plots.

THE TRADESCANTS'
AND ASHMOLE'S HOUSES

Fig. 19, plots 26–29 (plot 27 was not part of Vauxhall Escheat but for the sake of clarity is included here)

John "Treadeskant", who died in 1638,[144] was said to have been a Fleming or a Dutchman,[103] but as he had relations of the same name in Walberswick, Suffolk,[145] he may have been of East Anglian origin. He was a great traveller and botanist and introduced many new plants into England. After serving as gardener to several great houses he moved to South Lambeth and created a remarkable garden which was much visited and greatly admired.[103] Tradescant was also a collector of coins, medals and objects of natural history, which on his death passed to his only son, John.[144] The latter, also a gardener, bequeathed the collection to his wife, Hester, and instructed her to give it to either the University of Oxford or Cambridge.[145]

Elias Ashmole, the antiquary, was a friend and neighbour of the Tradescants and Hester gave the collection to him after her husband's death in 1662. She seems to have been an unstable person for shortly after giving the collection to Ashmole she accused him of robbing her.[146] But two years before her death in 1678[147] (she was drowned in the pond in her garden), she acknowledged before witnesses that she had wronged him by "fals, scandalous, and defamatory speeche and reporte".[146] The Tradescant collection was subsequently given by Ashmole to the University of Oxford; together with the manuscripts and books in the two top studies in his house in Lambeth, some medals and portraits, and the books in a closet in his lower study over the milk house,[148] they form the collection contained in the Ashmolean Museum.

The Tradescants' house stood on plot 29; in 1592 the plot was said to comprise a messuage, barn, orchard and garden in the occupation of Laurence Palmer;[83] it was subsequently occupied by Sir William Foster[141] (see page 66). The famous garden mentioned above occupied the site of plot 28, which was known as Walnut Tree Close and contained three acres.[83]

The house occupied by Ashmole, which he purchased in 1674 when it was said to have been previously in the tenure of Frances Bowyer, widow,[149] stood on plot 27 and adjoined the Tradescants' house. After Hester Tradescant's death Ashmole obtained a lease of the Tradescants' house and garden from their landlord Mr. Bartholomew,[146] the head lessee of Vauxhall Escheat.[89] According to his diary Ashmole added several rooms to his house, including the rear part of the Tradescants' house.[146] Plate 44b shows Ashmole's house on the right, set back a little and adjoining the Tradescants' house on the left. Ashmole also had the lease of plot 26 which was used as a pound for some years and is marked as such on the map of 1681.

The front part of the Tradescants' house was probably sub-let by Ashmole, for it was in the occupation of a Mr. Jones in 1681. In 1774 it was occupied by Dr. Ducarel, the antiquary and librarian of Lambeth Palace.[89] According to J. Nichols writing in 1786 "John Tradescant's house, though much altered of late years, was originally divided into two parts; the front thereof being that which is now the Doctor's [Ducarel's] own house; and the remainder making part of the offices of the great brick house built by Ashmole".[146]

Ashmole died in 1692 and left his estate to his third wife Elizabeth,[149] daughter of Sir William Dugdale.[103] At the beginning of the 18th century, when it was owned by Alexander Montgomerie, the house was known as the Turret House.[150] A plan of 1879[151] shows a house on the site of Ashmole's marked "Turret House" which probably incorporated much of the old building. It was then owned by Captain Francis Woodgate.[152]

In spite of the passing of the Act of 1810 plots 26, 28 and 29 were not let on building leases. The Ecclesiastical Commissioners sold plots 26 and 28 to Captain Woodgate in 1867[152] and plot 29 to Frederick Snelling, builder, in 1879.[151] The site of Ashmole's house was cleared about 1880 for the formation of Tradescant Street (now Road) and Walberswick Road which now cover plots 26, 27 and 28. Nos. 1, 3 and 5 Tradescant Road and some premises in the rear cover the site of the house. When Snelling purchased plot 29 there were then standing on the site, Stamford House, a school run by John Henry Hay[121] and six cottages in the rear.[151] Stamford House included the site of the Tradescants' house and may have included the old building. Meadow Place marks the northern boundary of this plot.

THE SEVEN ACRES

Fig. 19, plot 38

Though this plot is shown as two parcels on the map of 1681 it is consistently described in the records relating to the Escheat as one close containing seven acres. In a lease of the property to Benjamin White's trustees in 1802 two acres of waste land, part of South Lambeth Common which adjoined the seven acres, were inclosed and added to it.[142] This gave the seven acres a frontage to the present Lansdowne Way as well as Clapham Road.

PORTLAND GROVE, MURSELL ROAD, AND NOS. 192–220 (even) CLAPHAM ROAD

Formerly Nos. 1–15 (consec.) Portland Place

At the auction of the Escheat in 1821 the head lease of this parcel was purchased by William Bennett of Bartholomew Close, silversmith.[153] The land was divided into five lots and let on building leases between 1822 and 1830 to James Blake of Helmet Row, Old Street, carpenter and timber merchant,[154] John Barnes of Pentonville, carpenter,[155] and Richard Howard of St. Mary, Newington, carpenter and builder.[156] Blake had three of these leases. Each lease required the builder to erect four or more houses at a cost of not less than £3,000, making a total of £15,000 for the whole estate, and to construct new roads, i.e., Portland Grove and Mursell Road. Nos. 74 [63] and 76 Portland Grove, formerly Nos. 14 and 13 Sydney Place, are the two best examples of the small, but pleasant, cottage-type of houses erected on the estate, which consist mostly of two-storey brick houses with little ornament other than the fanlights over their entrances. Nos. 74 and 76 were built by James Blake under a lease granted in 1824.[153] The houses fronting Clapham Road [64] were more pretentious. Nos. 192–198 were erected by Richard Howard under a lease granted in 1822[156] (Plate 50c). Nos. 194–198 are plain box-like villas with three storeys and semi-basements, their centrally placed entrances being flanked by Greek Doric columns. No. 192 has [65] its entrance on one side. Nos. 200–220 were erected by Blake under leases granted in 1822[157] and 1823.[158] These are terrace houses grouped in twos and threes with semi-basements, three main storeys, and attics within mansard roofs. The front elevations have no interest other than the cast-iron balcony railings linking the first-floor windows. Excepting two pairs of two-storey houses, the houses facing Lansdowne Way are of the same height.

THE "PEAES" CLOSE

Fig. 19, plot 19

This close was described as the "Peaes" Close in 1592 and contained about one acre.[83]

NOS. 244–258 (even) SOUTH LAMBETH ROAD [66]

Formerly Nos. 224–238 (even) South Lambeth Road; previously Dean's Cottage and Nos. 1–7 (consec.) Dean's Place

These houses were erected under a building lease granted in 1824 to William Hearn of Nine Elms, miller, who covenanted to build two or more houses before Christmas, 1825, and another two or more before Michaelmas, 1829, at a total cost of not less than £2,000.[159] Nos. 246–252 form a plain terrace with semi-basements, three storeys and attics. Nos. 248–252 have entrances with attenuated columns at each side and patterned fanlights. They still have their original doors with key ornamented panels. No. 254, at the end of the terrace, and the detached pair, Nos. 256 and 258, are similar; their doorways have reeded surrounds with consoles supporting the transoms under the patterned fanlights. No. 244, which has the name "Dean's Place" painted on its front wall, has only two storeys and a semi-basement, and is narrower than No. 246. The arched heads of the doorway and ground-floor windows rise from plain imposts.

THE NINE ACRES

Fig. 19, plot 17

A faint line of dots on the map of 1681 indicates that this close was already divided at that date. In 1774 a footpath which ran along the line of the present Hartington Road divided the nine acres into a western portion, containing about five acres and planted with gooseberry and currant "trees", and an eastern portion, part grass and part ploughed land.[89] Another footpath on the line of Wilcox Road bounded the close on the north side. The western portion was let on two building leases to John Roupell, lead-smelter, in 1824[160] and 1825,[161] but it has been redeveloped in recent years with blocks of flats designed by Messrs. Clutton on behalf of the Church Commissioners.[162] The eastern portion was purchased by Thomas Allen at the auction of 1821[163] and was not let on building lease until after his death.[164] It was developed after 1857 by John Abbot, builder,[165] who laid out Brough Street and Kenchester Street. Since the houses between Hartington Road and Brough Street were destroyed by a flying bomb in the war of 1939–45, their sites have been covered with temporary single-storey prefabricated houses. On the rest of the land to the east the original development of two-storey terrace houses still stands. The houses are typical of the 1850s and 1860s, with stucco surrounds to the door and window openings and hoods over the ground-floor openings, all detailed in a debased Classical manner. Some houses have pilaster-flanked entrances.

THE TWO ACRES

Fig. 19, part of plot 6

This plot was described in 1592 as a close of meadow lying against "Woodbridge".[83] In 1802 it was in the occupation of Edward Shearing and was then described as a piece of land called "Battens" containing over two acres.[142] The two acres were sold in 1847 to the London and South Western Railway Company for the Nine Elms Extension Scheme.[166]

MINOR ESTATES

[67] Nos. 202–218 (even) South Lambeth Road

Formerly Nos. 182–198 (even) South Lambeth Road, previously Nos. 1–9 (consec.) Mawbey Place
Fig. 19, plot 18

These houses were built before 1791[78] on land belonging to Sir Joseph Mawbey, senior.[167] They form a three-storey terrace built in stock brick, each house being two windows wide. The elevation has no ornament save for the surround to the stone tablet incised "MAWBEY PLACE" set over No. 210, and the parapet raised over Nos. 210–214. A shop extends across the front garden of No. 202.

[68] Nos. 282–300 (even) South Lambeth Road

Formerly Nos. 260–278 (even) South Lambeth Road, previously Nos. 11–2 (consec.) Montpelier Row
Fig. 19, plot 22

These houses (Plate 46b) were erected in 1790–1[78] on a piece of land called Tom Fool's Field which then belonged to William Head,[138] a local builder.[168] Nos. 282–298 were erected by Head and form a regular terrace, each house being three storeys high and two windows wide. The entrances set forward slightly in brick surrounds which have mutule cornices, each doorway having a simple fanlight of radiating pattern. Joseph Greated of Ely Place, Holborn, carpenter, purchased a piece of the field from William Head in 1791 and erected Nos. 1, 2, 12 and 13 Montpelier Row.[138] Of these only No. 12 (now No. 300 South Lambeth Road) survives. It is similar to the other houses in the terrace, but has a semi-basement. With No. 302, now destroyed, it shared a pediment to its parapet.

No. 30 Wandsworth Road, Brunswick [69] House

Fig. 19, plot 7

This house (fig. 27) was built in 1758[39] on freehold land owned by the Dawson family, purchased by Richard Dawson in 1737 from Joseph Pratt.[169] In 1776 it was described as a mansion house, with offices, coach-house, and stable, lately erected by John Dawson (Richard Dawson's nephew and heir). The site of the house and gardens measured nearly three acres and included a piece of land with a timber dock on lease from the Dean and Chapter of Canterbury (part of plot 8). The property was bounded on the south by Belmont Row or Place (Nine Elms Lane). In 1791 the house, which was then called Belmont, was divided into two; the larger or south-western portion was leased to David Hunter and the other portion was leased to William Anderson. Hunter's half was sold to the Western Gas Company in 1845 and purchased by the London and South Western Railway Company in 1854. In 1811 Anderson's half was purchased by Friedrich Wilhelm, Duke of Brunswick, whose sister Caroline married the Prince Regent.[170] The Duke was a bitter opponent of Napoleon's domination of Germany, and fled to England after taking part in the battle of Wagram. He returned to Brunswick in 1813 to raise fresh troops, but two years later was killed at the battle of Quatre Bras.[171] His part of Belmont House was also purchased by the Gas Company and sold to the Railway Company in 1855. The two parts of the house were subsequently reunited under the name of Brunswick House and have been

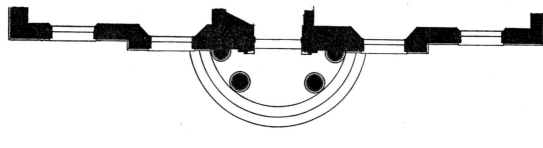

Fig. 27. No. 30 Wandsworth Road, 1758; front elevation

used ever since as an institute and club for railway workers.

This large three-storeyed house is almost square in plan, but the interior is so much changed that the original arrangements are obscure. The exterior, however, has survived with little alteration.

The entrance front towards Wandsworth Road is a pleasant formal composition with a central feature, three windows wide and crowned by an angular pediment, projecting slightly from narrow flanks, each one window wide. The rectangular window openings, originally correctly proportioned to the three storeys, are equally spaced in a stock brick face, horizontally divided by the deep plinth, the first-floor level platband, and the ogee-bracketed crowning cornice, all of painted stone. The cornice of the flanks is surmounted by a blocking course stopping against the central pediment, which has a circular shallow recess in its brick tympanum. The most interesting feature is the centrally placed porch (Plate 69d), which might well be a later addition, now painted but almost certainly of Coade's artificial stone. Semi-elliptical in plan and raised on steps, it has two free-standing and two engaged columns with enriched moulded bases, fluted and cabled shafts, and water-leaf capitals. The entablature has a frieze decoration of rams' skulls linked by floral festoons, and the cornice bedmouldings are enriched. The surmounting blocking-course continues the lines of the first-floor platband. The plain sill-band on the central feature's piers suggests that the first-floor windows have been lengthened.

While the side elevations are without interest, the river front has three tiers of five equally-spaced windows, and repeats the platband and bracketed cornice of the road front.

Internally, the most interesting feature is the south-west room on the first floor, where the dado and one section of the original ovolo-moulded panelling survives, together with a modelled plaster cornice. The stone staircase, rising between the front and back rooms on the west side, has a plain balustrade and handrail of late 18th century character. The basement below the front rooms is divided into two aisles by brick piers carrying intersecting vaults. A stone tablet incised with the date "1758" is set in the inner face of the front wall of the basement; this wall is built of red bricks which may have been used in a previous building on the site.

SPRINGFIELD METHODIST CHURCH,   [70]
FRIENDSHIP HOUSE, WANDSWORTH
ROAD

Fig. 19, plot 3

Most of the land covered by plot 3, on which this church stands, was a detached portion of Stockwell Manor. Springfield Hall was opened on March 18, 1902.[39] The builders were L. Whitehead and Company. Another block was added on the south side and opened in 1926.[39] Springfield Hall is used for worship and the ancillary buildings for a community centre. All the buildings are of red brick with stone dressings. The main hall has a wide entrance porch flanked by squat octagonal towers.

Nos. 238–246 (even) WANDSWORTH ROAD

Fig. 19, plot 2

These houses were demolished in 1953 to make way for a housing scheme. Mr. John Summerson attributes their design to the architect J. M. Gandy.[172] They were semi-detached villas of austere character, two storeys high and stucco-fronted. Each pair shared a flat-moulded pediment with a circular panel in the centre and the piers flanking the first-floor windows were adorned with Soanic frets. The ground storeys were hidden by shops built on the forecourts.

VAUXHALL BRIDGE

At the beginning of the 19th century there was no bridge across the Thames between Westminster and Battersea. A number of important roads (now known as Kennington Lane, South Lambeth Road, Wandsworth Road and Nine Elms Lane) converged on the river at Vauxhall, which was therefore a suitable place for a new bridge. Though the project was first discussed in 1806, ten years were to elapse before the bridge was opened.[173] In 1809 an Act of Parliament established the Vauxhall Bridge Company with powers to build a bridge and the necessary approach roads, collect tolls and raise capital up to £300,000.[174] John Rennie (1761–1821),[103] who was appointed engineer, prepared plans for a stone bridge with 11 arches,[175] and the foundation stone was laid by Lord Dundas on behalf of the Prince Regent on May 9, 1811. The bridge was to be named "The Regent's Bridge", but it very quickly assumed its present name.[173]

Rennie's estimate of the cost of the bridge had been £269,000, and the Company very soon began to feel that this figure was beyond its means.[176] In 1812 another Act authorizing the construction of a new bridge of iron or other material was therefore obtained,[177] and in November of the same year designs for an iron bridge were approved by the Company. These new plans were drawn up by Sir Samuel Bentham,[178] brother of Jeremy Bentham, and a naval architect and engineer of great experience. As Civil Architect and Engineer of the Navy, Sir Samuel had on two recent occasions seen his plans for naval works at Plymouth and Sheerness rejected in favour of those of Rennie, and the adoption of his plan for Vauxhall Bridge may therefore have given him considerable satisfaction. A contract for the erection of the bridge for £72,500 was signed with Mr. Grellier.[177] Sir Samuel's triumph was, however, short-lived, for doubts arose "as to the mode of constructing the foundation",[179] and he was dismissed.[180] He was replaced by James Walker, who prepared a new design differing little from that of Sir Samuel Bentham, and in May 1813 a new contract for £85,613 was signed with Grellier.[175]

The bridge (Plate 1a) was opened for pedestrians in June 1816, and for vehicular traffic in the following month.[176] The opening of the bridge led to a rapid increase in building development in Lambeth. The bridge was 36 feet wide and consisted of nine arches each of 78-feet span formed of cast-iron archribs. "The abutments, and the piers below springing-level, were of coursed masonry with rubble backing, the upper portions of the piers being of brickwork faced at the ends with masonry."[175] Accounts of the actual cost of the bridge vary very considerably. Despite Grellier's contract for £85,613, the Deputy Chairman of the Company stated in 1816 that Walker had undertaken the bridge "upon an estimate of 215,000 l. and had carried his estimate as nearly as the nature of things admitted into practical effect".[176] In 1854 the Director of the Company stated that his accounts did not show how much the bridge had cost, but that the outlay on the bridge and its approach roads amounted to "about 300,000 l., exclusive of about 70,000 l. for Parliamentary and legal expenses, conveyancing, etc."[181] In 1878 an accountant of the Metropolitan Board of Works who had examined the Company's books stated that the bridge had

cost £175,432, the approach roads £38,925, and that the total expenditure including legal and professional fees, compensation paid to the Battersea Bridge Company and others, had amounted to £296,998.[182] In the early 19th century bridge-building was indeed extremely expensive, but the scientific improvements which took place in the second quarter of the century considerably reduced costs for a number of years.[183]

The upkeep of the approach roads, which comprised Vauxhall Bridge Road and a short stretch on the Surrey side, remained the responsibility of the Company until 1858, when this duty was transferred to the local authorities.[184] Under the terms of the Metropolis Toll Bridges Act of 1877,[185] Vauxhall Bridge and a number of others were bought by the Metropolitan Board of Works and the tolls abolished. Compensation amounting to £255,000 was paid to the Company, and the ceremony of opening the bridge free of toll was performed by the Prince and Princess of Wales (later King Edward VII and Queen Alexandra) on May 24, 1879.[173]

The foundations of the bridge were repaired in 1887, but its narrowness and the steep gradients of its approaches soon made it inadequate for the steady increase of traffic. In 1895 the London County Council obtained statutory power to rebuild the bridge, and a temporary one was opened in 1898.[173] The present bridge (Plate 1b) was designed by the Council's Chief Engineer, Sir Alexander Binnie, who was succeeded in 1902 by Maurice Fitzmaurice, and the Council's Architect, W. E. Riley, assisted in the design of the superstructure.[175] The contract for the demolition of the old bridge and the construction of the piers and abutments of the new one was placed with Messrs. Pethick Bros.; C. Wall was the contractor for the superstructure.[175] Demolition began in September 1898, and the new bridge, which cost about £480,000,[175] was opened on May 26, 1906, by Evan Spicer, Chairman of the London County Council.[173]

The bridge has five arches and is 80 feet wide; the central span is 149 feet 7 inches wide, the two intermediate ones 144 feet 4¾ inches, and the shore spans 130 feet 5¾ inches. The piers and abutments are of solid concrete with granite facings and the superstructure is of open steel-framed construction. The simple parapet is heightened to form a balustraded screen so that when seen from a distance the arches do not appear as weak

[71]

at the crown as those of many bridges with flat spans. The bridge is decorated above the cutwaters with bronze figures of heroic size on both sides; these were executed by Alfred Drury, A.R.A., and F. W. Pomeroy, A.R.A., and represent from east to west Science, Fine Arts, Local Government, and Education on the downstream side, and Pottery, Engineering, Architecture, and Agriculture on the upstream side.[186]

CHAPTER III

Stockwell

THIS chapter covers the area of the former Manor of Stockwell, which extended further south than the relatively small area now known as Stockwell. The Manor was roughly diamond-shaped. The boundary in the north is uncertain, but on the east it probably ran from a point just north of Durand Gardens in Clapham Road to the junction of Stockwell Park Road and Groveway and down Stockwell Park Road. On the west it probably followed the southern boundary of Vauxhall Manor along Lansdowne Way and Wandsworth Road and thereafter the boundary between the parishes of Battersea and Lambeth to Clapham Road. In the south the Manor was bounded by the present Brixton Road and Brixton Hill on the east and Bedford and Lyham Roads on the west. A small detached portion of the Manor lay on the north-west side of Wandsworth Road (fig. 19).

STOCKWELL MANOR

The emergence of Stockwell and Vauxhall Manors as separate entities after the division of South Lambeth Manor has already been discussed on page 57. The evidence suggests, however, that although Stockwell achieved manorial status at about the end of the 13th century[a] the courts of Vauxhall Manor imposed their jurisdiction on Stockwell for centuries afterwards. In 1326 a rent of a head penny was payable by Stockwell Manor to the View of Frank Pledge of Vauxhall,[2] and was still being paid in 1528–9.[3] In 1722 the Dean and Chapter of Canterbury were presented by this (their own) court to put up new stocks in Stockwell as well as in Vauxhall.[4] Even as late as 1814, when a new pound was needed in Stockwell, it was the View of Frank Pledge of Vauxhall which ordered it to be erected, though on this occasion the responsibility for its erection was placed on the Lady of Stockwell Manor.[5] It is impossible to tell whether the Lords of Stockwell recognized the jurisdiction of the Vauxhall court, for the only manorial record

which has been found of an independent court being held for Stockwell is a draft minute of a Court Baron and View of Frank Pledge held in 1626 by Sir George Chute, then Lord of the Manor.[6] The minute records the election of a headborough, ale-conner, and constable, although before this date, tithing men, and after this date, headboroughs and constables, were elected for Stockwell liberty at the Views of Frank Pledge held at Vauxhall.[7] This evidence, though scrappy, does serve to confirm that Stockwell and Vauxhall had originally been linked closely enough for an association to continue, however weakly, until the 19th century; it also lends colour to the hypothesis that together they formed the ancient Manor of South Lambeth.

The descent of the Manor is described in some detail in the *Victoria County History of Surrey*,[8] published in 1912, but additional information has since been discovered. At the close of the 15th century, Stockwell Manor, together with Levehurst, Bodley, Upgrove and Scarlettes, and parts of Vauxhall and Lambeth Manors, was held by Sir John Leigh (Legh). Shortly before his death in 1523, he erected a chapel[9] in the parish church in which he and his wife were buried,[10] and a second chapel in Stockwell. He left instructions in his will that the chapel at Stockwell should be repaired out of the profits and revenues of Stockwell and Levehurst Manors, and bequeathed 66s. 8d. a year for a chantry priest and 53s. 4d. for ornaments; two vestments were to be made out of his furred velvet gown, with crosses from his jacket of crimson velvet.[9]

Sir John Leigh's heir was his nephew, John Leigh,[9] who in 1543 exchanged Stockwell and Levehurst Manors with the King for other property.[11] Stockwell was held by the Crown until 1555, when it was granted to Anthony Browne, Viscount Montagu, "for the better support of the estate and rank of a viscount",[12] in consideration of his services to Queen Mary during the rebellions of the Duke of Northumberland and Sir Thomas Wyatt. The Manor was held in chief for the service of half a knight's fee

[a] A deed of 1294 and an inquisition of 1326 both mention courts held at Stockwell.[1]

and charged with an annual rent of £8 12s. 11d. Viscount Montagu was succeeded by his grandson, the second Viscount Montagu,[13] who sold the Manor in 1598 to George Chute of Brede, Sussex.[14] Excepted from the sale were 30 acres called Great or (sic) Little Crowlands, seven acres called Paradise, Stockwell chapel, a forge and lands in the occupation of "Jukes", and Stockwell Wood.

Some of this latter property corresponds with certain lands which were let on long leases by the second Viscount Montagu before he sold the Manor. In 1580 he let the manor house, with part of Crowlands and other closes, to Henry Store of London, woodmonger, for 1,000 years, and in 1586 he granted a lease of some 44 acres for 2,000 years to John Pynder (Pindar) and John Thrayle, citizens and vintners of London.[15] John and/or Thomas Norton also had a lease of part of the Manor.[16] Most of these leasehold interests were acquired by Francis Goston, who after mortgaging them,[15] sold them in 1640 in three lots to Richard Rundell of Stockwell, yeoman, Edmond Dent, of South Lambeth, and Samuel Lewes, citizen and merchant taylor of London.[17]

Before he died, George Chute settled the Manor on Sir George Chute,[18] one of his younger sons. Sir George Chute was knighted in 1608[19] and died in 1649.[20] In his will he expressed a wish to be buried in the aisle in St. Mary's Lambeth where his predecessors, Lords of Stockwell Manor, had a right to be buried—presumably in the Leigh Chapel. Sir George's son, also a George Chute, of Stockwell[21] and Streatham,[22] inherited the Manor, but sold about 76 acres to John Howland of Streatham in 1683. Howland's daughter, Elizabeth, wife of Wriothesley, Duke of Bedford, inherited her father's estate and on her death it passed into the hands of her husband's descendants.[22] The estate is marked on the plan on Plates 74 and 75 as belonging to the Duke of Bedford. The rest of the Manor continued to be held by the Chute family until 1699, when the family's trustees sold it to (Sir) John Thornycroft.[23] When Sir John died he left the Manor in trust for his daughter Elizabeth, wife of Lieutenant-General the Hon. Roger Peter Handasyd, and only a shilling to his "undutiful obstinate and rebellious" son John. Nevertheless, when John Thornycroft junior made his will in 1739, he bequeathed his father's estate to Henry Forster

of Southwark, distiller, and five years later his sister Elizabeth had to pay £630 to regain the property. Her brother was then described as lately a prisoner in the King's Bench Prison.[24] The plan reproduced on Plates 74 and 75 represents the Manor of Stockwell in 1773 when it was owned by Henshaw Thornycroft. In 1781 Edward Thornycroft, then owner of the Manor, sold about 30 acres to Benjamin Robertson of Stockwell; this estate lay on the west side of Stockwell Road. An abstract of title relating to the estate mentions, but does not abstract, a deed of 1778 in circumstances which suggest that Robertson had already purchased another part of the Manor before 1781.[25] This may have been the site of Stockwell Park Crescent and part of Stockwell Park Road which Robertson's nephew and heir, John Bedwell, sold in 1806.[26]

The major part of the Manor remaining in the hands of the Thornycroft family was sold by auction in 14 lots in 1802;[24] it comprised all the land south of the present Ferndale Road and some adjoining it on the north side. Probably the last pieces of the Manor to be disposed of were Stockwell Green and Stockwell Common, which were sold about the same time as the auction took place, to William Lambert, who thus became Lord of the Manor.[27]

LANSDOWNE WAY AREA

Nos. 339–343 (odd) Wandsworth Road [72] and Nos. 141–149 (odd) Lansdowne Way

Formerly Nos. 1, 2 and 3 The Priory

This building originally comprised three houses and was built around 1843[28] in the Gothic taste of that time. The three-storeyed fronts towards Wandsworth Road and Lansdowne Way are faced with coursed stucco and form a balanced composition centred on the octagonal battlement-crowned bay at the corner, to which the three-sided bays terminating each front form responds. The windows have "Gothic" casements and over those to the first floor are moulded labels. Modern shop-fronts have obscured most of the ground storey, but No. 141 retains its original arch-headed doorway, framed by a moulded arch and rising from clustered and banded shafts. The property was owned in 1850 by John Cooke; it was purchased in 1866 by John Diplock of

Walworth, tea-dealer, whose descendants still retain a partial interest.[29]

[73] PRIORY PRIMARY AND SECONDARY SCHOOLS, PRIORY GROVE

This school was built for the London School Board; the contractor was W. Tongue of Plumstead, and his tender for a school for 1,200 children was for £11,675.[30] The architect was E. R. Robson[31] and the date of opening was January 11, 1886.[32] The school is a plain three-storey stock brick building with red brick and stone dressings.

[74] STOCKWELL GARAGE, LONDON TRANSPORT EXECUTIVE, LANSDOWNE WAY

This garage was erected in 1950–4, and was designed by Adie, Button and Partners, in association with Thomas Bilbow, architect to London Transport Executive. An illustrated article appeared in the *Architectural Review* for March 1954.

[75] ST. FRANCIS OF SALES and ST. GERTRUDE ROMAN CATHOLIC CHURCH, LARKHALL LANE

This church was erected in 1902[33] and is a plain stock brick slate-roofed building. It has stone lintels over the windows and over the two front entrances, the latter bearing carved crosses. The east elevation, with a corbelled gable and containing a large circular window, is surmounted by a tall metal cross. The architect was probably F. W. Tasker.

CLAPHAM ROAD WEST SIDE

[76] ST. AUGUSTINE'S CHURCH

This church stands on the site of a congregational chapel, an iron building erected in 1875 and called the Augustine Independent Church.[28] The latter was founded by Dr. Urijah Thomas[34] who was helped by his father, Dr. David Thomas, minister of Stockwell New Chapel.[35] The venture did not prosper, however, and in 1882 the building was purchased for a chapel of ease for the parish of All Saints, and dedicated to St. Augustine. A new building was erected on the site and opened on March 2, 1899.[34] The architect was Sir Arthur Blomfield, who had recently restored Southwark Cathedral. The church was

not consecrated until January 1, 1915.[34] On the alteration of parish boundaries in 1950 St. Augustine's was transferred to St. John's, Clapham, and now serves as a parish hall.

St. Augustine's is a Perpendicular Gothic building finished with red brick and stone dressings of plain and rather unimaginative design. It has a clerestoried nave and lean-to aisles with a lean-to entrance lobby across the Clapham Road front, the chancel being situated at the west end, all roofed with red tiles. On the flanking elevation a somewhat arbitrarily-placed gable is grouped with an awkwardly shaped bellcote. The interior, finished with red and stock brick, is architecturally very dull. The nave clerestory is carried on four-bay arcades which rest on circular columns.

TRINITY PRESBYTERIAN CHURCH [77]

The foundation stone of this church (Plate 26b) was laid by John Henderson of Park Glasgow on February 13, 1862. The architects were W. G. Habershon and A. R. Pite.[33] A Bath stone portico of coarse Roman Corinthian columns crowned by a massive pediment, forms the frontispiece to a plain stock brick building with tall arch-headed windows in its side elevations. At the time of writing the church is disused.

CLAPHAM ROAD, EAST SIDE

The plan of Stockwell Manor on Plates 74 and 75 shows an estate on the east side of Clapham Road marked "Mrs. Lads Ld." In 1736 Sir John Lade, baronet, purchased from Dennis Roundell 20 acres of land in Stockwell which abutted west on Martin Lane[36] (Clapham Road). Probably the property was originally part of Stockwell Manor. In 1782 Sir John Lade sold the estate to William Malcolm, nurseryman,[37] and for a time it was known as Malcolm's Nursery Grounds. William Malcolm also had a lease of land near the Oval.

NOS. 159 AND 161 CLAPHAM ROAD [78]
Formerly Nos. 9 and 10 Montague Place

This pair of houses appears to have been erected shortly before 1809.[38] The houses contain three storeys over a semi-basement, and exhibit an interesting variation from the normal plan in that the coach-houses are incorporated in the main structure. The front of each house, therefore, presents an unusual appearance, the dominant feature being the large arch-headed doorway to the coach-house. This is flanked by three smaller arched openings—the entrance doorway and two windows—all being set in a face of coursed stucco. Above the first-floor bandcourse the wall face is of stock brick and contains two tiers of four evenly spaced windows of rectangular form, those to the first floor being surmounted by stucco cornices and frieze panels with Soanic frets. A simple entablature and blocking-course completes the front.

[79] Nos. 163–169 (odd) Clapham Road
Formerly Nos. 11–14 (consec.) Montague Place

The site of these houses was conveyed by William Malcolm's son James to trustees in 1799. In 1807 the trustees sold it to Thomas Corpe of Kennington, builder,[39] and these houses were erected within the next few years.[38] They are grouped in pairs, originally uniform in appearance, and are nearly identical with several other contemporaneous houses in Clapham Road, all being probably the work of one builder. Each house has a semi-basement, three storeys, and a mansard attic. On the ground and first floors are two rooms, the back projecting in a segmental bow, and alongside is a coach-house wing, now generally altered. The exterior is of stock brick, the front being three windows wide. The ground-storey windows and doorway are set in recesses with arched heads rising from moulded imposts. The door is framed by elegant Doric columns supporting key-ornamented entablatures, and the arched head contains a fanlight of circular motifs (Plate 68b). The tall first-floor windows open to a balcony with a cast-iron railing of conventional fret pattern. The interior of No. 165 is probably typical and contains a cross-vaulted hall leading to the staircase which has a balustrade incorporating cast-iron standards of Classical and Gothic design used alternately. The doors and windows have reeded architraves with lion-head stops, and there are good Regency chimneypieces of grey marble.

[80] Nos. 171 and 173 Clapham Road
Formerly Nos. 15 and 16 Montague Place

These were originally built as one house (Plate 55a), which was erected in 1802–3 and first occupied by Edward Shewell[38] who moved here from No. 179 Clapham Road. Shewell purchased an estate to the east of Clapham Road in 1806 (see page 88) but by 1832 had moved to Notting Hill.[40] The division of the house into two separate dwellings dates from about this time. At the end of the 19th and beginning of the 20th century the house was occupied by an Anglo-French college for ladies;[28] it is now used by the Transport and General Workers' Union. When first built it was a large double-fronted house containing a basement and three storeys, spaciously planned with, on the ground floor, a large entrance hall leading to an oval staircase hall, flanked on either side by two reception rooms (fig. 28). Stock brick was used for the exterior facings except for the front which is of

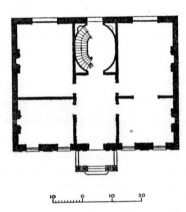

Fig. 28. No. 173 Clapham Road, ground-floor plan

"white" brick, and the design has the spare elegance typical of its period. The entrance front is a symmetrical composition with a slightly recessed centre, three windows wide, flanked by narrow wings, each one window wide, that to the ground storey being set in a recess with a segmental-arched head rising from moulded imposts. Before the centrally placed doorway is an imposing porch, finished in stucco, with paired Doric columns supporting a pedimented entablature. The shafts of these columns, and the respondent antae, have channels instead of the customary flutes. The wide eaves of the low-pitched slate roof are supported, at wide intervals, by plain mutules. From the east flank of the house projects a small two-storeyed extension, probably built when the property was subdivided, having a shallow porch of Ionic columns paired with antae and framing an arch-headed doorway.

[81] Nos. 175 and 177 Clapham Road

Formerly Nos. 19 and 18 Stockwell Common

These houses were erected between 1831 and 1840.[38] They are three-storeyed terrace houses of stock brick, with a coursed stucco facing to the ground storey which contains the arched doorway and two rectangular windows. There are two widely spaced windows in each upper storey and the fronts are finished with a simple entablature.

[82] Nos. 179–185 (odd) Clapham Road

Formerly Nos. 17–14 (consec.) Stockwell Common

About four acres of Malcolm's nursery grounds were bought in 1792 by Christopher Fall of St. Mary, Newington.[36] He had four houses, Nos. 179–185, erected in 1792–4.[38] The land in the rear containing about three acres was used as paddocks and was occupied together with No. 185. Christopher Fall died in 1811 and left his property in trust for members of his family. The three acres of land in the rear were purchased in 1867 from Henry Cheswright by the Trustees of Stockwell Orphanage.[36] These houses are in many respects similar to Nos. 163–169 described above, being grouped in pairs linked by coach-houses. Each house front is three storeys high and three windows wide, and built of stock brick with an arcaded ground storey containing two arch-headed windows and the doorway. This last has an ornamental radial-patterned fanlight over a door flanked by Ionic columns. The fronts finish with a mutule cornice and the mansard attic is lit by two lunette windows. A narrow recession marks the party wall between the paired fronts. Nos. 183 and 185 are now derelict.

[83] Spurgeon's Homes

Formerly Stockwell Orphanage

In 1866 Mrs. Hillyard, a clergyman's widow living in Islington,[41] gave C. H. Spurgeon £20,000 for the foundation of a home for fatherless boys.[42] Twelve Trustees were appointed to administer the fund.[43] In 1867 and 1879 land between Clapham Road and Stockwell Park Road was purchased by the Trustees for the site of the Orphanage.[44] Their plan was to accommodate the children in "family" houses,[42] which when completed were arranged in a quadrangle around a garden, approached by a narrow way from Clapham Road (fig. 29). The Trustees

were successful in 1867 in their appeal for subscriptions to augment Mrs. Hillyard's gift,[45] and they immediately started building on the north-east side of the quadrangle[46] (Plate 32b). The date of the foundation of each house is marked on fig. 29.

In the north-east block the houses were all designed by James Cubitt.[47] Those founded in 1867 were named the Silver Wedding House, to commemorate the gift of £500 by Mr. and Mrs. Tyson on the occasion of their silver wedding anniversary;[48] the Merchant's House, in honour of a benefaction from a London business man; the Workmen's House, after William Higgs, the builder, and his employees, who provided the materials and labour respectively;[49] and Unity House, which was paid for by Thomas Olney and his sons in memory of Mrs. Unity Olney.

Those houses founded in 1868 were called Wigner House, named after Pastor J. T. Wigner, secretary of the Orphanage, and erected by the Baptist brethren as a token of regard for C. H. Spurgeon; the two Testimonial Houses, presented as a testimonial of esteem for C. H. Spurgeon by the Baptist churches;[50] College House, built by the subscriptions of gentlemen educated at the Pastor's College; and Sunday School House, subscribed for by teachers and children of Sabbath schools. A building including a lecture -and dining-hall was also erected in 1868 at the north end of the north-west block.[50]

The acquisition of additional land in 1879 made expansion possible, and in 1880 the south-west block was founded for the accommodation of orphaned girls. The houses in this block were designed by Alfred Wright and called the Reading House in recognition of the liberality of friends in Reading; the Trustees' House, erected by the Trustees of the Orphanage; the Limes, given in memory of the five children of W. R. Rickett; Bray's Bricks, in memory of E. E. Bray; the Sermon House, given by C. H. Spurgeon and Messrs. Passmore and Alabaster; the Olives, given by Samuel Barrow and his friends; and the Liverpool House, named in remembrance of the help given to the Orphanage by friends in Liverpool.

The buildings in the south-east block were also designed by Alfred Wright.[47] They consisted of a girls' infirmary, given by Mr. and Mrs. H. Wood, and baths and play halls for the girls, and were opened on June 21, 1882. The block was

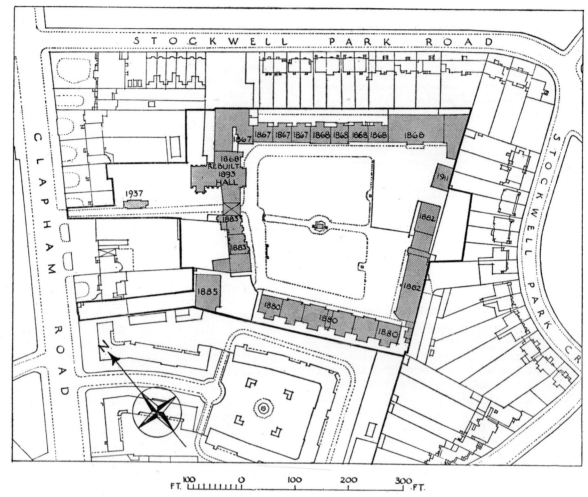

Fig. 29. Spurgeon's Homes, lay-out plan

completed by the addition of a library at the east end in 1911.

The north-west block, which had been started in 1868, with the dining-hall and gateway, was completed in 1883 by the addition of a Master's House; the architect was Alfred Wright and the builder W. Johnson. In the west corner of the quadrangle a laundry was opened in 1885. In 1893–4 the dining-hall was enlarged and re-named the Memorial Hall after C. H. Spurgeon. When finished the hall was cruciform, the transepts being formed by the ends of the old hall. At one end stood a large statue of C. H. Spurgeon, flanked by reliefs in terracotta; the group was modelled by George Tinworth and produced by Messrs. Doulton.[51] The architects

of the new hall were James Cubitt and G. F. Collinson, and the builders were Chessum and Sons. The cost was nearly £5,000.[52]

When completed the Orphanage accommodated some five hundred children between the ages of six and ten. A country home for younger children was opened at Birchington, Kent, in 1923.[51] On September 1, 1939, the children were evacuated from Stockwell to Reigate, and in 1953 they were all moved from Reigate to Birchington. The buildings at Stockwell were used by the secretary and office staff until April 30, 1953;[47] they are shortly to be demolished and replaced by a comprehensive high school.

The buildings of the Orphanage are grouped about a large open garden; they have two and three storeys and are built in red brick with stone dressings and are liberally banded and diapered in blue and yellow brick. The entrance archway and the houses on the north-west side of the square show northern Italian Gothic influence in their design while the Memorial Hall, which is surmounted by a galleried lantern and has a large oriel balcony at the south-east end, and the library, have simple English Gothic detail.

[84] No. 209 CLAPHAM ROAD

Formerly The Bays or No. 2 Stockwell Common

This is probably the oldest surviving house in Clapham Road, but unfortunately nothing has been discovered about its origin. It is a double-fronted house of three storeys, its painted stucco face clothing a front of mid or late 18th century date. The central doorway is surmounted by two windows and flanked on each side by a splay-sided bay rising through the three storeys. The wood doorcase is of charming design, the arched opening being framed by panelled pilasters with consoles supporting an open triangular pediment. The front finishes with a cornice and blocking-course.

[85] Nos. 355–363; 369–385; AND 391–393 (odd) CLAPHAM ROAD

Nos. 355–363, formerly Nos. 317–325 (odd) Clapham Road, previously Nos. 21–25 (consec.), originally Nos. 22–26 (consec.) Clapham Rise; Nos. 369–385, formerly Nos. 329–345 (odd) Clapham Road, previously Nos. 27–35 (consec.), originally Nos. 28–36 (consec.) Clapham Rise; Nos. 391–393, formerly Nos. 347–353 (odd) Clapham Road, originally Nos. 1–4 (consec.) Bedford Terrace

These houses were erected on that part of Stockwell Manor which came into the possession of the Dukes of Bedford at the beginning of the 18th century. Most of them, if not all, seem to have been built under an agreement made on December 31, 1791, between the then Duke of Bedford and Archer Willson, a Fulham builder.[53] The evidence suggests that Willson erected some of the houses (Nos. 391 and 393 were not built till after his death), and that they were then let by the Duke of Bedford to Willson's nominees. These nominees were undoubtedly Willson's financial backers, and in some cases they actually lived in the houses built with their money. This would account for the different tastes shown in the designs of the houses. Willson also had two mortgagees, Thomas Holloway of Chancery Lane, and Christian Kidd, widow, of Marylebone.

No. 357 was first occupied in 1792, and Nos. 359 and 361 in 1794; No. 355 does not appear in the rate books until 1806. The land on which Nos. 359 and 361 stand was let to Robert Robson by the Duke of Bedford and Robson himself occupied No. 359 between 1797 and 1808.

Nos. 355–361 are stylistically linked with Nos. 179–185, though they are not uniform in size. No. 355 alone retains intact the doorway with Ionic columns and elaborate fanlight that was probably common to all these houses. No. 359 has a wing with a segmental bow and an added entrance porch with anthemion-ornamented pilasters, while No. 361 has a five windows wide frontage with a central doorway from which the decorative fanlight is missing.

No. 363 was built in 1802. It is a much mutilated house, three storeys high and three windows wide, probably the survivor of a pair originally similar in style to Nos. 371–377. The site of No. 365 is now occupied by a garage.

No. 369 is the largest and finest of this group of houses. It was also built on Robert Robson's land and was first occupied by John Poynder, who lived there from 1815 until 1825, when he moved to No. 274 South Lambeth Road (see page 73). It is a detached house, spaciously planned and containing a semi-basement and three storeys. The exterior is faced with yellow stock brick dressed with painted stone or stucco. The unusual composition of the road frontage suggests that the original plans underwent enlargement at an early stage of the building's history, the first design probably being for a symmetrical composition with a wide central bay rising above and projecting from narrow wings, a further bay being added on the right. Each wing has one window to each storey, those of the ground and first floors being rectangular while that of the second floor is segmental-headed. There is a frieze-band and cornice above the first-floor window as well as at the parapet level, both being at lower levels than those ornamenting the two bays. From the ground storey of the first bay projects a segmental bow, containing two windows and surmounted by a cast-iron railing of lattice pattern. The flat wall face above contains two windows, that of the first floor being set within a segmental-headed recess, while that to the second floor is segmental-headed. Below the second-floor window runs a plain bandcourse, and the crowning cornice is surmounted by a pedimental blocking-course adorned with Soanic frets. The bay on the right of the recessed wing has the same projection but is slightly wider than that just described. It is also generally similar in design, except that the first- and second-floor windows are both rectangular and set within a round-headed recess. The house is entered on the north side, through a recessed porch of Regency Greek design, with unfluted Doric columns supporting a simple entablature having a frieze decoration of wreaths and key frets. The premises are now occupied by Messrs. Ashton Brothers and a garden with seats extends from the pavement edge back to the house.

Nos. 371–373 and 375–377 were let to John Burrup, stationer, as Archer Willson's nominee in 1802 and 1804 respectively. They are paired houses, originally similar in design. The front of No. 371 has been faced with stucco and a porch added to No. 373, but Nos. 375–377 are reasonably free from alteration. The stock brick front is of simple design, each house having three storeys with two windows, those to the ground floor being set in round-arched recesses. The entrances are contained in side annexes, and a porch has been added to No. 375.

Nos. 379 and 381 were also let at Willson's direction, to William Mitchell in 1803. Mitchell lived in one of them. They are a plain stock brick pair, each two windows wide, with narrow wings. The first-floor windows are set in round-arched recesses, and an attic storey surmounts the main cornice.

Nos. 383 and 385 were erected in 1806; they were let by the devisees of Willson to Thomas Rippon, who also occupied one of them. They are another plain pair with stock brick fronts.

Nos. 391 and 393 are a range of four terrace houses erected by William Novell of Clapham, builder, and let to him by Willson's devisees in 1825. They have been converted into two blocks of flats. They are four storeys high and each three windows wide. The houses are uniform and share a stock brick front of austere expression. Before conversion, the ground storey probably presented a range of round-headed door and window openings slightly recessed within an arcade, but the rhythm has been ruined by the replacement of each pair of doorways by a single entrance having a pedimented surround in stucco of coarse Victorian design. Each upper storey contains a range of twelve closely spaced rectangu-lar windows, those of the first floor also being set within an arcade.

STOCKWELL PARK CRESCENT AREA

In 1806 the land covered by Stockwell Park Crescent and part of Stockwell Park Road, formerly part of Stockwell Manor, was purchased by Edward Shewell, who then lived in Clapham Road, from John Bedwell,[26] the heir of Benjamin Robertson (see page 91). Though the northern part of Stockwell Park Road was laid out about 1832, development was delayed until after Shewell's death and was carried out by William Cox of Kennington, who purchased part of the estate in 1838.[26]

Nos. 44 and 46 Stockwell Park Road and Nos. 2 and 4 Stockwell Park Crescent [86]

Formerly Nos. 32 and 34 Stockwell Park Road and Nos. 1 and 2 Park Crescent

These houses (Plate 57) are grouped at the northern junction of the two roads, and though not identical they have similar characteristics which suggest they are the work of the same builder. Nos. 44, 46[54] and 4 were let by Cox in 1840 and No. 2 was let by him in 1841, for terms of 85 years, and as John Notley, a local builder, was a party to the lease of No. 44 he may have built all four houses.[36] They are all three-storey villas but whereas Nos. 44 and 46 are detached and have Ionic porches placed centrally, Nos. 2 and 4 are joined by a two-storey link containing their entrances. The side elevations of Nos. 44 and 46 and the fronts of Nos. 2 and 4 are stucco-faced and have an attractive late Regency flavour. The angles are emphasized by pilasters with incised Soanic frets, and the roof gable-ends are treated as open pediments containing small lunette windows. The other villas about the crescent are detached or in pairs. Some are stuccoed and treated similarly to Nos. 2 and 4; others are of stock brick and adorned with Greek detail—wreathed friezes over porches, Ionic columned entrances and hooded windows carried on consoles. The houses in Stockwell Park Road include many similar to those in the Crescent with a fair admixture of later houses which includes the large twin-gable fronted vicarage of St. Michael's.

[87] Nos. 14–24 (even) Stockwell Park Crescent

> Formerly Nos. 7–12 (consec.) Ben Lomond Place, Park Crescent

These houses exemplify the plainer variety of brick villa in the Crescent. They were erected at the costs of John Mackenzie of Crown Street, Westminster, bookbinder, in association with Frances Harrison, spinster, both of whom had building leases from William Cox in 1840–1.[36] Nos. 14 and 24 each bear a tablet "BEN LOMOND PLACE 1841".

That part of Stockwell Park Road south of Robsart Street was built on part of the Angell estate called Long Field towards the end of the 1840s.[55] South of its junction with Robsart [88] Street there are two *cottages ornés*, Nos. 86 and 99 (formerly Nos. 74 and 91, originally Vernon Cottage and Rodney Cottage), which have ornamented barge-boards to the gables of their central entrances and to the second-floor dormer windows.

[89] The Friendly Almshouses, Stockwell Park Road

The Friendly Female Society was founded in 1802 for the relief of aged women living within ten miles of St. Paul's. At first relief was given by means of small pensions to women living in their own houses, but in 1823 five almshouses for the accommodation of twenty women were built in the parish of Camberwell, and in 1863 seven houses accommodating 28 women were built on the east side of Stockwell Park Road.[56] They were built fronting the road, and not on the more usual quadrangular plan for almshouses. In 1940 and 1941 the houses were extensively damaged by enemy action, and in 1947–8 a new block was built to replace several of the old houses. Leslie Wyatt was the architect, and Messrs. Mitchell the builders.[57]

[90] St. Michael's Church, Stockwell Park Road

The site for this church was freely given in 1839 by William Cox[58] to the Commissioners appointed by the Act of 1818 for building additional churches in populous parishes.[59] William Rogers' design for the church was approved early in 1840, and to ensure that the building would be "substantially and honestly executed" Rogers was careful not to bind the Commissioners to accept the lowest tender. John Jay, of London Wall, was the builder selected, the estimated cost being £4,819 16s. 4d. (including commission, and salary for a clerk-of-works), of which sum £2,000 were to be provided by the Metropolitan Churches Fund.[58] The building was consecrated by the Bishop of Winchester on November 18, 1841, and a district was assigned in 1845.

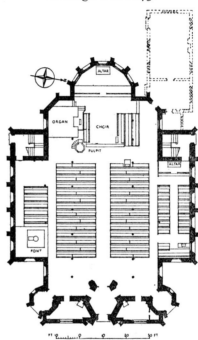

Fig. 30. St. Michael's, Stockwell Park Road, plan

The church (Plate 14a, fig. 30) as originally designed consisted of a wide nave with galleried aisles to the north and south, flanked by side chapels. An apsidal extension at the west end now forms the chancel, but the altar was originally placed within the arcaded base of the hexagonal steeple at the east end, being almost obscured from the congregation by the high pulpit. The steeple, placed axially with Lorn Road, is flanked by small vestries and octagonal lobbies added shortly after the completion of the building.

In 1880 a faculty was obtained to re-orientate the internal arrangements. The altar was then transferred to the west end, the porch there being demolished and the doorway built up.[60] Open pews replaced the box pews and the west gallery was removed, the organ being re-erected in the south aisle.

There are two inscribed tablets set in the tower buttresses. The first records the renewal of the pinnacles and the repair of the exterior in 1896, and the second records the internal renovation of 1920, carried out by the architect A. R. Powys. The church was severely damaged by a flying bomb in June 1944 and after its restoration by Thomas F. Ford was re-dedicated in 1952.

In every respect this is a typical Commissioners' "Gothic" church—that is to say, a capacious preaching-box with galleries, built of brick and meagrely dressed with stone detail of a wiry Early English character. Architectural interest centres on the east elevation, closing the vista along Lorn Road. This is a symmetrical composition balanced about the tower and spire of hexagonal plan, one half of which projects beyond the east wall of the nave. Each face of the tower is gabled and contains in its upper part a group of three lancets, one large glazed light between two blind arches. The angles are emphasized by offset buttresses rising to octagonal pinnacles. The present somewhat abrupt transition from tower to spire is due to the removal, in 1930, of the flying buttresses and inner ring of pinnacles at the base of the spire. Each flanking face of the nave wall contains a lancet group similar to those in the tower, and the parapet is sloped to accord with the roof pitch. The east end of each side chapel was treated as a low tower with an arcaded top stage and corner pinnacles, but these embellishments have been removed.

The interior has a spidery elegance due to the use of slender shafted columns of cast-iron for the arcades supporting the galleries and roof. The structural timbers of the roof were originally exposed but they are now concealed by a false ceiling. The windows of single lancet form generally have clear glazing, the exceptions being the five windows of the apse and the west windows in the side chapels. The stained glass for these was designed by John Trinick.

STOCKWELL GREEN AREA

Though there are few buildings in the neighbourhood which are even a hundred years old the centre of interest for the history of Stockwell Manor and hamlet still lies in the Stockwell Green area. The "stoc" or wood probably disappeared in the 17th century but there is still evidence of the plentiful supply of water which gave

the name of Stockwell its second component. On Stockwell Green there used to be a public well at the south-west corner[25] and there are still two wells on the site of Stockwell Congregational Church and two on the site of Hammerton's Brewery. The Barrett family's house in Stockwell Road opposite the Green was supplied with "remarkable fine water" from a spring nearby.[61]

This house was on the site of the old manor house which stood about sixty yards from the road and faced the northern extremity of the Green. Legend connects the manor house with Thomas Cromwell who may indeed have stayed there when it was in the hands of Henry VIII. In 1580 when it was leased to Henry Store for 1,000 years (see page 82) the house was surrounded by a moat and its gardens and orchards contained about four acres.

The leasehold interest in the manor house which had been acquired by Francis Goston was sold by him in 1640 to Samuel Lewes with about 42 acres of land.[62] The house was demolished shortly before 1756 and the lease was purchased in 1770 by Isaac Barrett, wax-chandler.[63] Barrett erected a large mansion on the site, but this was pulled down in the middle of the 19th century. Some parts of the moat, which was alleged to have been 30–40 feet wide,[64] were still visible at the beginning of the 19th century.[61]

The chapel built by Sir John Leigh stood a little to the south of the moat.[61] In 1598, when it was excepted from the sale of the Manor to George Chute, it had lately been demised to John Turbervile.[14] It was apparently still standing in 1801 when it was described as "a very antique building".[61]

PUBLIC HOUSES, STOCKWELL ROAD

There are four public houses in Stockwell Road which are still known by the names of older inns on whose sites they stand. The Swan [91] at the corner of Clapham and Stockwell Roads was rebuilt at the end of the 18th century[61] and again quite recently. Both the Swan and the Plough, on the west side of the road, are men- [92] tioned in a deed of 1781.[25] The Old Queen's [93] Head was rebuilt in 1882,[65] but a water-colour drawing of the old inn shows it as a long two-storey weather-boarded building lying back from the road.[66] The youngest of the four and the least altered is the New Queen's Head on the [94] west side of the road. It was probably erected at the same time as the houses adjoining it on the south in 1786.[61]

STOCKWELL COLLEGE, STOCKWELL ROAD

This college was founded by the British and Foreign School Society in 1859, the foundation stone being laid by Lord Granville. It was opened in 1861 by Lord John Russell. In 1843 the Society had admitted 20 women students into the Borough Road Training College, and from that time the number had increased until it was considered desirable to establish a separate college for them. Some 75 students were transferred to new premises on the east side of Stockwell Road in 1861; new practising schools were erected and in 1864 a kindergarten school was added. Further enlargements were made in 1871 and 1884. In 1922 the practising schools provided accommodation for 700 children. Training in Froebel methods was a prominent feature of the work of the college. In 1935 Stockwell College moved to its present home at the Old Palace, Bromley; the old site is now covered by blocks of flats.[67]

STOCKWELL PARK HOUSE AND THE BRIXTON TABERNACLE, STOCKWELL ROAD

Part of the estate in Stockwell Manor leased to Henry Store in 1580 included 11 acres called Harris Field and Long Field. They were sublet by Store together with a house erected by himself, to Nicholas Juxe or Jukes of Lambeth, yeoman, for 996 years. In 1702 both fields were purchased by Nicholas Hookes who conveyed them in the following year to Elizabeth Angell.[68] This transaction probably represented a marriage settlement on Nicholas Hookes's daughter Caroline who married Elizabeth Angell's son John. On part of Harris Field opposite Stockwell Common at the west end of the present Stockwell Park Walk, John Angell erected a large house.[69] The house later became known as Stockwell Park House, and the pleasure grounds attached to it extended as far as Brixton Road; they included Harris Field, Long Field and ten acres of copyhold land held of Lambeth Manor.[70] John Angell junior lived in the house after his father's death and stipulated in his will that either Stockwell or Crowhurst should be the chief residence of the family.[71] In 1790 his heir's widow leased the house to Thomas James of Stamford Street.[72] There is a plan of the house and grounds drawn in 1803, when part of the garden comprising the

ten acres of Lambeth Manor copyhold was sold.[22] By 1826 the house had been turned into a school;[73] it was pulled down about 1882 when Benedict and Speenham Roads were made.[74]

The Brixton Tabernacle, Stockwell Road, was erected on the site of the front garden of Stockwell Park House. Building began in 1883[33] and the chapel was opened on May 11, 1884. It is a dull pedimented building of red brick, with detail suggesting Jacobean influence. [95]

NOS. 40–46 (even) STOCKWELL ROAD [96]
Formerly Nos. 15–18 (consec.) Stockwell Place

These are some of the oldest surviving houses in Stockwell Road and were erected between 1781 and 1788[38] for Benjamin Robertson,[75] who purchased part of Stockwell Manor from Edward Thornycroft (see page 82). Originally there were nine pairs of houses and they were probably all erected by local craftsmen, two of whom were Joseph Buckmaster, plumber and glazier, and Samuel Burrows, plasterer, both of Lambeth.[76] Those remaining are plain grey brick houses, three storeys high above semi-basements, with plain parapets. Each house has a wing, of one or two storeys, containing a deep-set round-headed entrance. The gauged flat arches to the windows are of yellow brick. Benjamin Robertson also raised a botanical garden on part of his estate in Stockwell, though its exact site is not known. In his will, dated 1800, he left all his freehold estates to trustees, who included Adrias Hardy Haworth of Chelsea, William Acton of Kew, Alexander McLeay, secretary of the Linnaean Society, and Alexander Malcolm, a local nurseryman, to maintain and improve the garden which was to be called "Stockwell Botanic Garden founded by Benjamin Robertson Esq." After Robertson's death, however, this devise was held to be void and by a decree in Chancery dated July 6, 1801 his real estate was ordered to be vested in his next-of-kin. It was consequently divided in 1805 between his sister Esther, wife of William Moore, and his other sister's son, John Bedwell.[25]

KING GEORGE'S HOUSE, STOCKWELL ROAD [97]
Formerly Ingram House

This building was opened in 1905 as a residential club for young men;[77] it was subsequently used by the Y.W.C.A. and as a private residential club for ladies. Since 1937 it has been used by the John Benn Boys' Hostels Association for the accommodation of boys between the ages of 14 and 18 without a home in London.[78] The architect was Arthur T. Bolton and the builders were Rudd and Son.[33]

The building is skilfully planned in the form of a St. Andrew's cross, so that there are no internal courts and every room has a good outlook. As originally arranged it contained 208 bedrooms and many club-rooms including a dining-hall, lounge, library and smoking-room, together with such recreational facilities as a gymnasium, billiard-room, fives-courts, tennis-courts and a miniature rifle-range. This accommodation is arranged in a semi-basement and lofty principal storey for the club-rooms, with four uniform storeys of bedrooms above. The exterior is an impressive design, reflecting its author's deep interest in the work of Vanbrugh. It is almost entirely carried out in brickwork, generally stock, above a plum-coloured base and with red dressings. The large windows of the lower storeys are generally arch-headed. The flush-framed sashes of the bedroom windows are grouped in twos or threes within the framework of a giant order of Doric pilasters, the top-storey windows being contained within the high frieze of the triglyphed entablature.

[98] STOCKWELL PRIMARY SCHOOL, STOCKWELL ROAD

This school was built for the London School Board. The contractor was W. Brass of Old Street, whose tender for a school for 828 children was for £8,416.[79] The school was opened on August 13, 1877.[32] The architect was probably E. R. Robson, but T. J. Bailey remodelled the school in 1902.[31] It is a three-storey brick building with a narrow frontage to the road.

[99] NOS. 15–19 (consec.) STOCKWELL LANE
Formerly Nos. 6–2 (consec.) Park Place

Like Garden Close on the opposite side of Stockwell Road, Stockwell (formerly Love) Lane still retains a faintly rural air. It is a narrow thoroughfare with houses on the north side only. Nos. 15 to 19 are terrace houses of three storeys above a basement, having simply designed fronts of stock brick. The paired doorways are dressed with wooden architraves and hoods supported on

moulded brackets. The rendered reveals of the windows suggest that they once contained flush frames, while the details of the internal woodwork point to a building date of about 1750. The wall face of the top storey appears to be later than the rest and might replace a roof attic.

NOS. 10 AND 11 STOCKWELL LANE   [100]
Formerly Rose Cottage and White Rose Cottage

These houses stand back at the end of the lane. They are a pair of two-storeyed cottages built of stock and plum-coloured brick; they share a front crowned with a pediment which has a recessed quatrefoil in its tympanum. The first-floor windows are underlined by a continued sill-band, and the doorways have neat fanlights.

NO. 28 SIDNEY ROAD

This house stood at the east end of, and faced, Stockwell Lane; it was demolished in 1952 (fig. 31). At the time of its demolition it must

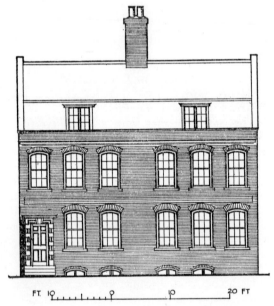

FT 10 |₁₁₁₁₁₁₁| 0   10   20 FT

Fig. 31. No. 28 Sidney Road. Demolished 1952

have been the oldest house then standing in Stockwell, for it was probably erected early in the 18th century. It stood on part of the land let with the manor house to Henry Store in 1580,[80] and was probably built as two houses.[a] In the

---

[a] Evidently an early example of twin houses. Others were Bridge House, Bermondsey, 1706 (see *The Antiquaries' Journal*, vol. XXXII, pp. 192–3), and The Grange, Fulham, 1713–14 (see *Fulham Old and New*, by C. J. Feret, 1900, vol. II, pp. 289–90).

19th century it was certainly used as two houses, which were called Grove House and Burnley House respectively.[80] They each contained a basement, two storeys, and an attic within a mansard roof. Sharing a uniform front of stock brick, each house was three windows wide; the flush-framed sashes were set in segmental-headed openings dressed with red brick. Burnley House had a doorway at the end of the front, which was framed by blocked architraves surmounted by a corniced hood resting on consoles; Grove House had an insignificant doorway on the flanking elevation.

[101] St. Andrew's Church, Stockwell Green

St. Andrew's church is the oldest church in Lambeth apart from the parish church of St. Mary. In 1711, a year after the establishment of Commissioners for building fifty new churches in London, Westminster and the suburbs,[81] the inhabitants of Lambeth presented a petition to the Commissioners praying that an additional church might be built in the parish.[82] Sir John Thornycroft, Lord of Stockwell Manor, offered to present two acres of waste ground,[83] and the consent of those freeholders of the Manor who enjoyed rights of common was obtained.[82] As a result of this offer the Commissioners resolved that "the new Church intended to be built within the parish of Lambeth, ought to be erected within the Liberty of Stockwell, upon the ground offer'd gratis by Sir John Thornicroft".[84]

For some undiscovered reason this project came to nothing and it was not until 1767 that a piece of land on the estate of the Duke of Bedford was obtained, and Stockwell Chapel erected[85] (Plate 13a). The cost of erecting the chapel was met by voluntary subscriptions. In 1788 the land on which the chapel was built, part of Stack Yard Field, was conveyed by Francis, fifth Duke of Bedford, to the Archbishop of Canterbury, the Bishop of Winchester and the Rector of Lambeth and their successors upon trust for use as a chapel of ease.[85] In 1844 it was stated that the chapel could hold 800 people.[86] It was drastically remodelled in 1867[87] and extended westwards by one bay so that the accommodation was increased to 1,043.[88] A tower was also built at the south-west corner at this time and the galleries were reconstructed. The architect for these works, which cost approximately £2,500, was Henry Edward Coe[89] (Plate 13b). The building was

opened on November 30, 1867, and consecrated on June 11, 1868, and dedicated to St. Andrew; a Consolidated Chapelry was assigned in the same year. Since then the fabric has remained in virtually the same form except that the grey brick of the exterior was rendered over in the 1880s[87] and the side galleries were removed in 1924 when an extensive restoration was carried out.[90]

When the church was remodelled in 1867 the plain body was elaborated with detail of an Italian Romanesque derivation, and the tower or campanile was erected in a similar style. The tower, which contains the entrance, is of three stages and supports a rendered pyramidal spire which is banded horizontally and surmounted by a stone gabled finial of squat proportions. The tower and the body of the church are covered in roughcast of a grey-brown colour, with red rendering above the upper windows and to the corner piers. The eaves of the tower and of the church, which has a slated roof, are corbelled, and the windows are simply detailed with stone mullions and surrounds. The large circular east window over the altar has plate tracery and at its centre is a round light, containing a St. Andrew's cross, surrounded by eight large and eight very small lights.

The plain interior has a small Lady Chapel on the north side of the nave and a gallery across the west end. The sanctuary and nave are separated by an arcade of three simple round arches, the centre arch being of wider span.

Stockwell Congregational Church [102]

Facing north-east towards Stockwell Green stands Stockwell Congregational Church, which is approached along a paved alleyway. Like St. Andrew's Church it is of particular interest because of its early foundation. Stockwell New Chapel was built in 1798,[91] but did not have a regular minister until 1801, when the Rev. Thomas Jackson was inducted as pastor; he remained there until his death in 1843.[92] He is buried in a vault in the graveyard behind the church and there is a tablet to his memory above the pulpit. The second minister to be appointed was the Rev. David Thomas. During his pastorate it was decided to enlarge the chapel. James Wilson was chosen as architect,[93] and the chapel was re-opened on October 8, 1850.[94] The building, which is of plain stock brick, was remodelled and extended on the south-east side. It was also refronted in stucco to a pretentious design with debased Ionic pilasters supporting a dentilled pediment, and a pedimented porch was added at the centre. At the same time a tower was built at the east corner, finished with a small dome surmounted by a finial; the top stage of the tower has splayed angles treated as pilasters. The interior has galleries on three sides. A tablet placed in the church on June 17, 1955 records the centenary of the marriage here on June 16, 1855 of William Booth, founder of the Salvation Army.

[103] No. 1 STOCKWELL GREEN

On the opposite side of Stockwell Green from the Congregational Church stands a building in Jacobean style now used for commercial purposes. It was opened on March 8, 1848 as an Educational Institute at the expense of the congregation of Stockwell New Chapel. Besides being used for non-sectarian schools it was also used for meetings and lectures.[95] Despite mutilation and disfiguring painting, the front survives as an interesting and fairly scholarly example of Jacobean revivalism. From the brick face project three flat bays, each of two lofty storeys. The ground storey of the middle bay has been altered, but that on each side contains an arched doorway between Doric columns that support an entablature, and a dwarf intermediate stage with a three-light window flanked by tapered Ionic pilasters carrying a second entablature. In the second storey is a large rectangular window divided by mullions and transoms into three tiers of three lights. The quoined angles rise to a crowning entablature and a parapet ornamented with quatrefoils in panels. A similar window forming the second storey of the middle bay is surmounted by a curved and stepped gable.

[104] STOCKWELL BREWERY (HAMMERTON'S) STOCKWELL GREEN

The plentiful supply of water around Stockwell Green made it a suitable site for a brewery. The date of establishment inscribed on the present brewery building—1730—is unsubstantiated. The earliest reference found to a brewery at Stockwell Green occurs in 1801 when it was said to belong to Robert Tyler and to be in the occupation of a Mr. Roberts.[96] Between 1831 and 1842 the brewery was put up for auction. It was said to have been established for more than 50 years and the trade was then about 12,000 barrels a year. There was attached to the brewery an "elegant freehold abode", with a bathroom "worthy of an emperor".[97] None of the early buildings survive.

Nos. 21–34 (consec.) STOCKWELL GREEN   [105]

These houses are of little architectural interest. They were erected singly and in twos and threes, at various dates from about 1790 to about 1840.[38] No. 21, probably late 18th century, is a two-storeyed cottage with a plain stock brick front, the upper part recently rebuilt. There are three round-headed openings in the ground storey, the middle one being the doorway, and above, correspondingly, are three rectangular windows. No. 22 is a much altered house of around 1800, containing three storeys over a semi-basement. The original portion of the stock brick front has two rectangular windows in each storey, and a Roman Doric doorcase of stucco. Nos. 23 and 24 are paired houses with their entrances in wings. The body of each house has an extremely plain stock brick front with a wide segmental-headed three-light window in each of the three storeys. Nos. 25 and 26 were erected between 1819 and 1821 on land belonging to Hannah Hughes, widow.[98] They are paired houses of three storeys with fronts of stock brick dressed with stucco. There are two rectangular windows to each storey, those of the first floor descending to a sill-band. The arch-headed doorways are contained in side annexes. Nos. 27 and 27A are two-storeyed cottages built at a right angle to the roadway, and might well be of late 18th century date. Nos. 28, 29 and 30 form a composed terrace of three cottages, with two storeys above a semi-basement. The two windows wide fronts are of stock brick, and the doorcases, ground-floor window architraves, and crowning cornice are of painted stucco. The blocking-course is raised over the middle house and inscribed "VICTORIA PLACE". They were built shortly before 1840. Nos. 31 and 32, dating from around 1815, are paired houses of three storeys with stock brick fronts. The ground storey of each house has two arched openings, the doorway having a stucco architrave, and there is a bandcourse at first-floor level. Each upper storey has two rectangular windows, those to the first floor opening to a cast-iron balcony of Regency character, missing from No. 31. No. 32 has a slightly recessed wing of three storeys, one window wide. No. 33 is a later house with a front of similar composition to No. 32 except that the upper windows are segmental-headed and the entrance is contained in the side wing. No. 34, a detached house of about 1810, has a stock brick front, three storeys high and three windows wide. The ground storey has been obscured by the addition of a shopfront, but the upper part is unchanged. The first-floor windows are arch-headed and set in recesses of the same form, linked by narrow impost-bands.

Building on the Green itself began in 1876, after a dispute as to the rights of the freeholder, a Mr. Honey, to appropriate the land for building purposes.[99]

[106] No. 22 Southesk Street
Formerly No. 16 Robertson's Place

In Stockwell Grove and Southesk Street there are several groups of working-class cottages dating from the early 19th century; they are all small and of very economical construction. No. 22 Southesk Street is the best example; it is two storeys high with a single pitched roof sloping away from the front, which is carried up to a parapet. Despite the cheapness of construction, the simple stock brick front shows regard for the niceties of late Georgian taste. The sash-windows are pleasantly proportioned and the narrow arched doorway admits a six-panelled door below a radial-patterned fanlight, while a recessed panel relieves the blank upper face of the wall.

[107] South Western Hospital, Landor Road

This hospital was built in 1869-70 by the Managers of the Metropolitan Asylum District under the provisions of the Metropolitan Poor Act, 1867, for the reception of patients suffering from fever and smallpox. It consists of two symmetrically arranged groups of stock brick buildings of two and three storeys joined by a wide central corridor. The blocks run approximately east and west across the long site, which extends north and south, and are plain and unprepossessing. The northerly group was designed by Thomas Henry Wyatt, and the southerly group by Frederick Marrable. William Howard was the contractor for both blocks.[100]

[108] St. Andrew's C.E. Primary School, Lingham Street

At a public meeting in 1815 it was decided to establish a school to be known as the Stockwell and Brixton Auxiliary Parochial School;[101] it was to be managed on the Madras system and on the principles of the Church of England in union with the National Society.[102] The foundation stone was laid by the Archbishop of Canterbury on June 9, 1818, and the school was opened on October 25, 1818, with 150 boys and 100 girls. The cost of the building was £1,000.[101] The school was restored and enlarged at the end of the 19th century.[103] The original hall is now in the centre of the group with later buildings flanking it on each side. The Lingham Street façade is of two storeys in red brick with stone mullioned and transomed windows grouped in horizontal bands across the front; it is crowned with a heavily bracketed cornice and has swept parapets over its two terminal and two medial projections.

An Infants' School was opened in South (now [109] Southesk) Street in 1838;[104] the undistinguished stock brick building, which is no longer used as a school, still remains.

FERNDALE ROAD AREA

City of London Almshouses, Ferndale [110] Road

After the passing of the Reform Bill of 1832 large sums of money were subscribed to celebrate the event by an illumination. A group of gentlemen in the City decided that the foundation of almshouses would provide a more useful and permanent memorial. They therefore determined "to induce the people in general to subscribe the money which they would have wasted in the glittering follies of a night to the establishment of a humane Institution, which reason could approve, and charity consecrate, as a lasting memorial of their united triumph over an absurd and dangerous custom".[105] The almshouses were intended "to afford a permanent asylum to aged and decayed freemen and householders of London, and their wives or widows, of good character and repute, . . .".[105] Subscriptions were received, including a gift of £1,500 from the Corporation of London,[105] and in 1834 the Trustees of the almshouses bought two plots of land in Brixton for £300 from John Alliston, and a third contiguous plot for £150 from Richard Boyman Boyman. Two years later they bought from Alexander

Ross a much larger piece of adjoining land with a frontage of over 800 feet along what is now Ferndale Road for £1,200, and 16 houses accommodating 31 residents were erected on the west side of the land at a cost of £3,000.[106]

This total outlay seems to have exhausted the Trustees' financial resources. They were unable to build any more houses, and had to resort to borrowing money; after 1841 they were unable even to pay the interest on the loans. At last in 1848 they handed over all the land and the 16 houses to Trustees acting on behalf of the City Corporation.[106]

In the reign of James I Robert Rogers had bequeathed £600 to the Corporation for the erection of almshouses. In 1856 the Court of Common Council decided to pull down the almshouses which had been built in Hart Street, Cripplegate, and erect others on part of the unused land in Brixton. This was done shortly afterwards.[107]

In 1882 the Corporation also removed to Brixton the almshouses founded by Sir Thomas Gresham in Whitecross Street; George Barnes Williams was the architect of this block of houses[33] (Plate 31b).

In 1884 the 16 houses built before the Corporation acquired the land in Brixton were pulled down and rebuilt, the foundation stone being laid on December 17, 1884, by the Chairman of the City of London Freemen's Orphan School Committee. The architects were Messrs. Davis and Emanuel, and the contractor Mark Gentry.[33] This group is now known as the Freemen's Houses.

The three sets of almshouses are grouped about an open quadrangle facing Ferndale Road. Rogers' Almshouses, which stand at the north end of the east side, are plain two-storey stock brick buildings gabled in pairs and of Gothic design. The Gresham Almshouses, at the south end of the east side, are built of red brick with stone dressings and form a single-storey terrace designed in quasi-Jacobean style. The entrances are grouped in pairs in recessed arcaded porches, and each house has a slightly projecting bay window. The Freemen's Houses are grouped in four blocks on the west and south sides. They also are built of red brick with stone dressings, but they have two storeys, the upper being galleried; there are pavilions flanked by short towers at each end of each block.

CITY OF LONDON FREEMEN'S ORPHAN SCHOOL, AND FERNDALE COURT

Before the removal of Rogers' and Gresham's Almshouses to Brixton the Corporation erected a school on part of the land which they acquired in 1848. An Act of 1829[108] had enabled the President and Governors of the redundant London Workhouse (a home for neglected and vagrant children) to dispose of their property and apply the proceeds towards the education and apprenticing of poor children. An Act of 1850[109] transferred the property of the President and Governors to the Corporation, and directed the latter to establish a school "for the maintenance and the religious and virtuous education of Orphans of Freemen of the City of London". That part of the land now occupied by Ferndale Court was appropriated for this purpose, and the first stone was laid on April 27, 1852. The school was designed by J. B. Bunning, the City Architect, and the contractors were Piper and Son; the initial cost was about £20,000.[110] The City of London Freemen's Orphan School, as it was then called, was opened on March 28, 1854, and accommodated 65 boys and 35 girls; the building was enlarged in 1863.[111]

In 1926 the school was removed to Ashtead Park, Surrey, and its name was changed to The City of London Freemen's School.[111] The school buildings at Brixton were demolished and the site was used for the erection of Ferndale [111] Court, blocks of flats for members of the City of London Police Force. The foundation stone was laid by the Lord Mayor on December 16, 1927, and the buildings were opened on October 11, 1929. The architect was Sydney Perks and the contractors were Cropley Bros. To the east of Ferndale Court is the City of London Police Sports Club ground.

ST. PAUL'S CHURCH, SANTLEY STREET   [112]

The site of this church formed part of an estate of some sixteen acres which was bought about 1865 by George Peabody, the philanthropist.[112] After his death in 1869[113] his Trustees decided to dispose of the property, and in the course of the next few years a large number of small houses was erected in the area between Ferndale Road and Acre Lane.[114] In 1874 a temporary iron church was erected on the site of the present parochial hall in Allardyce Street, and four years later a site for a permanent church was acquired.[115] St. Paul's was designed by W. G. Habershon,[115] of the firm of Habershon and Fawckner, of Bloomsbury Square,[116] and was consecrated by the Bishop of Rochester on July 29, 1881.[115] The builder of the church, which accommodates 1,500 people, was Mr. Jones of Gloucester.[116] A District Chapelry was assigned in 1882.[115]

The church is plainly designed in Decorated Gothic style and faced with yellow brick banded by courses of red brick. The clerestoried nave and the aisles each have separately gabled roofs, that covering the nave being of hammer-beam construction. The original design included a tower at the west end, but it has not been completed. The galleries in the aisles were removed during the war of 1939–45.

[113] SANTLEY PRIMARY AND SECONDARY SCHOOLS, SANTLEY ROAD

This school was built for the London School Board. A temporary iron building accommodating 450 children was opened on the site in April 1898.[117] The permanent school, which included a Special School for 40 children and a Manual Training Centre for 20 boys, and in all accommodated 1,082 children, was built by Holliday and Greenwood of Brixton for £28,230.[118] The architect was T. J. Bailey,[31] and the date of opening was January 6, 1902.[119] The school is a three-storey red brick building with ogee-capped towers defining the staircases, and a small centrally-placed cupola rising from the roof.

[114] KENYON BAPTIST CHURCH, SOLON ROAD

This chapel was erected by the Higgs family in memory of William Higgs,[33] builder (1825–83), whose son was one of the original partners in the firm of builders, Hill, Higgs and Hill (later Higgs and Hill).[120] Shortly before his death William Higgs senior presented the site to the London Baptist Association, of which he was Treasurer, and drew up plans for the chapel.[121] The foundation stone was laid by C. H. Spurgeon, who was a friend of William Higgs, on November 7, 1884. The building, designed in Decorated Gothic style, is faced with brown stone and cream-coloured terracotta dressings, the latter produced by J. Stiff and Sons, of Lambeth. The front has a central triple entrance over which is set a large five-light window.

H

EPIPHANY SOCIAL CENTRE, BEDFORD ROAD [115]
Formerly Church of the Epiphany

The Mission of the Epiphany was established in the western part of the parish of St. Andrew's in 1887, and a temporary church was erected in 1891.[122] The present church, which was intended for parochial activities as well as services,[123] was opened by the Bishop of Southwark in 1911;[122] it was designed in the Gothic style by F. H. Greenaway and J. E. Newberry.[124] The church is a plain building of multi-coloured brick with stone dressings. Its asymmetrical gabled front contains a seven-light traceried window. A staircase extends across the front and leads to the entrance, which is set to one side in a recessed porch.

ACRE LANE

Although Acre Lane was an old parish highway the only old houses still standing along it were erected after the auction of Stockwell Manor in 1802. George Wheeler purchased the Hither Six Acres Field (No. 54 on the plan on Plates 74 and 75), on which Nos. 24 and 26 and the Eighth Church of Christ, Scientist, stand, and the Further Six Acres Field (No. 49 on the plan on Plates 74 and 75), on which Trinity Homes and No. 46 stand.[125] Thomas Bailey purchased the Eight Acres Field (No. 48 on the plan on Plates 74 and 75), on which Nos. 48–50 and 86–92 stand.[126]

NOS. 24 AND 26 ACRE LANE [116]
Formerly Nos. 5 and 6 George Place

In 1802 George Wheeler sold a piece of the land which he had recently acquired to William Coward of Brixton Causeway, who became responsible for its development.[125] In 1822 Coward granted a lease of No. 24, then recently erected, to Samuel Clement of Great Suffolk Street, builder. Clement probably erected No. 26 as well, which was let in the same year to Richard Strong, who occupied it for several years.[125] They are a plain pair of three-storey stock brick houses, with entrances in narrow side wings. No. 24 has pilasters with festooned heads and a later semi-circular hood at its entrance. No. 26 has an identical hood and door pilasters of Corinthian type.

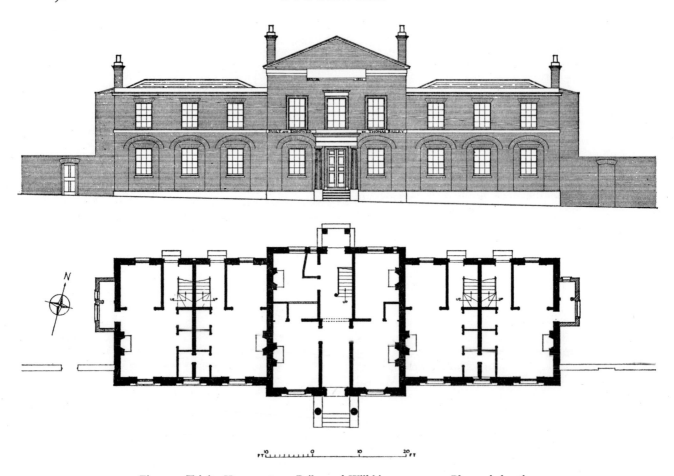

Fig. 32. Trinity Homes, 1822. Bailey and Willshire, surveyors. Plan and elevation

[117] THE EIGHTH CHURCH OF CHRIST, SCIENTIST, LONDON

A temporary church was erected at the rear of No. 20 Acre Lane in 1921 and extended in 1924.[127] The foundation stone of the permanent church, designed by T. E. Davidson, Son and Sherwood of Newcastle-upon-Tyne,[127] was laid in 1930, and the building completed in 1931.[128] It is a plain stock brick building with a three-storey front of red brick dressed with stone, gabled and of unostentatious design. The church was damaged in June 1944 by a flying bomb, and was restored in 1947–53 to the designs of Oswald P. Milne who made considerable modifications and also designed the reading room on the east side.[129]

TRINITY HOMES   [118]

Formerly Trinity Asylum

George Wheeler sold another piece of land to Thomas Bailey[130] of St. Paul's Churchyard[131] and Bethel House, Brixton,[132] on which Trinity Asylum was built in 1822 (Plate 31a, fig. 32). Bailey, "being desirous of establishing an asylum for pious aged women, whose lives and conversations give evidence that they have passed from death into life by faith in Jesus Christ",[132] had two blocks of houses built parallel with Acre Lane. The front block contained eight apartments and the rear block four. Each apartment consisted of two rooms fitted with a stove and an iron bedstead.[132] The work of erecting the two blocks was carried out under the supervision of

Messrs. Bailey and Willshire, surveyors.[133] In 1824 Bailey appointed seven Trustees to manage the asylum and endowed it with £2,000. Until his death in 1828,[134] however, he retained full control of the institution, for the subsequent management of which he provided a number of rules. Candidates for admission had to be members of the Church of England and be between 57 and 67 years of age. They had to have an income of their own of at least £20 per annum, in addition to which all inmates were to receive an annuity of £10 and twelve sacks of coal. They had to provide their own furniture and cooking utensils, and on Sundays they were required to go to church twice in summer and once in winter. They were not allowed to keep fowls or rabbits, and probably because there was a garden in the centre of the site, the rules also provided that "No flower pots or any thing whatever shall be allowed on the outside of any of the windows".[132]

Bailey bequeathed a further £500[134] to the asylum, whose management was taken over by the Trustees in 1828; another legacy was received from his widow a few years later.[135] In 1860 a third block containing four sets of rooms was erected on the east side of the plot. The architect was Samuel Field,[136] and Skinner Brothers, whose tender was for £575, were the builders.[137]

The block of almshouses fronting Acre Lane is an elegant two-storey building in yellow stock brick. The central feature, which is three windows wide, rises slightly higher and is pedimented. It has a central Greek Doric columned porch and bears the inscription "ERECTED 1822" beneath the plain panel under the pediment, and "BUILT AND ENDOWED BY THOMAS BAILEY" along the first floor sill-band. The side wings are set back slightly and the sill-band of the centre part continues beneath their three first-floor windows. All the ground-floor windows are set in shallow elliptical-headed recesses. The cornices of the wings have been marred by injudicious repairs.

The blocks at the rear are similar to the almshouses fronting Acre Lane, but plainer. The range on the north side of the garden has porches with unfluted Greek Doric columns sheltering each pair of entrances. The other range on the east side bears a tablet dated 1860.

NO. 46 ACRE LANE   [119]
Formerly Hambly House

No. 46 was erected about 1808[38] by Richard Curtis on a piece of land probably purchased from Thomas Bailey. Curtis occupied it until his death in 1843, when it passed to Elizabeth Hambly[138] who gave it the name of Hambly House. Since 1906 it has been used as a Church Army hostel for disabled men.[138] It is a plain three-storey stock brick building. On the road frontage pilasters rise through the full height to a cornice, and on the otherwise uninteresting side elevation there is a chaste porch with coupled Ionic columns.

NOS. 48 AND 50 ACRE LANE (THE CEDARS) [120]

In 1819 Thomas Bailey sold these two houses, which had been recently erected, together with about an acre of land, to John Illidge, stockbroker;[131] Illidge himself occupied No. 48.[38] In 1899 both houses were purchased by the School Board for London from John Betts Illidge[131] and a school for mentally defective children was established in them. They are also stock brick houses, three storeys high and have recessed porches in their wings framed by Ionic columns and flanking antae. The ground-floor windows are set in shallow segmental-headed recesses linked by unmoulded impost bands.

NOS. 86–92 (even) ACRE LANE   [121]
Formerly Nos. 4–1 (consec.) Melbourne Place

The land on which these houses stand was also part of the Eight Acres Field. The site was purchased by John Illidge from Thomas Bailey in 1825,[139] and the houses appear to have been erected between 1831 and 1839.[38] Nos. 86 and 88 are also three-storey stock brick houses, linked by a continuous sill-band below the first floor windows. Their entrances, in narrow side wings which are set back slightly, have simple pilasters on each side. Nos. 90 and 92 were similar until shops were built across their front gardens in 1884.

NOS. 47–53 (odd) ACRE LANE   [122]
Formerly Nos. 24–27 (consec.) Acre Lane

These houses are on the south side of Acre Lane. They are small two-storey brick villas erected between 1816 and 1824,[38] but are so marred by modern alterations that few of their original features remain intact. No. 49, Lynton

House, still has an Ionic columned porch and area railings of cast-iron with quatrefoil ornament.

BRIXTON HILL AREA

[123] LAMBETH TOWN HALL

In 1904, shortly after the constitution of Lambeth Borough Council, a site for a Town Hall on the corner of Acre Lane and Brixton Hill was purchased for £25,000.[140] A competition was held for a design for the new building and there were 143 entries,[141] that of Septimus Warwick and Herbert Austen Hall being chosen (Plate 36b). The builders, whose tender was for £38,274, were Messrs. John Greenwood, Ltd.[142] The foundation stone was laid on July 21, 1906, by the Mayor, Alderman F. A. Powell. In a cavity under the stone the Mayor placed a sealed bottle containing a copy of *The Times*, a map of the borough, a list of the members of the Council and its committees, and some coins.[143] The hall was opened by the Prince of Wales on April 29, 1908.[144] The clock in the tower was the gift of Edwin Jones, J.P.[145] In 1937–8 the original architects were employed to build an assembly hall fronting Acre Lane and make other extensions including an additional storey to the existing building.[146]

The Town Hall occupies a large site at the acute-angled junction of Brixton Hill and Acre Lane. The building is well planned with its main entrance at the corner of the site, where a vestibule leads past the staircase at the base of the tower, to a rotunda from whence the corridors branch left and right, opening to offices ranged along the two frontages. These ranges are linked by a transverse wing that contains the rates office with the council chamber above. There are two principal storeys, to which an attic has been added.

The building is a good example of the Edwardian Baroque manner, fairly restrained in the main but with occasional flourishes of opulent vulgarity. The exterior is faced with narrow red bricks of a fine quality, in conjunction with an extensive use of Portland stone, based on a grey granite plinth. The tall tower dominates the composition, its simple shaft of brick bounded by straight quoins supporting an octangular stage of stone. In each cardinal face is a louvred arch, containing a clock dial and surmounted by a pediment. Symbolic figures posture against the four angle faces and there is an extravagant terminal feature of inverted consoles supporting a pedestal with a crown-like finial. The main entrance is emphasized by its setting in a semi-circular feature that projects in front of the tower-base. This is entirely faced with stone and elaborately dressed with a giant order of plain-shafted Ionic columns, forming bays each containing a tall window below a circular one. The Brixton Hill front is a balanced composition with a central feature of three bays, and end pavilions each of one bay, also dressed with engaged Ionic columns and pilasters. Recessed within the middle bay of the central feature is an elaborate window with a swan-necked pediment, opening to a balcony beneath which is the secondary entrance to the building. The wall faces between the centre and end pavilions each have two tiers of seven windows, those to the first storey having arched heads. The windows in both tiers are linked by their stone setting, thus forming a series of vertical panels in the brick face. The crowning entablature is surmounted by a balustrade, broken by attic features over the centre and end pavilions. The Acre Lane front begins with a pavilion responding to that on the Brixton Hill front, but otherwise the monumental treatment is not repeated.

CORPUS CHRISTI ROMAN CATHOLIC [124] CHURCH, TRENT ROAD

In 1880 a mission was established in Brixton under the care of the Rev. Hendrik van Doorne, a Flemish priest who had lived in England for a long time. There was then no Roman Catholic church in the district, so in the following year a large house on the west side of Brixton Hill, known as No. 4 Gwydyr Houses, was purchased for £2,610. The house was re-named Corpus Christi House and one of the rooms was adapted as a small temporary chapel. A church building fund was opened, and in 1885 John Francis Bentley, the future architect of Westminster Cathedral, who had been associated with the scheme from its inception, suggested the purchase of Bethel House, with its large gardens, as a suitable site for a permanent church.[147] Bethel House is a large double-fronted house built in 1768 and formerly occupied by Thomas Bailey,[148] the founder of Trinity Homes, Acre Lane (page 98). The house was purchased for £3,550 and the foundation stone of the new church, which stands in the front garden of the house, was laid by Bishop Butt on July 14, 1886.[149]

Corpus Christi was Bentley's first important church-building commission. His plan (fig. 33) provided for a large church in the Early Decorated style, consisting of nave, chancel, ambulatory, north and south aisles, transepts, three side chapels and a tower. At the south-east corner there were to be two sacristies with an organ loft above, and at the south-west corner there was to be a presbytery. Owing to lack of funds only the chancel,

In its completed form the nave would have four arcaded bays and an aisleless extension towards the west, flanked on the north side by the porch below the steeple, and on the south side by the presbytery. The first three bays of the nave arcades open to aisles, that on the north side being flanked by a range of confessionals, while that on the south opens through another arcade to the Chapel of the Holy Ghost. The easternmost bay of the nave opens to the transepts, the northern having one bay and the southern two.

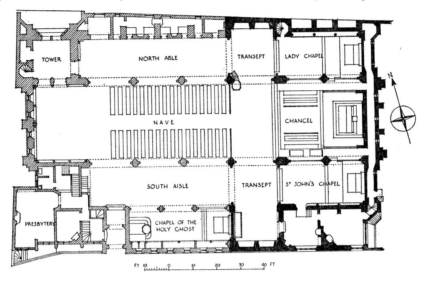

Fig. 33. Corpus Christi, Trent Road, plan. Hatched part not built

the two eastern chapels and the sacristies were built in 1886–7, the contractors being Laurenson and Sons. This first part of the church was opened by Bishop Butt on June 12, 1887.[147] The transepts were added in 1904, after Bentley's death.[150] His designs were modified, the rose windows being reduced in size.[147] Any further additions to the church will involve the demolition of Bethel House, most of which is now used as a school.

The Church of Corpus Christi (Plates 22, 23), in common with most buildings of Bentley's designing, has the character of an organic growth, the interior arising naturally from the plan and finding logical expression in the exterior. The building is well sited to take the fullest advantage of the site width between Trent Road and Horsford Road, with the east end set some distance back from Brixton Hill. The plan is asymmetrical, but balances on an east-west axis.

The square-ended chancel has two arcaded bays, opening on the north to the Lady Chapel and on the south to St. John's Chapel, the last being flanked by two sacristies with the organ loft over. A narrow ambulatory provides circulation space behind the reredos.

It will be seen that although the plan has transepts, there is no pronounced crossing, the nave and chancel being unified by the clerestory arcade, with two blind bays over each transept arch, and the pointed vault continuing unbroken from east to west. One very unusual feature of the design is the use made of different systems of bay spacing for the nave and aisle arcades, the latter having four arches to balance the three of the nave. In a similar way the outer walls of the chapels have three arches to balance the two of the chancel arcades. The resulting interplay of arcaded forms is most effective.

Bentley's design is a free interpretation of

Early Decorated Gothic, realized in brick with a generous use of Bath stone, the internal brickwork being plastered while fine red bricks are used for the exterior facings. Internally, an apparent over-elaboration of form arising from the conjunction of the differently-scaled arcades, and the effect of exaggerated height, are undoubtedly accentuated by the present incomplete state of the building and the absence of the rood-loft intended to enclose the chancel. The single completed bay of the nave arcade gives only a foretaste of the whole design. Faceted piers with engaged shafts on their lateral faces provide the springing for a two-centred arch with moulded and faceted reveals, having at its apex a carved corbel-head from which rises the shafted intermediate pier of the clerestory arcade, here bisecting the arch that terminates the pointed barrel roof of the transept. Against the main face of each pier, below the springing of the nave arches but level with that of the smaller-scale chancel arcade, is a similar corbel-head supporting a shaft which rises to the vault springing. Corbels and shaft-capitals are finely carved, the former with idealized heads and the latter with naturalistic foliage.

The chancel floor is raised by three steps above the nave level. The two-bay arcade is considerably smaller in scale than that of the nave, while the pier and arch profiles are more elaborate. The difference in height between the two arcades is taken up in the clerestory of tall two-light windows, three in number, set in deep splayed reveals with single shafts on the front faces, rising from corbel-heads to carry the vaulted roof. The east wall is a composition of three stages, the lowest containing the fine winged reredos setting (which was also designed by Bentley) for the high altar. Above is the triforium arcade of seven cusp-headed arches, arranged in groups of two-three-two and standing forward from the respondent range of seven lancet windows. The same spacing is adopted for the great east window, its triple arcade forming a splendid climax to the chancel clerestory. The body of the church is ceiled by a pointed barrel roof with groined intersecting returns to the clerestory arcade, constructed of closely-spaced wood ribs framing plaster panels.

By contrast with the well-lit chancel, the transepts seem shadowy, receiving their light through two tall single-light windows with trefoil heads, and the small traceried rose in the lunette above. The chancel side chapels have lateral arcades of three bays, the moulded arches rising from delicate shafted piers of quatrefoil plan. The north arcade stands free before a corresponding range of three-light windows. That on the south side opens to the organ loft. Each chapel has an east window of five lights. The arched heads of the windows generally are enriched with cusping and pointed trefoils are often introduced.

Externally, the quality of Bentley's design is best observed in the completed east front. The chancel end, bounded by massive frontal and lateral buttresses with gabled heads, is a tripartite composition dominated by the great three-arched window and crowned by a gable. The lower side chapels have recessed gables and are flanked by octagonal turrets with faceted conical roofs. The pronounced verticality of the design is checked by the introduction of several horizontal stone bands.

The completed portion of the north elevation includes the side of the Lady Chapel, with three triple-light windows between buttresses, and the north transept with its gable-end rising almost to the parapet line of the chancel, where the clerestory windows are linked by canopied panels. Chapel and chancel walls finish with simple corbel-tables behind which rise the steeply pitched roofs of slate. The south elevation is similar except that the chapel is here replaced by the twin-gabled wall of the sacristies and organ loft.

Bentley designed and supervised the execution of some very good stained glass for this church, some of which was unfortunately destroyed during the last war. There survive, apart from some fragments in the east windows of the two chapels, two complete windows in the Lady Chapel, and the seven lancets of the triforium of the east end of the chancel. The transept glass is by Osmond Bentley.[151]

CORPUS CHRISTI ROMAN CATHOLIC PRIMARY SCHOOL, TRENT ROAD [125]

This school was opened in 1902[152] in buildings standing in the back garden of Bethel House. More buildings have been added subsequently and the school now occupies a large part of Bethel House as well.

ST. SAVIOUR'S CHURCH, LAMBERT ROAD [126]

At a meeting held at St. Matthew's vicarage on March 24, 1873, a Committee was formed to build a new church. The proposed new district had a population of nearly 4,000, and a great deal of building was in progress. "The meadow-lands and brick-fields of a few years ago are now either covered with long rows of houses, or else marked out for fresh streets."[153] A site costing £775 was acquired and was conveyed to the Ecclesiastical Commissioners. The church (Plate 15b) was built to accommodate 938 people and was designed by E. C. Robins.[153] The first stone was laid on July 15, 1874, by James Watney, M.P.,[33] and the church was consecrated on September 29 of the following year. A Consolidated Chapelry was assigned shortly afterwards.[153]

St. Saviour's is designed in Gothic style and is faced with Kentish ragstone with Bath stone dressings. The tower at the north-west corner has four circular corner pinnacles and an octagonal louvred lantern, and is a conspicuous landmark in the neighbourhood. The nave has six arcaded bays, flanked by low aisles with lean-to roofs. The arches rest on circular columns with vigorously carved foliated capitals, and the clerestory windows contain plate-tracery.

[127] PARKSIDE PRIMARY AND SECONDARY SCHOOL, BARTLEY ROAD

This school was built for the London School Board by W. Downs of Walworth, whose tender for a school for 792 children was for £8,167.[154] The architect was E. R. Robson[31] and the date of opening was August 19, 1878.[32] The school was remodelled in 1913; it is a plain three-storey brick building.

[128] THE WINDMILL, BLENHEIM GARDENS

At the auction of Stockwell Manor in 1802, Christopher Chryssell Hall of the Borough of Southwark, merchant, purchased part of the Manor which was conveyed to him in the following year.[24] The property contained about 62 acres and lay south of the present Blenheim Gardens; it can be identified with the parcels of land marked 83–89 (inclusive) on the plan of the Manor on Plates 74 and 75. Very little development took place before 1850, most of the fields being used for digging brick earth until the 1870s.[155]

In 1817 John Ashby of Brixton Hill, miller, obtained a lease for 99 years from Hall of two acres of land (plot 84) on the south side of a new road to be called Cornwall Road (now Blenheim Gardens), together with a "Brick corn Mill" and other erections.[156] The windmill was erected in 1816–17 at the south-west corner of the two acres (Plate 43). Save for a brief period in 1862–4, when the sails of the mill were removed and new machinery installed, the windmill was in continuous use by the firm of Ashby until 1934.[157] It has been listed as a building of architectural and historic interest under the Town and Country Planning Act, 1947, and the London County Council is purchasing the site for an open space (1955). The mill is built of stock brick, painted over, and is surmounted by a gallery and a wooden boat-shaped cap; the gallery was added later. The ancillary buildings are of brick-nogged and weather boarded construction with pantile roofs.

NO. 47 BLENHEIM GARDENS [129]
Formerly No. 23 Cornwall Road

In 1843 John Ashby agreed with John Muggeridge of Brixton Road, builder, to let the eastern half of his property for building, and seven houses fronting Cornwall Road were erected by Muggeridge.[156] Only one, No. 47, has survived; it is a small single-storey house with a stuccoed front.

NOS. 49 AND 51 BLENHEIM GARDENS [130]
Formerly Nos. 25 and 25A Cornwall Road

No. 49, the Mill House, was erected as a family residence for the Ashbys;[156] it is a plain two-storey stock brick villa with a central entrance. No. 51, which stands in the yard approaching the mill, is a small two-storeyed villa, faced with stucco and of rustic appearance.

LAMBETH WATERWORKS, JEBB AVENUE [131]

The Company of Proprietors of Lambeth Waterworks was established in 1785 with works in north Lambeth.[158] In 1834 the Company obtained an Act of Parliament[159] in order to extend the area to which it might supply water. In the same year some 16 acres of land in Brixton were purchased from Christopher Chryssell Hall,[24] and a reservoir and works were built.

BRIXTON PRISON [132]

In 1818 the Justices of the Peace for Surrey decided to enlarge the prison at Kingston and to build two new Houses of Correction, one at Guildford and the other at Brixton.[160] About five acres of land forming parcel of the part of Stockwell Manor which had been acquired by Christopher Chryssell Hall in 1802 were bought for £400 per acre[161] from Florance Young.[24]

A further strip of land on the west side of the prison was bought in 1836 from the Lambeth Waterworks Company.[24] Designs for the prison were drawn up by Mr. Chawner, the County Surveyor.[162] His plan (fig. 34) bore some resemblance to the recently erected model prison at Millbank, for the central feature was a poly-

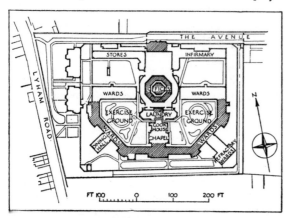

Fig. 34. Brixton Prison, lay-out plan based on the Ordnance Survey map of 1870. The shaded portions were built before 1853

gonal building from which the governor could watch the prisoners at work. But whereas the six main blocks of cells at Millbank were arranged like the petals of a flower round the governor's office, those at Brixton were arranged in the form of a crescent, and so provided for expansion at a later date, "should the encreasing Depravity of the lower Orders subject the County to that burthensome Obligation".[163] The whole prison was surrounded by a high wall with a large gatehouse on the north side.

The wall and the gatehouse were built in 1819,[164] and when they were finished 25 prisoners were sent to help in the construction of the main blocks.[165] The experiment was not altogether successful, for three prisoners escaped in 1820 and the governor was dismissed.[166] When completed the prison contained 149 single cells and 12 double ones, the capacity of the single ones being 360 cubic feet, which compared very unfavourably with the 911 cubic feet of the cells at Pentonville Prison, erected in 1840–2.[167] Estimates of the cost of the building vary considerably; Mayhew, quoting figures supplied by the Clerk of the Peace for Surrey, says that the cost of the land, the building and the erection of the treadmill was £51,780;[168] but a report pre-

sented to Quarter Sessions in 1852 says that the original cost of the building and fittings was £32,000 exclusive of the cost of the land and treadmill.[169] The first figure probably includes the cost of later works.

During discussion of the plans of the prison the Surrey Justices asked for the advice of Mr. Orridge, governor of the new House of Correction at Bury St. Edmunds.[163] A treadmill had been installed there in about 1818 by (Sir) William Cubitt[170] and in 1820 he was asked to prepare plans for a similar machine for Brixton House of Correction.[171] His plans were approved by the Justices, and in 1821 a tender from John Penn to erect a treadmill and keep it in repair for five years for £2,910 was accepted; Cubitt was offered £400 for his services.[172] Radiating out from the governor's office in the centre of the prison were the airing yards in which the tread-wheels worked by the prisoners were established[173] (Plate 37a). These tread-wheels were connected to the mill-house which contained the machinery for grinding corn. Each wheel could be adjusted to the strength of the class of prisoner in the yard. At Brixton the space stepped over by each man in one hour was 731 yards. The advantages of the wheel as a method of employment were considerable; the prisoners required no instruction, they could not shirk their share of the labour nor waste or misapply materials, and there was endless work which could be started or stopped at a moment's notice.[173] Nevertheless the tread-wheel was immediately denounced by some writers as inhumane; Thomas Allen, the historian of Lambeth, for instance, wrote that for women it was "only fit to be used in the dungeons of the Spanish Inquisition".[174]

The House of Correction was frequently very overcrowded. By 1846 as many as four prisoners sometimes slept together in a single cell. In the following year the Justices resolved to build a large new House of Correction at Wandsworth.[175] After this prison had been completed the Justices decided to sell the Brixton House of Correction, and in 1852 they offered it to the Government.[169] An Inspector of Prisons reported very favourably on the possibility of using it as a criminal lunatic asylum,[169] but no action was taken, and on September 8, 1852, the prison was sold by auction to (Sir) William Tite, the architect of the South Metropolitan Cemetery at Norwood, for £8,450.[176]

Tite bought the prison as an investment, and intended to demolish it and sell the materials. He was therefore quite prepared to sell the prison as it stood to the Government, provided that he made a reasonable profit. Discussions for the purchase of the prison began immediately after September 8, 1852, and in November Tite gave the Government one month's option to buy it for £12,930.[169] But in December Lord Derby's ministry resigned, Lord Palmerston succeeding Spencer Walpole as Home Secretary.[177] Owing to the change of government nothing was done about Tite's offer, and in January 1853 Colonel Jebb, Surveyor General of Prisons, reported against the purchase of the prison. Meanwhile Tite was becoming justifiably impatient and arranged for an auction of the fabric to take place on February 28, 1853.[169] Lord Palmerston was, however, intending to introduce a Bill for the partial abolition of transportation, which would require a considerable expansion of prison accommodation at home.[178] On February 16 Colonel Jebb suggested that Brixton prison might be very useful for this purpose, and nine days later a provisional agreement for the purchase of the gaol for £13,000 was signed.[169] The formal conveyance was dated May 14, 1853, and left Mr. Tite with a profit of £4,550.

The prison was intended for use as a convict prison for women. A new block of cells was built at each end of the crescent, and other additions made in 1853 included a chapel, wash-house, baths, infirmary, kitchens and houses for the officers; these alterations provided accommodation for 700 women. The first prisoners entered on November 24, 1853. New prisoners were confined to the old part of the prison for probationary discipline.[179]

The prison has been considerably altered and enlarged since 1853. It is now largely used for the confinement of unconvicted prisoners and debtors.

Nos. 176–182 (even) Brixton Hill [133]

Formerly Nos. 9–12 (consec.) Upper Brixton Rise

These houses stand on part of the Nine Acres Field purchased by Florance Young of Southwark from Christopher Chryssell Hall in 1818.[180] They were erected between 1824 and 1830[38] and were left by Young on his death in 1835 to his four sons.[180] There were originally twelve houses but only Nos. 176–182 survive. They are two pairs of stock brick houses of three storeys and semi-basements, with wings of the same height which contain the entrances. Each pair shares a poorly detailed pediment, and the houses are devoid of ornament except for the Victorian gabled porches added to the entrances of Nos. 176 and 178.

CHAPTER IV

Brixton

THIS chapter covers the central of part the parish between the Manor of Stockwell on the west and the Manor of Milkwell on the east. The greater part of the area formed part of the Archbishop of Canterbury's Manors of Lambeth and Lambeth Wick, and was the scene of a great deal of undistinguished speculative building in the first half of the 19th century.

THE WRIGHT ESTATE

Nothing is known about the early history of the land between Prima Road, South Island Place, Clapham Road and Brixton Road. The area formed a no-man's land bounded by the Manor of Kennington and Vauxhall Creek on the north, by Vauxhall Manor on the west and by Lambeth Wick Manor on the east and south. It may perhaps be identified with 18 acres held by Robert Addison of St. Saviour's, Southwark, butcher, who was presented in 1640 to the Court of the Commissioners of Sewers to scour the sewer which lay along his ground near Hazards Bridge.[1] Hazards Bridge crossed Vauxhall Creek at the north end of Brixton Road. The land must have been very marshy at all times until the sewer was closed in, for the area around Kennington Common, the Oval and Claylands Road formed a shallow depression through which the river flowed, and indeed often overflowed. Development of these 18 acres started at the beginning of the 19th century but only along the frontages to the main roads. Prima Road, formerly Church Row or Street, was laid out about 1794, when the property belonged to John Wright of Esher, banker.[2] Wright granted several building leases of plots fronting Clapham and Brixton Roads and a few of the houses erected under these leases survive and are described below. In 1870 another John Wright, who was then owner of the estate, disposed of it in two parts. The northern part, between Prima Road and the present gardens of houses in Handforth Road, was sold to Philip Edward Sewell of Norfolk, civil engineer.[2] The southern portion was acquired by Robert and

Isaac Crewdson,[3] and Handforth and Crewdson Roads were subsequently laid out across it.

No. 5 PRIMA ROAD [134]
Formerly Severn House

This house was erected under a building lease granted in 1801 to William Broadhurst[2] but has probably been altered since. It is a three-storey stock brick villa raised above a semi-basement and finished with a cornice and blocking course to the parapet. It has a rusticated stuccoed ground storey and is set forward slightly at each side of the central entrance. The entrance is sheltered by a broad Ionic-columned porch which has rectangular corner piers with anthemion-ornamented heads. There are bearded male mask keystones over the windows which are identical with those on No. 57 South Lambeth Road (Plates 70a, b, c). The villa is partially masked by later houses which abut it at each side on an advanced building line.

THE BELGRAVE HOSPITAL FOR CHILDREN, CLAPHAM ROAD [135]

This hospital was founded in 1866 in Pimlico.[4] At the end of the 19th century the Governors decided that the need for hospital accommodation in south London warranted its removal from Gloucester Street, Pimlico, and in 1899 they took a lease of its present site from P. E. Sewell.[5] The buildings which then occupied the site were pulled down and the foundation stone was laid by Princess Henry of Battenberg on June 27, 1900.[6] The east wing, centre block, outpatients' department and the ground floor of the south wing were finished in 1903[4] and opened on July 20 of that year.[7] The south wing was completed in 1924 and the west wing two years later.[4] The plan of the hospital was the work of H. Percy Adams, but the elevations, which show the influence of Philip Webb, were prepared by Charles Holden, who had joined Adams in October 1899.[8] The builders were Messrs. Gough and Co. of Hendon.[9]

The hospital has a simple cruciform plan and is symmetrically arranged about the Clapham

Road front. The building, which is mostly of four storeys, is faced with red brick and has mullioned and transomed windows of Portland stone. Its entrance wing at the centre is surmounted by a steep gable flanked by low square battlemented towers, and the wards in the north and south wings are galleried, with plain towers at each corner containing necessary services.

[136] Nos. 13 and 15 Clapham Road

Formerly Nos. 4 and 5 Clapham Road Place or Lambeth Place

A plan on the lease of the adjoining property dated 1805 shows these houses on lease to Henry Wood,[2] who may have erected them about this time. They are paired three-storey houses and have a stock brick front of simple design. A narrow recession defines the party wall between the houses, each of which has two rectangular windows in each storey. Those to the ground floor are set in shallow recesses with arched heads rising from moulded imposts. Each house is flanked by a single storey annexe containing the entrance, the door being set with a radial-patterned fanlight in a segmental-arched opening.

[137] Nos. 17–25 (odd) Clapham Road

Formerly Nos. 6–10 (consec.) Clapham Road Place

These houses were erected in 1805 at the costs of James Medland of St. Mary Newington, surveyor, and were let to him in that year by John Wright's trustees.[2] They are a terrace of five houses sharing a stock brick front that presents a balanced composition. All the houses are three windows wide and each end house forms a slightly projecting pavilion, four storeys high, the last being an attic above the mutule cornice. The three intermediate houses are three storeys high, and the cornice is surmounted by an open balustrade. A bandcourse marks the first-floor level. The windows generally are rectangular excepting those to the ground floor, which have flat segmental heads. Each house has a wood doorcase of simple design, except for No. 21 where the stucco surrounds are later.

[138] Nos. 27–33 (odd) Clapham Road

Formerly Nos. 11–14 (consec.) Clapham Road Place

No building lease of these houses has survived, but again by comparing the leases of adjoining houses it can be deduced that their site was on lease to Head,[10] probably William Head, a local builder (see page 76), in 1805. These are paired houses similar to Nos. 13 and 15, but with two-leaved doors and elaborated parapets to the annexes, which are now heightened or altered. The ground floor of No. 27 has been partly cut away to provide access to the rear, and the upper part of No. 29 has been rebuilt.

Nos. 35–41 and 61–77 (odd) Clapham [139] Road

Formerly Nos. 15–18 and 25–33 (consec.) Clapham Road Place

In 1809 the trustees of John Wright, then deceased, let the whole of the frontage of Clapham Road between and including the site of No. 35 and the site of the present South Island Place, on building lease of 80½ years.[3] The lessees were the trustees of Richard Wooding, surveyor, who probably had an agreement for the building lease before his death in 1808. The trustees included Mary, wife of Richard Wooding, his executor Robert Roberts, who was also a surveyor, and Isaac Bates of Kennington, brickmaker (see page 21). Nos. 35 and 37 are built of stock brick, three storeys high, and form a six-bay block with end bays recessed and containing the doorways. The upper windows are square-headed and on the ground floor round-headed in shallow arched recesses, which, like the arched entrances, have rectangular impost blocks. Nos. 39 and 41 are a pair of three-storeyed stock brick houses with semi-basements. The two ground-floor windows and the entrance to each house are round-headed and recessed beneath shallow arches springing from moulded imposts. Above, the windows are rectangular, two to a storey, and there is a sill-band at first-floor level. The doorcases have pilasters with reeded panels, capped by wreathed blocks. The street railings to No. 41 remain in part. They are spear-headed, the principal uprights having elegant urn finials. Nos. 63–73 form a symmetrical group of three linked pairs, the centre pair being considerably larger than the other two. No. 61 is nearly identical with the right-hand house in either of the smaller pairs, but has suffered some alteration. All are built of stock brick, of three storeys raised on a rendered semi-basement. Nos. 67 and 69, the centre pair, have each three windows to a floor, square-headed upstairs and round-headed on the ground floor where they are set in arched recesses with moulded imposts, to match the entrance. Both their doorways have plain fanlights and are flanked by very slender Roman Doric columns. No. 69 retains its original frieze, cornice and blocking course. Nos. 63 and 65 and Nos. 71 and 73 are flanked by one-storey links containing the doorways and each house is two windows wide. Otherwise they are treated in the same way as the centre pair. No. 75 is a two-storey stock brick house with a semi-basement, its front finished with a cornice and blocking course. It is three windows wide and there is a centrally placed porch resting on columns. The basement is faced with stucco. No. 77 is a narrow three-storey house wedged in between Nos. 75 and 79. It is very similar to Nos. 39 and 41, but has a cast-iron balcony across the full width of the house at first-floor level.

[140] Nos. 22 AND 24 BRIXTON ROAD

Formerly Nos. 28 and 30 Brixton Road, previously Nos. 6 and 7 Spencer Place

In 1802 a building lease of the land on which these houses stand was granted to William Broad-hurst,[2] who also built No. 5 Prima Road. They are a pair of modest, stock brick houses of three storeys, each two windows wide. Single storey extensions, now altered, contain the round-headed doorways, that to No. 22 having a reeded stucco architrave. The windows have segmental heads and lattice pattern iron guards on the first floor. No. 24 has an attic in a mansard roof and No. 22 has been extended to the side.

LAMBETH WICK ESTATE

The origin of the Manor of Lambeth Wick (Wyk, Wyke or Wykecourt) is obscure, but it seems to have been appurtenant to the Manor of Lambeth which was granted to Hubert Walter, Archbishop of Canterbury, by the Prior and Convent of Rochester in 1197.[11] The earliest mention of it which has been found is in 1271,[12] when "Lametheth with La Wyk" was in the king's hands during the vacancy of the See of Canterbury caused by the death of Archbishop Boniface. In the chartulary belonging to St. Thomas' Hospital there are grants of land "in Wike" and "at la Wyke".[13] Only one of these is dated (1338) and as no deeds relating to this land have survived among the hospital's archives it is impossible now to identify it. The only surviving record of courts held for the Manor of Lambeth Wick occurs in a roll for the years 1385–6.[14]

"Farmers'" accounts for Lambeth Wick and references to repairs of the grange there[15] suggest that the property was administered as a separate unit from the end of the 13th century to the beginning of the 15th. But from 1480[16] to the beginning of the 19th century it was the practice of successive Archbishops to demise the Manor for short terms at an annual rent of £8, reserving to themselves all courts, etc., but allowing the lessees 20 loads of wood a year.[17] In 1701 the Manor was let to Sir Stephen Fox,[18] father of the first Baron Holland of Foxley and grandfather of the famous Charles James Fox; various members of the family continued as lessees of the property till the beginning of the 20th century. The estate was developed by Henry Richard Vassall, the third Baron Holland, who adopted his wife's maiden name of Vassall in 1800.[19] Holland Grove, Foxley, Vassall and Lilford[20] Roads commemorate the family's connection with the area.

The land belonging to the Manor lay in three separate parcels. The most northerly extended from Kennington Common south and west to the site of Melbourne Square and across Brixton Road to Clapham Road; to the south of this lay a second parcel, separated from the east side of Brixton Road by copyhold land of Lambeth Manor (part of the Angell and Slade estates), and extending south across Coldharbour Lane almost to the junction of the present Mayall and Shakespeare Roads; the third and smallest parcel abutted on the north-west side of Coldharbour Lane and is now covered by parts of Lilford Road, Flaxman Road and Kenbury Street. In a survey of the Archbishop's possessions in Lambeth made in 1647 Lambeth Wick Manor was said to be "divided into Twenty small Closes . . . (containing) . . . in all about two hundred and thirty Acres".[21] Just before its development at the beginning of the 19th century the land was used chiefly as pasture and market garden ground.[22]

Although an Act of Parliament was passed in 1807 enabling the Archbishop to grant building and repairing leases of this and other of his estates,[23] the development of Lambeth Wick Manor did not start till 1820. This delay was probably due to the slow progress of the project which was first mooted in 1806 to build a bridge across the Thames at Vauxhall with connecting roads into Middlesex and Surrey (see page 78). Such a scheme would and did have a tremendous effect on the development of Kennington and Brixton, and it seems likely that building in Lambeth Wick was delayed until it was known definitely what direction the new roads would take. Vauxhall Bridge was eventually opened in 1816 and two years later an Act of Parliament was passed providing for the formation of a road from the bridge foot to Camberwell,[24] i.e., Harleyford Road and Camberwell New Road, the latter passing across the northern parcel of the Manor. The estate thus acquired valuable frontages to both sides of the new road, which was subsequently linked with the Brixton and Clapham Roads by Caldwell Street and Vassall Road.

Between 1820 and 1824 the whole of the Manor was let to Henry Richard Vassall, third Baron Holland, under 15 different building leases for terms of 99 years, due to expire by 1923.[25] Under the covenants of these leases brick houses were to be erected of at least the third rate and were to be kept in good repair; the outside wood and ironwork were to be painted every fourth year and offensive trades were prohibited. For developing each plot £1,000 were to be expended on building in the first five years of the term and another £1,000 by the end of the following fifteen years.

Building began first in the northern parcel of the Manor where prospects had been considerably improved by the opening of the Camberwell New Road. The frontages to Clapham, Brixton and Camberwell New Roads, and later to the new roads in between, were let in small parcels by Lord Holland to both builders and speculators for terms of 80 years. This policy of piecemeal letting, especially in the Brixton Road, resulted in unrelated groups of villas and terrace houses which, in spite of the charm of individual members, gave to the whole an untidy and haphazard appearance. In some cases the reserved rents of the plots sub-let by Lord Holland were sold by him for the duration of the sub-lease to persons not actively engaged in developing the property.[26] This practice provided the vendor with fresh capital to re-invest in further development, while the purchaser of the rents and his dependants enjoyed an annuity for some time to come.

The long thin shape and isolated position of the southern parcel of the Manor made develop-ment more difficult, and building started later. There were no roads on the east side and there was no access to Brixton Road except by Loughborough Lane (now Road) and across the fields of the Slade and Angell estates (see page 128). Coldharbour Lane was the only other road running across the estate and though on the south side the frontage was considerable, on the north side only a narrow neck of land fronted the road. The whole of the southern portion of the Manor, let on building leases to Lord Holland in 1824, was immediately let by him to Lt. Col. Randall Gossip of Thorp Arch Hall, Yorkshire.[27] Gossip was probably acting as a steward, for in 1829 he surrendered all the property which he had succeeded in sub-letting for development, to Lord Holland's trustee.[28] Most building in this area took place between 1830 and 1850. A plan[29] for the layout of St. James's Crescent, Millbrook Road and Barrington Road was prepared by Henry Currey,[a] and building lots fronting these roads were offered to the public by advertisement in 1843. Loughborough Park was formed in the years 1844–57, and the detached portion of the Manor on the north-west side of Coldharbour Lane was built up in the early 1830s.

On the triangular-shaped piece of ground now covered by Evandale, Claribel, parts of Loughborough, Lilford and Akerman Roads, stood Loughborough House and grounds. The house itself, shown on a plan of 1825[33] as an oblong range of buildings facing west with its south side abutting on Loughborough Lane, stood on the site of the south-east corner of Evandale Road and part of the roadway. It was supposed to have derived its name from its occupation by Henry Hastings, first Baron Loughborough, and younger son of the fifth Earl of Huntingdon. His biographer states that in 1664 his residence was "an old mansion in . . . Lambeth".[34] This may have been the house which was occupied by a Mr. Younge in 1661 with ten acres of land "most part of yt planted".[35] In 1820 Loughborough House was described as a "very large old house of light construction" and the grounds comprised about 11 acres.[22] Henry Hastings fought on the Royalist side during the Civil War and at the Restoration was appointed Lord Lieutenant of Leicestershire. In 1664 he promoted a Bill in

[a] Henry Currey, architect, 1820–1900,[30] became architect to St. Thomas' Hospital and designed the hospital buildings on the Embankment. His father Benjamin was solicitor and steward to Lord Holland for his Lambeth estate,[31] and Clerk Assistant in the House of Lords. Frederick Currey, one of Henry's brothers, was a prominent mycologist.[32]

Parliament for making a navigable river from Brixton Causeway to the Thames. The Act[36] received the Royal Assent but perhaps because Hastings died two years later[37] no advantage was taken of the scheme. In spite of the insistence of the Act that the proposed waterway would "tend much to the increase of Trade" it is difficult to imagine how the scheme would have benefited such a sparsely populated area. Towards the end of the 18th century Loughborough House became a "superior Academy"[38] and in 1787 the second edition of a collection of elocution lessons was published by R. Turner dedicated "To the Young Noblemen and gentlemen receiving their education at Loughborough House School".[39] In 1825 Thomas Willett, who had lived at Loughborough House for some years, purchased the leasehold interest of the house and grounds, which included a field called Shoulder of Mutton Close, from Randall Gossip for £5,000.[33] Willett was not bound by this contract to erect any buildings on the land, and it is probable that he made the purchase to prevent its development. He died in 1846[40] and the house was pulled down about 1854.[41]

The dates and names which follow the architectural description of the houses mentioned below are the dates of the building leases granted by Lord Holland—presumably when building was nearing completion—and the names of the lessees. When known, the occupation and address of the lessee is given on the first occasion he is mentioned; thereafter only his name is repeated. All the houses are built of stock brick unless otherwise stated.

[141] Nos. 97–113, 119, 121, 127–133, 135 (odd) CLAPHAM ROAD

Formerly Nos. 3–11, 14, 15, 17–20, 22 (consec.) Holland Place

No. 97 is a house of two storeys and a semi-basement, its three windows wide front finished with a cornice and blocking course. The centrally placed entrance has a patterned fanlight. March 4, 1824; Skinner Chart of Kennington Lane, builder.[42]

Nos. 99–107 form a terrace of houses containing three storeys and semi-basements with the centre house, No. 103, rising to four storeys. The entrances and ground-floor windows are round-headed and set in arched recesses. Nos. 99 and 101 have cast-iron window guards at the first floor. January 4, 1823; Arnold Heath of Kennington Cross, corn-dealer.[43]

No. 109 is similar to No. 97; it originally had a hood over the doorway, but this has been removed. No. 111 is a narrow two-storey house with a semi-basement, its front finished with a cornice and blocking course. March 20, 1821; William Gummer of Kennington, plumber.[44]

No. 113 is similar to No. 97. Its centrally placed entrance has attenuated columns and a patterned fanlight. September 11, 1820; James Crundall of Clapham Road Place, timber merchant.[45]

No. 119 is a two-storey villa, three windows wide, with overhanging eaves and a slated roof. The centrally placed doorway has slender columns and is round-headed. April 16, 1821; Jane and Eliza Sorel of Kennington, spinsters.[46]

No. 121 is a narrow house of two storeys and semi-basement with an attic in a mansard roof. It is two windows wide and the round-headed doorway has a patterned fanlight. March 23, 1822; William Richard Self of Clapham Road Place, plumber.[47]

Nos. 127 and 129 are paired three-storey houses with semi-basements. The front of each house is two windows wide and finished with a cornice and blocking course. The ground-floor openings have semi-elliptical heads and No. 129 has a patterned fanlight. The entrances are in single- (No. 127) and two-storey (No. 129) annexes; the latter is joined to No. 131 by a two storey link which is set forward slightly. Nos. 131 and 133 are similar but three windows wide, and the entrances are set in the body of the houses; No. 133 has no annexe. No. 131 has a patterned fanlight. March 20, 1821; William Bird of Clapham Road Place, builder.[48]

No. 135 is another three-storey house with a semi-basement, but has been mutilated. October 18, 1821; John Lett of Montague Place, Bedford Square.[49]

Nos. 11–43 (odd) SOUTH ISLAND PLACE   [142]

Formerly No. 4 and Nos. 23–8A (consec.) South Island Place

Nos. 11–43 form a continuous terrace of plain two-storey cottages. The front of each cottage contains a rectangular window and a round-arched doorway on the ground floor, two rectangular windows on the first floor, and finishes with a plain coped parapet. The four cottages at the east end have their ground-floor windows set in elliptical-headed recesses, and there are apron panels above the upper windows. Nos. 31 and 41 alone have simple fanlights which are respectively of radiating and circular pattern. Nos. 11–41, March 23, 1822; William Richard Self.[47] No. 43, July 29, 1823; James Collins of Kennington, mason.[50]

[143] Nos. 37–61 (odd) HILLYARD STREET
Formerly Nos. 11–23 (consec.) Russell Street

Nos. 37–61 form a continuous well-maintained terrace of three-storey houses, each two windows wide, of which Nos. 37–47 form one group and Nos. 49–61 another (Plate 48c). The groups are similar and of the same height to their parapets. The former group has a linking band at first-floor sill level while the others are linked at first-floor level. The ground floor windows and doorways have round arches springing from stone imposts; the first-floor windows have gauged flat arches set in shallow semi-circular headed recesses. The terrace is devoid of ornament except for the cast-iron guards protecting the first-floor windows of Nos. 49–61. December 31, 1822; James Crundall.[51]

[144] Nos. 91–115 (odd) BRIXTON ROAD
Formerly Nos. 1–13 (consec.) Bowhill Terrace

Nos. 91–109 (Plate 50b), form a long, plain three-storey terrace with five houses at the centre joined by single-storey entrance links to two houses at the north end and three at the south end. The end houses of the centre and south blocks are set forward slightly. At ground-floor level all the houses are faced with rusticated stucco and have round-headed recessed windows and deep-set entrances. The majority of the houses have first-floor cast-iron window guards with anthemion and wave ornament, and some have entrance fanlights of radiating pattern. The crowning cornice has been removed. Nos. 91–103, January 4, 1823; Thomas Hill of Harleyford Place, Kennington.[52] Nos. 105–109, January 4, 1823; John Muggeridge of Harleyford Place, builder.[53]

Nos. 111–115 are plain three-storey stucco-fronted houses with semi-basements. There are pilasters on the lines of the party walls and at the

corners, and all the openings have architraves. The crowning cornice has been removed. August 26, 1823; James Crundall.[54]

[145] Nos. 117–141 (odd) BRIXTON ROAD
Formerly Nos. 1–13 (consec.) Minerva Terrace

Nos. 117–137 (Plate 48b), form a three-storey terrace in which the centre house, No. 127, is stuccoed, and the end houses are set forward slightly. All the houses have depressed semi-elliptical arches over the ground-floor openings, and the doorways (Plate 68d) have patterned fanlights and fluted quadrant reveals. Most of the ground-floor windows have their original glazing bars with marginal panes; those at No. 23 retain their original amber glass. The first-floor windows have cast-iron guards. Nos. 139 and 141 are both stucco-fronted, and are divided by pilasters which, with the friezes under the consoled window hoods, are somewhat coarsely ornamented. July 29, 1823; James Crundall.[55]

[146] Nos. 147, 149 AND 155 BRIXTON ROAD
Formerly Nos. 3, 4 and 7 Vassall Place

These houses are simple two-storey villas with overhanging eaves and slated roofs; they are very similar to No. 112, on the opposite side of the road. No. 149 has a Greek Doric porch, and No. 155 is stucco-fronted. Another villa in this group, No. 151, was demolished in 1950. Nos. 147, 149, 151, January 23, 1822; James Crundall.[56] No. 155, January 26, 1824; John Keith of Camberwell (New) Road.[57]

[147] Nos. 167–179 (odd) BRIXTON ROAD
Formerly Nos. 1–7 (consec.) Claremont Place

No. 167 is a large three-storey house with a semi-basement and attics, and is finished with a cornice and blocking course. It is three windows wide and has a centrally placed doorway with a projecting porch supported on columns. There is a coach-house at the side. Nos. 169 and 171 are similar but have only two storeys. June 13, 1823; Evan Roberts of North Brixton, slate merchant.[58]

No. 173 is another two-storey villa finished with a cornice and blocking course; it is three windows wide and has a centrally placed entrance. There is no porch, attic or coach-house. Nos. 175 and 177 are paired two-storey houses with semi-basements and overhanging eaves; the roofs are slated and have small projecting attic windows. No. 179 is similar to No. 173; the doorcase is illustrated on Plate 68c. Nos. 175 and 177, January 26, 1824; George Grove Unwin of Kennington.[59] Nos. 173 and 179, October 15, 1821; William Woods of Kennington, builder.[60]

[148] Nos. 195–211 (odd) BRIXTON ROAD
Formerly Nos. 1–9 (consec.) Alfred Place

Nos. 195–203 form a three-storey terrace with basements, the ground storey being faced with rusticated stucco. The centre and end houses are set forward slightly and are flanked on the upper storeys by pilasters with key ornament; they also have continuous cast-iron balconies on the first floor, while those on the intermediate houses are separate. May 8, 1824; James Crundall.[61]

No. 205 is a two-storey villa with windows set in segmental arches on both floors. The central entrance has quadrant reveals and in the inflected blocking course of the parapet above there is a ribboned wreath. No. 207 is another two-storey villa but it has an attic storey in the mansard roof, and a two-storey projecting bay on one side. These two houses were both designed as detached houses, but were built on such narrow plots that they are actually joined together (Plate 55b). Nos. 209 and 211 are a pair of three-storey houses with semi-basements and two-storey annexes, which in the case of No. 211 contains the entrance. Each house is three windows wide and the fronts are finished with a cornice and blocking course. April 16, 1823; William and Thomas Cox of Playhouse Yard, St. Luke's, Middlesex, paper stainers.[62]

[149] Nos. 98–112 (even) BRIXTON ROAD
Nos. 98–110, formerly Nos. 2–8 (consec.) Elizabeth Place

Nos. 98–108 form a three-storey terrace well raised above stuccoed semi-basements. Nos. 98 and 100 are a pair joined to the others by a two-storey link. Nos. 102 and 108 are set forward slightly and the round-arched ground floor windows are linked by moulded imposts. The entrances have patterned fanlights and are flanked by attenuated Greek Doric columns. Each house has steep steps with cast-iron balustrades. May 15, 1823; William Bird.[63]

No. 110 abuts No. 108 and is a plain three-storey house with semi-basement, its ground floor faced with stucco. It is slightly lower than Nos. 98–108, and the entrance is contained in a single storey annexe. No. 112 (Plate 55c) is a neat well-maintained two-storey villa with wide overhanging eaves to its slated roof. It is three windows wide, and its central entrance and ground-floor windows are set in shallow elliptical arched recesses. The doorway has a fluted surround and a delicate fanlight. March 20, 1821; William Bird.[48]

Nos. 120–124, 130–142 (even) BRIXTON [150] ROAD
Formerly Nos. 1–3 (consec.) Carlton Terrace, and Nos. 1–7 (consec.) St. George's Place

Nos. 120–124 were similar to Nos. 98–108, but stucco-fronted. They were demolished in 1955. (The building lease cannot be found.)

No. 130 is a three-storey stucco-fronted house, three windows wide and with a two-storey wing. There is a projecting porch supported on columns. Nos. 132–138 are two-storey houses with semi-basements, the fronts being finished with a cornice and blocking course; Nos. 134 and 136 have attics in a mansard roof. Each house is two windows wide, and the doorways and ground-floor windows are round-headed, the latter being set in arched recesses. No. 138 has a two-storey annexe which was probably built at the same time as the house and served as a coach-house. August 16, 1824; Peter Daly of Margate.[64]

Nos. 140 and 142 are a pair of three-storey houses with semi-basements. They are faced with channelled stucco at ground-floor level and the original doors, ornamented with Maltese crosses, survive. May 2, 1824; the Hon. James Abercromby of New Street, Spring Gardens.[65]

Nos. 152–160 (even) BRIXTON ROAD [151]
Formerly Nos. 5–1 (consec.) St. Ann's Terrace

These houses (Plate 49a) are the survivors of a terrace of seven large four-storey houses with semi-basements; Nos. 148 and 150 were destroyed in the war of 1939–45. All are stucco-fronted at ground-floor level and are finished with a cornice and blocking course. The centre house, which is three windows wide, and the end house, No. 160, are set forward slightly, and the entrance to the latter is set in a single storey annexe. There are cast-iron balustrades with anthemion and wave ornament enclosing the areas and guarding the first-floor windows. Nos. 152, 156, 158, February 7, 1828; Robert Stevens of Burnham, Berkshire.[66] Nos. 154 and 160, February 7, 1828; William Thorowgood of Acre Lane.[67]

[152] Nos. 162–168 (even) BRIXTON ROAD

No. 162 is a two-storey villa with a stucco fronted semi-basement. The front is finished with a cornice and blocking course and the house is three windows wide with the doorway in the centre; the ground-floor windows have cast-iron guards, and there is a coach-house at the side. Pediments have been added to the dormer windows in the mansard roof. Nos. 164 and 166 are a plain three-storey pair with semi-basements. The ground floors are faced with channelled stucco, the upper storeys are set forward over the entrances at the end, and the fronts are finished with a cornice and blocking course. No. 168 is very similar to No. 162, but has a Tuscan columned porch at the centre with a mutule cornice. Nos. 162 and 168, January 1, 1823; William Woods.[68] Nos. 164 and 166, September 1, 1824; the Hon. James Abercromby.[69]

[153] Nos. 32–48 (even) FOXLEY ROAD

Formerly Nos. 10–2 (consec.) Foxley Cottages

Nos. 32–48 are three-storey detached villas, linked in pairs by recessed annexes, of one or two storeys, that contain the entrances. The uniform fronts are unusual in composition and severe in expression (Plate 51b). The semi-basement is faced with horizontally channelled stucco, but the stock brick face above relies for effect on the arch-headed shallow recess that rises almost to eaves level and is centred between the two windows of each storey. This recess is echoed by a further break at each end of the front. The ground-floor windows are round-headed and set in arched recesses; those on the first floor are rectangular and on the second floor square. The slated roofs are low pitched and overhanging. The entrances are recessed in stuccoed porches, with pilasters at each side. The doors are surmounted by patterned semi-circular fanlights. January 1, 1824; Nicholas Phillipps, Rothery of Exeter.[70]

No. 34 was occupied between 1827 and 1841 by David Cox (1783–1859), the water-colour artist; his residence there is confirmed by entries in the rate books for 1830–40. Cox was born in Birmingham, but came to London in 1804 where he was employed at Astley's Amphitheatre in Westminster Bridge Road, painting scenery. For a few years he taught at Hereford but returned to London in 1827, when he began "the most arduous and the most rewarding period" of his life.[71]

I

Nos. 15–37 (odd) FOXLEY ROAD   [154]

Nos. 21–37, formerly Nos. 9–1 (consec.) Eltham Place

No. 15 is a plain two-storey villa raised above a stucco-fronted semi-basement. It has eaves and a slate roof, and there is a centrally placed Doric porch. No. 17 is similar, but slightly higher. No. 19, which is now derelict, is a three-storey stucco-fronted house with a flat pediment carried on consoles over the architrave-lined central entrance. Nos. 21–37 form a plain three-storey terrace with basements. The end and centre houses are set forward slightly and have an extra storey. Each house is two windows wide and cast-iron balconies link the first-floor windows of each house. The ground storeys are stuccoed and channelled, and contain entrances with panelled door frames and simple segmental fanlights. The cornices to the parapets have been removed. Nos. 15–31, January 1, 1824; N. P. Rothery.[70] Nos. 33–37, January 1, 1824; John Williamson of Fleet Street.[72]

Nos. 3–41 (odd) VASSALL ROAD   [155]

Nos. 7–41, formerly Nos. 1–18 (consec.) Mitford Place

Nos. 3 and 5 are uninteresting two-storey buildings with shop fronts; they abut a long terrace consisting of Nos. 7–41. These houses have three storeys and semi-basements and are finished with a cornice and blocking course; the ground storey is faced with channelled stucco. Some of the doorways have simple semi-circular fanlights and there are window guards at first-floor level. Nos. 3–7, July 29, 1823; James Crundall.[55] Nos. 9–41, July 15–22, 1825; James Crundall.[73]

Nos. 57–87 (odd) VASSALL ROAD   [156]

Formerly Nos. 4–19 (consec.) Clarendon Place

Nos. 57–73 form a plain three-storey terrace. Each house is two windows wide, and the ground-floor windows and doorways are round-headed; most of the latter have patterned fanlights. The whole range is unified by a first-floor sill-band. Nos. 75–87 are similar to the above, but the entrances of Nos. 77–87 are paired and protected by shallow hoods borne on consoles. September 1, 1823; James Crundall.[74]

Nos. 89–93 (odd) VASSALL ROAD   [157]

No. 89 is an unprepossessing two-storey house with semi-basement and an attic in a mansard roof. It is three windows wide and there is a projecting porch borne on columns. No. 91 is similar, but the semi-basement is faced with stucco. May 24, 1831; Benjamin Currey of Old Palace Yard.[75]

No. 93 also resembles No. 89, but the whole of the front is faced with stucco and the centrally-placed entrance has a pediment. April 23, 1828; Benjamin Currey.[76]

[158] Nos. 95–123 (odd) VASSALL ROAD

Formerly Nos. 1–5 (consec.) Kendal Place, and Nos. 1–10 (consec.) Winterslow Place

Nos. 95–103 and 105–113 form two plain four-storey terraces of which the end houses in each block project forward slightly. The ground storeys are faced with channelled stucco and contain recessed windows and doorways. The end houses have annexes containing the entrances, which are flanked by Greek Doric columns. Cast-iron balconies extend across the full width of the first floors of the end houses; on the intermediate houses they are separate. Nos. 115–123 are similar but only three storeys high. Nos. 95–103, March 1, 1824; John Gullett of Devon.[77] Nos. 105–111, January 1, 1824; John Williamson.[72] Nos. 113–123, January 1, 1824; John Adolphus Snee of Bartlett's Buildings, Holborn.[78]

[159] Nos. 125–133 (odd) VASSALL ROAD

No. 125, formerly No. 11 Winterslow Place, and No. 133, formerly No. 3 Vassall Road

Nos. 125 and 127 are a pair of three-storey houses with basements. Each house is two windows wide, the ground storey is faced with channelled stucco, and the fronts finished with a cornice and blocking course. The doorways, which have Greek Doric columns, are contained in two-storey annexes. A cast-iron balcony extends across the width of both houses at first-floor level, and there are iron railings enclosing the areas. No. 127 has a two-storey extension flanking the entrance annexe. Nos. 125 and 127, January 1, 1824; John Adolphus Snee.[78]

No. 129 is a two-storey villa with overhanging eaves and a slated roof. It is three windows wide and has a centrally placed porch supported on columns. There is a low two-storey annexe at one side. Nos. 131 and 133 are a pair of three storey houses with eaves and slated roofs. The first-floor windows of No. 131 have standard cast-iron window guards of anthemion and wave ornament; those of No. 133 were probably re-

moved when its shop front was built. May 9, 1823; Benjamin Tapley of London Road, Blackfriars.[79]

Nos. 48–52 AND 64–82 (even) VASSALL [160] ROAD

Formerly Nos. 22–24 (consec.) Devonshire Place, and Nos. 11–2 (consec.) Ampthill Place

Nos. 48–52 form a two-storey terrace with shop fronts. The latter are neatly detailed with swept ends to the fascias and there are projecting panels with aprons over the first-floor windows. August 30, 1824; James Crundall.[80]

Nos. 64–80 form a line of small two-storey detached houses with slated roofs. They are raised on high semi-basements and are only two windows wide; the entrances, which are at the side, are approached up narrow flights of stairs. The ground-floor windows have hoods borne on consoles and those on the upper floors are architrave-lined. May 25, 1831; Benjamin Currey.[81]

No. 82 is similar but is three windows wide and has a centrally placed entrance with a patterned fanlight. The ground floor windows are round headed and set in arched recesses. The first floor windows are taller than those of Nos. 64–80. November 16, 1826; the Hon. James Abercromby.[82]

Nos. 86, 88 AND 90, 98, 100–110, 114 [161] AND 116 (even) VASSALL ROAD

No. 86 is St. John's vicarage; the other houses were formerly Nos. 11 and 10, 6A, 6–1 (consec.) Langton Place, and 4 and 3 Union Place

No. 86 is a four-storey house with semi-basement. It is two windows wide with a two-storey annexe, and has a Greek Doric porch. The ground-floor windows flanking the porch have hooded architraves. The conspicuous return elevation overlooking the church of St. John the Divine has three windows on each floor; the centre ones are blind. September 1, 1824; the Hon. James Abercromby.[83]

Nos. 88 and 90 are a plain two-storey pair with semi-basements; No. 90 has an attic in a mansard roof. Each house is one window wide and the entrances are set in low two-storey wings. The ground- and first-floor windows are set in shallow round-headed recesses springing from little stone imposts. Both houses have patterned fanlights and ground-floor window guards. No. 98 is a two-storey villa with a slated roof. It is three windows wide, and the square-headed ground-floor windows are set in recessed round-headed arches. September 1, 1824; William Jennings of Dorset.[84]

Nos. 100–104 form a three-storey terrace with semi-basements, the fronts being finished with a cornice and blocking course. No. 102 has a mutilated Ionic porch, and the entrances to Nos. 100 and 104 are contained in recessed porches flanked by pilasters with vase heads. Nos. 106–110 are plain three-storey houses raised above semi-basements. Each house is two windows wide, and the entrances to the end houses are contained in two-storey annexes. All three houses have cast-iron railings to the stone entrance stairs. Nos. 100–106, June 21, 1824; John Woods of Vassall Road.[85] Nos. 108–110, September 1, 1824; William Jennings.[86]

Nos. 114 and 116 are a plain three-storey pair. Each house is two windows wide, and there are recessed rectangular panels above the third-floor windows. No. 114, December 6, 1830; Francis Scrimes of Pimlico.[87] The house was erected by George Gadsby. No. 116, December 6, 1830; George Gadsby of Grays Walk, Lambeth, carpenter.[88]

[162] Nos. 9–27 (odd) COWLEY ROAD
Formerly Nos. 1–10 (consec.), Cowley Road

Nos. 11–21 are two-storey stucco-fronted houses (Plate 48a). They form a terrace which has a front of considerable distinction, being in effect a continuous wall arcade. Each house has three elliptical-headed arches, the middle one containing the arched doorway and that on either side a ground- and first-floor window, the latter adorned with a cast-iron guard. Each house is separated from its neighbours by a narrow round-headed recess. The front of No. 9, which is similar though set back and narrower, and the fronts of Nos. 11–21 are uniformly finished with a delicate cornice and blocking course which is continued above the more orthodox fronts of Nos. 23–27. August 30, 1824; James Crundall.[80]

[163] Nos. 29–67 (odd) COWLEY ROAD
Formerly Nos. 1–20 (consec.) Cowley Place

These are rows of two-storey houses, the centre group being raised on a semi-basement. All are two windows wide and the wall face sets back for the entrances and to mark the party walls.

The doorways are framed by architraves and those in the lower houses have fluted quadrant pilasters. At first-floor level there is a sill-band and the fronts finish with a cornice and blocking course. There are variations in several of the houses. May 25, 1831; Benjamin Currey.[81]

Nos. 69–107 (odd) COWLEY ROAD   [164]
Nos. 89–107, formerly Nos. 1–10 (consec.) Cowley Terrace

No. 69 was built as a detached two-storeyed villa, three windows wide, with single-storeyed wings. It has a slated roof and the long ground-floor windows are in round-arched recesses with moulded imposts. October 30, 1830; George Henry Rickards of Vassall Road.[89]

Nos. 71–87 are undistinguished stock brick or stucco-faced houses of two storeys, mostly built in pairs. May 25, 1831; Mrs. Mary Currey, widow, of Charterhouse Square.[90]

Nos. 89–107 form a row of two-storeyed houses of the poorest type. May 26, 1831; Benjamin Currey.[91]

Nos. 4–16 (even), 22 AND 24 NORMANDY [165]
ROAD
Formerly Nos. 1–7 (consec.), 9 and 10 Addison Place

Nos. 4–14 are two-storeyed houses, built as a terrace, with the end houses set slightly forward and with recessions marking the party walls. Each house has a central square-headed doorway and round-arched ground-floor windows. The upper storey has two windows and a panel above the door. Part of the ground floor of No. 4 is used as a shop. No. 16 is a crudely elaborated stucco version of one of the above. Nos. 22 and 24 are very plain two-storeyed houses, with a brick cornice and parapet. No. 22 has a central round-headed doorway and one window on each side. No. 24 is two windows wide. August 30, 1824; James Crundall.[92]

Nos. 4–10 (consec.), 14 AND 15 MEL- [166]
BOURNE SQUARE

Nos. 4–10 and 14–15 are paired houses of two storeys on a semi-basement, linked by lower two-storeyed blocks set well back. Each house is two windows wide and has stucco dressings, the slate roof being partly hidden by a cornice and blocking course. No. 3, which paired No. 4, has been destroyed. Nos. 11 and 12 differ in having

no parapet and being each three windows wide.
May 26, 1831; Benjamin Currey.[91]

[167] Nos. 65–99 (odd) CAMBERWELL NEW ROAD

Formerly Nos. 3–20 (consec.) York Terrace

Nos. 65–77 are three-storey houses with semi-
basements; they have a sill-band at first-floor level,
and the round-headed doorways have fluted
quadrant reveals. Nos. 79–99 are plain three-
storey terrace houses with semi-basements, the
ground storeys being faced with channelled stucco.
Nos. 79, 81, 89, 91 and 99 are set forward
slightly, and all the houses have elliptical-headed
doorways and windows, the latter set in arched
recesses. Nos. 65–79, June 11, 1824; Jonathan
Hawkins of Albany Street, Albany Road, builder.[93] Nos. 81–99, August 8, 1825; Benjamin
Tapley. The latter houses were erected by John
Wise of Vassall Place.[94]

[168] Nos. 101–107 (odd) CAMBERWELL NEW
ROAD

Formerly Nos. 1–4 (consec.) Cambridge Place

These three-storey houses are raised on high
semi-basements; there is a sill-band at first-floor
level and the fronts finish with a cornice and
blocking course. Nos. 103 and 105 form a pair
and are linked to the flanking houses by two-
storey wings containing the double entrances.
Nos. 101 and 103 have heavy porticoes with
balustraded parapets, but those of Nos. 105 and
107 have been removed. All the windows are
square-headed except those on the ground floor
of Nos. 103 and 105 and those above the porticoes, where they are round-headed. December 14,
1825; Isaac Bates of Brixton.[95]

[169] Nos. 109–137 (odd) CAMBERWELL NEW
ROAD

Nos. 109–135, formerly Nos. 1–14 (consec.) Grosvenor
Place; No. 137, formerly No. 5 Surrey Place

Nos. 109–127 are similar to Nos. 101–107,
but they are grouped in pairs and their elliptical-
headed doorways have no porches. Some of the
doorways have patterned fanlights, and all the
ground floor windows are round-headed; those of
Nos. 121 and 123 have cast-iron guards. Nos. 129
and 131 were probably built as one plain two-
storey cottage, three windows wide, with a
centrally-placed doorway, overhanging eaves and
a slated roof. No. 133 is similar to Nos. 129 and
131, but has small single-storey wings and a porch

enclosed by cast-iron trelliswork. No. 135, Grosvenor Lodge, is another two-storey house, three
windows wide and flanked by low two-storey
wings. There is a sill-band at first-floor level and
the front was originally finished with a cornice,
now removed. The centrally placed entrance has
a coarse stucco surround and a semi-circular fanlight, and the round-headed ground-floor windows
are set in arched recesses. No. 137 is a two-storey
stucco-fronted house surmounted by a pediment.
At ground-floor level there is one window and a
segmental-headed doorway with a patterned fanlight and fluted quadrant reveals. On the first
floor there are three windows and a sill-band; all
the openings have architraves. August 14, 1823;
John Shelton of Gravel Lane, Southwark.[96]

Nos. 62–76 (even) CAMBERWELL NEW [170]
ROAD

Nos. 64–76, formerly Nos. 1–7 (consec.) Olive Place or
Olive Terrace

Nos. 64–76 are formally grouped three-storey
houses with semi-basements. The end and centre
houses, which have band courses at second-floor
level, are set forward slightly, and the blocking
course above the cornice of these houses is inflected
and contains the inscription "OLIVE TER-
RACE 1825". The ground storey of the terrace
is faced with channelled stucco, and all the first-
floor windows have anthemion-ornamented
guards. Nearly all the entrances have patterned
fanlights and retain their original fret-ornamented
doors. No. 62 abuts No. 64 and has an identical
cornice and blocking course. There is a shop
front on the ground floor. No. 62, May 7, 1825;
Nos. 64–70, August 30, 1824; Nos. 72–76,
June 16, 1825; Edward Kilsby of Nine Elms,
ship breaker.[97]

Nos. 78–100 (even) CAMBERWELL NEW [171]
ROAD

Formerly Nos. 1–12 (consec.) Orchard Place

Nos. 78–82 form a two-storey terrace with a
rendered semi-basement and attics in a slated
mansard roof. Each house has a cornice and
blocking course and is three windows wide, No. 80
being brought forward slightly. The ground-floor
windows and doorways are round-headed, and the
latter have patterned fanlights. No. 82 contains
a blank arched recess on the ground floor and the
doorway is contained in a slightly recessed additional bay of the same height. Nos. 84–90 are

similar but paired. Each pair is flanked by lower wings of two storeys. These wings are recessed and contain the doorways, which have patterned fanlights and fluted quadrant reveals. Nos. 92 and 94 are a pair of two-storey villas raised on high stuccoed semi-basements and with overhanging eaves. Each house is three windows wide, the outer one contained in a set-back with the doorway below. The doorways are segmental-headed with panelled pilasters and patterned fanlights. All the windows are round-headed, those on the ground floor being set in arched recesses. No. 96, Russet Lodge, is a two-storey villa three windows wide with a centrally placed doorway. The latter has a round-headed fanlight and a key-ornamented door frame, and there is a projecting Greek Doric porch. The ground-floor windows, which are also round-headed, are set in arched recesses and there is a sill-band at first-floor level. Nos. 98 and 100 are a pair of two-storey houses with semi-basements and finished with a cornice and blocking course. Each house is two windows wide and the doorways are set in much altered annexes. The ground-floor windows and the doorways are round-headed, and the latter have slender Greek Doric columns. May 9, 1823; Benjamin Tapley.[79]

[172] Nos. 102–114 (even) CAMBERWELL NEW ROAD

Nos. 102–112, formerly Nos. 1–6 (consec.) Holland Place

Nos. 102 and 104 formed a pair similar to Nos. 98 and 100; No. 104 has been demolished. Nos. 106–112 are also paired two-storey houses with semi-basements. Each house is three windows wide, the outer one contained in a set-back with the doorway beneath. The doorways are round-headed and Nos. 108 and 110 have patterned fanlights. The ground-floor windows have cast-iron anthemion-ornamented guards. No. 114 is a three-storey house, its front finished with a cornice and blocking course. It is two windows wide and there is a two-storey wing containing the doorway. The window above the doorway and those on the ground floor are round-headed, the latter being set in arched recesses. There is a small cast-iron porch with a tented roof. August 14, 1823; Thomas Gibbons of Belvidere Place, Southwark.[98]

Nos. 116–142 (even) CAMBERWELL NEW [173] ROAD

Nos. 122–142, formerly Nos. 11–1 (consec.) Bath Terrace

No. 116 is a three-storey stucco-fronted house with a slate roof. There is a two-storey annexe containing the segmental-headed doorway which has fluted quadrant reveals. Nos. 118 and 120 are a pair of two-storey cottages with overhanging eaves and slated roofs. Each house is two windows wide, the outer one contained in a set-back, with the doorway below. The ground-floor windows and the doorways are round-headed and set in arched recesses. Nos. 122–142 form a long two-storey terrace with semi-basements. The end houses are set forward and the two centre houses have an extra storey with a mansard roof. The ground storey is faced with rusticated stucco and the entrances, most of which have patterned fanlights, are flanked by fluted pilasters. The ground-floor windows are set in arched recesses with panels beneath. Some of the areas are enclosed by good cast-iron railings. The front gardens are bounded by square stuccoed piers with flat pedimented stone cappings. May 9, 1823; Benjamin Tapley.[79]

Nos. 289–299 (odd) COLDHARBOUR LANE [174]

These are three pairs of two-storeyed stock brick "Gothic" houses with stuccoed fronts and slated roofs containing attics. Nos. 289 and 291, and Nos. 297 and 299, are identical pairs with shallow gabled projections, small bay windows and a central chimney stack corbelled out from the wall face. The imaginatively arranged entrances are at the side and all the openings have label mouldings, those on the ground floor with well-modelled stops in the form of male and female heads, while there is a single enriched corbel to each window-sill. Nos. 293 and 295 share three Dutch gables and have oriel windows on the first floor. January 29–31, 1844; George Sturge of Kent Road. The houses were erected by Charles Wyatt of Walcot Place, Kennington Road, builder.[99]

Nos. 12–50 (even) SUSSEX ROAD [175]

Formerly Nos. 1–20 (consec.) Sussex Road

Sussex Road, lying west of, and parallel with the north–south branch of Loughborough Park, has on its west side a terrace composition containing twenty cottages of early 19th century date, built of stock brick and without ornament, but presenting a remarkable example of monumental design applied to housing of the most humble description. Each cottage is uniformly two storeys high and two windows wide, but the middle pair are set slightly forward and crowned with a triangular pediment, while the first and fourth house at each end of the terrace is similarly accented with a smaller pediment. Standing in their well-kept front gardens, these utilitarian cottages present a picture of undeniable charm. January 25, 1825; the Hon. James Abercromby. These were let by Randall Gossip[100] (see page 109).

[176] LOUGHBOROUGH PARK

The layout of Loughborough Park appears to date from about 1844 when Lady Holland began to grant building leases of one or two plots in the road.[101] In 1846 Benjamin Currey (see page 109n.), in association with William A. Loch, a conveyance and equity draughtsman,[102] granted some more leases with the consent of the estate trustee. Thereafter leases were granted by Loch with the consent of the trustee up to 1857.[103] In view of his father's connection with the estate, and his own connection with the development of the estate north of Coldharbour Lane, it is possible that Henry Currey designed Loughborough Park. Most of the houses were erected by Edwin Heritage of Loughborough Park, builder. Loughborough Park is an attractive and well-planned development consisting of single and paired houses with spacious front gardens lining a wide roadway that leads south from Coldharbour Lane, each side then expanding in a convex sweep to meet another similar roadway running from the south-west to the north-east. There is an enclosed garden in the triangle thus formed.

The houses on the east side of the first branch are generally detached, two storeys high over semi-basements, and with stucco-faced fronts of simple Italianate design, three windows wide and with a central porch. Those on the west side are mostly built in pairs, two storeys high and two windows wide, with fronts of grey brick dressed with stucco, generally with Regency Greek detail. The most striking houses are the two pairs on the south-east side of the second branch, Nos. 89–91 and 93–95. Their combined fronts are faced with stucco and treated to form a balanced composition, each house being defined by giant Doric pilasters supporting a simple entablature.

This frame contains a ground-floor window of three lights, dressed with an architrave, plain frieze and triangular pediment on consoles, over which is a single unadorned first-floor window. The recessed portion of the front contains the doorway, framed by pilasters and a simple entablature, with an arch-headed window above. The low-pitched slate roof has a wide overhang. Nos. 89–95, formerly Warburton Villas, December 31, 1846; Benjamin Bates Cowell of Old Kent Road, coal meter (sic).[104]

CHRIST CHURCH, BRIXTON ROAD   [177]

In 1823 the Rev. Dr. John Styles obtained a sub-lease from Lord Holland of a piece of land on the west side of Brixton Road on which he had recently erected Holland Chapel.[105] At first the chapel was used for Independent worship, but about 1836 Dr. Styles and part of the congregation seceded and moved to a new chapel in Claylands Road[106] (see page 61). In the 1840s Brayley described Holland Chapel as "a neat stuccoed edifice, with a bell-turret over the central part" and said that it had been a proprietary Episcopal chapel for some years.[107]

Owing to the efforts of the Rev. J. McC. Hussey, who purchased the leasehold interest in 1854, the chapel became vested in the Church Building Commissioners, and was consecrated in 1855 and renamed "Christ Church". Hussey gave the leasehold interest to the Commissioners and enlarged the chapel out of his own private funds. He also acquired the advowson and presented himself to be the first vicar; he held the living until his death in 1891. During the incumbency of the next vicar, W. R. Mowll, the chapel proved inadequate for the increased congregation. A printed appeal for funds reported that "The congregations attending the Church, more particularly on Sunday evenings, are immense; . . . The building has been packed from floor to roof; and . . . the adjoining Church Room has also been filled with eager listeners." Plans for a new church to accommodate 1,200 persons were provided by Professor Beresford Pite but were not finally approved until January, 1900. Meanwhile two houses at the rear of the church in Chapel (now Mowll) Street were purchased for the erection of a hall (also designed by Pite) which was to accommodate the congregation during the rebuilding of the church. The foundation stone of the new hall was laid on July 24, 1897, and the building was completed in 1899. The foundation stone of the new church was laid on December 13, 1898, by Princess Christian, and the old church was demolished in the following year. The house adjoining the old church in Brixton Road (No. 96) was also pulled down and the land on which it stood was incorporated in the site of the new building. At the same time a six-foot strip of land was given up for the widening of Chapel Street.[105] The church was built by Alfred A. Webber of Mortimer Street, St. Marylebone, at a cost of about £17,000[108] and was consecrated by the Bishop of Rochester on December 5, 1902.[109] The outside pulpit at the south-west corner was designed by Weir, Burrows and Weir and was erected without reference to Pite;[110] it was dedicated on November 3, 1907 (Plate 17, fig. 35).

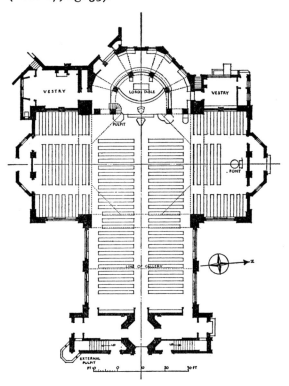

Fig. 35. Christ Church, Brixton Road, plan

The church is designed in an eclectic style with Byzantine motifs predominating, and has a cruciform plan. It is built of yellow stock bricks banded by courses of Berkhamsted purple bricks and has window arches of red brick. Stone dressings are used extensively on the Brixton Road front. At the centre of this front rises a dome-capped octagonal tower of unusual appearance, flanked by lower square towers. The crossing is roofed by a dome with a small louvred lantern, carried above an octagonal brick drum. The plainness of the exterior is relieved by diverse arrangements of round-headed recesses and windows. The sanctuary is at the west end in an apsidal chancel surrounded by an ambulatory. The altar which stands below a semi-domed ceiling borne by eight Byzantine columns, is unusually arranged, with the communion rail completely surrounding the Lord's Table. The lectern is set directly in front of the altar and flanked by the pulpit and reading desk. The bold plain vaulting at the crossing and the wall surfaces are plastered, the walls being relieved by interlinking arches and arcading on different planes. The north transept contains the font which is of well figured polished green marble and has a large round bowl. The organ gallery is over the east end. The floor of the church slopes towards the altar. The hall at the rear of the church, built of yellow stock brick, has a bold round-arched north window divided by vertical buttresses in a manner characteristic of the church windows. The fabric was damaged during air-raids in the war of 1939–45 but was restored in 1954. Several uses in this church recall its origin as a place of Independent worship. Communicants kneel all round the communion rail and the officiating minister wears a black preaching gown with Geneva bands for preaching his sermon. The lectern has a reversible top and the Bible is always presented to the congregation before the lessons are read.

CHURCH OF ST. JOHN THE DIVINE, VASSALL ROAD [178]

In the 1860s the south-east portion of the parish of St. Mark's, Kennington, which until then had consisted of strawberry beds, market gardens and exhausted brick fields, became the scene of widespread building. In 1866 a district mission was established under the Rev. D. T. W. Elsdale in a school in Bolton Street (now Crescent).[111] In 1867–8 a building was erected to the designs of C. A. Gould[112] on the corner of Elliott Road and Frederick Crescent; a lower room served as a temporary church and an upper room was used for a school.[111] The present site of St. John's Church was obtained from the Ecclesiastical Commissioners, in whom the Lam-

Fig. 36. St. John the Divine, pencil sketch drawn by G. E. Street to explain his plans

beth Wick Estate was then vested, in 1871; George Edmund Street (1824–81) was commissioned to design the church and his plans were approved in 1872[112] (Plates 18, 19, fig. 36). It was originally intended to complete the east end of the church first, and then to make do with a temporary iron nave until funds were available to complete the building.[113] The foundation stone was laid by Samuel Wilberforce, Bishop of Winchester, on July 4, 1871, and the chancel, vestries, organ chamber and chapel were completed by September, 1873. Consecration was delayed, however, as an anonymous gift of £10,000 made the building of the nave possible and the church was eventually consecrated on November 14, 1874, by Bishop Harold Browne who had suc-

ceeded Wilberforce at Winchester.[114] The tower and spire were built in 1888 to Street's original design and dedicated on May 4, 1889.[115] The church was built of specially manufactured red brick with Bath stone dressings[116] and according to Elsdale was "glaringly pink and white at its birth".[113] The graceful iron grilles in the chancel and baptistery, which were designed by Street, the clock, and the peal of eight bells (cast by Messrs. Mears and Stainbank, Whitechapel) were all added shortly after the dedication of the tower and spire in 1889.[117] G. F. Bodley was responsible for work carried out between 1890 and 1892 when the nave roof was painted, the chancel elaborately decorated and a wooden reredos added. The latter, depicting the Annunciation and the

Crucifixion, was carved by Messrs. Brindley and Farmer.[118] The stained glass included work by Clayton and Bell, C. E. Kempe, Burlison and Grylls and Herbert Bryans. There were also three memorials to past vicars. The font cover in the baptistery was given in 1923 by the nieces of the Rev. D. T. W. Elsdale (vicar 1866–81); in 1913 a bronze bas-relief on a marble ground in memory of Canon C. E. Brooke (vicar 1881–1911) was erected on the north wall of the Sanctuary; the Deedes Memorial Chapel, commemorating the incumbency of Canon A. C. Deedes from 1911 to 1916, was completed in 1920 to the design of Sir Charles Nicholson.[118]

The church was heavily damaged by enemy action during the war of 1939–45. Restoration was started in 1955 under the superintendence of Mr. H. S. Goodhart-Rendel.

The Church of St. John the Divine is an outstanding masterpiece of the Gothic revival, a remarkable example of its architect's genius for deriving inspiration from the Gothic churches of Italy and Spain, as well as France and England, yet producing a building that is completely homogeneous and highly personal to its author, fully expressive of the time and circumstances of its creation.

The church contains an apse-ended chancel, flanked on the south by a chapel, and on the north by cloisters with vestries and the organ chamber. The wide hall-nave is flanked by aisles, that on the south opening to the baptistery at its west end, that on the north side having a corresponding porch. At the west end of the nave is the great steeple, containing the vestibule and belfry.

The brick-vaulted vestibule opens through a high arch to the finely proportioned nave, some 110 feet long and 24 feet wide. The first bay is narrow and aisleless, each side wall containing a tall window of two lights. Then follow arcades that open to the aisles, 13 feet wide, and have four wide bays and one narrow, the last canted inwards to meet the chancel arch. The moulded two-centred arches rise from shafted piers with rich foliage capitals, only the single shaft on the front face rising unbroken to the level of the arch-crowns to support the transverse ribs of the pointed vault of wood. This rests on the corbelled and crested wallplates above the brick spandrels, and over its surface decorative ribs trace a pattern of groining. The transition from the wide and lofty nave to the smaller-scaled chancel is beauti-

fully contrived, the wood ceiling following the inward splay of the last bay and then returning with a groined intersection to form a lunette over the chancel arch, which is a larger and more splendid version of those forming the nave arcades. The chancel, measuring some 46 feet in length by 24 feet in width, has one wide and two narrow bays, the former arcaded, and terminates in a three-sided apse, the whole being ceiled with a simple groined vault of brick with moulded stone ribs and carved bosses. The south chapel and the cloisters are similarly vaulted. There is no clerestory, but each aisle wall contains a range of finely traceried windows, two to each wide bay and one to the narrow. All are divided into three lights, their heads being filled with different patterns of Decorated tracery. The windows of the eastern apse are of two lights with foliated heads beneath a cinquefoil. From the westernmost bay of the south aisle projects the semicircular apse of the baptistery, lit by three trefoil-headed windows and ceiled with a groined brick vault. The circular space is completed by a wrought-iron grille projecting into the aisle.

The elements composing the plan are perfectly expressed in the elevations and general grouping of the exterior, which is dominated by the western steeple, rising to a total height of 212 feet. The tower consists of two lofty stages, the first corresponding in height with the nave roof ridge. This stage has flat gable-terminated buttresses on each exposed face, on the west flanking the great doorway, and on the north and south a tall window with two tiers of two lights and a Geometrical traceried head. Against the north side is a circular stair turret, its conical cap rising into the upper stage of the tower where each face has two tall two-light louvred windows in an arcaded and gabled setting. The brick face is then corbelled out to receive the tall broach spire of stone, which is finely adorned with three rings of gabled dormers, diminishing in scale towards the capstone.

The north and south elevations are generally similar, the main interest being provided by the aisle wall where the main bay divisions are marked by massive buttresses surmounted by niched and crocketed pinnacles, while the buttresses marking the secondary divisions rise only to the window-arch springing level, all having weathered offsets. Between the pinnacles runs a stone parapet that is adorned with various Geometrical patterns, such as blind arcades, quatrefoils and cinquefoils. Behind the parapet the lean-to roof of the aisle extends to meet the plain parapet of the nave wall, above which rises the immense roof of the nave, its slated expanse broken only by a range of minute dormers. The gabled wall of the chancel arch carries a gabled bellcote flanked by crocketed pinnacles. The buttresses of the eastern apse again rise only to the springing level of the window arches, and the chancel roof rests on brick corbelling. The vestries on the north side have a lean-to roof, while that to the south chapel is gabled.

[179] CHRIST CHURCH C.E. PRIMARY SCHOOL, CANCELL ROAD

The site of this National Society school formed part of Lambeth Wick Estate and in 1860 was freely granted by the Archbishop of Canterbury, Lord John Russell and the Duke of Devonshire to the minister and chapelwardens of the district chapelry of Christ Church, Brixton Road. In 1864 a small piece of this land was sold to the Governors of Queen Anne's Bounty as a site for a parsonage house.[119] The school buildings were erected in 1860 by Henry Currey, architect. The infants' school was designed in 1876 but was rebuilt in 1904; the original building was remodelled in 1909. The school is in two single-storey brick buildings with slate roofs. It was damaged by enemy action in the war of 1939–45.[120]

[180] KENNINGTON SECONDARY SCHOOL, HACKFORD ROAD

This school occupies a plain three-storey brick building which was built for the London School Board by H. Hart of Southwark, whose tender for a school for 996 children was for £10,249.[121] The architect was T. J. Bailey[122] and the date of opening was May 9, 1887.[123] The south wing was added in 1894.[122]

[181] DURAND PRIMARY SCHOOL, DURAND GARDENS

This building adjoins Kennington Secondary School and was erected for the London School Board in 1888 as a Pupil Teachers' School. The contractor was H. Hart of Southwark, whose tender was for £6,230.[124] The architect was T. J. Bailey.[122] The building was later used as a secondary school for girls, and a second floor was added in 1906, Bailey being the architect.[122]

The south wing was damaged in the war of 1939–45 and has since been rebuilt under the supervision of Mr. Richard Nickson.

STUART SECONDARY SCHOOL, SUSSEX ROAD [182]

This school was built for the London School Board and included a Cookery Centre and a Manual Training Centre. The contractors were J. T. Chappel of Pimlico, whose tender for a school for 798 children was for £15,811;[125] owing to a breach of contract the work was completed by W. Downs of Walworth.[126] The architect was T. J. Bailey,[122] and the date of opening April 9, 1894.[123] The school comprises an irregularly arranged group of three- and four-storey stock brick buildings.

THE JACKSON ESTATE

In 1804 Robert Slade, proctor-at-law, and Randle Jackson, barrister-at-law and an expert on Indian affairs,[127] were admitted tenants to 23 acres of copyhold land near the Washway on the west side of Brixton Road.[128] They partitioned the estate in 1806, Jackson taking the northern half (fig. 37) and Slade the southern.[129]

NOS. 186–192; 194, 196, 198–204; 206, [183] 208–220 (even) BRIXTON ROAD

Formerly Nos. 1–4 (consec.) Grove Place; Grove House, Elm House, Nos. 4–1 (consec.) Fir Grove Place; Fir Grove House, Nos. 7–13 (consec.) Grove Place

Although Jackson immediately obtained licence to demise his land for building purposes, only a few houses were erected before his death in 1837; these are illustrated in a water-colour, dated 1820, reproduced on Plate 47a. This shows the layout of the Brixton Road frontage as originally intended, with two terraces of six houses each, flanked by two pairs of houses at the north and south ends, all three storeys high with attics. The northerly terrace was not built until a few years after 1837,[130] when Nos. 194–204 were erected; their design differs considerably from that shown in the water-colour. Two piers incised "Grove House" and "Elm House" respectively, still stand in front of these houses, the latter retaining its anthemion finial (not shown on Plate 47a). The two pairs of houses flanking the southerly terrace were pulled down about 1928 to make room for a three-storey row of shops.[131] The rest of the houses illustrated still stand. Nos. 186–192 are

Fig. 37. Jackson estate and neighbourhood, lay-out plan

linked by their coach-houses and each has a segmental bay projection at the rear. Their attractive verandahs have long since been removed, but they retain delicate lattice guards to the first-floor windows. The southerly terrace comprises Nos. 208–218 (Plate 47b), but two houses were added, one at each end, i.e. No. 206 and No. 220. Together they form a plain undistinguished terrace with unhappily designed Greek Doric porches to the entrances and light bowed cast-iron window guards of lozenge pattern on the first floor. A shop has been built across the front garden of No. 220. No. 206, erected by Randle

Jackson for his own occupation,[132] is built on the same line as the rest of the terrace but on the north side there is a projecting wing with rounded corners. The entrance is on the north side of the wing and is relieved above and on its flanking pilasters by key ornament. The house has been divided and is now numbered 206 and 206A. The pier illustrated on the extreme right of the water-colour marked the boundary between the Jackson and Lambeth Wick estates; it is still standing. Nos. 186, 188 and Nos. 208–214 were let on lease to various tenants between 1810 and 1831.[132] Robert Pledge and Skinner Chart were connected with the erection of Nos. 208 and 210, so the whole terrace may have been built by the firm of Pledge, Chart and Mason which had the contract for building St. Mark's school, Harleyford Road (see page 26).

[184] Nos. 2–8, 12–34 (even); 15, 17–29 (odd), 31, 33, 37, 39 LORN ROAD

   Formerly Nos. 1–4 (consec.) Swiss Cottages, 32–43 (consec.) Lorn Road; Nos. 19, 9–15 (consec.), 11A, 10, 9A, 8 Lorn Road

The land at the back of the houses in Brixton Road was used as pleasure ground and garden to the house called Fir Grove. In 1835 Jackson was granted licence to demise this land on building leases for 99 years, but in 1837 when James P. Macdougall was admitted as trustee of the property on Jackson's death it was still undeveloped.[133] Macdougall was granted licence to make roads, i.e. Lorn Road and Groveway, to pull down the greenhouse, stables, and out-buildings which stood on the land, and to cut down trees. Groveway and Lorn Road were laid out about 1840,[134] Lorn Road forming an approach road to St. Michael's Church from Brixton Road. Most of the houses in Lorn Road are of the *cottages ornés* type (Plate 56).

Nos. 15, 25, 27 and 29 are the survivors of four pairs of houses (Nos. 17–23 were destroyed in the war of 1939–45) which were built by William Ball Docter of Cowley Road about 1843.[135] They are two-storeyed stock brick villas, with rendered semi-basements, and attics in the slated roofs. The main windows are architraved but surmounted by Gothic cresting on the ground floor, which also appears, inverted, below the main cornice and in the frieze of the linked Classical entrances. The angular-headed attic windows are set in hipped and barge-boarded gables. Nos. 31, 33, 37 and 39 are two pairs not unlike the last but with no Classical features. The gables are very steeply pitched, with finials, the central parapet is battlemented and the windows have either label mouldings or arched heads. The porches are buttressed and pinnacled and have sharply pointed arches. Nos. 2–8 are two pairs similar to Nos. 25–29 but with no basements or attics and with shallow pitched gables, those to Nos. 2 and 4 being hipped. Nos. 6 and 8 have a very high central parapet and the linked entrances are topped with small obelisks. All four houses have been altered.

Nos. 12–34 are well designed pairs of stock brick houses, three storeys high on semi-basements and with two-storeyed wings containing the entrances. The latter are ornamented with incised fret patterns and with wreaths in the frieze. The detail generally is Greek and very restrained.

All these houses were erected shortly after the street was formed.

GROVEWAY   [185]
   Formerly Grove Road

The houses in Groveway vary considerably but with some exceptions they are built of stock brick, two or three storeys high above a semi-basement and either singly or in pairs. They all have architraved windows, many have rendered and coursed ground floors, and parapets and eaves appear in equal numbers. Several houses have the flank walls brought forward to form antae, an idea which, like the treatment of Nos. 40 and 42 with open pediments containing lunette windows, can be seen in Stockwell Park Road and Crescent. No. 16 is exceptional in having a pilastered front and Ionic portico. Other entrances have incised frets or wreaths in the frieze while several larger houses have free-standing Roman Doric porticos.

Nos. 33–41 (odd) STOCKWELL PARK ROAD [186]
   Formerly Nos. 25–33 (odd) Stockwell Park Road

In 1832 Randle Jackson added a piece of freehold land, part of Stockwell Manor, to his copyhold estate;[135] it is now covered by these houses. No. 33 is a rather dull two-storey villa with a semi-basement. It is fronted with grey brick and has a recessed porch flanked by pilasters with wreaths in the frieze above. Nos. 35–39 form a symmetrical yellow brick terrace with an extra storey. The porches are like that of No. 33 except that the pilasters are coupled at the end houses. No. 41 is of the same height as No. 33. It is stuccoed on two sides and has a Greek Doric recessed porch wedged against a semi-circular bay at the south-west corner. The house is pedimented on the Groveway elevation and the composition is unified by a scroll-ornamented band at first-floor level.

THE SLADE ESTATE

Robert Slade's part of the 23 acres which he divided with Randle Jackson is now covered by Ingleton, Halstead, and Thornton Streets and

Ingleborough Road, named after places in Yorkshire where the family also owned property. Slade let part if not all of this piece of copyhold in 1808 to Simon Vowell, who erected a row of houses fronting Brixton Road called Loughborough Place.[136] In 1805 Slade purchased another copyhold estate consisting of seven acres on the east side of Brixton Road between the present Burton and Loughborough Roads, from William Brown Angell.[137] This land had previously been part of John Scaldwell's estate (see page 127). The White Horse public house on the corner of Loughborough Road and Brixton Road stands on the site of an older building of the same name first mentioned in 1786.[138] Robert Slade's youngest son Felix inherited the property after his brother William's death in 1858. Although both his father and brother were distinguished for their public service in Lambeth, Felix Slade is better known for the professorial chairs which he endowed at Oxford and Cambridge, and for the School of Art which he founded at University College, London.[32]

[187] St. Michael's C.E. Primary School, Halstead Street

This school was probably founded shortly after the completion of St. Michael's Church in 1841.[139] The one-storey building, which is of brick with a low-pitched slate roof, was considerably altered in 1892, when Elphicke and Howell were the architects.[140]

[188] St. Helen's Roman Catholic Church, Robsart Street

This church was probably designed by F. W. Tasker and was opened in 1905.[141] It was extended in 1938 by the building of a Lady Chapel on the west side of the nave. The architect for this extension was J. O'Hanlon Hughes.[142] The congregation moved to the disused Independent Church in Brixton Road (see page 130) in 1953 and St. Helen's is now (1955) being converted for use as an annexe to Corpus Christi Primary School. It is a plain stock brick gabled building with slated roofs, and lean-to entrance lobbies across the whole street frontage. There is a large circular window above the lobbies, and the gable is surmounted by a cross.

MASTICKS AND THE FOURTEEN ACRES

These lands comprised the northernmost part of John Scaldwell's copyhold estate (see below). Masticks was bounded by the northern parcel of Lambeth Wick Manor on the north and west, the Manor of Milkwell on the east and the fourteen acres on the south. Together with the half of the fourteen acres on which Mostyn Road now stands Masticks was inherited by Scaldwell's grandson Thomas Fox,[143] who sold the property in 1735 to James Wall.[144] At the beginning of the 19th century all these lands comprised the Washway Farm, in the occupation of Robert Martin; they were then part of the Thurlow estate.

Mostyn Road Methodist Church   [189]

The foundation stones of this building (Plate 27a) were laid on June 23, 1868. The architect was John Tarring, and the builders George Myers and Sons.[145] The church is designed in the Decorated Gothic style and faced with Kentish ragstone. At the north-west corner there is a tower surmounted by an octagonal spire. The church was heavily damaged in the war of 1939–45, and was restored in 1954–5.

THE ANGELL ESTATE

The Angell family has owned land in Lambeth since the latter part of the 17th century. An estate at Crowhurst in Surrey, which had been purchased earlier in the century by William Angell, formed the nucleus of the family's property.[146] One of William Angell's grandsons, Justinian Angell, married Elizabeth Scaldwell,[147] daughter of John Scaldwell, junior, who owned extensive lands in Lambeth, including Heathrow Manor, freehold and copyhold in Lambeth Manor and leasehold land in Stockwell Manor. By his will,[148] which was proved in 1679, John Scaldwell left almost all his lands to his wife for life, and upon her death they were to be divided between his two grandsons, Thomas Fox and John Angell. It seems likely that some family arrangement was made after Scaldwell's death in 1679, for part of the property which he left to Thomas Fox came into the hands of John Angell.[149]

Thomas Fox inherited a copyhold estate in Lambeth Manor called Masticks and half of fourteen acres (see above) and the farm of Heathrow, in which his grandfather lived (see page 136). A piece of freehold land on the south side of Cold-harbour Lane marked on the Inclosure map of 1810 as being held by William Brown Angell, and which was still part of the Angell estate in 1916,[150] may originally have been part of Heathrow Farm.

In Lambeth Manor John Scaldwell's other grandson, John Angell, inherited three acres of freehold land called Water Leys or Burdin Bushes[151] and a copyhold estate consisting of a farm called Mallams,[152] later called Stiles Farm,[153] containing about fifty acres, the other half of the fourteen acres,[154] and three acres called Pound Close;[155] all this property lay on the east side of Brixton Road. On the west side of Brixton Road he inherited ten acres.[154] He also held two leasehold estates in Stockwell Manor.[156]

John Angell died in 1750.[157] Eight years later his copyhold estate in Lambeth was seized by the Lord of the Manor because his heir had failed to claim it.[158] In fact it had been settled by John Angell on his son William in 1733,[159] but William had pre-deceased his father.[157] In 1764

William's brother, John Angell, junior, was admitted to the estate by special grace and favour of the Lord of the Manor,[160] though no doubt he had enjoyed possession of the lands in the meantime. The eccentricities of this John Angell achieved considerable notoriety. Samuel Denne published his will in full and commented that he was "marked by the legislature for a person inflexibly obstinate", and had "by a self-drawn will, perpetuated the name of Angell in Westminster-Hall, and in the records of assise for the counties in which he had possessed estates".[161] Moreover, "The propensity of Mr. Angell to litigations at law, and his disposition to perpetuate them after his decease, appear from the clauses of his will that enjoin large sums of money to be reserved out of his estates, and appropriated to that use", and from "his random devise of his estates to the heirs male (if any there be) of his remote ancestors".[162]

As was to be expected several law suits began after the death of John Angell, junior, in 1784,[162] and again the copyhold estate was seized by the Lord.[163] In 1786 Benedict John Angell Brown

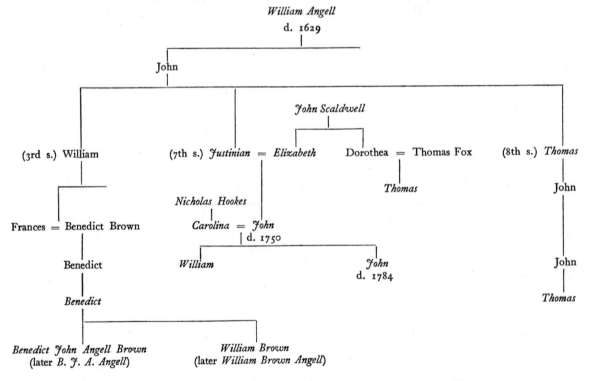

Fig. 38. Abridged pedigree of the Angell, Scaldwell and Brown families.
The names in italics are mentioned in the text

was admitted to the estate,[153] but in 1790 an entry in the court rolls proclaimed that this admittance was a mistake and that by the custom of the Manor, William Brown, Benedict's brother, was the rightful heir, being the youngest son of Benedict Brown, who had been John Angell's heir.[164] Both William and Benedict adopted the name of Angell (which had been stipulated by John Angell in his will)[165] and were subsequently known as William Brown Angell and Benedict John Angell Angell.

At the beginning of the 19th century the copyhold estate was reduced by two sales. In 1803 the ten acres on the west side of Brixton Road and the three acres called Pound Close on the corner of Coldharbour Lane and Effra Road were sold to Thomas Woodroffe Smith,[166] and in 1805 seven acres, consisting of half the fourteen acres on the east side of Brixton Road, were sold to Robert Slade[137] (see page 125). The rest of the copyhold estate was surrendered by William Brown Angell to his brother Benedict in 1823 in exchange for an annuity.[167]

Stiles Farm had been let by John Angell, junior, to William Westcombe in 1776 for 61 years;[168] in 1810 the area was still undeveloped and included a gravel pit and tenter ground.[169] Benedict John Angell Angell's title to Stiles Farm was challenged in 1827 in Lambeth Manor court by Thomas Angell as the youngest lineal descendant of Justinian Angell's younger brother Thomas.[170] As Justinian had never had a title to the property except in right of his wife, the claim was based on a false premise; even so, the court took a year to decide the issue, but finally awarded judgement to Benedict.[171]

Extensive development on this estate did not take place till the middle of the 19th century, but a few earlier houses still stand.

[190] Nos. 285, 287 and 299–313 (odd) Brixton Road

Nos. 285 and 287, formerly Effra Lodge and Westbourne Cottage; Nos. 309–313, formerly Nos. 1–3 (consec.) Brixton Ville

In 1631 three acres of land, lying on the east side of Brixton Road and called Water Leys or Burdin Bushes, were purchased by Edmond Dent.[172] The land passed into the hands of John Scaldwell in 1675[173] and after his death became part of the Angell estate.[151] William Westcombe, who had a lease of Stiles Farm which

adjoined it on the north, east and south, apparently purchased Water Leys from the Angell family. Unfortunately no records relating to the building of the houses on this estate have survived.

Nos. 285 and 287 are shown on the Inclosure map of 1810, and probably date from about this time. They form a pair of single-storey stucco-fronted cottages which have slate roofs with deep overhanging eaves. There is a trace of Gothic influence in the pointed heads of their windows.

No. 299 Brixton Road can be traced back in the rate books beyond the date when the architectural evidence suggests it was erected. As the house was occupied from 1815 to 1830 by Evan Roberts,[174] a slate-merchant who erected several houses in Brixton, it may have been rebuilt by Roberts on the site of an older house. It is a rather uninteresting stucco-fronted villa of two storeys, with an attic in a slated mansard roof. Attached to the north side is a taller three-storey wing and on the south side is a former coach-house. The middle part is three windows wide with a central entrance, and the upper and lower windows are set in round-headed recesses, the upper tier being underlined by a continuous sill-band. The middle part and the north wing are finished with a cornice and blocking course.

Nos. 301–307 appear to have been erected between 1816 and 1830.[174] No. 301, a compact stock brick villa of two-storeys with a semi-basement, is three windows wide with its entrance at the centre. The entrance has a flat wooden doorcase, with key-ornamented pilasters supporting a plain frieze and cornice. No. 303, of the same height and materials, has its entrance in a later side wing protected by a small valanced tent-roofed porch. This is supported on ornamental cast-iron standards. No. 305, another villa of the same height and materials, has an uninteresting central porch borne on square piers. The canted two-storey bay extension on the south side is a later addition. No. 307 has been altered almost beyond recognition.

Nos. 309–313 appear to have been erected in 1801–2, though No. 311 was unoccupied until 1810.[174] They (Plate 51a, fig. 39) are set at an oblique angle to Brixton Road and have a slightly curved front. They may form the southern section of a crescent-shaped layout which was not completed. They are a stock brick group, with a semi-basement, two storeys and a mansard attic. The middle house, No. 311, is set forward slightly and elaborated on the ground storey, so that the other houses have the appearance of being wings. It has an entrance set in a grooved frame with wing lights at each side.

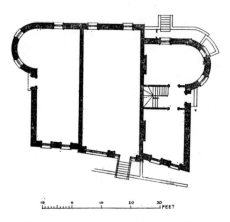

Fig. 39. Nos. 309–313 Brixton Road. Interior measurements of Nos. 309 and 311 not available

Foliated blocks at the head of the frame support a delicately festooned cornice, with vases over the heads, and a mutule transom. The doorway, and the similarly detailed window of three lights to its north, are set in elliptical-headed recesses which spring from anthemion-ornamented impost blocks and have keystones with crowned and bearded male masks. The entrance to No. 309 is on the flanking elevation, which suggests that there was never any intention that the houses should have a continuous façade. This entrance is set tightly against a semi-circular two-storey projecting bay and has a neat wooden doorcase with engaged acanthus-headed columns at each side. There are vases to the frieze blocks above. The doorway has a simple patterned fanlight and panelling to the linings and arch soffit. No. 313 lost its original entrance when additions were made at the south end of the terrace.

[191] No. 26 Villa Road

This house is shown on the Inclosure map of 1810 as one of a pair, but the other house, on the west, was pulled down to make room for the later terrace houses in the road. It is a small stucco-fronted two-storey house, with a central entrance protected by a cast-iron trellised tent-roofed porch. The window above and those at each side on the first floor are set in shallow elliptical-headed recesses, while on the ground floor there is a segmental bay on the east side and a semi-elliptical one on the west. The entrance has a delicate rectangular fanlight, patterned with three ellipses, and a reeded surround with lion-head stops at the corners.

Angell Town   [192]

Stiles Farm was enfranchised in 1847[175] and its present layout took shape in the 1850s. The Lambeth Wick Estate on its eastern boundary was already laid out for development, but owing to lack of collaboration between the landlords the Lambeth Wick Estate had been planned depending on Loughborough Road for access to the main highway of Brixton Road (see page 109). Angell Town, as the area subsequently became known, was consequently laid out with a long principal road (Wiltshire Road) connected by short linking roads to Brixton Road and the roads on the Lambeth Wick Estate.

This layout shows something of the influence of Repton's theories of landscaping, avoiding any suggestion of a geometrical plan and presenting a careful arrangement of wide curving streets contrived to give effective cross vistas and generally to centre on the focal point of St. John's Church tower. The houses are all set in gardens and mostly built in pairs, but there is occasionally a short terrace and a number of single houses, usually placed at road junctions.

The houses are, in essentials, standardized types. There are the single houses of three storeys over semi-basements, with central porches and three widely-spaced windows in each upper storey. Then there are the smaller pairs, with semi-basement, two storeys and a roof attic, the fronts being two windows wide. But perhaps the commonest type is the paired house of three storeys over a semi-basement, with linked porches, a basement and ground-floor bay window, and either three windows or a three-light and single window to each upper storey. Some fronts are completely stucco-faced, while many others are of grey brick liberally dressed with stucco quoins, porches, window-surrounds, etc. All the detail is coarse and presents a veritable ragbag of motifs, some windows having Jacobean crestings and others Italianate pediments. There are debased Louis Quinze guilloche balconies, Doric entablatures to porches and bay-windows, and some hideous doorway arches with cable mouldings and vermiculated spandrels. Near the church, however, the houses in Wiltshire Road are respectfully Gothic, having bays with segmental-headed windows, crudely gabled porches, and twin-arched windows to the upper storeys, all the arches rising from coarsely designed foliage capitals. Some, at least, of the houses were erected by James Barker of Bath Road, Peckham,[176] who was responsible for Angel Terrace (see below).

[193] ST. JOHN'S CHURCH, ANGELL TOWN

The site of St. John's Church was freely given to the Church Building Commissioners by Benedict John Angell Angell in 1852,[177] and the cost of the building was met by William Stone of the Casino, Herne Hill.[178] The architect was Benjamin Ferrey[a] and the contractors were Messrs. H. and R. Holland whose tender was for £5,302. The church accommodated about 1,150 people[178] and was consecrated by the Bishop of Winchester on April 30, 1853; a district was assigned in the same year.[179] In 1876 the building was extensively restored and a vestry or parish hall was added on the north side to the designs of Sextus Dyball in 1882.[180] The church was severely damaged by fire in 1947 but has since been restored to the designs of Thomas F. Ford with the altar standing beneath the chancel arch; the east end of the church is now used for parochial purposes.[181]

The church (Plate 16), which stands with the vicarage on an island site, is designed in Perpendicular Gothic style, and faced with Kentish ragstone and Bath stone dressings. Axially at the west end there is a substantial three-stage tower which is battlemented and finished with octagonal corner pinnacles. The battlements have a chequerwork pattern of red and cream-coloured stone. There are lean-to aisles flanking the nave and a gabled porch on the north side. Excepting in the nave clerestory the windows have arches with alternating cream and grey ragstone voussoirs.

The interior is simple and dignified with nave arcades of four plain pointed arches resting on octagonal piers. There is a small organ gallery beneath the tower.

[194] ST. JOHN'S C.E. PRIMARY SCHOOL, CANTERBURY CRESCENT

The site of this school was freely given by Benedict John Angell Angell. The buildings (Plate 34c) were designed in Tudor style by Benjamin Ferrey and built in Rochester brick with Bath stone dressings by Messrs. Holland in 1853; the cost was £1,600. As originally planned the school contained three large rooms and provided accommodation for 180 boys, 120 girls and 100 infants. There was also a house for the master.[182] Later additions have been unsympathetic. The school was severely damaged in the war of 1939–45, and was reopened in 1947.

NOS. 341–361 BRIXTON ROAD [195]
Formerly Nos. 1–11 (consec.) Angell Terrace

This terrace was erected by James Barker of Peckham, builder, who executed an agreement to build it with Benedict John Angell Angell on January 1, 1855.[176] Barker borrowed money from Angell and Samuel Copping but shortly afterwards was declared a bankrupt. This led to a delay in the finishing of the houses and only Nos. 1, 2, 4, 10 and 11 were occupied in 1860, the whole terrace being occupied by 1868.[174] The terrace (Plate 49b) is boldly conceived and consists of four-storey stock brick houses of Classical design with the two end and three centre houses set forward slightly and contained by quoins at the corners. A substantial appearance is given by the ornamental stucco work which is liberally applied to the window surrounds and throughout the ground storey where it is channelled. The two end houses have enclosed entrances with side arched openings. The others have open Roman Doric porches which are separate except in the case of the two houses at each side of the centre portion, where they are linked; all have a full order with mutules, triglyphs and guttae to the cornice, frieze and architrave respectively. This decoration is continued as an ornamental band between the porches. All the windows are architrave-lined and are either eared or consoled at the sills. The first- and second-floor windows are elaborated variously with plain, triangular-pedimented, and segmental-pedimented hoods conforming to a regular pattern throughout the façade; on the second floor the windows are further ornamented with pulvinated, ribboned and rosetted friezes. Above the architraves of some of the windows on the third floor there is a type of Jacobean strap ornament which occurs elsewhere

[a] Benjamin Ferrey was a pupil of Augustus Charles Pugin and author of *Recollections of A. W. N. Pugin and Augustus Pugin.*

K

on the Angell estate. The terrace is finished with a vigorous festooned and bracketed cornice with a deep blocking course to the parapet above.

[196] BRIXTON POLICE STATION

Brixton Police Station was erected in 1858 to the designs of Charles Reeves, Metropolitan Police Surveyor, at a cost of £2,974; the building was extended in 1909.[183] The design has a distinct flavour of Vanbrugh and is very like other police buildings by the same architect, for example, No. 10 Gipsy Hill. Built of stock brick, five bays wide with a two-bayed extension to the south, it is three storeys high on a semi-basement and formerly had a mansard roof. The quoins and all other dressings are of brick except the bracketed cornice which is rendered in cement. On the ground floor the windows are rusticated and round-arched with triple bays. There is a band course at first-floor level and another beneath the second-floor windows and all the upper openings have segmental keyed heads and lugged architraves. The doorway was altered in 1909.

No. 372 COLDHARBOUR LANE (demolished c. 1933)

Formerly Halnaker Lodge

This charming Regency house stood on the north side of the road opposite Somerleyton Road. It was a two-storey stucco-fronted house with overhanging eaves, and flanked by single-storey wings. In the centre was a semi-circular projecting porch with unfluted Greek Doric columns, which supported the delicate ironwork of the verandah above. The house is illustrated by a photograph in *Small Houses of the Late Georgian Period 1750–1820* by Stanley C. Ramsey, and by photographs and measured drawings in a supplement to *The Architect and Building News* for July 1, 1932.

[197] Nos. 314–320 (even), 332, 334, 340 AND 342 BRIXTON ROAD

Formerly Nos. 1–4 (consec.) Park Place, and Nos. 2, 3, 6 and 7 Park Terrace

The ten acres of copyhold land held of Lambeth Manor which lay on the west side of Brixton Road were sold in 1803 by William Brown Angell to Thomas Woodroffe Smith.[166] A small portion of the land was let under a licence to demise granted in 1807[184] but Nos. 314–320, 332, 334, 340 and 342 Brixton Road were

erected by Evan Roberts of north Brixton,[185] slate-merchant, under a licence granted in 1826 to Smith's trustees. Nos. 314–320 are two plain pairs of stock brick houses, well elevated above the road. They are of three storeys with semi-basements and are set forward at the ends above their Greek Doric porches. No. 318 is ruinous. Nos. 332 and 334 are another plain pair, and have coupled antae flanking their recessed entrance porches. Nos. 340 and 342 are a pair of larger villas of three storeys above semi-basements. Their fronts were almost identical until the central Ionic porch of No. 342 was mutilated. Both have round-arched windows over the porches, and their ground floor windows, set in shallow elliptical-arched recesses, have moulded linking impost bands.

OUR LADY OF THE ROSARY ROMAN   [198]
CATHOLIC CHURCH, BRIXTON ROAD

At the southernmost point of the ten acres stands the present Roman Catholic Church of Our Lady of the Rosary (Plate 27d). The building was formerly known as Brixton Independent Church, and was erected by means of subscriptions raised by the congregation of Claylands Chapel[186] (see page 61), and opened in June 1870.[187] The architect was Arthur J. Phelps and the contractors were Myers and Son.[145] During the war of 1939–45 the building was heavily damaged, and its use as an Independent place of worship discontinued. It was restored in 1952–3 for the Roman Catholic congregation of St. Helen's, Robsart Street, and opened for worship on December 8, 1953.[188] The architects for the restoration were Justin Alleyn and John Mansel.[189] The church is built of red brick interspersed with vitrified bricks which give a striped appearance to the pointed door and window openings. It has stone dressings and is designed in a style showing Early English Gothic influence. There is a bold three-stage tower of rectangular plan at the north-east corner. The present crown of battlements replaces the original termination, which comprised a solid brick chisel spire rising from the parapets. The high altar stands at the west end of the church in an apse which is lit by six long lancet windows, and there are short transepts on either side. The nave and aisles are separated by slender cast-iron arcades which also supported the side galleries, removed at the time of restoration. The hall on the south side of the church, in the same style and materials, was demolished in 1955. A new hall and vestry were built and alterations to the forecourt carried out in the same year.

RUSH COMMON

Rush Common (sometimes Rushey Common or Rushey Green) and Norwood Common were the two main areas of common land in the Manor of Lambeth. Most of Rush Common lay in the triangle formed by Brixton Hill, Effra Road and a line drawn in a south-westerly direction from the junction of Effra Road and Water Lane to Brixton Hill; there was also a long narrow spur extending up the east side of Brixton Hill, and shorter spurs along the northern end of Tulse Hill and the southern end of the east side of Brixton Road.

An Act of Parliament[190] of 1806 provided for the appointment of Commissioners who were empowered to divide and inclose the common lands of the Manor; the Act also forbad any building on certain parts of Rush Common (Plate 72a). In the 18th and early 19th centuries turnpike and other local Acts often proscribed building in parts of the areas to which they applied; in 1756, for instance, the Act authorizing the building of what are now Marylebone, Euston and Pentonville Roads forbad the erection of any buildings within 50 feet of either side of the road.[191] The proscriptions contained in the Lambeth Manor Inclosure Act were incorporated in the Inclosure Commissioners' Award of 1810, and the subsequent history of their enforcement has an important bearing on the development of the area.

The Act of 1806 stipulated that "no Buildings or Erections above the Surface of the Earth"[192] should be erected upon Rush Common within 150 feet of the London to Croydon Turnpike Road (now Brixton Road and Hill), nor within 200 feet of the old inclosures which formed the south and east boundaries of the Common, nor within 100 feet in front of any building already erected on adjoining land without the owner's consent. Persons injured by any infringement of these proscriptions were empowered to proceed against the offender. Section 33 of the Act provided, however, that encroachments which had been made at least twenty years before 1806 should not be considered as part of the Common; by implication they were therefore exempt from the clauses which forbad building in the areas described above.

By their Award of 1810[193] the Commissioners divided and allotted the Common, and provided for the layout of the roads now known as Effra Road and St. Matthew's Road. By an amending Act passed in 1821[194] these two roads were made parish highways, and the building proscriptions were modified to permit the erection of a church (St. Matthew's) with a burial ground and parsonage house only; the latter was in fact never built. The Award also provided for a projected canal from Croydon to Deptford to run across the Common; the canal was not made.

As long as the Act of 1806 remained within the memory of the inhabitants of the area the building proscriptions appear to have been observed; in 1859, for instance, a corn-chandler in Brixton Place (now Brixton Road between Coldharbour Lane and the high-level railway bridge) attempted to erect a building on his forecourt, but "the feeling of the neighbours was so strongly manifested and legal proceedings threatened that the intention was abandoned".[195] Although the Metropolitan Board of Works had power to regulate building lines, it was not able to enforce the building proscriptions contained in the Act of 1806, and in 1875 one-storey shops were erected in defiance of the Board on the sites now known as Nos. 421–427 Brixton Road. In 1885, however, the continuation of this encroachment southwards was successfully prevented, probably through the legal action taken by an adjoining property owner.[196]

Between Josephine Avenue and Arodene Road the position was complicated by the existence of a house there before the Act of 1806. The house (which still stands at the back of No. 95 Brixton Hill, Plate 72b), must originally have been an encroachment on the Common, but if it were erected twenty years or more before the Inclosure Act, it and its curtilage were exempt from the proscriptive clauses. In 1880 the Metropolitan Board of Works granted permission for the erection of a one-storey shop upon the forecourt of No. 95,[197] and during the next five years seven other buildings whose fronts extended to the public way were erected;[195] their sites were presumably considered to be part of the exempted curtilage of No. 95. In 1899–1900, however, the London County Council received protests against the erection of three shops and houses[195] adjoining the south side of those erected between 1880 and 1885. In this case there appears to have been some doubt as to whether the site of these buildings formed part of the original curtilage of No. 95. Proceedings were taken against the builder of the three shops and houses, and the Council's Superintending Architect of Metropolitan Buildings defined the building line as being at a greater distance than 50 feet from the highway. The Tribunal of Appeal, however, decided that the building line was the back edge of the pavement of Brixton Hill.[198] A continuous line of buildings projecting up to the pavement still exists between Arodene Road and Josephine Avenue.

In 1891 the London County Council consented to the formation of Arodene Road and Helix Road provided that no buildings were erected "upon any of the ground forming a portion of Rush Common".[199] Five years later the Council received several protests that houses were being erected in Arodene Road on proscribed land. But the Council was not a party injured by the encroachment and could not therefore take action under the terms of the Act of 1806.[195] The houses still stand.

During the early years of the 20th century acute difficulties over the enforcement of the provisions of the Act of 1806 frequently arose at the north end of the old Common, nearly all of which lay between the low-level railway bridge and Coldharbour Lane. Here the original houses had been built outside the proscribed area but gradually they had been turned into shops whose proprietors constantly erected stalls, kiosks and temporary structures on the forecourts. The London County Council (General Powers) Act of 1924 therefore contained a clause whereby the building line of Nos. 429–467 (odd) Brixton Road might be moved forward provided that all the owners agreed to surrender the part of their forecourts nearest to the road, which could then be widened.[200] The unanimous agreement of the frontagers was not obtained until 1935. In 1938 another Act[201] authorized the Council to permit building on part of the proscribed land occupied by Nos. 415–427 (odd) Brixton Road, subject to such conditions as might be agreed upon by the Council and the owners; these powers have not yet been applied. In 1939[202] similar statutory powers were granted for the proscribed land between Coldharbour Lane and Rushcroft Road, where the Public Library had been erected in 1891–3 and a theatre in 1900–1,[102] both partly on proscribed land.

The total area proscribed from building by the Act of 1806 was about 34½ acres, of which only a very small proportion had been dealt with by these three Acts. In the remaining area south of the junction of Effra Road and Brixton Hill many difficulties arose over the interpretation of the Act of 1806. In Effra Road there appeared to be a contradiction between the wording of the Act and the Award of 1810; moreover the original plans of 1810 had probably shrunk or stretched, and the thickness of their lines represented four to eight feet. Problems such as these could only be solved by fresh legislation, and in 1947 the Council was empowered both to enforce the prohibition in the Act of 1806 and to consent to the erection or retention of buildings in the proscribed area, subject to agreement between the Council and the owners.[203] These powers will eventually result in the widening of Brixton Hill and Effra Road; most of the long and often neglected gardens (Plate 72c) which the Act of 1806 produced are designated as private open spaces in the County of London Development Plan of 1951. The proscribed area south of the junction of Brixton Hill and Upper Tulse Hill is in the Borough of Wandsworth, and blocks of flats set well back from the roadway have recently superseded the private houses; the land in front of these flats is designated as public open space. Thus in due course the whole area will once again acquire the spaciousness which was originally intended and which is so conspicuously absent in many parts of Lambeth.

ST. MATTHEW'S CHURCH, BRIXTON   [199]

By their Award of 1810 the Lambeth Manor Inclosure Commissioners allotted three parcels at the northern end of Rush Common to the Archbishop of Canterbury, the Rector of Lambeth and Robert Stone. After the establishment of the Church Building Commissioners in 1818 the Lambeth Church Building Committee decided that these three plots would form a fine site for a church and burial ground.[204] The building restrictions contained in the Inclosure Act of 1806 had to be modified by an amending Act of 1821 to permit the erection of the church.[194] The land belonging to the Rector was then conveyed to the Commissioners gratuitously for the site of the church.[205] The Archbishop's land was made into a burial ground[206] and £88 was paid to Robert Stone's Trustees for their piece.[205]

The architect of the church was C. F. Porden.[205] The first stone was laid by the Archbishop of Canterbury on July 1, 1822,[207] but work on the foundations was started in the previous autumn by Mr. Mercer of Millbank. The soil proved looser than the architect expected, and extra foundations were needed. Mercer then became insolvent and his contract was completed by Messrs. Thomas Want and John Richardson. J. and H. Lee of Chiswell Street, who were well known "as builders of the greatest respectability",[204] shared in the completion of the church, whose total cost was £16,150, of which the Church Building Commissioners contributed £7,917; the remainder was raised by the parish of Lambeth.[208] The church (Plates 5–9, 11b, 12) was consecrated on June 21, 1824 by the Bishop of Winchester.[207] There were 904 rented sittings and 1,022 free seats. By an Order in Council gazetted on March 29, 1825, a District Parish was assigned.[205]

In 1829 the *Gentleman's Magazine* described St. Matthew's as "one of the few chaste specimens of classical architecture to be found amongst the various new Churches in the environs of the Metropolis". The writer went on, however, to deplore the use of the Grecian style for churches, and criticised the siting of the church, whereby "the portico is lost, in consequence of the sides being closed; until the spectator arrives opposite to the building, he can only imagine there may be a portico".[207] Nevertheless, St. Matthew's is the finest early 19th century church in the area under review.

In plan St. Matthew's is a simple rectangle, with a portico fronting the vestibule and flanking staircase-lobbies at the west end, and a tower projecting centrally from the east. By so disposing his portico and steeple, Porden gave architectural interest to both the important road frontages. Furthermore, he forestalled the adverse criticism usually levelled against any attempt to combine these two essentially disparate elements.

The severe Doric exterior, impressive in scale, is built of grey brick dressed generally with Bath stone. Pedestals flank the wide steps that ascend to the portico, tetrastyle in antis, where Portland stone columns are combined with Bath stone antae, entablature and pediment. The entablature continues as a unifying motif right round the building. The rear wall of the portico is a plain brick face containing three doorways with tapered jambs and straight heads, the middle opening being slightly higher and wider than the others, which are not centred with the intercolumniations. Framed by an eared architrave of Bath stone, each door has two wooden leaves, with three tall panels within a running band of ivy-leaf ornament.

The portico, being in antis, is not expressed on the side elevations, hence the criticisms made in the *Gentleman's Magazine*. Here the only ornament is provided by the entablature, the narrow antae at each end, and the single tier of five equally spaced windows, which have architraves of similar form and detail to those of the portico doorways. Centred beneath the westernmost window on each side is a low pedimented porch, projecting and approached by steps descending to the crypt.

The east front is by far the most original feature of the whole design. The steeple, consisting of a square two-stage tower surmounted by an octagonal lantern, projects well forward from the flanking two-storeyed porches, framed by antae that support the continued entablature. The first stage of the tower, of equal height with the body of the church, rises from a steeply stepped podium of granite and contains in its east face a tall window. This has a tabernacle frame with its flattened pediment superimposed on the architrave of the main entablature which here is without triglyphs. The second stage, housing the belfry, is raised on a stepped plinth. Each face is identical in having a tall louvred opening recessed between Doric columns which are coupled with the antae at the angles. The plain entablature of this stage is surmounted by a pedestal parapet broken by a clock dial on each face. From a small square plinth rises the octagonal open lantern, a charming feature reminiscent of both the Lysicrates Monument and the Tower of the Winds. Its pyramidal roof has stone ornamental ribs that converge in an acanthus crown supporting the cross.

The middle doorway in the west portico opens to an aisled vestibule leading to the floor of the church. Each side doorway gives access to a lobby with an open staircase to the gallery. The very spacious and airy interior has a gallery on three sides, and a flat single-span ceiling. The minimum of ornament has been used to considerable effect, and architectural interest is rightly focused on the setting for the altar, where the plain wall faces of the gallery are terminated by pilasters, framing a recess containing a tall rectangular window flanked by Doric columns. A simple cornice adorns the gallery fronts and the supporting square piers have delicately moulded caps. Moulded ribs intersect to form a pattern of alternating wide and narrow panels on the ceiling.

Most of the box pews survive, together with some of the original furnishings. The simple Doric organ-case in the western gallery, and the communion rail of iron, with tall Doric column balusters and an open frieze of laurel-wreaths, are well worthy of notice. A series of chaste Grecian memorial tablets, in white and grey marble, relieves the severity of the plain wall surfaces.

At the north end of the churchyard, which has recently been converted into a public open space, is a remarkable monument (Plate 71a) erected by Henry Budd in memory of his father Richard Budd (1748–1824). It was designed and executed by R. Day in 1825, and was described by Thomas Allen, the historian of Lambeth, as "without doubt the finest sepulchral monument in the open air in the metropolis, and perhaps not equalled by any one in the kingdom".[209] It is of Greek derivation in its parts, with some Egyptian features, and shows the influence of Soane. Square in plan, it is built apparently of Portland stone, in three main stages, on a stepped granite base. The four faces are identical except for a low sunk doorway with a projecting pedimented lintel, which cuts into the base on the west side. The lowest step has vermiculated rustication on its face. The main stage consists of four broad pedimented stele projecting from the central block, with classical urns set in the re-entrant angles thus formed. The stele are ornamented with paterae and egg and dart moulding, and contain white marble slabs carrying inscriptions to members of the Budd family. The pediments are surmounted by acroteria at the corners. The second stage has a cornice of considerable projection with scrolled acroteria, the square panels below containing openings with fretted iron grilles and carvings of the serpent with its tail in its mouth, symbol of eternity, and the winged globe, the Egyptian hieroglyph for the Almighty Creator. Flanking these panels are low relief carvings of angels in side panels which are returned on to the adjoining face. The top stage is stepped back and has carvings of the Holy Dove in its four panels. The acanthus-leaved cornice supports segmental pediments topped by two blocking courses and a large anthemion finial.

NOS. 1–21 (odd) ST. MATTHEW'S ROAD [200]
Formerly Nos. 1–11 (consec.) Church Road

In 1825 Robert Stone's Trustees agreed to lease a plot of land between Effra Road and St. Matthew's Road to William Brass of Wood Street, Cheapside, builder.[210] This land was formerly part of Rush Common, and the building restrictions contained in the Act of 1806 forbad the erection of houses on much of it; the most northerly house was given a disproportionately large garden in consequence (fig. 40). Nos. 1–5 were built by Brass between 1825 and 1827.

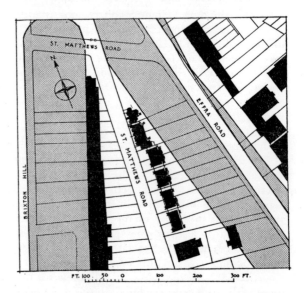

Fig. 40. St. Matthew's Road, lay-out plan. Shading denotes the area proscribed from building by the Act of 1806

No. 1, a stucco-covered villa of two storeys and a semi-basement, has a central entrance which is attended by Greek Doric columns. The columns, which have poorly detailed abaci, support a moulded transom and have a plainly patterned fanlight above. The doorway sets forward slightly and is finished with a dentilled cornice and blocking course, the latter continuing as a sill-band linking the first-floor windows. There is a semicircular ground-floor bay projection on the north side finished with a dentilled cornice, like that over the entrance, and a balustraded parapet.

Nos. 3 and 5 (fig. 41) form a pair of stock brick houses of the same height as No. 1, and have similar entrances. These are set in two-storey wings which project forward slightly and are

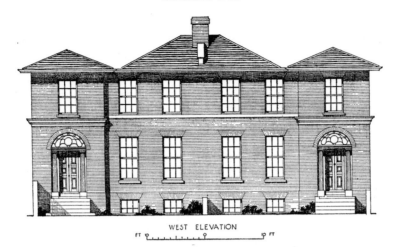

WEST ELEVATION

Fig. 41. Nos. 3 and 5 St. Matthew's Road, 1825–7. Lessee, William Brass, builder

divided by cornices at first-floor level. Like No. 1, their upper windows are underlined by a continuous sill-band. This pair has a slated roof of less steep pitch. No. 5 is the vicarage of St. Matthew's Church. The curious plan of No. 3 (fig. 42) was probably adopted to prevent any encroachment on the area proscribed from building.

William Brass subsequently got into financial difficulties, and Nos. 7–21 were erected shortly after 1840 by William Lawrence of Hoxton,

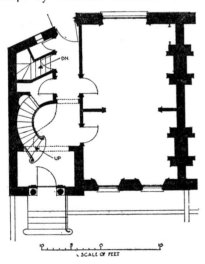

SCALE OF FEET

Fig. 42. No. 3 St. Matthew's Road, ground-floor plan

builder. All these houses have recently been demolished. They formed four pairs of severely detailed stucco-fronted houses of three storeys with semi-basements, and almost hidden roof

attics. Each house had a wing, slightly set back, of full height, containing a recessed porch guarded by a pair of Greek Doric columns. The fronts were finished with a cornice and blocking course, the latter inflected to form an unmoulded pediment over each pair. The porches were flanked by flat piers and the houses were given an appearance of added strength by the channelling of their ground storeys and by the joining of their upper-floor windows with deep sill-bands. The pairs were linked by simply pilastered screen walls containing entrances to the back gardens.

TRINITY CONGREGATIONAL CHURCH, ST. [201] MATTHEW'S ROAD

The foundation stone of this church was laid

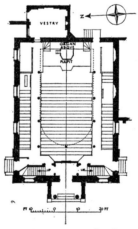

Fig. 43. Trinity Congregational Church, St. Matthew's Road, plan

on September 23, 1828. The church (Plate 25a, fig. 43) is almost square in plan, austere in character, and built of yellow stock brick. The two-storeyed front is divided into three bays, the centre being slightly recessed. Each outer bay contains a ground- and semi-circular headed first-floor window, both framed in a shallow arched recess. From the central bay projects the one-storey Greek Doric porch. The crowning entablature is surmounted by a blocking course inflected to form a low pediment over the central bay. A U-shaped gallery extends round three sides of the nave and is supported by Greek Doric columns; the windows are segmental below and round-headed above the gallery.

[202] ST. MATTHEW'S C.E. SCHOOL, ST. MATTHEW'S ROAD

This school was founded in 1828.[211] By 1870 the building had become very dilapidated,[211] and it was entirely rebuilt in the following year,[212] Joseph Gale being the architect.[213] This new building, which accommodated 600 children, was heavily damaged during the war of 1939–45, and is not now used as a school. It is a two-storey brick building dominated by a tapering rectangular tower at the north-east corner. The tower has a chisel roof crested with ornamental ironwork.

[203] NOS. 4–12 (even) AND 18 EFFRA ROAD

In the 1820s a number of detached houses of various sizes were built along the west side of Effra Road; all of them were set well back in order to comply with the building restriction contained in the Inclosure Act. Only four of these houses survive. Nos. 6 and 8 are two-storey stock brick cottages with central doorways and one window on each side. No. 6 has round heads to the ground-floor windows and entrance, with an impost band and sill-band above. No. 8, which is illustrated in a supplement to *The Architect and Building News* of October 7, 1932, is faced with stucco and has a trellised porch.

Nos. 10 and 12 are stuccoed, two-storey villas, three windows wide, No. 10 being raised on a semi-basement and having an extra storey in a mansard roof at the rear. Its central doorway has a long narrow fanlight and is flanked by attenuated Greek Doric columns. There are iron guards to the ground-floor windows and those above are square with a sill-band. No. 12 has traces of a portico but both houses are now in ruins. Nos. 4

and 18 Effra Road, both now demolished, are illustrated in supplements to *The Architect and Building News* of May 6 and September 2, 1932, respectively.

TATE CENTRAL FREE LIBRARY, BRIXTON [204]

This building and its site were presented to the Lambeth Public Libraries Commissioners by (Sir) Henry Tate, and cost about £15,000. The library was opened by the Prince of Wales on March 4, 1893; the architect was Sidney R. J. Smith,[214] and the builders were F. and H. F. Higgs.[215] A brass tablet in the entrance hall records that the garden in front of the library was given in 1905 by Amy, Lady Tate in fulfilment of a wish of her husband Sir Henry Tate, bart.

The library is a boldly conceived building of two storeys in Classical style, built in Elham Valley red brick with Portland and Beer stone dressings. The central entrance and the end pavilions are slightly set forward and the ground storey brickwork is rusticated. The entrance has a coffered round arch and there are freely carved panels at either side. The balcony above is borne on pairs of consoles. The centre and end pavilions are pedimented, the former being elevated on coupled pilasters. The roof is of slate with a central wood lantern.

THE MANOR OF HEATHROW

The small Manor of Heathrow or Knight's was held as freehold of the Manor of Lambeth, to which a quit-rent of 12d. a year was paid.[216] The name "Knight's" suggests that the area was formerly occupied by the Knight family, who held much land in Lambeth in the sixteenth century. The Manor passed into the possession of Thomas Wiseman and after his death to his son Thomas.[217] The latter was a Jesuit priest in Rome and by 1594 he had sold the Manor to William Wiseman who in his turn had sold it to Francis Fitch.[218] It was subsequently acquired by Sir Francis Goston[216] in whose family's ownership it remained until 1658 when Francis Goston conveyed it to John Scaldwell.[219] By his will, which was proved in 1679, Scaldwell left the Manor and three adjoining acres of copyhold of Lambeth Manor to his wife Dorothy for life and then to his grandson Thomas Fox.[148] No later reference to this Manor has been discovered, but by tracing the descent of the adjoining copyhold in the Court Books the position of Heathrow has been identified.[220] It comprised some 70 acres south of Coldharbour Lane on the east side of Effra Road and the north-east side of Dulwich Road. The parcel of land now covered by Geneva and Somerleyton Roads may also have been part of Heathrow Manor; on the Lambeth Manor Inclosure map of 1810 it is shown as freehold land belonging to W. Angell. Between 1791 and 1806 Robert Stone bought Heathrow in four parts; it was then known as Effra Farm.[221] The value of the land was greatly enhanced by the layout of Effra Road in 1810 by the Lambeth Inclosure Commissioners, and again a few years later by the building of St. Matthew's Church. Stone divided the northern part of the area into plots and granted long leases. A few detached houses (none of which now survives) were then built. Robert Stone died in 1820, leaving a widow and seven children, all minors. His estate was so heavily burdened with debts that his executors refused to act, and his affairs were finally settled under Chancery supervision by a private Act of Parliament.[222] Some 33 acres were sold by auction in 1824. The rest of the property was afterwards let on building leases and sold at another auction in 1826.[223] The southern portion of the estate was bought by the Westminster Freehold Land Society in 1855,[224] and what are now Effra Parade, Chaucer Road, Spenser Road, Shakespeare Road and Milton Road were laid out on a much humbler scale than the northern portion of the estate.

[205] BRIXTON UNITARIAN CHRISTIAN CHURCH, EFFRA ROAD

In 1840 the congregation of Brixton Unitarian Chapel obtained a long lease of a site on the east side of Effra Road;[225] the chapel which was subsequently built there was destroyed by enemy action in 1940, and was replaced by the present temporary building.

[206] BRIXTON SYNAGOGUE, EFFRA ROAD

The foundation stone of this synagogue was laid by Sir Robert Waley Cohen on May 1, 1921; Cecil Masey was the architect and W. J. Mitchell and Son were the builders.[145] The walls of the building are rendered and painted white, and there is a Tuscan-type columned porch extending across the front which is flanked by pedimented pavilions. There is a gallery round three sides of the interior.

ST. JUDE'S C.E. PRIMARY SCHOOL,   [207]
RAILTON ROAD

An inscription on the original building of this school stated that "This Building dedicated by Mr. and Mrs. Simpson and other contributors to the Christian Education of the Infant Poor was erected A.D. MDCCCXXXIV". The school was originally known as St. Paul's Infant School, but on the formation in 1869 of the ecclesiastical district of St. Jude's, the management of the school was transferred from St. Paul's, Herne Hill, in the parish of Camberwell, to a committee of the vicar and parishioners of St. Jude's.[226] The original building (Plate 35a), which is now dwarfed by later additions, is a single-storey stock brick structure with a slate roof; the wall facing Railton Road is pierced by five groups of three lancet lights.

RAILTON METHODIST CHURCH, RAILTON [208]
ROAD

This church was erected in 1874, R. Cable being the architect and Richardson Bros. the builders.[145] Three years later schools were built at the rear, the architects being R. and J. Cable, and A. Peacock the builder. The church (Plate 27c) is built of stock brick with a steeply pitched slate roof. The front, which is faced with coursed Kentish ragstone, contains a centrally placed Decorated Gothic window above the dual entrance, and two narrow flanking windows above the secondary doorways.

MILKWOOD AND WICKWOOD

This portion of Lambeth Manor comprised some 86 acres on either side of Coldharbour Lane; one piece lay between the Lane and the east side of Loughborough Junction, and the other piece was bounded approximately by Poplar Walk, Lowden Road and Milkwood Road. Until the middle of the 17th century the whole area was woodland reserved to the Archbishop of Canterbury, but the trees were uprooted during the Commonwealth[227] and after the Restoration the land was leased for successive terms of 21 years.[228] In

1711 a lease was granted to William East of the Middle Temple,[229] whose descendants continued as tenants until 1837,[230] when the lease was surrendered to Rice Richard Clayton. When it expired in 1865 the whole neighbourhood was being transformed by the construction of railways.

The development which took place shortly afterwards was architecturally undistinguished, but is of interest through its connection with the Suburban Village and General Dwellings Company. The purpose of this Company was "to provide at the most rapid rate possible, healthy, pleasant, and comfortable abodes, for the overcrowded population of the metropolis. The company will purchase estates in all the suburbs near to and having direct railway connexion with London, and erect thereon complete villages. The houses erected will contain from four to eight rooms with every domestic convenience, each house to have a piece of garden ground. Educational establishments, etc., will be provided, as also a limited number of shops. . . ."[231] Money was subscribed by 250 working men in hopes of obtaining houses, and Edward Vigers, Chairman of the directors of the Company, applied to the Ecclesiastical Commissioners for a lease of part of Milkwood and Wickwood. Meanwhile the Secretary of the Company had spent nearly all the available funds and the shareholders refused to pay the calls for extra money needed to implement the scheme. The directors were all deposed and an attempt was made to wind up the Company.[232]

At this unpromising moment W. G. Habershon, partner in the well-known firm of architects, Habershon and Pite, of Bloomsbury Square, offered to take over the estate for its original purpose. In 1868 he and his partner, A. R. Pite, reached an agreement with the Ecclesiastical Commissioners. They were to receive a 99 year lease of 24 acres, and covenanted to build roads and sewers and between 480 and 650 houses; as soon as any houses were completed, separate leases were to be granted to them or their nominees.[233] The first stone of the new village was laid on March 30, 1869, by Lord Shaftesbury.[234] The two main streets were Milkwood Road and Lowden Road, and the houses were to be "very pretty specimens of cottage dwellings in ornamental brick, and built in six, eight or ten rooms, exactly as the shareholder and intending occupier may wish".[234] (Plate 73d, fig. 44).

[209]

Houses could be purchased by a lump sum payment, or by instalments spread over 21 years.

By 1872 the project was well under way. The cheapest houses cost £200, but many were more expensive. Five houses built in Lowden Road in 1872 cost £1,739, while four shops elsewhere on the estate cost £2,559.[235] Builders were

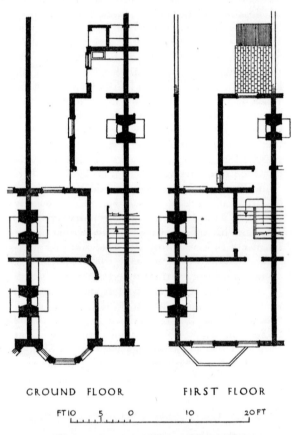

GROUND FLOOR   FIRST FLOOR

FT 10   5   0   10   20 FT

Fig. 44. Houses in Milkwood Road, plans

attracted by the proximity of the estate to the new railway lines, and by promises of advances of up to 60 per cent on the cost of every house covered in,[236] while purchasers were attracted by the cheap workmen's fares which the London, Chatham and Dover Railway Company was compelled to provide. Within four years of the signature of the agreement with the Ecclesiastical Commissioners, *The Builder* reported that the estate provided "a striking instance of the new suburban neighbourhoods rising up in succession in different places around the metropolis. About the present time last year the greatest portion of the land forming the estate was occupied as market gardens, but the entire area has now been laid out in wide and spacious streets, all drained and paved, and provided with ample footpaths, and upwards of two hundred private houses and shops have already been erected and occupied, whilst a large number of new dwellings are at present in course of erection."[237]

The houses on the estate are built in terraces of stock brick with red brick dressings and slated roofs. Most of them are two-storeyed, a few three, and some of each type are raised on semi-basements. The majority are two windows wide, with an arched doorway and bay window on the ground floor, and generally stone is used for lintels, arches and mullions, often with incised designs. Some mullions have cast-iron columns with enriched caps and a few houses have gables. Later development up the hill is distinguished by more gables, more red brick, square two-storey bay windows and ornamental terracotta.

BRIXTON HILL, EAST SIDE

The northern section of the road now called Brixton Hill was formerly called Brixton Causeway. The name Brixton (with many variations) dates from at least the 11th century, and its derivation has been suggested as "(At) the stone of Beohtsige (Brightsige)".[238] Manning and Bray suggested that the Causeway derived its name from this stone,[239] but they also quoted another explanation that in the 14th century Sir John de Burstow (or Bristow) repaired this piece of road with stone, and that it was subsequently known as Burstow or Bristow Causeway.[240] The earliest known reference to a causeway is contained in a will of 1530, when Hugh Acton left £20 for making and repairing the highway from Streatham Church to the foot of "Bristowe Cawsey".[241] The names Rush Common, or Rushey Green, and Watery Lane (now Brixton Water Lane) both suggest that the area was marshy. At some date before 1530, and possibly even in Roman times (see page 5), the road was evidently embanked or paved.

Rush Common bordered the whole length of the east side of Brixton Hill, and the Inclosure Act of 1806 provided that no buildings should be erected on the Common within 150 feet of the road. When building began in the 1820s at the south end of the road, the houses were set well back with long narrow front gardens.

Nos. 123–129 (odd) Brixton Hill [210]

These houses were erected between 1824 and 1830.[174] Nos. 123 and 125 are a plain uninteresting pair of stock brick houses of two storeys with an attic storey in a slated mansard roof. They also have semi-basements and their entrances are in side wings of slightly less height. No. 127, a stucco-fronted detached villa of the same number of storeys, has a central pedimented porch with Tuscan-type columns which are grossly moulded at their bases. The house is dilapidated and empty. No. 129 is finished with overhanging eaves; it is a poor stucco-fronted villa with a badly detailed Greek Doric porch at the centre.

Brixton Hill Methodist Mission Church [211]

Formerly Elm Park Methodist Chapel

The first chapel to be erected on this site was built in 1824; it was entirely rebuilt in 1856–7, William Wesley Jenkins being the architect.[242] This second chapel was totally destroyed by enemy action in the war of 1939–45.

Nos. 139–167 (odd) Brixton Hill [212]

Nos. 139–145, formerly Nos. 1–4 (consec.) Brixton Hill Terrace; Nos. 151–161, formerly Nos. 1–6 (consec.) Brunswick Place

These houses were erected between 1816 and 1824;[174] Nos. 155, 157 and 159 were described as empty in 1824, and an inscription on No. 163 states that it was erected in 1820 (Plate 59a).

Nos. 139–145, a stucco-fronted three-storeyed terrace finished with a cornice and blocking course, are plain houses devoid of ornament except for the fluted quadrant reveals to the entrances. The houses are joined by a plain band at first-floor level and are channelled through the ground storey. Nos. 147 and 149 are a plain pair of stock brick houses of three storeys which have their entrances contained in recessed wings of the same height. Except for the first-floor lattice-type cast-iron balconies at No. 147, the houses lack ornament. No. 151, another plain three-storey stock brick house, is only of interest in the unusual treatment of the ground-floor windows on each side of the entrance. They are of gauged flat type set in shallow rectangular recesses which also have gauged heads. No. 153, slightly taller than No. 151, is stucco-fronted, plain and of little interest. There is a rectangular panel set in the middle of the blocking course above the parapet cornice. Nos. 155 and 157 form a stucco-fronted pair of three storeys and are finished with a cornice and blocking course. They are joined by a plain first-floor band and the ground storey is channelled. The two first-floor windows of each house have splay-ended guards of cast-iron with standard wave and anthemion ornament. Each doorway has fluted reveals.

The abutting terrace, Nos. 159–167, sited at a slightly higher level because of the slope of Brixton Hill, is similar, though No. 163, which has a long architrave-framed panel inscribed "BRUNSWICK HOUSE. 1820." at second-floor level, is of greater width and has three instead of two windows on the upper floors. This terrace also differs in having a mansard-roofed attic storey behind its balustraded parapets. Except at No. 167, the first-floor windows of each house are joined by balconies borne on shaped brackets.

[213] St. Matthias Church, Upper Tulse Hill

The site of this church formed part of the Manor of Lambeth and was bought in 1881 from the Trustees of Stockwell Orphanage. The cost of the land was borne by a relative of the minister. Owing to lack of funds a temporary iron church was erected to serve the needs of the locality. This building proved unsatisfactory, the heat in the summer becoming so intense that members of the congregation were sometimes unable to sit through a whole service.[243] The foundation stone of the permanent church was laid on June 2, 1894, by Mrs. Selina Lingham. The architects were John Thomas Newman and William Jacques and the builders Messrs. James Longley and Co.[145] The church provided accommodation for 780 people, and was dedicated in December of the same year; owing to outstanding debts it was not consecrated until March 25, 1899. A Consolidated Chapelry was assigned in the same year.[243]

The church stands on a sloping site and is a plain red brick building sparingly dressed with stone; the roofs are tiled. All the windows are lancets and there are lean-to aisles at each side of the clerestoried nave. There is a tall gabled vestry projecting on the south side. The interior, which is also of red brick, has five bays of stone arcading with alternating circular and octagonal piers flanking the nave; the chancel is apsidal, and the altar has a stone canopied reredos with panels at each side inscribed with the Lord's Prayer, the Creed and the Commandments.

CHAPTER V

Myatt's Fields Area, Denmark Hill and Herne Hill

THIS district probably formed part of the Manor of Milkwell, a relatively small Manor which lay partly in Lambeth and partly in Camberwell; its history is so obscure that its position cannot be indicated with any precision.

In 1291 the Manor of Milkwell belonged to the Hospital of St. Thomas, Southwark, and was taxed at £1 5s.[1] In 1305 it was granted by the Hospital to St. Mary Overy Priory at a yearly rent of 10s.[2] At the Dissolution it was valued at £5 2s.[3] In 1540 the Manor "and the wood called Mylkewell woodde, in the parish of Lambeth, belonging to the said late monastery" of St. Mary Overy, was granted to Sir Thomas Wyatt, to be held by knight service for a rent of 10s. 9d.[4] In 1550 custody of the Manor was granted to Richard Duke during the minority of Thomas Duke, son and heir of George Duke deceased.[5] It was described in 1609, after the death of Thomas Duke, as consisting of six messuages, eight cottages, five barns, five gardens, 150 acres of land, 20 acres of meadow, 200 acres of pasture, 30 acres of wood in Milkwell, Camberwell and Lambeth, parcel of lands of the late Priory of St. Mary Overy. Duke also died seized of 20 acres of land, seven acres of pasture, three acres of meadow in Camberwell and Lambeth, formerly parcel of the lands of the monastery of Bermondsey (St. Saviour's). Save for 25 acres the Manor was held of the King in chief for a tenth part of a knight's fee at an annual rent of 40s. 9d.[6] Thomas Duke's heir, Sir Edward Duke, sold a small portion of the Manor to Edward Alleyn of Dulwich,[7] and the remainder to Robert Cambell, alderman of London.[8] By his will[9] the latter left his lands in Lambeth Dean and Camberwell to his son James, whose widow Theophila was granted letters of administration of his estate in 1660.[10] Theophila Cambell, who was commonly called Lady Cambell, died in 1670 or 1671, leaving three daughters, Theophila, Philippa and Isabella.[11] The Manor of Milkwell appears to have been divided amongst these three daughters, for one third descended to Theophila[12] and in 1672 Richard Bassett, husband of Philippa, suffered a recovery of another third of the Manor.[13]

The later history of the Manor is very confused. One of the three daughters, Theophila, married Sir John Corbett, and in 1691 their son Robert Corbett sold his third of the Manor to John Godschall of London, merchant, for £3,680.[12] This property comprised some 124 acres in the areas later known as Denmark Hill and Herne Hill, and included a farm or Manor called Betton's. Despite its description in the deed of sale as part of the Manors of Betton's and Milkwell, an annual quit-rent of 6s. 8d. was payable to the Manor of Lambeth.[14] The Godschall family continued to hold this land until 1783, when William Man Godschall sold it to Samuel Sanders,[15] a timber merchant with premises on Pedlar's Acre, Lambeth. Shortly after the passing of the Lambeth Manor Inclosure Act of 1806, objections were raised that Sanders' property was not part of the Manor, but he and one of his tenants attended one of the Inclosure Commissioners' meetings "and made it appear that the property was within the Manor of Lambeth and paid a quit-rent to the Lord".[16]

The descents of the other two-thirds of the Manor of Milkwell are less clear. In the latter part of the 17th century Abraham Harrison, a goldsmith of Covent Garden, was buying land in Kent,[17] and by his will, dated 1717, he bequeathed a farm called Lambeth Dean Farm, then said to be part of an ancient manor, with 109 acres in Lambeth and Camberwell, to his son Thomas.[18] The property passed to Thomas's nephew James Harrison who sold it in 1747 to the executors of the will of Thomas Lord Wyndham, formerly Lord High Chancellor of Ireland, for £3,352.[19] In 1762 the property was conveyed to the use of Sir Wyndham Knatchbull Wyndham,[20] and a recovery was suffered to bar the entail.[21] Shortly afterwards Sir Wyndham

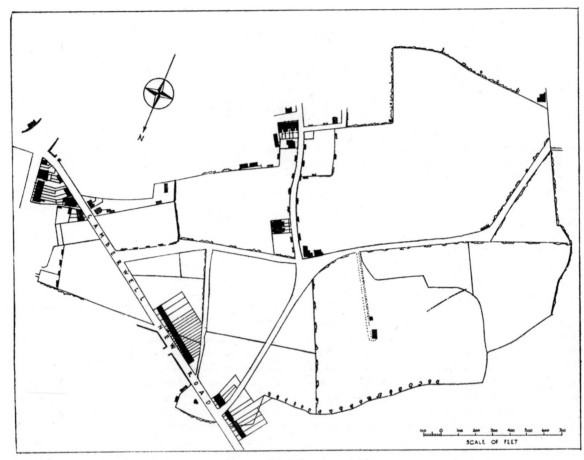

Fig. 45. The Minet estate, 1841

died, leaving all his lands to his uncle Sir Edward Knatchbull.[22] In 1770 the latter sold the property to Hughes Minet,[23] whose descendants still own the greater part of it. Although no direct connection has been traced, it is probable that the Minet property was formerly part of the Manor of Milkwell.

Manning and Bray state that Milkwell Manor was acquired from the Cambell family by the Bowyers, from whom it descended to the Wyndhams and Smyths.[24] These last three families successively owned extensive property in Camberwell, together with a small piece in Lambeth south-east of Kennington Common. Part of their estate probably represents the final third of Milkwell Manor.

Building development in the area of the former Manor of Milkwell began at the end of the 18th century. In the Denmark Hill and Herne Hill areas it took the semi-rural form of large detached houses with large gardens. North of Coldharbour Lane there was not much development until after the formation of Camberwell New Road in 1818; building was on a more modest scale here, and mostly took the form of small terrace houses.

MYATT'S FIELDS AREA

Much of this district is comprised in the Minet estate. The Minets were a French Huguenot family. After the Revocation of the Edict of Nantes in 1685, Isaac Minet, whose parents had kept a pharmacy in Calais, was imprisoned with his mother. They managed to escape to England, where some of Isaac's brothers had already established themselves. Isaac Minet had spent some months at Dover in his boyhood learning English, and he and his brother Ambroise set up a shop of

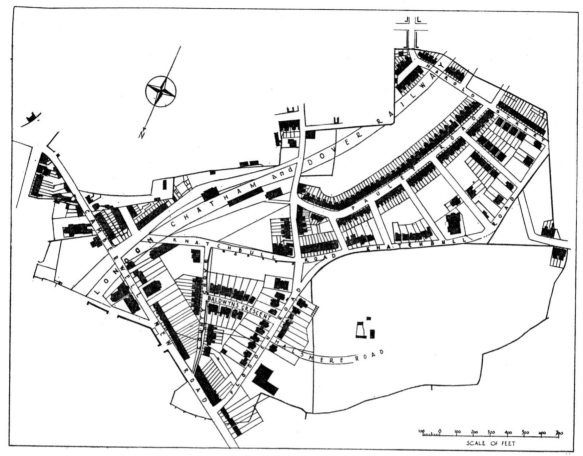

Fig. 46. The Minet estate, 1885

"licors and parfumes" in London. Isaac's grandson, Hughes Minet, was born in Kent in 1731[25] and it was he who in 1770 bought 109 (by a later measurement 118) acres of land from Sir Edward Knatchbull.[23] Most of the estate was in the parish of Camberwell, but the greater part of it is now in the borough of Lambeth. The relatively short frontage to Camberwell New Road was partially developed shortly after the authorization of the road in 1818 (fig. 45), but the flat, low ground did not attract the more prosperous classes who were migrating to the suburbs in the first half of the 19th century. In 1863 the opening of the Metropolitan Extensions of the London, Chatham and Dover Railway Company quickly created a very large demand for small suburban houses. Several acres along the southeast side of the estate were bought by the Railway Company, and the remainder was carefully laid

out for residential use (fig. 46). Builders applied for plots which were granted on long leases; when the houses were finished they were sold by the builder and a direct lease was granted to the tenant by the freeholder, James Lewis Minet, or after his death in 1885, by his son William Minet. By 1871 most of the estate had been divided into plots and building was going on in Paulet Road, Knatchbull Road and the connecting streets.[26] James Lewis Minet provided a site for the Church of St. James's, Knatchbull Road, and bore the entire cost of building. In 1889 his son, William Minet, gave some 14½ acres known as Myatt's Fields to the London County Council for use as a permanent open space. The Minet Public Library was opened in the following year. The history of the estate provides a good example of the benefits which a public-spirited family of landlords could confer on their tenants.

[214] CHURCH OF ST. JAMES THE APOSTLE, KNATCHBULL ROAD

The site of this church was freely given by James Lewis Minet, who also bore the entire cost of the building.[27] The foundation stone was laid on June 19, 1869, and the church was consecrated on June 27, 1870; a consolidated chapelry was formed in 1874.[27] The architect was George Low and the builders Dove Brothers of Islington.[28] The church, which accommodates 780 people,[27] is designed in Decorated Gothic style with unusual detailing, and is faced with Kentish ragstone with Bath stone dressings. It has a clerestoried nave flanked by lean-to aisles terminating in short gabled transepts. At the northwest corner there is an almost free-standing steeple; the tower has octagonal corner buttresses finished with canopied pinnacles, and there are dormer windows in alternate faces of the octagonal stone spire. The interior of the church is plain and detailed in a rather mechanical manner; the sanctuary has an apsidal end and the transepts are separated from the aisles by two-bay transverse arcades.

[215] MYATT'S FIELDS

In 1889 William Minet gave $14\frac{1}{2}$ acres of land to the London County Council for use as a permanent open space, and after the Metropolitan Public Gardens Association had spent some £10,000 on the layout of the park, it was opened on April 13, 1889. In 1935 Miss Susan Minet presented a further quarter of an acre near the junction of Knatchbull Road and Calais Street.[29] The name Myatt's Fields commemorates Joseph Myatt, a former tenant who had been famous for the rhubarb which he grew there.

[216] THE MINET LIBRARY, KNATCHBULL ROAD

The building which now houses the library was originally intended by William Minet to serve as a hall for the use of the tenants of the estate and as a church hall for St. James's, Knatchbull Road. Mr. Minet's wife died in 1887 before the hall was finished and he then decided to turn it into a library in memory of her. After building work had been interrupted for a time by the contractor's bankruptcy, Mr. Minet, who was much interested in the co-operative movement, conceived the idea of forming a private company on co-operative lines. The experiment proved successful and the library, which was designed by George Hubbard, was finished and opened in 1890.[30]

Until the constitution of the metropolitan boroughs in 1899 the library stood in the parish of Camberwell; it is now in the borough of Lambeth. In 1889 Mr. Minet offered to present it to the Camberwell Libraries Commissioners.[31] The latter asked the Lambeth Commissioners to share in the cost of maintenance, and application was made to the President of the Local Government Board, by whose help the necessary powers were inserted in the Public Libraries Amendment Act, 1889.[32] An agreement was then reached that there should be a Joint Committee consisting of equal numbers of Commissioners from the two parishes. This arrangement was in the first instance to last for ten years, after which it was to be terminated on either side by one year's notice, the building and contents then passing to the Commissioners to whom the notice was given. On June 25, 1890, Mr. William Minet conveyed the site and buildings to the two bodies of Commissioners.[31] In later years he gave to the library his important collection of Surrey archives. Many additions have been made to this valuable collection and the library is recognised by the Master of the Rolls as a repository for manorial records. The library was partially destroyed by incendiary bombs on December 8, 1940, but the entire Surrey collection was preserved.

The building is designed in Gothic style and is octagonal with the ground floor raised above a semi-basement. It is built of red brick with stone dressings, and has a wing at the rear. Within the shell of the ground storey a temporary building has been erected to serve as a children's library.

CORMONT SECONDARY SCHOOL, CORMONT [217] ROAD

This school was built for the London School Board. The contractors were Holliday and Greenwood of Brixton, whose tender for a school for 894 children was for £18,601.[33] The architect was T. J. Bailey,[34] and the date of opening was January 10, 1898.[35] The school is a more elaborate version of Kennington Manor School. It comprises a lofty three-storey central block flanked by six-storey towers, which are linked to three-storey end pavilions by five-storey lavatory blocks.

[218] ST. GABRIEL'S COLLEGE, CORMONT ROAD

The foundation stone of St. Gabriel's Church Training College for women teachers was laid by Lady Cranborne, later Marchioness of Salisbury, in July 1899. The architect was Philip A. Robson, and the contractors for the main block were Messrs. J. Garrett and Son of Balham Hill. The chapel, which was the personal gift of Canon C. E. Brooke, vicar of St. John the Divine, Vassall Road, was erected shortly after the main block, and was dedicated in 1903.[36]

The building is typical of its period and employs mixed Gothic and Renaissance motifs. It is built of a hard red brick with sparingly used Portland stone dressings and is five storeys high, the top storey being a very recent addition. In the centre is a gabled porch with a three-centred arch and above a statue of St. Gabriel. It is approached by a double flight of steps supported on a wide segmental brick arch. The chapel comes forward at an angle to the main building and is more competent and more decidedly Gothic in character. It has gabled buttresses, lancet windows with traceried heads slightly recessed under stone relieving arches, and a canted east end where the three light window has curvilinear tracery. The steeply pitched roof is covered with green slates.

CAMBERWELL NEW ROAD

Camberwell New Road was a Turnpike road authorized by Act of Parliament in 1818. A large number of uninteresting two- and three-storey stock brick terrace houses were built along either side of the road during the course of the next twenty years. Those which were built on the Lambeth Wick Estate are described on pages 116-117, and the remainder of the houses which are within the borough of Lambeth are dealt with here. Part of the road is in the borough of Camberwell, and the houses facing that part of the road are not included in this volume.

[219] NOS. 185, 187, 189; 191–199 (odd); 201–205 (odd); 207–223 (odd) CAMBERWELL NEW ROAD

Formerly Nos. 11 and 12 South Place, Clifton Cottage; 1–5 (consec.) Clifton Place North; 1–3 (consec.) Victoria Place; 9–1 (consec.) Chancery Place

All these houses were erected between 1830 and

L

1840;[37] only No. 189 has any distinction (Plate 55d). It is a double-fronted house of two storeys with a stock brick front of charming design. The entrance, flanked by Greek Doric columns, is set in a stucco channelled surround with an arched head. The windows of both storeys are set in arched recesses joined by plain impost bands. Above the first-floor windows the wall face is adorned by shaped panels of stucco containing the name "CLIFTON COTTAGE" and the date "1833". The parapet has a cornice and blocking course.

NOS. 154–166 (even); 168–198 (even); [220] 200–228 (even) CAMBERWELL NEW ROAD

Formerly Nos. 7–1 (consec.) Norfolk Place; 1–16 (consec.) Clifton Place; 1–15 (consec.) Chepstow Place

On the south side of the road between Vassall and Lothian Roads are a number of uninteresting two- and three-storey houses. Nos. 154–166 were erected between 1824 and 1830.[37] Nos. 168–198 were all built before 1840; six of them were already completed in 1830.[37]

Between Lothian and Flodden Roads Nos. 200–204 were erected between 1837 and 1839, and Nos. 206–210 were erected in 1835–6.[38] Together they form two groups of three with the cornice and blocking course of the end houses at a slightly lower level. Nos. 202–208 are unified by a continuous sill-band on the first floor and by the linking of the moulded imposts of the ground floor doorways and windows. The houses have fluted quadrant reveals to the doorways with mutule transoms, and the long landings before the entrances have anthemion-ornamented cast-iron railings. No. 212 was erected in 1826–7.[38] It is a severe and well-proportioned three-storey house with semi-basement and flanked by single-storey wings. The wings and main façade are finished with stone cornices and blocking courses. The recessed elliptical-headed doorway and window in each wing and the three round-headed windows between them, are linked by impost bands. The entrance doorway has plain wooden Doric columns. No. 214 was erected in 1830–2, Nos. 216 and 218 in 1839–40, Nos. 220 and 222 in 1836–7, and Nos. 224–228 in 1830–2.[38] No. 224 is a detached two-storey house; the remainder have three storeys and semi-basements.

[221] ST. JOHN THE APOSTLE JUNIOR MIXED AND INFANTS' SCHOOL, WARHAM STREET

This school was opened on August 5, 1872,[39] in premises in James (now Warham) Street;[39] the original buildings accommodated 400 children.[40] A number of later additions have been made[41] including the three-storey red brick and Portland stone front to Camberwell New Road. Part of the buildings are now occupied by St. Michael and All Angels' Secondary Modern School.

DENMARK HILL AND HERNE HILL

Denmark Hill is said to have acquired its name from Queen Anne's husband, Prince George of Denmark, who hunted there.[42] No example of the name Herne Hill has been found earlier than 1789.[43] The greater part of the land on the west side of the roads now known as Denmark Hill and Herne Hill was bought in 1783[15] by Samuel Sanders, a wealthy timber merchant whose will contained bequests of over £100,000.[44] Shortly afterwards he built himself a large house at Denmark Hill,[45] and began to grant long leases of the land fronting the road. By 1843 an almost unbroken line of large houses stretched from St. Matthew's Church, Denmark Hill, to the south end of Herne Hill.[46] Only three of them survive in a recognizable form.

[222] Nos. 150–154 (even) DENMARK HILL

Formerly Nos. 156–160 (even) Denmark Hill; in 1875 No. 158 was called The Elms, and in 1938 Pentamar

These three houses, which are now occupied by King's College Hospital, are important examples of late 18th century suburban development; they are illustrated in Plates 52–54, and fig. 47. Details are shown in Plate 69c and figs. 48 and 49. No. 150 was erected in 1785–6, and No. 152 in 1787–8;[47] the first occupier of No. 152 was John Christian Schreiber, a wealthy merchant engaged in the Hamburg trade,[48] whose offices were in Budge Row, Cannon Street;[49] after his death his widow Louisa continued to live there until 1816.[50] No. 154, which is perhaps the finest house in the area reviewed in this volume, was built in 1785–6,[47] and was designed by William Blackburn[45] (1750–90), a native of Southwark and architect of the Unitarian Chapel, Lewin's Mead, Bristol, and of a number of

prisons.[51] It was first occupied by Edward Henshaw, a linen draper in Southwark,[52] and later by Richard Lawrence, who may perhaps be identified with Richard Lawrence, broker, of Throgmorton Street.[53]

No. 150 Denmark Hill is a house of three storeys, raised on a semi-basement and flanked on the south by a large addition of two lofty storeys with an angular bay projecting from the front. The original portion of the house has a stock brick front of simple design, its two stages defined by the wide bandcourse above the semi-basement, the sill-band below the first-floor windows, and the crowning mutule cornice with its blocking course. The first stage contains the doorway, flanked by one window on the left and two on the right. The upper stage has two tiers of four evenly spaced windows, corresponding to the ground-floor openings. All the windows are rectangular and without architraves, their heights being proportionate to the three storeys. The wooden doorcase is of unusual and interesting design, the six-panelled door being flanked by attenuated Doric columns that support an architrave, its outer fascia being returned down each side. Above is a frieze panel with a Flaxmanesque relief of classical figures, and the cornice is returned on each side round scroll-shaped brackets that rise from pilasters to support an open segmental pediment-hood (Plate 69c).

No. 152 Denmark Hill consists of a central block of three storeys, flanked by narrow wings each originally of one storey, the whole being raised on a semi-basement. The stock brick front has many points of similarity to that of No. 150, the central block having four windows to each storey and the wings two. Again there is a basement bandcourse, a first-floor sill-band, and a crowning mutule cornice. The coarsely detailed entrance porch, placed left of the centre, is certainly a later addition and fronts an arch-headed doorway, but the elegant wrought iron balustrade of the double stair approach is probably original. The right-hand wing has been heightened by one storey, and each wing bears in the centre of its parapet an ornamental vase. The garden front is remarkable for its fine verandah in the Chinese taste (fig. 48b) and the interior still retains some fine decorative features in the refined Grecian style of the period.

No. 154 Denmark Hill is a detached villa consisting of a three-storeyed central block flanked

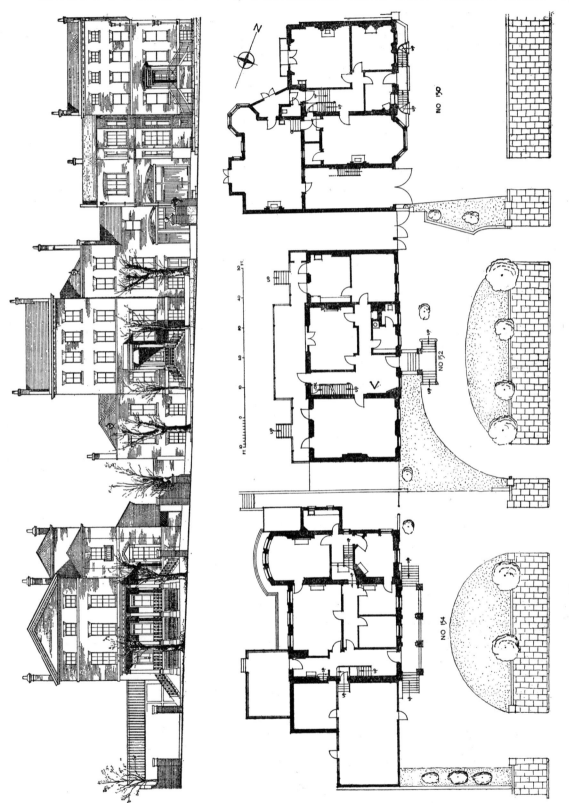

Fig. 47. Nos. 150–154 Denmark Hill, 1785–8: ground-floor plan and elevation

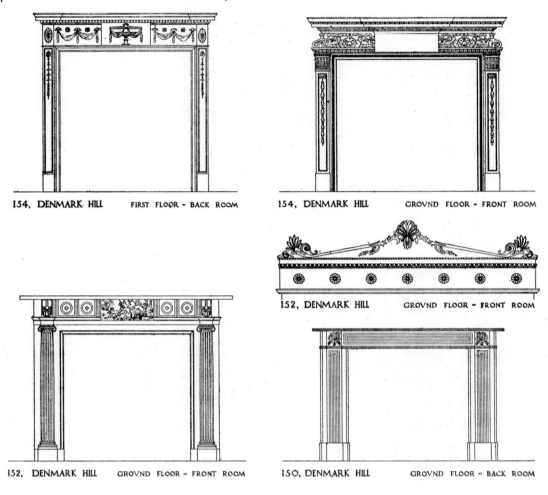

154, DENMARK HILL   FIRST FLOOR - BACK ROOM

154, DENMARK HILL   GROVND FLOOR - FRONT ROOM

152, DENMARK HILL   GROVND FLOOR - FRONT ROOM

152, DENMARK HILL   GROVND FLOOR - FRONT ROOM

150, DENMARK HILL   GROVND FLOOR - BACK ROOM

SCALE OF 12 9 6 3 0 ⎹⎹ 1 2 3 4 FEET

Fig. 48a. Nos. 150–154 Denmark Hill, 1785–8, chimney pieces and overdoor

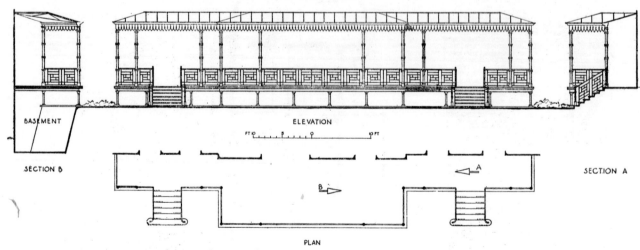

BASEMENT

ELEVATION

FT 10 ⎹ 0 10 FT

SECTION B

B

A

SECTION A

PLAN

Fig. 48b. No. 152 Denmark Hill, 1787–8, verandah

by two-storeyed wings, that to the south having been demolished, the whole raised on a semi-basement.

Before maltreatment, the front towards Denmark Hill was a design of great charm and distinction, carried out in stock brick with stone dressings. The three-storeyed centre projects slightly forward from the two-storeyed wings and its ground storey has a wooden portico-verandah of three bays, approached by stone steps at each end. The four equally spaced columns have stone

INS 12   O   I   2 FT.

Fig. 49. No. 154 Denmark Hill, balustrade

pedestals and bases, slender wooden shafts, and composed capitals of Ionic derivation. The delicately moulded entablature has a frieze decoration of husk-festoons linking vases and paterae The stucco-faced wall behind the colonnade has pilasters responding to the columns and in each bay is a tall rectangular opening, respectively a door and two windows. The three tall rectangular windows of the first floor, and the three almost square windows of the second floor are equally spaced in the brick wall face, without architraves but underlined by narrow sill-bands. Above is a triangular pediment with a mutule cornice and a plain brick tympanum. The brick face of the surviving wing has a slightly recessed centre, containing on the ground storey a tall rectangular

window dressed in wood with Doric pilasters and a triangular pediment. The sill-band continues below the plain first-floor window, and the crowning cornice is moulded. The cast-iron balustrade to the verandah is probably Victorian.

Inside, the house has been considerably altered, but some of the original decorative features remain. Most noteworthy is the staircase, of charming form and design, its iron balustrade of vase-profile standards supporting a mahogany handrail with the newel terminals inlaid with ebony stars (fig. 49). Some of the rooms retain their plaster cornices and chimneypieces of wood and composition.

No. 164 Denmark Hill   [223]
Formerly No. 180 Denmark Hill

South of No. 154 the only survivor of the original houses is No. 164, a two-storey house which has been refaced but retains its original Greek Doric porch.

Houses on Denmark Hill and Herne Hill now Demolished

When John Ruskin was four years old his parents went to live at Herne Hill and later moved to Denmark Hill. Ruskin's account of his childhood there goes far to explain the urge which seized so many wealthy Londoners to move out into the country in the early 19th century (see page 11). In 1823 Ruskin's father took a long lease of a semi-detached house at Herne Hill.[54] The house was later numbered 28 and was demolished in or shortly before 1923. Its site is now occupied by Nos. 26 and 28 Herne Hill, and a tablet commemorating John Ruskin's association with the place stands in the garden of No. 28. In 1842 the Ruskin family moved to a larger detached house at Denmark Hill, whose site—for it too has been demolished—was in the parish of Lambeth but is now in the borough of Camberwell, and is occupied by a block of flats. This house remained Ruskin's home until 1871. In the latter part of his life a cousin lived at 28 Herne Hill, and John Ruskin frequently stayed there.[54]

Eight of the original houses facing Denmark Hill were demolished for the formation of Ruskin Park. There are photographs of all of them in the Photographic Library of the London County Council.

No. 162 was a late 18th century house which

in size, general form and some details, closely resembled No. 152. The body of the house contained a basement and three storeys, and was flanked by narrow one-storey wings. The stock brick front was three windows wide with the doorway on the left, while each wing contained a single window. All the windows were rectangular and without architraves, their heights being proportionate to the three storeys. There was a plinth-band to the ground storey, a sill-band to the first-floor windows, and a crowning mutule cornice with a blocking course, while each wing had a parapet with an open balustrade of equal width to the window below. The chief ornamental feature was the Coade-stone surround to the arch-headed doorway, consisting of vermiculated rustic-blocks and a mask-keystone, the door being flanked by side-lights and surmounted by a finely detailed radial fanlight.

Nos. 164 and 166 were detached houses of heavy Victorian design, very similar and of small interest.

No. 168 was a large detached house of late 18th century date, with a wide-fronted centre of three storeys and one-storey wings fronted by colonnades of three bays. The stock brick front was a balanced design in which paired windows flanked the central porch and an elaborated first-floor window, the windows generally being rectangular and without architraves, their heights proportioned to the three storeys. There was a continued sill-band to the first-floor windows and a crowning mutule cornice with a blocking course. The wide entrance porch had two pairs of slender columns, with water-leaf capitals, supporting a triglyphed entablature. Single columns of the same design were used for the wing colonnades where the entablature was surmounted by a balustrade. The middle first-floor window, set in a wide segmental-headed opening, was divided into three lights by attenuated columns supporting an entablature and a lunette adorned with an outer ring of fan ornament. The garden front, to which considerable additions had been made, was faced with stucco and adorned at ground-floor level by a long verandah of "Gothic" design.

No. 170 was nearly identical to No. 168. The columns of the porch, however, were more widely spaced and the doorway was arch-headed, while the entablature of the central first-floor window was replaced by a simple transom. The ground storey of the garden front projected from the body of the house, having at its centre a recessed portico.

No. 172 was again similar to No. 168, the variations here being chiefly confined to the design of the porch which had single Doric columns supporting a plain entablature, while the mutules of the crowning cornice were spaced at very wide intervals. This house also had plain single-storey wings.

No. 174 was a late Georgian house with a plain stucco-faced front. The central portion, three storeys high and three windows wide, was flanked on the right by a segmental bow of the same height, and on the left by a wing of two lofty storeys, two windows wide. The ground-storey windows in the central portion and bow were arch-headed and set in recesses, while a cumbrous porch projected on the left of the bow. The simply moulded crowning cornice was surmounted by a blocking course. The garden front, of stock brick, was of no architectural interest.

No. 176, another late Georgian house, had a wide front of two storeys, faced with stucco. The pedimented central feature, three windows wide, was flanked by unequal wings, the left being one window wide and the right two. A Doric porch projected from the central feature. On the garden front both wings projected well forward from the pedimented centre.

No. 18 Herne Hill was demolished shortly after the war of 1939–45. It was a large detached house with a stucco-faced front of Regency Greek design. The central block, three storeys high, was flanked by single-storey wings. The projecting ground storey consisted of a Doric porch centred between flanking faces each containing a single window, framed by an eared architrave, the whole finished with an entablature having a frieze decorated at wide intervals with wreaths. Each upper storey had three widely-spaced windows framed by architraves, the middle first-floor window having in addition a cornice resting on scroll consoles. The crowning cornice was surmounted by a blocking course.

In the absence of contrary evidence, it is suggested that William Blackburn might well have designed Nos. 168, 170 and 172, Denmark Hill, for details in their elevations can be matched in Blackburn's authenticated works. For example, the three-light window treatment occurs in his Unitarian Chapel at Lewin's Mead, Bristol, while the attenuated delicacy of the porches recalls the portico at No. 154 Denmark Hill.

[224] ST. MATTHEW'S CHURCH, DENMARK HILL

In 1792 many of the inhabitants of the Camberwell Green area "found it very difficult or impracticable to procure Seats or accommodation to attend Divine Service in the Parish Church of Camberwell";[55] they therefore decided to build a proprietary chapel. A committee was elected and in 1794 Claude (later Sir Claude) Champion de Crespigny granted a 99 year lease of the site now occupied by St. Matthew's; the land formed part of four acres which de Crespigny had bought from William Man Godschall in 1783. The chapel accommodated 750 people and was built between 1792 and 1794, the cost being met by twenty to thirty subscriptions of between £100 and £150 each. Each subscriber was entitled to a pew for six persons; part of the remaining accommodation was allotted to the use of the poor.[55]

In 1814 a surveyor reported that the chapel required "very considerable repair & that the roof was in danger of falling in".[55] After several of the subscribing proprietors had refused to contribute towards the cost, a majority of them apparently bought the shares of the more reluctant minority at £30 each. The repairs were then presumably carried out for the chapel continued in use until 1846. By that time the chapel was inadequate for the needs of the growing population of the neighbourhood, and there were 250 applications for sittings which could not be provided. In 1848 both the freehold and the leasehold interests were freely conveyed to the Church Building Commissioners. The chapel was rebuilt at a cost of £6,547 (excluding the tower and spire) and was consecrated on July 15, 1848, A. D. Gough being the architect (Plate 14b). An Ecclesiastical District was assigned shortly afterwards.[55] The tower and spire were completed by 1858.[56] The building was destroyed by enemy action in 1940.

This church, of which only the steeple and part of the east end remain, was a Victorian Gothic building of ragstone with Bath stone dressings. The design had one unusual and ingenious feature, for while the east end presented in effect a five-sided apse with a narrow ambulatory, the latter formed in fact a pair of entrance passages leading left and right from the high gabled entrance arch. The elongated windows of the apse clerestory were surmounted by elaborate hoods and placed between thin buttresses with crocketed pinnacles. The tall and slender steeple, standing against the north side of the church, has a French flamboyant character and consists of a two-stage square tower surmounted by an octangular spire.

NOS. 136–142 (even) DENMARK HILL   [225]

These houses stand on a small piece of land which formerly belonged to the de Crespigny family; they were erected between 1810 and 1824.[37] They form two plain pairs of semi-detached houses, built in stock brick, of three storeys with semi-basements. Their entrance wings, set back slightly at the sides, are a storey less in height. The ground-floor windows are recessed in round-headed arches linked by plain imposts. Each entrance has fluted pilasters, a mutule transom and a simple fanlight of circular pattern. No. 142, now serving as a temporary church for St. Matthew's parish, has a later ground-floor bay window.

DENMARK PLACE BAPTIST CHURCH, COLD-   [226]
HARBOUR LANE

In 1802 a small Baptist chapel was erected at the junction of Coldharbour Lane and Denmark Hill.[57] By 1823 the congregation had almost dwindled away, but under the leadership of a new minister, Dr. Edward Steane, its fortunes revived so quickly that a larger building was needed.[58] The present church, which was designed by Mr. Burrell[a] and built by Mr. Humphries, cost £3,700, and was opened on June 29, 1825.[57] Side galleries were added in 1832, and further alterations were made in 1869.[59]

The church is a plain stock brick building, and has a front with three round arches supporting a pediment. The arches have keystones, the centre one being incised "A.D. 1823", probably in commemoration of the renewal of the chapel by Dr. Steane. There are four entrances, each of which has a segmental or triangular pediment borne on consoles.

NOS. 125 AND 127 COLDHARBOUR LANE   [227]
Formerly Nos. 3 and 4 Adelphi Place

These houses stand on a piece of freehold land formerly in the possession of Susannah Vaughan,

[a] Probably J. Burrell. See *A Biographical Dictionary of English Architects, 1660–1840*, by H. M. Colvin, 1954, p. 108.

and are the survivors of Adelphi Place, a row which was probably erected between 1830 and 1834.[60] The easternmost house, which was numbered 119 and was formerly known as White Cottage, was a detached two-storey stucco villa. It has now been demolished, but is illustrated in a supplement to *The Architect and Building News* of December 2, 1932. Nos. 125 and 127 are a pair of houses now very much mutilated. Built of stock brick with slated mansard roofs they are three storeys high with a semi-basement, and an attic in the roof. The party wall is marked by a recession in the wall face and each house is one window wide, the entrance being at the side. The windows are square-headed, there is a sill-band at first-floor level and the simple cornice is finished with a blocking course. On the side elevation of No. 125 a semi-circular patterned fanlight of a former front door remains.

Nos. 121 and 123 were probably similar.

[228] HERNE HILL RAILWAY STATION

The decline of Denmark Hill and Herne Hill as wealthy residential areas began in the 1860s when the railways invaded the neighbourhood. Herne Hill became the junction of the two arms of the Metropolitan Extensions of the London, Chatham and Dover Company. The whole scheme, of which Herne Hill Station (Plate 39a) forms part, was completed in 1863, Cubitt and Turner being the engineers, and Peto and Betts the general contractors. In 1866 a loop line connecting Victoria and London Bridge Stations was built through Denmark Hill. With quick and cheap access to London, large numbers of small houses were soon afterwards built in the neighbourhood.

[229] LOUGHBOROUGH PARK CONGREGATIONAL CHAPEL, COLDHARBOUR LANE

This chapel, whose foundation stone was laid in 1860, is a plain building built in grey brick with stone dressings and designed in quasi-Norman style. It has long lancet windows at the sides and a large wheel window set in the north front. There are vigorously carved foliated pilasters flanking this window and at the corners of the building, and machicolations to the north gable and the eaves as well as to the tower. The latter, built some years after the rest of the chapel, is sited at the north-west corner and is capped by a sharply-pitched chisel-type slated roof. The main

roof, also of slate, is punctuated by ventilating dormers. There is a small entrance porch in the centre of the north front. The chapel is used for storage purposes at the present.

ST. SAVIOUR'S CHURCH, HERNE HILL ROAD [230]

In 1864 a temporary church to serve this neighbourhood was erected on the north side of Coldharbour Lane. Shortly afterwards the Ecclesiastical Commissioners offered a site for a permanent church at the corner of Coldharbour Lane and Flaxman Road, but the plans drawn up by the local church building committee were rejected by the Commissioners. Owing to lack of money the whole project was abandoned. In 1865 James Lewis Minet offered to present an acre of ground in Herne Hill Road and fifty pounds towards the cost of building a church there. In 1866 the land was freely given to the Ecclesiastical Commissioners, who contributed £500 to the building fund. The foundation stone was laid by Melicent, wife of William Henry Stone, M.P., on June 29, 1866. The church accommodated 938 people and was consecrated by the Bishop of Winchester on June 25, 1867. The architect was A. D. Gough,[61] the chancel and south transept being added later to the designs of W. Gibbs Bartleet (Plate 15a).[62]

St. Saviour's is an uncouth Victorian building of ragstone dressed with Bath stone. The aisled nave of four bays, a hybrid design with late Norman and Early English characteristics, is the earlier portion to which were added double transepts and an apsidal-ended chancel, more consistently Gothic in style with Geometrical and plate tracery in the windows. The tower at the north-west corner has five offset stages, the topmost being arcaded and surmounted by a pyramid roof, and there is a tall round pinnacle at the north-west angle. The interior calls for little comment—the nave arches are Norman in style, there is no chancel arch, and the windows of the eastern apse have two lights with a six-foil above.

ST. SAVIOUR'S C.E. PRIMARY SCHOOL, [231] HERNE HILL ROAD

This school was built in 1868, shortly after the completion of St. Saviour's Church. The cost was £1,550, of which £1,062 was raised by local voluntary contributions.[39] The school was enlarged in 1892.[63] It occupies a stock brick building designed in the Gothic style.

[232] CARNEGIE PUBLIC LIBRARY, HERNE HILL
ROAD

In 1901 the Lambeth Borough Librarian, F. J. Burgoyne, applied to Andrew Carnegie for financial help to build a library in the Herne Hill area and so complete the library system of the borough. In the following year Carnegie promised to grant £12,500.[64] A site was then acquired and H. Wakeford and Sons were appointed architects.[65] A tender for £11,316 from Messrs. Holliday and Greenwood was accepted,[64] and the library was opened by Lady Durning Lawrence on July 9, 1906.[66]

The library consists of an imposing formal group of buildings of two and three storeys designed in free Renaissance style. It stands on a sloping site and is built of red brick, brown unglazed terracotta also being used extensively as a facing material. The central entrance is slightly set forward and has a broken pediment and gable above. The pavilion ends, which are similarly detailed, are flanked by coupled Ionic columns. The three-storeyed wings each have two pedimented gables and their entrances are hooded. All the roofs are of green slate and each wing is surmounted by a small octagonal lantern.

[233] ST. PHILIP AND ST. JAMES ROMAN
CATHOLIC CHURCH, POPLAR WALK

This church was erected in 1905[63] and is a simple stock brick building with open pedimented east and west gables and a slate roof. A large circular west window, with transoms and mullions forming an open cross within it, is set above the entrance. A five-bay round-arched arcade built on the north side was intended to lead to an aisle but this extension has never been made. The architect was probably F. W. Tasker.

[234] RUSKIN PARK

The site of Ruskin Park was acquired by the London County Council in two portions. The first portion cost £48,000,[67] and was opened on February 2, 1907;[68] the second portion cost £24,000[67] and was opened on February 19, 1910.[69] Generous subscriptions were received from the Metropolitan boroughs of Camberwell, Lambeth and Southwark and a local committee collected voluntary contributions for both purchases. A small piece of land was added in 1929.[67] Eight of the original houses facing Denmark Hill

were included in the new Park, and have subsequently been demolished (see page 149). One of these houses, formerly No. 170, was the home of Captain James Wilson, and its portico has been retained as a shelter. A commemorative tablet records that "In the house of which this shelter is a remainder lived 1799–1814 Captain James Wilson, who was born at Newcastle-on-Tyne 1760 and after an adventurous life at sea during which he was present at the Battles of Lexington and Bunker's Hill and was confined nearly two years in the Black Hole at Seringapatam, served the London Missionary Society 1796–98 as Honorary Commander of the 'Duff', the first British Missionary Ship of modern times". Nearby is a sundial commemorating Mendelssohn's stay at Dane House (formerly No. 168), which was then the home of F. C. Benecke. An inscription on the sundial states "Here stood the house where Mendelssohn wrote the Spring Song 1842".

KING'S COLLEGE HOSPITAL   [235]

In 1839 the Council of King's College, London University, realizing that facilities for clinical training for the medical students of the College were needed, took on lease the former workhouse of the parish of St. Clement Danes. This building was converted into a hospital by Sir Robert Smirke;[70] in 1852 a new building was erected near by to the designs of Thomas Bellamy.[71] By the end of the 19th century changes in the character of the locality had deprived the hospital of much of its usefulness, and the idea of removing it elsewhere was already being discussed.[72] In 1904 the Hon. W. F. D. Smith, M.P., purchased 11 acres of land at Denmark Hill[73] which he presented to the Governors of the hospital. A competition limited to six leading architects[74] for the design of the new buildings was won by William Alfred Pite,[75] and the foundation-stone was laid by Edward VII on July 20, 1909.[63] The contractors were Messrs. Foster and Dicksee of Rugby;[70] the first portion of the hospital to be completed was opened by George V on July 26, 1913.

The private patients' wards were erected in 1937 to the designs of Messrs. Colcutt and Hamp. The tower over their entrance was erected by Sir Connop Guthrie, bart., K.B.E., to commemorate the success of his son Giles in the 1936 Portsmouth–Johannesburg Air Race.

The hospital is arranged with the main administration block, which is five-storeyed and dominates the group, situated at the centre of the north or Bessemer Road front. This block extends back as far as the main corridor which is the spine of the scheme and runs east–west bisecting the site. Southward at right angles from this corridor run various ward blocks of two and three storeys.

The older parts of the hospital are designed in a Classical style characteristic of the early 18th century with a particular Vanbrughian flavour in the low pedimented pavilions flanking the administration block. The hospital is built mostly of stock brick but has some red brick, and Portland stone dressings are used freely.

The Denmark Hill entrance to the private patients' wards, adjoining No. 150, is surmounted by a tower of modernistic design with neo-Georgian elements. At each side of the entrance, which has a cantilevered hood, there are four stone panels carved with various drug-producing flowers. In front of this entrance stands a marble statue to Dr. Robert Bentley Todd, 1809–60, who was Professor of Physiology at the hospital.

The chapel is in effect a simple basilica with round-headed windows designed to receive the good late Victorian stained glass windows removed from the former hospital; it is situated at first-floor level on the axis southward of the administration block.

CHAPTER VI

Tulse Hill and Brockwell Park

THE areas now known as Tulse Hill and Brockwell Park correspond roughly with the Manor or Manors of Bodley, Upgrove, and Scarlettes,[1] the boundaries of which cannot be established with any precision.[2] A family called de Bodyleys held lands in Lambeth in the 13th century, and in the first half of the 14th century lands at "Bodele" in Lambeth were held by a family called Hardel.[3] In 1352 the Crown granted a licence to the hospital of St. Thomas the Martyr in Southwark to receive 130 acres of land and the reversion of another 67 acres,[4] all of which had belonged to the Hardel family, for the health of the souls of the grantors and the "sustentation of the poor sick".[3] In 1379 the hospital also acquired 20 acres of land in Lambeth from Nicholas de Carreu.[5] Five years later the latter was granted lands in Lambeth which had previously belonged to Stephen Skarlet.[3] In 1456 a lease of the Manor of Bodley was granted to Ralph Leigh and in 1537 a lease of the Manors of Bodley and Upgrove with all the lands called Scarlettes was granted to William Peter of London.[6] The property was surrendered to the Crown in the following year and passed with the hospital's other lands rapidly through various private hands, until in 1545 it again entered the possession of the Leigh family.[7] In 1634 the property was described as "All those the mannors called or knowne by the names of Bodyleyes Upgroves and Scarlettes", containing about 250 acres.[8]

During the Commonwealth, Bodley, Upgrove and Scarlettes were held by the Tulse family,[1] from whom Tulse Hill gets its name. Sir Henry Tulse's daughter, Elizabeth, married Richard (the first Lord) Onslow, Speaker of the House of Commons from 1708 to 1710.[9] After his death in 1717 the lands in Lambeth passed to his son Thomas Onslow,[10] who died in 1740, and then to his grandson, Richard Onslow,[11] who died in 1766 without issue.[9] The property was then shared between the descendants of two of the first Lord Onslow's daughters,[12] and in 1789 the greater part of it was sold to William Cole;[13] the rest, comprising the northern and western parts of what is now Brockwell Park, was apparently sold at about the same time to William Winter.[14] In 1766 and 1769 William Cole had been admitted to two moieties of 16 acres of adjoining copyhold land, part of Lambeth Manor, which were known as Page's Fields.[15] By his will dated June 5, 1807, Cole divided his property; the western portion, comprising Tulse Hill and his copyhold in Page's Fields were left to Mercy Cressingham, spinster, while the eastern half comprising his capital messuage known as Brockwell Hall, with its lands and appurtenances were left to Richard Ogbourne of Bishopsgate Street, stationer.[16] In 1809 Richard Ogbourne sold Brockwell Hall and 60 acres of land to John Blades,[17] a glass manufacturer who later also bought part of Winter's land.[18] The western or Tulse Hill part of the estate was developed for residential purposes by Mercy Cressingham's husband, Dr. Thomas Edwards, while most of the eastern half remained the private grounds of the Blades-Blackburn family until it was eventually bought for a public park.

But before the two estates assumed their very different characters there seems to have been a short-lived attempt by Blades and Edwards to co-operate in developing the whole area as a less grandiose version of John Nash's schemes in Regent's Park. Amongst the Papworth Collection of drawings in the library of the Royal Institute of British Architects is a plan (Plate 64) drawn in 1823 and marked with the name of Chandler and Buckingham, a firm of nurserymen in Vauxhall,[19] in which a few well-sited roads covering both estates were to provide access to large detached houses with ample gardens. The roads now known as Tulse Hill and Upper Tulse Hill (marked on the plan as Lower Tulse Hill Road and Upper Tulse Hill Road) had already been built by Dr. Edwards before 1821[20] and the subsequent development on his estates followed the lines shown in the plan. But Blades was evidently not attracted by the scheme, and the history of the two estates diverged.

TULSE HILL ESTATE

The development of Tulse Hill was largely the work of Dr. Thomas Edwards (1775?–1845), a legal writer who married Mercy Cressingham, probably in 1811. Edwards studied at Trinity Hall, Cambridge, and took the degrees of LL.B. and LL.D. in 1800 and 1805 respectively. He later became a Fellow of his College and was admitted advocate at Doctors' Commons. He was a member of the Lambeth Church Building Committee which supervised the erection of the four "Waterloo" churches in the parish, and as a Justice of the Peace for Surrey he interested himself in social questions. He died at The Grove, Carshalton, on October 29, 1845.[21]

In 1810 there was only one house on the Edwards' land, Tulse Hill Farm, and there were only very short frontages to the existing roads. At first sight, therefore, it might have seemed likely that no successful development would take place so far south in the parish for some decades. But in fact its pleasant situation on high ground, combined with the enterprise of Dr. Edwards, soon made Tulse Hill a flourishing residential suburb.

Who designed the layout of the estate for Dr. Edwards is not known. Chandler and Buckingham, the nurserymen whose plan of the Brockwell and Tulse Hill estates has been mentioned above, may have been responsible, but Daniel Gould was employed by Dr. Edwards as a surveyor from 1813 until at least 1842; Tulse Hill was "parcelled out . . . for building ground"[22] by Gould, and it is therefore more likely that he suggested how the roads should run.

Dr. Edwards' first step was taken in 1814 when he paid £500 for a thin strip of ground connecting Brixton Hill with his land on Tulse Hill.[23] Before 1821 he laid out two private roads, now Tulse Hill and Upper Tulse Hill, which provided access to a large part of his estate. They evidently fulfilled a need, for they were both taken over by the parish as early as 1822, and the tolls were abolished.[20] At the north-west end of Upper Tulse Hill the land alongside the road did not belong to Dr. Edwards, and here a number of small terrace-houses were erected on the western side, mostly between 1843 and 1850. The Edwards' estate was, however, exclusively for the well-to-do. The land fronting the roads was divided up into plots of varying sizes, and was let on long leases of up to 99 years. Some of the lessees took several adjacent plots and assigned their interest immediately after the houses were completed; but the plots were more often leased singly, most of the houses on the estate being detached. All the leases contained safeguards for the preservation of the exclusive character which the estate was intended to provide. No house costing less than a certain figure (usually £700) was to be built, a minimum distance from the road was prescribed for each house, and no school, shop, trade or manufactory was to be established without permission; in some cases the lessee had to undertake to pay a reasonable share of the cost of making such drains and sewers as might be needed in the future.[24]

In Upper Tulse Hill most of the early houses were on the west side of the road and building progressed southwards. In Tulse Hill building began at the Brixton end of the road and progressed southwards, chiefly on the west side, where by 1843 there was a continuous line of houses, nearly all detached and many with coach-houses at the side, stretching up to the top of the hill; all of these have now been demolished. By 1843, or just over 20 years after the development of the estate began, there were some 125 houses on the Edwards' property.[25] The success in the 19th century of this type of suburban development, catering for large families with ample domestic service, was as striking as the rapidity of its disappearance in favour of flats in the 20th century.

After the death of Dr. Edwards in 1845 and of his wife in 1851, most of the estate passed to Mercy Edwards' brother, Jonah Cressingham. The most important part of the estate still to be developed was Page's Fields, comprising some 16 acres between Tulse Hill and Norwood Road. This land was former copyhold land, part of Lambeth Manor, which had been enfranchised in 1844.[26] A road (now called Trinity Rise) was built shortly afterwards connecting Tulse Hill with Norwood Road.

UPPER TULSE HILL

The houses on the Edwards' property on the west side of this road and north of Roupell Road were formerly in the parish of Lambeth but are now in the borough of Wandsworth; they are included in this volume because they have no historical connection with Wandsworth. In 1829

Thomas and Mercy Edwards leased a plot of land on the west side of the road to Sophia Pearce, widow, together with a house lately erected thereon. This house has since been demolished, but in 1840 and 1841 Mrs. Pearce mortgaged her property and Nos. 54 and 56, formerly Elm Cottage and Scotia Cottage, were probably erected shortly afterwards;[27] they were certainly standing in 1843.[28] They are an undistinguished pair of two-storey brick houses finished with a cornice and blocking course. In 1820 the site of Nos. 58 and 60 was leased by Michael Gamon of Somerset Street, St. Marylebone (who already had a head lease of a larger area from Dr. and Mrs. Edwards) to John Hebbes of Brixton Hill, builder, together with the two cottages then in course of erection; Hebbes was subsequently ejected and in 1824 the two houses were leased to John Tame, yeoman.[27] They are a stucco fronted two-storey pair sharing a pediment. In 1823 Thomas and Mercy Edwards granted a 99 year lease dating from March 25, 1822, to Michael Gamon of land and three houses "now erected and built or partly erected and built thereon".[29] Of these three houses the sole survivor is No. 66, a two-storey villa with wings which project forward at each side of the central entrance; the stucco-faced front is finished with a cornice and blocking course. In 1822 Simon Dodd Guthrie was granted a 96 year lease of land together with two houses, Nos. 92 and 94 (Plate 59b, fig. 50) "then erecting and building thereon".[30] These are semi-detached houses of three storeys above semi-basements, with stucco-faced fronts unified by a first-floor balcony and finished with a cornice and blocking course. No. 92 was formerly known as Eldon House; No. 94 is derelict. In the 1820s houses of this type were being put up in large numbers along Clapham and Brixton Roads, but in the more prosperous neighbourhood of Tulse Hill they were quickly superseded by detached villas, mostly of two storeys. No. 100 Upper Tulse Hill, formerly Laurel Bank (Plate 61b), was erected under a 99 year lease granted to William Andrews in 1824;[31] it is a two-storey villa with a stucco front and a central porch with Roman Doric columns; at the side is a coach-house with an arched entrance. Nos. 102 and 104, formerly Leckhampton Villa and Percy Cottage, were built under a lease granted to John Gamon in 1820, when they were described as "lately erected".[32] No. 102, which has been altered,

[236]
[237]
[238]
[239]
[240]
[241]

retains an Ionic columned porch; engaged columns of the same order flank the service entrance. No. 104 has wreaths on the frieze beneath its eaves and a porch with coarse Greek Doric columns. The land on which No. 106 stands was leased in

[242]

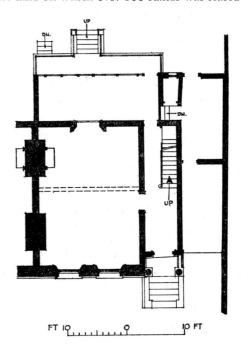

Fig. 50. No. 92 Upper Tulse Hill, ground-floor plan

1826 to George Simson, upholsterer, together with the house "erected and built or now erecting and building thereon".[32] It has a stock brick front with canted bays at each side of a simply pilastered entrance. The cast-iron gate standards have anthemion and acanthus ornament. No. 108, formerly Mountfield and now Kingsdown Cottage (Plate 60b), was built under a lease of 1830 granted to Daniel Wilson Davidson,[32] a solicitor of Clement's Inn who also occupied the house.[33] It has a neat stock brick front with round-headed openings on the ground floor; the entrance is in the centre and is flanked by Greek Doric columns. Nos. 110, 112, and 114 (No. 112 formerly Fitzroy Villa, No. 114 formerly Leiston House) were built under one lease granted in 1843 to Daniel Chambers of Brighton Terrace, Brixton;[34] they were then described as lately erected. Nos. 112 and 114 have recently been demolished, but they were very similar to No. 110, which is a three-storey house having a central porch with

[243]
[244]

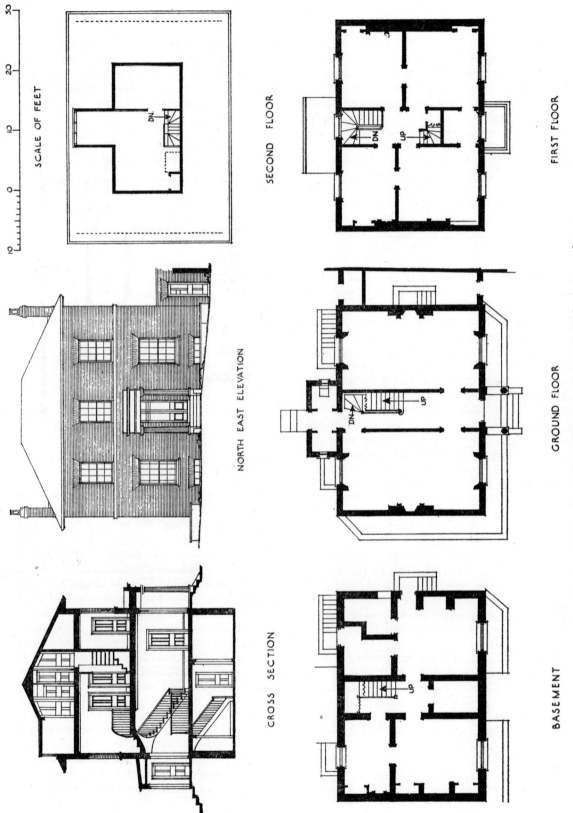

SCALE OF FEET

SECOND FLOOR.

FIRST FLOOR.

NORTH EAST ELEVATION

GROUND FLOOR

CROSS SECTION

BASEMENT

Fig. 51. No. 122 Upper Tulse Hill, 1841. Lessee, W. White, hat manufacturer

[245] coarsely detailed Tuscan columns. No. 116, formerly Parel Lodge, was built under a lease of 1826 granted to John Gubbs, an insurance broker of Lloyds;[35] it is a two-storey house with a semi-basement, stucco-fronted and having a central [246] porch with Greek Doric columns. No. 118, formerly St. James Villa, is identical in appearance and was built under a lease of 1826 granted to William Macfarland, who may perhaps be identified with "Wm. M'Farland", an umbrella manu-[247] facturer in the Strand.[36] Nos. 120 and 122 (Plate 61a, fig. 51), formerly Ormesby Cottage and Nottingham Cottage (now Hollyhurst) respectively, were both built under leases granted to William White, who is variously described as of "Tulse Hill, gentleman", and of Cheapside, hat manufacturer. The lease of No. 122 was granted in 1841.[37] It is a double-fronted house of two storeys and a semi-basement, exceptionally well maintained and very free from alteration. The brick front is a simple and elegant composition, the designer's care for detail being evident in such things as the marginal panes of the ground-floor windows, which flank the Greek Doric porch. A continued sill underlines the three first-floor windows, and the low-pitched slated roof has wide overhanging eaves. All the remaining houses on this side of Upper Tulse Hill were built shortly before 1843 and are not of much interest; [248] Nos. 134 and 136 are a pair of detached two-storey villas raised above semi-basements; both have Greek Doric porches placed centrally, and the ground-floor windows have marginal panes.

On the east side of Upper Tulse Hill there was [249] no building until the 1840s, when Nos. 55, 57, 61, 67–75 (odd), formerly Nos. 41–55 (odd), were erected. The standard of building was much lower than on the west side, and the houses erected are uninteresting; most of them have two storeys with semi-basements and central entrance porches carried on debased Tuscan columns.

TULSE HILL

On the east side of the road the only surviving [250] example of early building is No. 47, formerly No. 13 and known as Adelaide Lodge, now occupied by Sir Henry Tate's Nurses' Home, which was probably erected about 1824. It is a two-storey stock brick building with a semi-basement, and has been much altered and enlarged. Its central porch has key-ornamented pilasters, and the windows have moulded architraves; the

ground-floor windows also have bracketed hoods with paterae in their friezes. For the next quarter of a mile there are no 19th century houses left on this side; higher up the hill where the original houses survive, the development was later, most of Nos. 107–147 (odd), formerly Nos. 73–113 [251] (odd), being built between 1850 and 1870. No. 107 (Plate 63a), formerly No. 73 and called St. David's, was designed by Charles Hambridge of Guilford Street, Russell Square, for Thomas Cree, a solicitor in the firm of Cree and Last, of Gray's Inn Square. The house was erected in 1865, and the lowest tender, which was submitted by Messrs. Brown and Robinson, was for £4,223;[38] it is now used by the London County Council as a Day Nursery. The house has three storeys and a semi-basement and is built of stock brick and stone. Its full-blooded Victorian Gothic appearance is further enlivened by red and yellow bricks used in the first-floor window arches, and by vigorous foliated carving. Nos. 109–129 are large three-storey houses of unostentatious design with central porches carried on columns. Nos. 131–141, The Lawn, three identical pairs of houses, have grey brick fronts of austere design with narrow windows; there are Greek Doric porches at the end of each pair. Nos. 143–147 are similar to Nos. 109–129 though No. 145 has been much mutilated.

On the southern side of the hill sloping down towards Norwood, most of the houses are of late date and larger than the earlier ones. No. 153, [252] formerly No. 119 and called Egremont House, was designed by Charles Gray for Mr. R. Griffiths, publican of the Duke of Sussex, Gibson Street, Waterloo Road,[39] and was built in 1853. The lowest tender, submitted by Rowland and Evans, was for £2,101.[40] It formerly exhibited the mixture of styles characteristic of mid 19th century architecture, but after being severely damaged by enemy action in the war of 1939–45 it was refronted and now has a Neo-Georgian porch; the architect was Alister G. MacDonald.[41] No. 155 (Plate 62b), formerly No. 121, origin-[253] ally called Berry House and later known as Silwood Hall, is now occupied by the St. Martin-in-the-Fields High School for Girls. It was built in 1856–7 and its first occupier was Edward Groves. Although much altered and enlarged, it is still the most imposing house in the road. It has a white stucco front of Italianate Classical design, with three-storey pavilions at each side of the two-storey entrance; the return elevations are plain and faced with stock brick.

[254] No. 157, called Kenilworth (Plate 63b), was built in 1888 and was the last large house to be erected in this once favoured area; the builder was W. Rowe of Lansdowne Road, S.W.,[42] and its occupier in 1892 was Miles Simpson. Its red brick exterior illustrates the rising influence of Norman Shaw's "Queen Anne" revival. Lower down the hill stand two pleasant two-storey

[255] detached houses with semi-basements. Nos. 181 and 183, formerly Nos. 145 and 147 and known as Osborne Lodge and Woodlands respectively, were built shortly before 1843. Both have central porches, with Tuscan columns at No. 181.

Of the surviving houses on the west side of

[256] Tulse Hill, No. 122, formerly No. 128 and known as Fairfield or Fairfield House, is the earliest. In 1825 Thomas and Mercy Edwards granted a 99-year lease to William Macfarland (see page 159) of land at Tulse Hill on which already stood three houses.[43] The much-mutilated survivor is of two storeys with semi-basement and an attic. The stucco-faced front has shallow projecting bays flanking a central porch supported by Greek Doric columns.

Lower down the hill there formerly stood a house built in 1847 by John Deane, a member of the firm of G. and J. Deane, wholesale and retail hardwaremen, cutlers and jewellers, of King William Street; John Deane had ten shares in the Independent Benefit Building Association, and the cost of the house was partly met by an advance of £750 from the Association.[44] Nos.

[257] 144–154 (even), two-storey houses with semi-basements and attics (Plate 62a), were built in 1843, and were originally known as Prince of Wales Crescent; No. 144 has lately been demolished, and No. 150 was totally destroyed in the war of 1939–45. This group of houses was probably an unsuccessful speculation; the Tithe map marks them all as empty, and they were still being disposed of in 1847, when James Bailey, silk mercer, and Charles Hodgson, printer, were granted a joint lease for 92½ years of No. 152 (formerly Guildford Lodge) and No. 158 (formerly Selwood Lodge); the latter is now

[258] demolished.[45] In 1827 No. 166 (formerly Silverdale Lodge) was leased by Dr. and Mrs. Edwards to Robert Wiss of Fleet Street, engineer; the house was enlarged in 1866.[46] It is a detached house of two storeys and a semi-basement,

with a stucco front. No. 168, formerly Woodbine [259] Cottage, is similar, and was probably erected shortly before 1824; it has later enlargements.

Owing to the depleted state of the Rate Books it has not been possible to plot the position of a few houses whose origins have been discovered from other sources. Two prosperous publicans speculated on the Tulse Hill estate. In 1841 William Crow of the Prince of Wales, Brixton, was granted a lease of a plot,[47] and in 1865 Ezekiel James Bailey of the George Canning, Grove Lane, Camberwell, and the Lord Palmerston, Lordship Lane, Dulwich, erected an unspecified number of houses. The latter commissioned an architect, Frederick Chadwick of 71 High Street, Croydon, and Westminster Chambers, Victoria Street, to design the houses, which were built by Walker and Co. at an estimated cost of £10,500.[48] In 1867 Mr. O. Mullett, who lived at No. 108 Upper Tulse Hill, commissioned J. D. Hayton, architect, to design a house whose estimated cost was £1,115. John Daniel Hayton of 5 Whitehall, was probably a relation of Daniel Hayton, builder, of Effra Road.[49]

HOLY TRINITY CHURCH, TRINITY RISE [260]

A church was needed to complete the development of the estate, and in 1855 Jonah Cressingham freely gave to the Church Building Commissioners the sites of what are now Holy Trinity and the adjoining parsonage house. The church accommodated 1,000 people and cost about £6,000, Cressingham contributing over two-thirds of the money. It was consecrated on February 5, 1856,[50] and the architect was T. D. Barry[51] (Plate 14c, fig. 52).

The proposal to build this church and to assign a Particular District to it evoked the vigorous opposition of the incumbents of St. Matthew's, Brixton, and St. Luke's, Norwood. The former protested that he had already lost the eastern part of his District to St. Matthew's, Denmark Hill, and Angell Town to St. John's, leaving his large church with the poor area of Brixton and the well-to-do area of Tulse Hill, now to be removed. He alleged that Cressingham desired a church merely as an adjunct of the development of his estate. The incumbent of St. Luke's, Norwood, petitioned the Church Building Commissioners three times, protesting that there was no need for the church (the population of the proposed district being only 1,500 in 1853), that there were no poor people in the proposed district, and that the pew-lettings of his church would be greatly diminished. But the Church Building Commissioners overruled all these objections, and a Particular District was assigned in 1856. The unfortunate incumbent of St. Luke's could only protest again at what he termed "so unjustified a concession to private individual interest".[50]

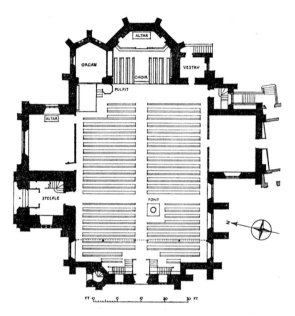

Fig. 52. Holy Trinity, Trinity Rise, plan

The church is in the Early Geometric Decorated style, with nave, transepts and a shallow chancel with an apsidal east end. The nave is spanned without intermediate supports. At the west end there is a small organ gallery. The tower, surmounted by a stone broach spire, stands at the north-west angle of the north transept, with the entrance lobby to the church at its base. The church has a brick carcase faced with Kentish ragstone; the dressings are of Corsham Down Bath stone, and the steeply-pitched roofs are slated. In 1951 three stained glass windows representing the Creation, Redemption and Sanctification were put in the three-light windows of the apse, to replace those destroyed in the war of 1939–45. The artist was Miss Clare Dawson.

The adjoining parsonage was built at the same time and in the same style as the church.

M

BROCKWELL ESTATE

John Blades (c. 1751–1829), who in 1809 purchased 60 acres of land in Brixton from Richard Ogbourne (see page 155), was a wealthy glass-manufacturer with premises at Ludgate Hill.[52] His business was founded in 1780–2 and, after his death, was carried on under the name of Crook and Jones, and later of Jones and Sons.[53] Blades was Sheriff of London and Middlesex in 1812–13. At his death in 1829 he left personal property valued at about £140,000, as well as Severndroog Castle near Shooter's Hill, premises in St. Bride's Avenue, Fleet Street, and the estate at Brixton.[52]

BROCKWELL HALL   [261]

The Lambeth Manor Inclosure map of 1810 shows that the only building standing on Blades' estate at Brixton was Brockwell Hall, which stood near the present Norwood Road. Shortly afterwards Blades demolished this house,[54] and the Rate Books show that between 1811 and 1813 he erected the present house (Plates 66, 67, figs. 53, 54) on top of the hill to the north-west. The design of this house has been attributed to J. B. Papworth, but there seems no reason to doubt that D. R. Roper was the architect. In the *Dictionary of Architecture* Papworth's son, Wyatt Papworth, stated that between 1825 and 1832 his father "designed and superintended Brockwell hall",[55] but as the house was undoubtedly built before 1825 this statement cannot be correct; moreover in a later memoir Wyatt Papworth stated that between 1824 and 1829 his father only "directed repairs at Brockwell Hall, with some furniture".[56] Amongst the extensive collection of J. B. Papworth's drawings in the library of the Royal Institute of British Architects there is only one of Brockwell Hall—a copy of an original drainage plan made in 1813. In *Topographical Surveys through Surrey, Sussex and Kent* (1818) by James Edwards, it is stated that Roper designed the house;[54] Blades was a subscriber to this work and paid for an engraving of Brockwell Hall to appear in the book. The attribution to Roper must therefore be regarded as reliable.

Brockwell Hall is prominently sited on the highest ground in the south part of Brockwell Park. The main building consists of a residential block, a deep oblong in plan with its entrance front facing north-west, and a service wing forming a narrower oblong extending centrally from the south-west side. The small stable range, lying parallel to the south-west face, is linked with the wing by the walls enclosing the service court (fig. 53). The residential block is compactly planned, the accommodation being contained in two lofty storeys raised on a basement and having a small top-lit attic in the roof. The service wing is also of two storeys and a basement, but here the floor heights are less.

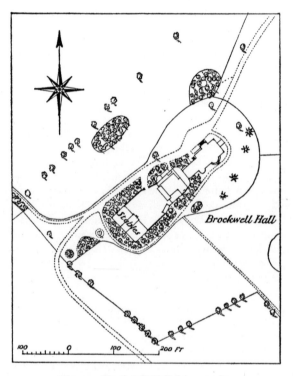

Fig. 53. Brockwell Hall, lay-out plan

Within the centrally placed portico on the north-west front is a doorway opening into a square vestibule, on the right side of which are two doors, the first leading to the staircase hall, and the second to a large room. The corresponding doors on the left side open to the large and small drawing-rooms, these being linked by sliding doors. The door facing the entrance opens to the segmental-ended room that is expressed by the central bow on the south-east front. The bed- and dressing-rooms on the first floor follow an arrangement similar to that of the ground floor.

The exterior of the house is a slightly meretricious design in the free Grecian manner of the early 1800s. Generally, the walls are of "white" brick, stone being used for the deep plinth, the window-sills, the portico and balustrades, and the main cornice with its blocking course. The north-west, or entrance front is a symmetrical composition of three wide bays, the main wall of the middle one being slightly recessed. Centrally, on the ground storey, projects the portico, raised on steps and having two pairs of Ionic plain-shafted columns supporting the entablature and surmounting balustrade. The inside wall contains the segmental-headed entrance, set in a rusticated stone face. The ground storey of each flanking bay has a large rectangular window of three lights, one wide between two narrow. Below the delicately detailed wood frame is a stone panel adorned with a fret, and above is a segmental lunette of stucco modelled with scroll ornaments, the whole being enclosed by a segmental-headed opening in the brick face. Above is centred a single rectangular window without any adornment. The middle bay has a similar window above the portico, but this is set in a segmental-headed shallow recess. The simply moulded main cornice is surmounted by a blocking course.

The north-east elevation contains two tiers of three equally-spaced rectangular windows, those to the ground storey having the simple dressing of a cornice supported on scroll-brackets. The south-east elevation is similar to the north-west, described above, except that instead of the portico there is a segmental bow containing three tall and narrow rectangular windows. The bow is finished with a simple cornice and surmounted by a balustrade. At the junction of the residential and service blocks is a two-storeyed bay surrounded by a cast-iron verandah of Victorian design. The service wing elevations are extremely plain, with two tiers of segmental-headed windows and a brick cornice. The strange howdah-like turret on the roof ridge is probably a Victorian addition.

Without the brilliance of Papworth's original furnishings, the interior is disappointing. The rooms generally have plaster cornices and ceiling borders of stock Grecian pattern, common to many houses of the period. The doors, of painted deal, are more interesting in their detail and have moulded architraves with ornamented stops. By far the most charming feature is the square vestibule, with its shallow domed ceiling rising from pendentives.[a]

[a] At the time of writing this room is divided by a partition screen.

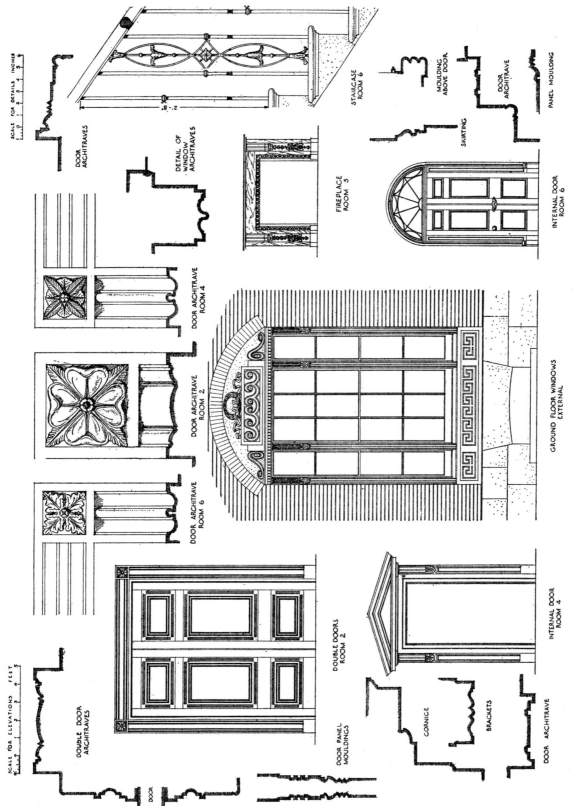

SCALE FOR DETAILS INCHES

DOOR ARCHITRAVES

DETAIL OF WINDOW ARCHITRAVES

DOOR ARCHITRAVE ROOM 4

DOOR ARCHITRAVE ROOM 2

DOOR ARCHITRAVE ROOM 6

SCALE FOR ELEVATIONS FEET

DOUBLE DOOR ARCHITRAVES

DOOR

FIREPLACE ROOM 5

GROUND FLOOR WINDOWS EXTERNAL

DOUBLE DOORS ROOM 2

DOOR PANEL MOULDINGS

CORNICE

BRACKETS

INTERNAL DOOR ROOM 4

DOOR ARCHITRAVE

STAIRCASE ROOM 6

MOULDING ABOVE DOOR

DOOR ARCHITRAVE

PANEL MOULDING

SKIRTING

INTERNAL DOOR ROOM 6

Fig. 54. Brockwell Hall, 1811–13, details. The plan on Plate 66 shows the position of the numbered rooms

The stable range, a balanced composition with a narrow two-storeyed centre flanked by three-bay wings, has segmental-headed windows similar to those of the service wing. The courtyard front, now altered, had two-bay loggias flanking the central feature. At a short distance from the house, near the lake, is a garden shelter consisting of a four-bay portico with offices behind, a simple and attractive design combining Classical and Gothic motifs.

In the 1820s J. B. Papworth did a great deal of work for Blades. He designed some elaborate glassware which the latter was making for the Shah of Persia, and in 1825 he designed a new front for Blades' shop at Ludgate Hill. At the Brockwell estate he directed the formation of roads, drains and fences in preparation for the development of the estate for building purposes. [262] Brockwell (later Clarence) Lodge (Plate 65a) was erected to his designs in 1825–6[57] for the occupation of Mrs. Emma Murray at a cost of £5,000;[56] after Blades' death in 1829 the house was left to his daughter Caroline Prodgers, wife of the Rev. Edwin Prodgers,[58] first vicar of St. Matthew's, Brixton. In 1828 Papworth designed and superintended the erection of a pair of semi-detached houses (Plate 65b) in an intended row running parallel with Dulwich Road and called Brockwell Terrace; the builder of this pair, which was demolished in 1908,[59] was Thomas Burton of Crispin Street, Spitalfields.[57] The death of John Blades in 1829 put an end to further development.

By his will Blades left Brockwell Hall to his daughter Elizabeth Blackburn, wife of Joshua Blackburn, of Russia-mat warehouse, Wormwood Street, Bishopsgate, for their lives, and Clarence Lodge to his daughter Caroline Prodgers and her husband for their lives. Subject to these provisions the whole Brockwell estate was left to Blades' grandson, Joshua Blackburn.[58]

[263] BROCKWELL PARK

Towards the close of the 19th century large numbers of houses were being erected in the Brixton and Herne Hill area, and the population was increasing by leaps and bounds. In 1888 the Lambeth Vestry and the Metropolitan Board of Works obtained statutory powers to buy land and form a small park to be known as Raleigh Park on the east side of Brixton Hill.[60] This scheme was abandoned, however, in favour of acquiring part of the very much larger Blackburn estate. The property was now being administered by Trustees on behalf of Joshua Blackburn. After protracted negotiations the London County Council bought 78 acres of the estate in 1891 for £117,000.[61] Of this sum, the London County Council contributed £61,000, Lambeth Vestry £20,000, Camberwell Vestry £5,000, Newington Vestry £6,000, the Charity Commissioners £25,000, and the Ecclesiastical Commissioners £500; the rest was provided by private subscription. The land, which was opened to the public on Whit Monday, 1892, lay between Tulse Hill and Norwood Road and included the mansion built by John Blades which had hitherto been known as Brockwell Hall.[62]

There was at first no entrance to the park from the Brixton direction. The problem of improving the access was complicated by the fact that the large gardens of Clarence Lodge and Brockwell House (erected between 1860 and 1870) which barred the way to Brixton and Herne Hill were still in private hands. In 1895 the tenant of Clarence Lodge agreed with the Trustees to exchange three much-needed acres of his garden for three acres elsewhere on the estate. The London County Council then bought this and a very small piece of land on the Herne Hill side and made a new entrance from Arlingford Road.[61] The formation of the park was completed in 1901 when the London County Council bought the remaining 43 acres of the Blackburn estate for £64,500.[61] Of this sum the Council contributed £32,250, the Camberwell Borough Council £8,000, the Lambeth Borough Council £20,000, Southwark Borough Council £2,500 and the Brockwell Park Extension Committee £1,750. This extension to the park was opened on February 28, 1903.[63]

This handsome addition comprised the northern part of the present park. Unfortunately nearly half of the 43 acres was still subject to leases granted by the Blackburn Trustees. The lease of Clarence Lodge expired in 1907 and some $13\frac{1}{4}$ acres were then added to the park.[64] The undistinguished buildings 100 yards south-east of the southern end of Brailsford Road are all that now remain of Clarence Lodge and its appurtenances. The lease of Brockwell House expired in 1919 but owing to exceptional circumstances created by the war it was renewed until 1922. Upon the expiry of this new lease the house (which was of no architectural interest) and most of its outbuildings were demolished; the lodge a few yards south of the swimming pool is the sole survivor.[65]

Nos. 46, 48, and 56–66 (even) BRIXTON WATER LANE

The Lambeth Manor Inclosure map of 1810 shows William Winter as the owner of the land on which these houses stand. The Land Tax

slender cast-iron columns extending across its ground storey. No. 62 (fig. 55) has an entrance porch with Roman Doric columns supporting an entablature adorned with triglyphs. No 64, formerly Norwood Cottage, has a ground storey trelliswork verandah with wreaths in the panels of its frieze. No. 66 is somewhat coarsely detailed and has canted bays at each side of its porch.

Nos. 46 and 48 Brixton Water Lane, formerly [265] Bayham Cottage and Meadow View respectively,

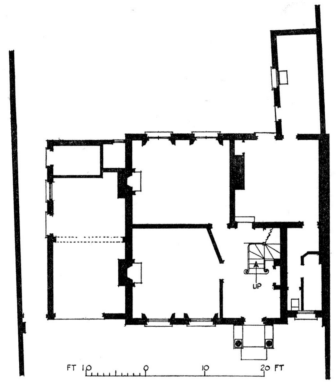

FT 10 0 10 20 FT

Fig. 55. No. 62 Brixton Water Lane, ground-floor plan

[264] Assessment books suggest that about 1787–8 he purchased what is now the north-west section of Brockwell Park and the site of these houses from the descendants of the first Lord Onslow's daughters. John Blades bought the site of Nos. 56–66 (Plate 60a) in 1819–20. These houses were erected between 1816 and 1823.[66] They are small two-storey terrace houses with stuccoed fronts. No. 58, formerly Sussex Cottage, has a porch with Tuscan-type columns; No. 56, formerly Kent Lodge, had a similar porch but it is now mutilated. No. 60, formerly Olive Lodge, has a valanced verandah borne on

stand on an adjoining piece of Winter's land which was not bought by Blades; they were erected between 1830 and 1839.[66] This semi-detached pair of two-storeyed cottages is chiefly remarkable in having a front elevation that must be related to Papworth's design for the larger pair of houses of Brockwell Terrace (Plate 65b). The composition is similar although the expression is much simpler. Plain pilasters divide the central feature into two wide bays, each containing a ground- and first-floor window. These rectangular openings are set without architraves in a plain stucco face, horizontally divided by narrow channellings, a sill-band, and the simple cornice below the eaves. On each side, slightly recessed from the central feature, is a lower two-storeyed wing containing the doorway, with a rusticated surround, and one ground-storey window.

[266] ST. JUDE'S CHURCH, DULWICH ROAD

In 1867 Joseph Moore and Herbert Dalton bought the land on which this church and parsonage house now stand from Joshua Blackburn for £736, and in the following year they freely conveyed it to the Ecclesiastical Commissioners.[67] On August 3, 1867, the foundation stone of the church was laid by Joshua Blackburn,[68] who made a generous contribution towards its cost.[69] The architect was E. C. Robins, whose plans were chosen after a competition in which twelve designs were submitted.[70] The contractor was John Kirk,[68] and the cost of the church, which accommodated over 1,000 people, was £7,300.[71] Mr. Plows carved the pulpit, reading-desk, and font from designs by Robins.[72] The church was opened for Divine Service on October 28, 1868,[71] and a District Chapelry was assigned in 1869.[73]

The building was severely damaged by fire in 1923, and was restored by G. H. Fellowes Prynne.[74]

Despite the fact that the design was chosen in preference to eleven others, it is disappointing to find that St. Jude's is a nondescript Victorian Gothic church of conventional plan, having its major axis running south-east to north-west in alignment with Dulwich Road. The nave of five bays is flanked by aisles ending in shallow transeptal projections, and the aisleless chancel is at the north-west end. The exterior is of Kentish ragstone with Bath stone dressings, the roofs of slate having cast-iron crestings. The walls are buttressed and finished with corbel-tables, while the windows generally are filled with Geometrical tracery. In the north angle formed by the chancel and transept rises a squat two-stage tower, surmounted by an ashlar-faced broach spire. The arches of the nave arcades have voussoirs alternately of red brick and stone, rising from columns with foliated capitals. Three bays of the east aisle were enclosed in 1952 to form a chapel. The rest of the church is still disused while extensive war damage repairs are being completed.

CHAPTER VII

Norwood

SOUTH of Tulse Hill and Brockwell Park lies Norwood, a name derived from the North Wood which formerly covered the hilly country of north Croydon and the southern parts of Lambeth. The Lambeth portion of Norwood comprises West (formerly Lower) Norwood and part of Upper Norwood; it consists of a number of low hills, Knight's Hill, Salter's Hill, Gipsy Hill, which slope gently up to the ridge along which runs the road from Streatham to Sydenham. Until the beginning of the 19th century the area was remote and inaccessible, the roads from the north tapering off into winding tracks; indeed the name Norwood is itself a reminder that it had closer connection with Croydon than with Lambeth or London. As late as 1802 a hermit known as "Matthews the hairyman" lived in the wood in a cave or "excavated residence".[1] The neighbourhood was so lonely that at about the same date Dr. Leese, who lived on Central Hill, used on winter nights to "fire off a pistol to let people know he had firearms in the house";[2] even in the 1840s Norwood Lane (now Road) was so unfrequented that it provoked the dread of a youth walking home from his work in London.[3]

About three-quarters of the Lambeth portion of Norwood, including all the area south of St. Luke's Church, formed part of the Archbishop of Canterbury's Manor of Lambeth. The remaining quarter consisted of two pieces; one, bounded by Norwood Road, Croxted Road and part of Thurlow Park Road, was a detached portion of the parish of Streatham and of the Manor of Leigham Court, the rest of which lay in Streatham; the other, approximately bounded by Leigham Vale, Norwood Road, the parish boundary and a line parallel with and about one hundred yards south of Canterbury Grove, formed the bulk of the small Manor of Levehurst.

Much of the Archbishop's land in Norwood was wooded until the 18th century. Gipsy Hill gets its name from the gipsies who encamped in the woods there for many years and to whom Pepys may refer in the following entry: "This afternoon my wife and Mercer and Deb went with Pelling to see the gypsies at Lambeth, and

have their fortunes told; but what they did, I did not enquire".[4] The Gipsy House stood on the north side of the railway near Oaks Avenue. At the time of the Parliamentary Survey in 1647 that part of the wood in Lambeth covered some 300 acres with about 6,300 trees, but many of them were felled in the next 150 years. They were mostly pollard oaks which were lopped every 30 years; the herbage, bushes and thorns belonged to the tenants of the Manor. Within the wood were three inclosed coppices, Elderhall coppice, Great Clayland coppice and Little Clayland coppice, covering about 130 acres at Salter's Hill and Gipsy Hill. These three coppices were felled at ten years' growth and then inclosed for seven years; "And then the commoners have had their common therein for three yeares till ye next fall".[5]

At the south-eastern corner of the parish, where Westow Hill and Crystal Palace Parade now meet, stood the Vicar's Oak, "an ancient remarkable tree" which still stood in 1647, but which was probably felled soon afterwards.[6] The tree marked the junction of four parishes— Lambeth, Croydon, Camberwell, and a detached portion of Battersea—and was a favourite spot for the inhabitants of Lambeth to pause for refreshment when they beat the bounds of the parish; in 1586–7, for instance, the churchwardens spent 2s. 6d. "for makinge honest men drinke when we went to vicars oke in perambulacion".[7] The tree was so famous that the term "Vicar's Oak" survived as a place-name until well into the 19th century.

The south-west extremity of the parish was much more open; the Parliamentary Survey of 1647 only mentions a small common wood called Knight's Hill, containing 40 pollard oaks and two elms,[5] while to the west of St. Luke's Church there was a heath called Little Blabbs Heath.[8]

The land between St. Luke's Church and Herne Hill was formerly part of the area known as Lambeth Dean. The history of this district, and of the rest of Norwood lying in Lambeth parish is greatly complicated by the existence of two areas both called Knight's Hill. The southerly Knight's Hill formed part of Lambeth Manor and lies to the south of St. Luke's Church, while the other comprised the detached portion of the Manor of Leigham Court and of the parish of Streatham mentioned above, and lies between Norwood Road and Croxted Road. The confusion dates from the 16th century when both areas were occupied by members of the Knight family, who held a great deal of land in Lambeth and Streatham. The Manor of Leigham Court lay in the latter parish, and its descent has been traced in the *Victoria County History of Surrey*.[9] Only the detached portion referred to above, containing some 160 acres, falls within the area covered by the present volume. In the 16th century it was part of the copyhold of the Manor of Leigham Court, and was usually held with an adjoining capital messuage which formed part of

the copyhold of Lambeth Manor.[10] In 1786 the Manor of Leigham Court was held by the Duke of St. Albans.[9]

On the south side of the Knight's Hill belonging to Leigham Court lay the Manor of Levehurst, which in 1471 was held by Ralph Leigh (Legh).[11] In 1543 Sir John Leigh conveyed Levehurst and Stockwell Manors and certain copyhold lands in Lambeth Manor to Henry VIII.[12] Unfortunately Sir John Leigh had no right to sell the copyhold, for he had a younger brother, Ralph, to whom by the custom of Lambeth Manor it rightly belonged. In 1552 the Archbishop obtained a decree of the Court of Augmentations returning this land to him.[13] Levehurst remained in the hands of the Crown, but the position must have been obscure even then, for in 1563 a Commission was set up to

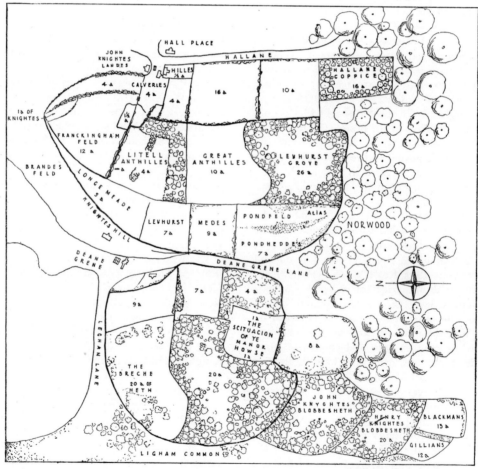

Fig 56. Levehurst Manor in 1563; re-drawn from a map in the Public Record Office

inquire whether the lands conveyed by Sir John Leigh to Henry VIII had been held by him as freehold or as copyhold of the Archbishop's Manor of Lambeth. The jury empanelled by the Commissioners described the boundaries of Levehurst (fig. 56) and reported that Sir John Leigh had held the Manor subject to a rent of 10s. per annum to the Archbishop; but they could not say whether the adjoining land belonging to the Archbishop was freehold or copyhold, or even by what right parts of it were held.[14] A likely cause of their doubt may have been that much of the land in dispute was recently-felled woodland whose boundaries had hitherto not been accurately defined.

Two years later Queen Elizabeth granted Levehurst to Richard Barnard and Robert Taylour,[15] who in 1566 conveyed it to Sir Richard and Lady Wenefride Sackville.[16] In 1578 their son Sir Thomas Sackville conveyed it to Dr. Robert Forth,[17] and his son Thomas sold the greater part of it to Samuel Weller in 1600.[18] In 1616 William Weller conveyed this portion to John Bingham,[19] and in 1628 the latter's brother William sold it to Thomas Overman.[20] In 1703 another Thomas Overman and his wife Mary conveyed it to Samuel Lewin.[21] In 1744 it was in the possession of James Wall.[22]

That part of Levehurst Manor which lay on the east of Norwood Road was conveyed by Thomas Forth to Henry Dalton, citizen and joiner of London, in 1600.[23] George Dalton conveyed it to Christopher Woodward, citizen and vintner of London, in 1616.[24] This land descended to Christopher Woodward's grandson Edward, upon whose death in 1725 it was divided. Subsequently James Wall bought up both interests in 1731[25] and 1744,[26] so that by the latter date the whole Manor had been reunited.

In addition to acquiring Levehurst Manor, James Wall acquired a large copyhold estate in the adjoining parts of Lambeth Manor. In 1733 he was admitted to some 124 acres in the south-west part of the Manor, comprising Blackmans and Julians (the latter name being still in use in St. Julian's Farm Road), Little Blabbs Heath and Fuzzey Field or Oxenleys, and to some 52 acres called Berrys Grove and Colwood coppice lying in the area between the south side of the South Metropolitan Cemetery and the eastern boundary of the parish.[27] In 1745 Wall was also admitted to the greater part of the remaining land

between Norwood Road, Croxted Road and Knight's Hill, including two fields known as "Anthills".[28] These last and Berrys Grove, which was formerly known as Levehurst Grove, had in the 16th century been part of Levehurst Manor,[14] but had subsequently become incorporated in the Manor of Lambeth.

The Wall estate was, however, soon superseded by an even larger one whose history coincided with the beginning of the development of modern Norwood. In 1772 Edward (later Lord) Thurlow was admitted to Knight's Hill House and 100 acres of copyhold land in Lambeth Manor between Norwood Road and the south-west side of Knight's Hill.[29] This land formed the nucleus of the vast estate in Lambeth and Streatham which Lord Thurlow acquired during the next 23 years. In 1778 he took a lease from the Duke of St. Albans of the Knight's Hill which formed a detached portion of the Manor of Leigham Court, and in 1785 he bought this land, comprising some 160 acres and then called Brockwell Green Farm,[30] for £3,255.[31] Two years later he was admitted to the entire copyhold estate held by the Wall family in Lambeth Manor.[32] In 1789 he bought the Manor of Leigham Court in Streatham (the detached portion of which he had already acquired in 1785) from the trustees of the late Duke of St. Albans,[30] and in 1795 he rounded off his enormous property by acquiring Levehurst Manor from James Wall, junior, a Lieutenant in the Navy.[22] The entire estate comprised 594 acres of freehold in Streatham, 355 acres of copyhold in Lambeth Manor, 123 acres of freehold in Lambeth and 48 acres of land allotted after the Lambeth Manor Inclosure Act of 1806.[33]

Lord Thurlow (1731–1806) was one of the most eminent lawyers of the late 18th century. He became Solicitor-General in 1770, Attorney-General in 1771, and was Lord Chancellor from 1778 to 1792 (except for the short period of the Fox-North Coalition). His distinguished appearance made him the victim of Charles James Fox's famous remark that "no man ever was so wise as Thurlow looks".[34]

Near the junction of Thurlow Park Road and Elmcourt Road Lord Thurlow built a large mansion designed by Henry Holland (Plate 44c). Thurlow did not mean to spend more than £6,000, but Holland built an "ill executed" house costing about £18,000.[35] The two men quarrelled and the house, which was built between 1792 and

1795, was finished by Samuel Wyatt of Chelsea, "architect and builder".[36] Lord Thurlow never moved into the house, but continued to live at Knight's Hill Farm, a very much smaller house near Norwood Road. Lord Chancellor Eldon told the story that, as Lord Thurlow was coming out of the Queen's Drawing Room, a lady "asked him, when he was going into his new house? 'Madam', said he 'the Queen has just asked me that impudent question; and as I would not tell her, I will not tell you' ".[37]

The development of modern Norwood may be said to date from 1806, the year in which the Lambeth Manor Inclosure Act was passed and Lord Thurlow died. By his will[38] Lord Thurlow devised his entire property in Lambeth and Streatham to trustees to sell. The trustees at once tried to sell the mansion and part of the land, but no purchasers came forward. They therefore obtained an Act of Parliament in 1809 empowering them to demolish the mansion, to sell or lease the land, and to make certain roads to accelerate building in the area.[39]

Under the terms of this Act Norwood Road was improved, and what are now Leigham Vale, Canterbury Grove and Palace Road were built. Meanwhile in their Award of 1810[40] the Lambeth Manor Inclosure Commissioners provided for the inclosure of Norwood Common and for the construction of the roads now known as Norwood High Street, Elder Road, Chapel Road, Gipsy Road, Salter's Hill and Gipsy Hill. In 1810 the trustees of Lord Thurlow started to disperse their estate and put up 160 acres of land for sale by auction.[41] This process went on gradually, the sales being sometimes by private treaty but usually by auction, until 1846, when all the Lambeth property had been sold.[42] The mansion was demolished in 1810, and the materials sold for £7,230.[43] Thus between 1806 and 1810 the fundamental obstacles to the development of Norwood had suddenly been removed; the Common had been divided amongst individual owners, greatly improved access had been provided, and the break-up of the principal estate had begun.

Most of the houses which were built in the area immediately after the Award of 1810 were cheap and small, probably because the Archbishop had no power to grant long leases on his own property, nor was he able to grant copyholders licence to demise their property for more than 21 years. A few of these unremarkable houses survive in a much mutilated condition in Norwood High Street. By two Acts of Parliament of 1824 and 1825,[44] however, the Archbishop was enabled to provide the necessary security of tenure for a better type of development, and no doubt the decision of the Lambeth Church Building Committee to erect St. Luke's Church (consecrated in 1825) in what was still open country provided an additional attraction for the wealthier classes. Between 1824 and 1843 a line of houses similar to those being erected at Tulse Hill, Herne Hill and Denmark Hill was built on the north side of Crown Lane;[45] all of them have now been demolished. On the west side of Knight's Hill there were two houses on an even grander scale. Both have now been demolished; both were originally erected in the 18th century but the more northerly one was entirely rebuilt shortly before 1840, when it became known as St. John's Lodge (Plate 45). A description of it written in 1884[46] on the eve of its final demolition illustrates the lavish scale on which wealthy business-men lived in the 19th century. The house stood in 21 acres of ground and commanded extensive views. On the ground floor there were two drawing rooms, a dining room, morning room, library, conservatory, two kitchens and a servants' hall; on the first floor there were ten bed chambers, and four more on the upper floor. Outside there was a coach-house, granary, two cottages, a lodge and stabling for six horses. There was also a farmyard with cow houses, piggeries, fowl houses and mushroom houses. The garden included a lake with an island, a boat house, summer house, heated peach houses, tennis lawn, an Italian garden, a rosery, a pheasantry, asparagus beds, two vineries, melon grounds, a fish reservoir and three kitchen gardens. The house was at first occupied by Bazett David Colvin,[47] an East India Agent,[48] and after 1850 by Thomas Tredwell, a railway contractor of the firm of Tredwell Brothers in Parliament Street.[49] The house and grounds were sold by auction in 1884; the house was shortly afterwards demolished and the entire area covered with small houses. Portobello House, the more southerly of the two, and its grounds suffered a similar fate when the Lambeth Borough Council made use of the site for a housing estate in 1949.[50]

St. John's Lodge, Portobello House and the houses in Crown Lane all finally succumbed before the inexorable advance of later and more modest development. Another part of Norwood was the scene of an ambitious scheme which never got under way at all. In 1825 George Mills of Norwood bought the Manor of Levehurst, which then contained 94 acres, from Lord Thurlow's trustees. This area was bounded by Leigham Vale on the north, Norwood Road on the east, the parish boundary on the west, and a line parallel with and about 100 yards south of Canterbury Grove on the south. In the following year Mills sold (at considerable profit) the bulk of this land to John Wilson, builder, and the remainder to Allen Perring.[22] By this time the plan for the layout of the roads now known as York Hill,

Lansdowne Hill, Royal Circus and the eastern part of Knollys Road had been settled (fig. 57) and Wilson very probably built them; they had certainly been built by 1843.[45] Wilson at once mortgaged his property and built and disposed of a number of houses; in 1834 he sold his entire interest to his mortgagee, who died three years later. The whole area was then sold off in small lots.[22]

The significant point in this otherwise totally undistinguished piece of development was the idea of building a circus. Royal Circus stood in a superb position on top of a steep hill, and in the late 1820s a speculator may well have thought

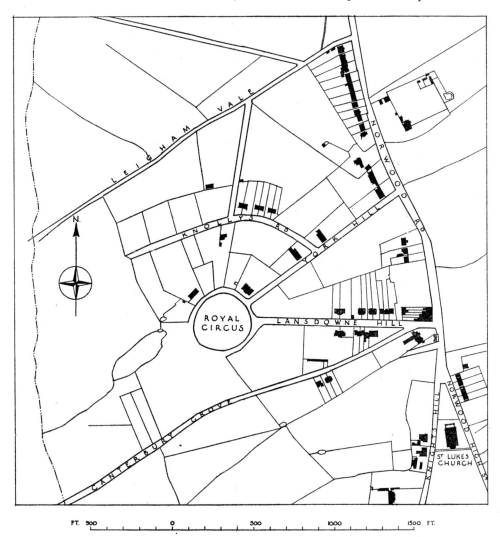

Fig. 57. Royal Circus area in 1843, lay-out plan

that he could attract wealthy people to live there as Dr. Edwards was already doing at Tulse Hill. Unfortunately he did not realize that the advent of the detached or semi-detached suburban house in the early 19th century had already killed the use of the circus in suburban development. Royal Circus proved a complete fiasco. In 1860 it still contained only three houses, all detached, and building along the other estate roads had been at a standstill for nearly twenty years. The steepness of the hill may have discouraged purchasers; the railway which was opened in 1856 and ran round the north-east side of the hill must have provided a further deterrent. The development of the estate was not completed until the early 20th century.[51]

The rapid development of Norwood began shortly after the opening of the West End of London and Crystal Palace Railway in 1856. In 1851 the population of the district of St. Luke's, Norwood, was 3,977, and there were 647 houses.[52] By 1901 the population had increased nearly tenfold to 35,888, and there were 6,431 houses.[53] (The figures for 1901 include Knight's Hill and a small part of Tulse Hill not included in the return of 1851.) The demand for land became so great that in 1857 a jury valued at £500 some two acres of land which the railway company wished to acquire and which the owner had bought for only £60 in 1839.[54] Detailed treatment of the vast quantity of building which took place in the second half of the 19th century is impossible, but a few points of general interest may be noted.

Much of the land sold by Lord Thurlow's trustees between 1810 and 1846 was bought by successful London business-men. In Norwood one of the largest of these commercial investors was John Roupell, a lead-ash smelter of Cross Street, Blackfriars Road;[55] the occupations of other purchasers include those of pocket-book maker, gunmaker and several "merchants". Some of the purchasers styled "gentleman" prove on further investigation to have a commercial origin, such as "tripe butcher".

These were the people who often became the landlords of the second half of the 19th century. In the case of copyhold land capable of development before about 1850, the owner obtained a licence to demise from the manor court and then let all or part of it to a builder; when the houses were finished, he granted a lease varying usually from 24 to 99 years to the builder's nominee.

From about the middle of the century, however, land was often enfranchised before development began. An Act of 1841 established Copyhold Commissioners with whose consent Lords of Manors might enfranchise copyholders upon receipt of a lump sum payment.[56] That enfranchised land was considered a better foundation for development than copyhold is shown by the fact that in 1843 R. P. Roupell was willing to pay £1,239 for the enfranchisement of 55 acres.[57] In the following year Lord Thurlow's trustees paid £2,845 for the enfranchisement of the remaining 156 acres of their estate;[58] a plan providing for the building of what are now Rosendale Road (as far south as Park Hall Road only), Thurlow Park Road, Lancaster Avenue and Park Hall Road was then drawn up, and the entire area was sold in freehold lots in 1845 and 1846.[42]

The size of estates ready for development varied greatly. Whatever the extent of their operations may have been, many landowners and builders seem to have lacked a sense of their own limitations—usually financial. In 1868 there were over thirty firms of builders in Lower (now West) Norwood,[59] most of them probably quite small businesses without the necessary capital to undertake large contracts; bankruptcies were exceedingly common, and many of them must have been caused by excessive ambition.

Norwood provides a spectacular example of catastrophe overtaking a landowner. The Roupell Park estate, whose two main arteries were Christchurch Road and Palace Road, was formed out of the former Thurlow estate and lay in Lambeth and Streatham. It was merely one of several estates in the Home Counties which were acquired by John Roupell and his son Richard Palmer Roupell. The latter had for many years lived with a woman by whom he had several illegitimate children; one of these, William Roupell, had managed the estates in Streatham and Lambeth on a grand scale with their own brick-works. Subsequently, however, R. P. Roupell had married his mistress and had a legitimate son, Richard. Upon his father's death in 1856, William Roupell forged a will by which the entire property (valued at over £200,000) was left to his mother, with himself as sole executor. In 1857 William Roupell was elected one of the Members of Parliament for Lambeth, but five years later suspicions of his deception were aroused and he fled to Spain. He returned voluntarily after a few months and in September, 1862, he was convicted of forgery at the Old Bailey and sentenced to penal servitude for life.[60]

Land companies and building societies which actually built houses for their members were also active in Norwood in the second half of the 19th century, though the scope of their work in this area was small compared with that of private landowners. In 1867, for instance, the London and Suburban Building Society was erecting five pairs of villas costing £6,745[61] (these houses have not been identified), and in 1871 the United Land Company was laying out roads in Gipsy Hill.[62] At a humbler level on the social scale the

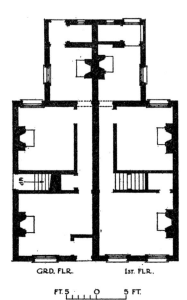

GRD. FLR.   1st. FLR.

FT. 5   0   5 FT.

Fig. 58. Nos. 25 and 29 Dunbar
Street, plan

Lower Norwood Co-operative Building Company erected working-class cottages on the Elm Grove estate, now known as Dunbar Street. The land on which these houses stood was formerly copyhold of Lambeth Manor but had been enfranchised before the Company bought it.[63] The [267] first houses were built in 1865. Each pair contained four lettings with separate entrances, and cost £330, so that each letting cost £82 10s.[64] (Plate 73c, fig. 58.) In general, however, building societies did not play a dominant part in the

development of the area until the 1870s, by which time most of them had ceased to erect houses themselves. By advancing money for the purchase of houses they nevertheless played a very important part in the development of Norwood, as of all other Victorian suburbs.

CHURCHES OF THE ESTABLISHMENT

ST. LUKE'S CHURCH   [268]

The Lambeth Manor Inclosure Commissioners evidently foresaw the impending development of Norwood, for in their Award of 1810 they set aside 1½ acres of the Common for the erection of a church.[65] After the establishment of the Church Building Commissioners in 1818, the Lambeth Church Building Committee decided to make use of this site.[66] Legal difficulties arose, however, for the Inclosure Act had provided that on the land to be inclosed no building should be erected within 100 feet of any existing building without the owner's consent.[65] It seems to have been the original intention of the Commissioners that the church should be orientated east and west like St. Mark's, Kennington, and St. Matthew's, Brixton, but the west end of the building would then have come within less than 100 feet of the Horns Tavern on the west side of Knight's Hill;[65] the Commissioners were therefore forced to agree that it should be built on a north–south axis.[67]

The first plan proposed by the Lambeth Church Building Committee was rejected by the Commissioners; three more plans were then submitted and eventually that of Francis Bedford was chosen.[67] His first proposal provided for the altar to be at the south end, but the Commissioners decided that even if the church could not face east the congregation should do so, and a very odd arrangement whereby the pews stood facing the altar in the middle of the east side of the church was approved.[68] Building started in November 1822, the contractor "for the whole of the Works"[69] being Elizabeth Broomfield of 1 Marlborough Place, Walworth,[a] who at about the same time was also responsible for the brickwork at the churches of St. Peter's and Holy Trinity, Walworth.[71] At St. Luke's her contract

[a] Elizabeth Broomfield may have been the widow of James Broomfield, builder, whose business she took over in 1821–2. She was no longer in business in 1826.[70]

was for £10,392.[69] In 1824 it was decided that, owing to "the very unexpected and extraordinary encrease of Buildings"[72] in the neighbourhood, galleries should be added. These were erected by Richard Humphries at a cost of £1,650.[73] The total cost of the church was £12,947, of which the Commissioners contributed £6,448, and the rest was raised by the parish of Lambeth. Accommodation was provided for 1,412 persons, and the church was consecrated by the Archbishop of Canterbury on July 15, 1825.[65] Thus of the four "Waterloo" churches in Lambeth, St. Luke's was the last to be completed.

In 1838 £557 was spent on repairing the roof and replastering the cornices. In 1852 the churchwardens asked the Church Building Commissioners, who had been responsible for the inconvenient arrangement of the interior, to contribute to the cost of re-arranging the pews and the altar.[65] Unfortunately no record of the outcome of this request has been found, and it is likely that no major internal alterations were made until 1870, when George Edmund Street undertook the complete re-arrangement of the interior.[74]

Architecturally the church is not an outstanding example of the work of the Commissioners (Plates 3, 4b, 10). Its similarity to Holy Trinity, Newington, which was also designed by Francis Bedford, was criticised at the time, but of the three Classical churches in Lambeth which stand on important sites at road junctions (St. Matthew's, Brixton, and St. Mark's, Kennington, are the others), St. Luke's is the only one whose portico appears to great advantage.

St. Luke's has a simple rectangular plan, its major axis running north–south, with the entrance portico at the north end. Apart from such structural features as the original vestibule forming the base of the steeple, nothing of the original internal planning survived Street's drastic remodelling.

Fortunately, Street's commission did not extend to the exterior, beyond some minor changes to the windows. Superbly placed from the architectural standpoint, the church is dominated by its portico and related steeple. Hexastyle and of the Corinthian order, the portico is of picturesquely weathered Bath stone. Respondent antae mark each end of the inner face, which is of grey brick and contains a range of five doorways with windows over them. Doorways and windows have architraves of similar form, with tapered jambs and straight heads.

The portico entablature is continued on the side elevations, each presenting a grey brick face containing a range of six arch-headed windows, framed by architraves rising from a continued sill-band. The pilastered bay at the north end is a weak attempt to echo the placing of the steeple which rises from the roof ridge, and is in general form and details closely akin to Bedford's steeples at St. John's, Waterloo Road, and Holy Trinity, Newington. The high square pedestal stage contains a clock dial in each of its rusticated faces, and the succeeding belfry stage, also square in plan, has on each face a louvred recess between Doric columns coupled with corner antae. The entablature frieze has wreaths centred over the columns and there are acroteria at the corners. A smaller square pedestal, each die adorned with an anthemion panel, is surmounted by the octangular lantern, with eight "Tower of the Winds" columns supporting the entablature and flat pyramidal roof that mitres to a square pedestal finial. This is surmounted by an acanthus crown and a cross.

Within the shell of Bedford's pseudo-temple, Street contrived a High Victorian church interior, comprising a four-bay nave with aisles, and a chancel flanked by a chapel on the west and a choir vestry with organ chamber on the east. The style is Street's very personal Italianate Romanesque; the materials are harsh and polychromatic. The stilted round arches of the nave arcades rise from plain shafted columns with stiff foliated capitals. An arcaded frieze supports the wall-plate of the panelled waggon roof, which is tied by moulded beams. The lunette above the chancel-arch is pierced by a triple arcade, and the wall behind the altar has two tiers of blind windows consisting of a range of five lights above two twin-lights. The high altar is now placed beneath a wide baldachino of simple Classical design. In the two blind windows above are tempera paintings executed in 1885 by W. Christian Symons, to designs by John Francis Bentley.

CHRIST CHURCH, GIPSY HILL   [269]

In the 1860s Gipsy Hill was the scene of considerable building development and an iron church erected there in 1862 was soon filled to capacity every Sunday. Two years later the parson applied to the Ecclesiastical Commissioners, who owned much of the land in the district, for a freehold site for a permanent church, £1,600 having already been promised by his congregation as at contribution to the cost of building.[75] The site of the present church, which was designed by John Giles,[76] was freely given by the Ecclesiastical Commissioners, and the church (Plate 14d) was consecrated by the Bishop of Winchester on June 7, 1867. The builder's contract was for under £7,500, including 40 feet of the tower.[76]

Christ Church is designed in Gothic style, and faced with Kentish ragstone with Bath stone dressings. The church comprises an apsidal chancel and nave with lean-to aisles; at the north-east corner there is a three-stage tower, surmounted by a short octagonal spire; the top stage, very French in inspiration, and more elaborate in treatment, was added in or before 1889, Messrs. Giles, Gough and Trollope being the architects.[77] The interior of the church is of simple design. There are six bays of arcading on each side of the nave, the arches rising from polished grey granite circular pillars with stiffly carved foliage capitals. The chancel arch has similar capitals with short pillars resting on corbels. The windows generally have plate tracery, that in the nave clerestory being very peculiar in design and proportion.

[270] St. Peter's Church, Leigham Court Road

In or shortly before 1866 a temporary church accommodating 300 people was erected on the west side of Leigham Court Road opposite the present church. In 1870 land for a permanent church was freely given to the Ecclesiastical Commissioners by George Henry Drew and Richard Drew.[78] The new church was designed by Richard Drew, but only the eastern portion, comprising the chancel, vestries and three bays of the nave, was built.[79] In this unfinished state the church was consecrated on July 2, 1870. A Particular District was assigned in the same year, despite the opposition of the incumbent of St. Luke's, Norwood, who protested that the new District would strip his parish of its last well-to-do area.[78]

In 1882 the parochial committee instructed G. H. Fellowes Prynne to prepare designs for the completion of the church. His first plans (which are illustrated in *The Builder*, July 17, 1886) provided for the addition of two more bays to the nave, a tower at the north-west corner and a terrace at the west end with a crypt below. On

the north side there was to be an enlarged vestry, and on the south side a chapel with groined apsidal sanctuary. At the junction of the chancel and nave roofs he placed a flèche, which was to house the sanctus bell and form part of the ventilation system. These plans were put out to tender but the committee found it impossible to carry out the work. A second set of plans was also abandoned. A new committee was then formed, and Fellowes Prynne received fresh instructions "to make out a new scheme on somewhat hard and fast lines, rendering it necessary for him to make a building more picturesque than imposing".[79] These plans provided for the addition of two bays to the nave and a projecting octagonal baptistery at the west end. The work was carried out in 1886–7, and the contractors were J. and C. Bowyer of Upper Norwood.[79]

St. Peter's (Plate 20, fig. 59) is sited on a con-

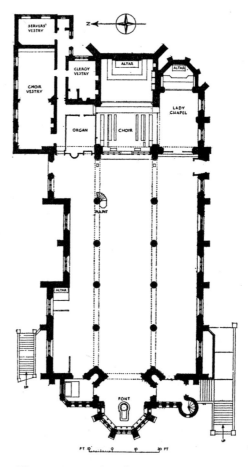

Fig. 59. St. Peter's, Leigham Court Road, plan

fined plot of ground, rising towards the south-east and having a frontage on the west to Leigham Court Road. The west end of the church is therefore raised on a basement storey containing parish rooms, with an open staircase ascending to the principal porch at the south-west corner. The plan is simple, consisting of a nave of five arcaded bays opening to aisles, and a short square-ended chancel flanked on the south by the Lady Chapel and on the north by the organ chamber, with vestries beyond.

The original design was for a Decorated Gothic building in yellow brick banded and diapered in red, with Bath stone dressings. This scheme was followed in the additions by Fellowes Prynne, whose own distinctive style is more clearly seen in the highly picturesque west front. This balanced but slightly asymmetrical composition centres on the gabled end wall of the nave and the semi-octagonal baptistery that projects below it. This has two storeys and in each of the three outer faces is a two-light window for the basement and a triple-arcade of lancets lighting the baptistery. Buttresses with weathered offsets mark each angle, stopping at the corbel-table from which rises the steeply-pitched and hipped roof of red tile. Against the north and south faces of the semi-octagon are gabled buttresses linked by flyers to the octagonal turrets that flank the nave gable-end, with its great wheel-window of Geo-metrical tracery. Each turret finishes with a stage of small louvred lancets and a cone-shaped stone roof. The two-storeyed wings to the semi-octagon differ in their fenestration, and that on the south side has a circular stair-turret projecting from its outer angle. The end wall of each aisle contains a window of two lights below a traceried head, and has at the outer angle a frontal and lateral buttress, the former rising to an octagonal pinnacle. The straight stone-coped parapets are linked by flying buttresses to the octagonal turrets flanking the nave.

The simple dignity of the interior arises from the general harmony of its proportions and the honest decorative use of building materials similar to those of the exterior. Stone columns with simply moulded bases and caps support the wide pointed arches of the nave arcades, which are formed in brickwork. Above each arch is a plastered panel, now whitened but probably intended for painted decoration, between engaged shafts rising from corbels to support the trusses

of the open wooden roof. The aisles have lean-to roofs of low pitch, and to correspond with each bay of the arcade there is a three-light traceried window set with a plain reveal in the brick outer wall.

The east wall of the nave has a lunette with three foliated openings above the chancel-arch, the chancel being entered through a filigree screen of gilded wrought-ironwork below an oak rood beam. The Lady Chapel, which has a three-sided apse, is entered through a wrought-iron screen of more robust design.

In the west wall of the nave, beneath the wheel-window, is an arch opening to the baptistery, where the lancet windows are screened by delicate arcades. The font is a handsome one of tawny alabaster and green marble. The pulpit, designed by F. E. Howard and executed by the Warren Guild in 1930,[80] and high-altar reredos are fine examples of design and craftsmanship based on traditional West Country models.

EMMANUEL CHURCH, CLIVE ROAD   [271]

The land for this church was freely given by John Westwood in 1876; a temporary church accommodating 430 people had already been erected in the vicinity in 1872.[81] The foundation stone of the permanent church was laid on July 8, 1876, by Francis Peek[82] and the first part of the church was consecrated on September 8 of the following year by the Bishop of Rochester.[81] The architect was E. C. Robins[81] and the builders T. H. Adamson and Sons.[82] A District Chapelry was assigned in 1878.[81] In 1893 the church was completed when the baptistery and the two westernmost bays of the nave were built.[83]

The church is a Gothic building faced with Kentish ragstone and Bath stone dressings. It has a clerestoried nave, with plate-traceried windows, flanked by lean-to aisles terminating in transepts. There is a small baptistery at the centre of the west end with entrance lobbies at each side. The sanctuary has an apsidal end and there is an incomplete buttressed tower at the north-east corner.

The interior is plain and faced with white gault bricks. There are four bays of stone arcading with foliated capitals separating the nave and aisles. The chancel and transept arches are tall and rest on engaged shafts borne by stone corbels.

[272] St. Jude's Mission Church, Berridge Road

This building was erected in 1880 as a mission church for the parish of Christ Church, Gipsy Hill. The architect was Frederic W. Ledger.[84] It is a small plain stock brick building of little architectural pretence. There is a small porch fronting the road; over the east gable there is an open bellcote surmounted by a cross. The low projecting wings were designed for use as schoolrooms.

[273] All Saints' Church, Rosendale Road

Despite its present unfinished state All Saints' is an impressive example of late 19th century church building, and represents the mature work of an architect, G. H. Fellowes Prynne, whose personal style was distinctive enough to survive the strong influence of his master, G. E. Street.

In the 1880s parts of West Dulwich were still undeveloped, and a temporary iron church in Rosendale Road supplied the spiritual needs of the district. Proposals to build a permanent church were first put forward by the West Dulwich New Church Building Committee in 1887, and shortly afterwards the Estates Governors of Dulwich College promised to present a site.[85] The foundation stone of the church was laid by the Bishop of Rochester on October 31, 1888, and the completed portion of the building was opened under licence on October 31, 1891. The entire cost, amounting to about £16,000, was met by gifts from the inhabitants of the district. The site was conveyed free of charge to the Ecclesiastical Commissioners in 1893, and the church was consecrated on November 13, 1897. A Consolidated Chapelry was formed in 1899.[85] The church was damaged by enemy action in 1944, and when the work of restoration was carried out in 1952 a belfry designed by J. B. S. Comper was erected in memory of the parishioners killed in the war of 1939–45.

The church (Plate 21, fig. 60) was designed on a generous scale for a congregation of some 1,400, with a plan probably derived from the great hall churches of Catalonia (also a favourite prototype with Street) consisting of a wide and long nave joined to a short and narrow apsidal-ended chancel. Here the nave was intended to have seven arcaded bays, the westernmost four opening to narrow aisles while the easternmost

three open to chapels. The Lady Chapel on the north side forms in effect a small church, being wider than the south chapel of All Souls and having a narrow chancel of three arcaded bays with a three-sided apse and an ambulatory.

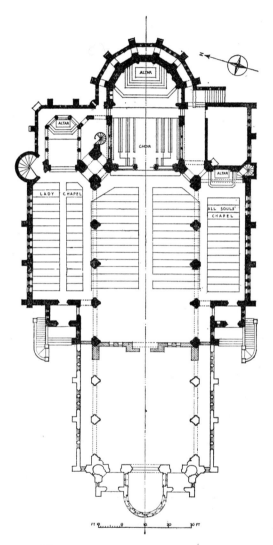

Fig. 60. All Saints', Rosendale Road, plan.
West end not built.

Splayed bays link the nave to the chancel, which consists of one wide bay terminated by a seven-windowed apse and surrounded by an ambulatory. The three westernmost bays of the nave, with the semi-circular baptistery and flanking porches, remain unbuilt.

The building is correctly orientated and sited

N

along the south side of a large triangular plot of ground that falls sharply towards the east, lying between the two roads that converge from different levels to meet at the north-west point of the triangle. Consequently, the chancel end is raised on a lofty basement, with fine dramatic effect, and the whole composition was designed to appear at best advantage from the north viewpoint.

In style the building is Gothic of an eclectic nature; the east end, for instance, might well have been inspired by the cathedral at Erfurt. The exterior, of red brick dressed with stone, is dominated by the chancel apse, where the elongated three-light windows are ranged between offset buttresses, linked near their bases by flyers to the gable-ended buttresses of the ambulatory and basement. The ambulatory is lit by small lancets, three in each bay, and the basement windows are deeply recessed behind open arches. Ambulatory and basement arcade continue as a unifying motif around the Lady Chapel chancel, beneath its small-scale clerestory of two-light windows, stopping against a round cone-roofed stair turret. Chancel and chapel walls are finished with coped parapets, the former being underlined by a corbel-table, and above them rise the steeply-pitched slated roofs. The side elevation of the Lady Chapel nave is simple in treatment, with two tiers of lancet windows grouped in threes within the three buttressed bays, and a steep gable-ended roof that conceals the clerestory of the main nave. This last has a wide-spreading roof that continues the pitch and ridge-line of the chancel roof, although the junction is defined by the base of an intended flèche, approached by open stairs on the roof slope. The architect originally intended to flank the body of the church with two tall and slender towers, placed anglewise and rising off the splayed junction walls between nave and chancel. These would have combined with the flèche to produce the skyline relief for which the present pyramidal-roofed belfry can only be regarded as an inadequate substitute.

The interior is spacious and very impressive, a finely controlled design carried out in yellow and red brick dressed with stone, with a pointed waggon vault of wood. The nave bay divisions are strongly articulated by moulded brick piers with stone shafts on their cardinal faces, those on the nave side rising to carry the groined sections of the vault. The nave arcades have moulded brick arches of nearly semi-circular form. Over each arch is a large panel intended for colour decoration and above this the three lancets of the clerestory, the middle one rising into the lunette formed by the groining. Superimposed arches penetrate the splayed walls flanking the great chancel arch which contains the most striking feature of the interior—a stone screen of three tall arches with foliated heads rising from slender shafts of Devonshire marble, the lunette being filled with tracery consisting of a cinquefoil between two quatrefoils. The shafts are linked by girders of delicate wrought-ironwork forming a rood-beam. This screen, which has its counterparts in several of Prynne's churches, was probably inspired by the late-Gothic stone screens in the Essex churches of Stebbing and Great Bardfield. Each side wall of the chancel has a wide and lofty arch, its moulded head dying into massive piers. Within the arch is a gallery supported on a light screen of three arches, the north gallery being intended for musicians and the south containing the organ. A climax of light is produced by the seven tall three-light windows of the apse, where the high altar stands against a simple background of draped walls flanked by interlacing arcades containing the statues of sixteen saints.

In the Lady Chapel architectural interest is centred on the chancel, with its arcade of pointed arches rising from round columns and its clerestory of two-light windows ranged between shafts that rise from corbel-heads to support the groined intersections of the wood vault. Here, and in All Souls' Chapel, is the best of the stained glass remaining in the church, which includes examples of the work of Burlison and Grylls, B. Barber and Sir Ninian Comper.

ST. PAUL'S CHILDREN'S CHURCH, ELDER ROAD [274]

This church was originally a Mission Hall for St. Luke's, Norwood. It was built in 1897, James C. Wright being the architect and Mr. Bugg the builder, and cost £1,335.[86] It is a plain stock brick building of no architectural pretence. The west gable has a tablet inscribed with the date 1897.

CHURCH OF ST. JOHN THE EVANGELIST, GUERNSEY GROVE [275]

In 1902 the Ecclesiastical Commissioners voted £350 from the City Parochial Charities fund towards the cost of purchasing a site for a mission church for the parish of Holy Trinity, Tulse Hill; another £350 was raised by local subscriptions, and a temporary iron church was erected in 1905. The foundation stone of the present church was laid on June 17, 1911, by the Rev. H. Woffindin, vicar of Holy Trinity. The architect was Leonard Martin, and the estimate of the contractors, Messrs. F. and H. F. Higgs, was for £3,925. The church was dedicated by the Bishop of Southwark on January 20, 1912.[87]

St. John's Church (Plate 15d) is a simple red brick building having a nave and chancel with three-light Perpendicular Gothic east and west windows. Its liturgical arrangement is reversed with the altar at the west end and the entrance porch on the Guernsey Grove frontage. The red tiled roof is punctuated by an octagonal shingled flèche near the east end. The floor of the nave is raised well above street level, and there is a church hall beneath.

ROMAN CATHOLIC CHURCH

[276] ST. MATTHEW'S ROMAN CATHOLIC CHURCH, NORWOOD HIGH STREET

St. Matthew's was opened on April 2, 1905; the architect was probably F. W. Tasker. The church has a nave and sanctuary flanked by lean-to aisles; it was lengthened at the east end in 1937. After damage by enemy action in 1940 the west end was rebuilt in 1949–50 with a two-storey brick front containing a central entrance with side lobbies; the architect was Donald Plaskett Marshall. Set in a round arch over the entrance is a stone statue of St. Matthew carved by Joseph Cribb, an associate of Eric Gill.[88]

NONCONFORMIST CHURCHES

[277] CHAPEL ROAD CONGREGATIONAL CHURCH

This building was erected between 1819 and 1821 on land bought by William Salter from Benjamin Shaw, to whom it had been allotted by the Lambeth Manor Inclosure Commissioners.[89] The church (Plate 26a) has a plain stock brick body made more imposing by a taller pedimented front which is stuccoed and contains a recessed Ionic porch at the centre. The flanking stuccoed wings have round-arched windows and were built as Sunday schools.

PRIMITIVE METHODIST CHAPEL, WINDSOR [278] GROVE

This chapel was erected by the Wesleyan Methodists in 1838; the congregation soon outgrew the building and built a larger chapel at Knight's Hill (see below). The chapel in Windsor Grove was subsequently occupied by the Primitive Methodists[90] but is now used for commercial purposes. It is a small stock brick building with three narrow round-headed windows on the road front.

CONGREGATIONAL CHURCH, PARK HALL [279] ROAD

The foundation stone of a small Congregational chapel in Rosendale Road was laid on October 7, 1851, by the Rev. J. Burnet. The building soon proved too small and a larger chapel was erected at the corner of Chancellor Grove and Park Hall Road, and opened in 1855.[91] The foundation stone of the chapel in Rosendale Road was incorporated in the fabric of the new chapel, and two inscribed stones record that "THE STONE BENEATH THIS IS THE FOUNDATION STONE OF THE FIRST CONGREGATIONAL CHAPEL IN DULWICH"; and below "THIS STONE WAS LAID BY THE REV. J. BURNET, OCTOBER 7TH 1851". The chapel was destroyed by enemy action in the war of 1939–45.

WEST NORWOOD METHODIST CHURCH, [280] KNIGHT'S HILL

This church was erected in 1852–3; a chancel was added in 1894.[92] It is a small stock brick building with a ragstone front in Norman style.

BAPTIST CHAPEL, CHATSWORTH WAY [281]

This chapel was erected in 1876–7 at a cost of about £6,000, including £500 for the site. The architects were Edward Power and Wheeler and the builders were Newman and Mann. In 1900 a hall was built at the back, the architect being R. W. Moore and the builders Higgs and Hill.[93] The chapel and hall were destroyed by enemy action in 1944.

UPPER NORWOOD METHODIST CHURCH, [282] WESTOW HILL

This church occupies a stock brick building designed in the Early English Gothic style and erected in 1874;[82] the south front is faced with Kentish ragstone. At the south-west corner there is a tower surmounted by a stone spire.

[283] ROUPELL PARK METHODIST CHURCH, NORWOOD ROAD

The foundation stone of this church (Plate 27b) was laid on June 11, 1879, and the building was completed in the following year.[94] The architect was Charles Bell and the builders J. and C. Bowyer.[82] The church is designed in Early English Gothic style and is faced with Kentish ragstone with Bath stone dressings. At the north-east corner there is a tower supporting a stone spire. The side aisles have transverse roofs which are gabled, and the west end is apsidal. A clock was erected in the tower in 1888. The cost of the church amounted to about £15,000.[95]

[284] GIPSY ROAD BAPTIST CHURCH

This church was erected in 1881–2 at a cost of £5,000, probably by Richard Henry Marshall, builder. The church was extended in 1890.[96] It is a brick building of simple Gothic character, with a Kentish ragstone front, and is approached by a steep staircase.

[285] ST. CUTHBERT'S PRESBYTERIAN CHURCH OF ENGLAND, THURLOW PARK ROAD

This church was erected in 1901 to the designs of Arthur Owen Breeds.[97] The building is prominently sited above the road and is built of red brick with stone dressings. At the north-west corner there is a tower surmounted by a short copper spire.

[286] SOUTH METROPOLITAN (OR NORWOOD) CEMETERY

The terrible overcrowding in many of London's graveyards prompted Parliament to authorize the establishment of eight commercial cemetery companies in the vicinity of London[98] between 1832 and 1847. The first of these cemeteries was opened at Kensal Green, and the second was established at Norwood in 1836.[99] The South Metropolitan Cemetery Company was empowered to open a cemetery of up to 80 acres' extent in Surrey, within 10 miles of London, to build two chapels, and to raise capital up to £75,000. The land bought by the Company in 1836 and 1837 consisted of some 41 acres of copyhold land in Lambeth Manor which had formerly belonged to Lord Thurlow, and which had subsequently been surrendered by his trustees.[100] The land was enfranchised immediately after its purchase by the Company, and the great surrounding wall which still stands was built shortly afterwards. The cemetery was consecrated by the Bishop of Winchester on December 7, 1837.[101]

The Company's Surveyor was William (later Sir William) Tite, and the Church of England and Nonconformist Chapels standing on the summit of the hill at the east end of the cemetery were designed by him (see frontispiece).

CHURCH OF ENGLAND MORTUARY CHAPEL [287]

The Church of England Chapel (Plate 28a), prominently sited on the highest ground of the cemetery, is an austere building of Gothic design with Decorated and Perpendicular detail. The materials used are grey brick with stone dressings. The west front contains a large five-light window deeply recessed within a wide and lofty archway, gabled and flanked by octagonal turrets rising into open lanterns with battlemented crowns. From either side of this front extend cloisters, each of five bays, the extreme north and south bays being emphasized by octagonal buttresses rising into pinnacles. The side walls of the chapel are pierced by five tall, narrow, two-light windows equally spaced between buttresses, and the walls are finished with plain parapets. The east end is dominated by a large five-light window and there are small octagonal piers at each corner.

The chapel has a lofty interior with two rows of panelled stalls at each side and a gallery across the west end. The roof is supported by shallow wood trusses carried on plain corbels with pendant terminals. The side walls are divided into bays by pairs of thin engaged shafts which correspond with the roof truss spacings. The chapel is heated by an embattled cast-iron stove of Gothic design. There are extensive catacombs beneath the chapel.

Included among the tablets on the wall is one to Sir William Tite, "Member of Parliament for the City of Bath, and Architect of the New Royal Exchange of London", who died April 20, 1873, and was buried in a family vault here. The tablet, which is of white marble and bears Tite's coat of arms, has an inscription panel with a cusped head in Decorated style; it was designed by W. Harding.

[288] NONCONFORMIST MORTUARY CHAPEL (now CREMATORIUM)

The former Nonconformist Chapel (which was demolished in 1955) was a smaller and less imposing building erected in the same materials and style as the Church of England Chapel; there were catacombs beneath. It was orientated approximately north–south and on the east and west sides were five two-light mullioned and transomed Decorated windows, placed between buttresses; at the south end a short battlemented tower containing a flue was added later. At the north end cloisters extended east and west. The interior was similar in design and detail to the Church of England Chapel. The whole building was severely damaged by enemy action in the war of 1939–45 and is now being rebuilt to the designs of Alwyn Underdown.[102]

The stone gateway leading into Norwood Road which was designed by Tite, bears on either side the arms of the Sees of Canterbury and Winchester. The original lodge stood to the south of the gate. It was rebuilt in 1936 and destroyed by enemy action in 1944. The present offices were built in 1950. Upon the small square piece of land to the south of the lodge there formerly stood two pairs of large semi-detached houses built between 1824 and 1836. The houses were bought by the Company in 1936, and were destroyed by enemy action in 1944.[103]

[289] GREEK MORTUARY CHAPEL

In 1842 a small piece of land in the north-east corner of the cemetery was acquired by the Brotherhood of the Greek Community in London. In 1872 an adjoining piece, making about one acre in all, was added, and in the same year Stephen Ralli obtained the permission of the Brotherhood to erect a small chapel dedicated to St. Stephen in memory of his son[104] (Plate 28b).

The chapel, which may have been designed by John Oldrid Scott, the architect of the Greek Cathedral of Saint Sophia, Bayswater,[105] is a correctly detailed small stone building having at its north and south ends a Greek Doric tetrastyle pedimented portico with columns in two rows. Low wings, with rusticated faces and pilasters at the corners, flank each side. The north portico, which contains the main entrance, has the further adornment of sculpture in the metopes and in the tympanum of the pediment. The interior has grey-painted walls and a richly

coloured coffered ceiling with fret ornamentation. On the west wall is a white marble tablet commemorating the building of the chapel by Stephen and Marietta Ralli in memory of their eldest son Augustus, who died of rheumatic fever at Eton in 1872 aged 15 years. There is a simple etched window at the south end of the chapel which portrays Our Lord with two angels at His feet; it was executed by H. Warren Wilson in 1952. In the wings leading off the chapel are burial vaults, that on the west side belonging to the Ralli family.

The chapel is surrounded by many monuments of considerable size and diversity of design; one of them (Plate 29d) was erected by the Ralli family and designed by G. E. Street.[106]

In 1847 the parish of St. Mary-at-Hill in the City of London, one of whose churchwardens was then a director of the South Metropolitan Cemetery Company, acquired a small piece of land in the south-east corner of the cemetery.[107]

This cemetery was one of the first to install a crematorium. The first gas furnace was built by a French firm, Toisal Fraudet of Paris, and the first cremation took place in 1915.[108]

The experiment of establishing commercial cemetery companies was not widely followed after 1850. Up till then the idea was favourably viewed, and in 1847 a Cemetery Clauses Act was passed whose purpose was to supply general rules applicable to all public companies which might establish cemeteries in the future.[109] Shortly afterwards there was a sharp change of outlook. A Parliamentary Report summed up the new feeling when it stated that "the interrment of the dead is a most unfit subject for commercial speculation".[98] In 1850 an Act of Parliament[110] constituted a Metropolitan Burial District and granted the General Board of Health power to provide burial grounds and to purchase the commercial cemeteries which had already been established. Only one—the Brompton—was acquired and the Act of 1850 was repealed in 1852, when the Vestries were permitted to establish Burial Boards.[111]

VOLUNTARY SCHOOLS

ST. LUKE'S, WEST NORWOOD, C.E.   [290]
PRIMARY SCHOOL, ELDER ROAD

In 1810 the Lambeth Manor Inclosure Commissioners awarded a piece of land abutting on

Elder Road to the Lambeth Vestry. When the church of St. Luke's was in course of erection in 1825 it was resolved at a meeting of the Vestry that the minister and churchwardens of the new church should be authorized to take possession of the land and make use of it for a school. The school (Plate 34b) was erected and opened in 1825, the cost being met by voluntary contributions. In 1850 an adjoining piece of land was leased for 99 years, and an infant school was built there; the freehold was acquired in 1895.[112] The single-storey building has a front of three bays with rusticated segmental arches and piers in stucco, surmounted by a stucco cornice and parapet, the central portion of which is raised and panelled to accommodate the original name, Norwood Infant School. The panels within the rusticated segmental arches are of brown brick, pierced by segmental-headed windows with bracketed stone sills. The stucco facing and parapet are returned one pier's width along the gable end, which is pierced by one large semi-circular window.

[291] JOHN WESLEY PRIMARY SCHOOL, EDEN ROAD

In 1860 a Methodist day school was opened in a loft over a stable at the corner of Chapel Road and Woodcote Place. In the following year a permanent building was erected at the rear of West Norwood Methodist Church, and the school was named Eden Road Wesleyan Day School. In 1951 the school was leased to the London County Council and re-named John Wesley Primary School.[92] It occupies an unpretentious stock brick building.

SCHOOLS BUILT BY THE SCHOOL BOARD FOR LONDON

[292] KINGSWOOD PRIMARY SCHOOL, GIPSY ROAD

This school was built by G. Ward of Dulwich to accommodate 600 children; the contractor's tender was for £5,978.[113] The architect was E. R. Robson,[114] and the date of opening was April 12, 1880.[115] The school was extended in 1904–5.

[293] PAXTON PRIMARY SCHOOL, WOODLAND ROAD

This school was built by Walls Bros. of Kentish Town, whose tender was for £9,879, for a school for 800 children.[116] The architect was T. J. Bailey,[114] and the date of opening January 10, 1887.[115]

GIPSY HILL PRIMARY SCHOOL, GIPSY ROAD [294]

A school was originally opened on this site in 1875,[115] E. R. Robson being the architect.[114] In 1895–6 a Junior Mixed School was added;[117] T. J. Bailey was the architect,[114] and the builder, whose tender for a school for 410 children was for £10,254, was C. Cox of Hackney. This school was opened on August 24, 1896.[115] All of the buildings erected in 1875 have been replaced by later additions.

ROSENDALE PRIMARY SCHOOL, ROSENDALE [295] ROAD

The site of this school was bought in 1894 for £2,800. The inhabitants of the adjacent houses protested unsuccessfully that the school would depreciate the value of their property and that there were "no poor children anywhere near". Temporary iron school buildings for 360 children were opened in January 1897. The permanent school provided accommodation for 476 children and 276 infants, and was built by Treasure and Son of Holloway for £15,589.[118] The architect was T. J. Bailey[114] and the school was opened on January 8, 1900.[115]

INSTITUTIONS

ELDERWOOD, NORWOOD HOUSE AND WOOD [296] VALE

The scattered buildings covering several acres in the angle of Elder Road and Crown Dale are the descendants of the House of Industry for the Infant Poor which the Vestry established there in 1810. The old parish workhouse, which stood in Kennington on the south side of what is now Black Prince Road, was overcrowded and unhealthy, so the Vestry decided to move the pauper children away to the rural outskirts of the parish. Slightly over one acre of land on the west side of Elder Road was bought from John Barnard (to whom it had been allotted under the Inclosure Award)[119] and in 1810 the first children were admitted to a newly-built workhouse or school of industry.[120] More land was acquired in 1820 and the building was enlarged in 1824 and 1828; a school was formed in 1834.[121] Shortly afterwards the premises were taken over under the

Poor Law Amendment Act by the Lambeth Board of Guardians.[122] In 1837 all the adult paupers whose labour had been used to run the workhouse were removed, hired labour being used instead.[123] In 1849–50 a new schoolhouse was built, Mr. Rogers being the surveyor[124] and Joshua Higgs and Son the contractors.[125] This building survives as Elderwood; it is a two-storey stock brick building with long rows of neatly-proportioned windows facing Elder Road.

By 1882 the accommodation was no longer adequate and more land was bought and very large new three-storey buildings (now Wood Vale) were erected in 1883–4, Mr. Coe being the architect and Mr. Lucas the builder. The estimated cost of these buildings was £55,000.[126] They consist of a symmetrically arranged stock brick group sparsely ornamented with Classical detail. The centre block is surmounted by an open campanile with a ball finial. A number of buildings were erected later by the Board of Guardians, but only an Outdoor Relief Station facing Elder Road, designed in 1887 by Sidney R. J. Smith,[82] is of any architectural note.

In 1930 the entire group of buildings passed under the Local Government Act of 1929 to the London County Council. Besides the school (which was renamed Norwood Children's Home) there were then a home for the aged poor, a nursery and a children's infirmary. In 1949 the name of the school was changed to Wood Vale; it comprises a children's home and a primary school. The remainder of the buildings are now known as Elderwood and Norwood House, and are used as homes for the aged; Norwood House also accommodates homeless families.

[297] NORWOOD TECHNICAL COLLEGE, KNIGHT'S HILL

In 1851 the Trustees of the Society of Friends of Foreigners in Distress bought two acres of land on the east side of Knight's Hill from Henry Bacchus for £950.[127] Almshouses were erected on part of the land a few years later, but they had a short life and were demolished when Rothschild Street was formed in 1898.[128] In 1858 the trustees leased the southern part of their land for 80 years to Arthur Anderson, who erected Norwood Institute, the purpose of which was "to promote the moral, intellectual and social

improvement of the Inhabitants residing within a radius of five miles" of the Institute.[129] In 1862 Anderson appointed trustees to superintend the Institute, and in 1894 they offered to transfer the lease to the Technical Education Board. This offer was accepted; the Institute was renamed Norwood Technical Institute, and was used as a school of domestic economy and commerce. After the freehold had been bought in 1901, the buildings were considerably enlarged by the Board,[130] and in 1904 the Institute passed to the London County Council Education Committee. Further additions to the buildings have since been made. In 1948 the name was changed to Norwood Technical College. The College occupies an asymmetrically arranged three-storey building with ragstone facings. There is a short battlemented tower at the south-west corner.

JEWISH ORPHANAGE, KNIGHT'S HILL [298]
Formerly the Jewish Hospital and Orphan Asylum

The Jews' Hospital in Mile End Road, Stepney, was founded in 1795.[131] In 1859 and 1860 Barnett Meyers conveyed to trustees some nine acres of land between Knight's Hill and Canterbury Grove; six acres of this land were formerly part of Lord Thurlow's copyhold in Lambeth Manor, while the part fronting Canterbury Grove was part of Levehurst Manor, which had also formerly been the property of Lord Thurlow. The trustees were to use the land for the maintenance of the aged poor and the education and employment of children, as described in the foundation deed of the Mile End Hospital.[132] The foundation stone of the new hospital was laid on June 6, 1861[82] by one of the trustees, Sir Anthony de Rothschild. Owing to the slope of the ground considerable excavations were needed, and the building cost some £23,000. The architects were Tillott and Chamberlain, and the builder was John Willson (Plate 32a). The entrance gate (now demolished) from Knight's Hill was the gift of Henry Keeling, the treasurer.[133] In 1862 a porter's lodge costing £323 was built by a builder named Wills, and £650 was spent on laying out and draining the grounds and building roads, Winn being the builder. Tillott and Chamberlain were the architects for both these schemes.[134] Further additions were made in 1874,[135] and in 1876 the Mile End and Norwood Asylums were amalgamated under the name of the Jews' Hospital and Orphan Asylum. A Centenary Hall and two wings were opened by the Duke of Cambridge on May 3, 1897.[136]

The orphanage is an imposing three-storey building with an attic storey set in a slated mansard roof. It resembles a Jacobean mansion and is built of red brick diapered with black brick, the window surrounds, corner quoins and other dressings being of Portland cement. The central projecting arcaded porch gives access to the entrance hall, above which is a synagogue. The north and south wings are fronted by canted bays extending through three storeys. An ogee-capped tower punctuates the south elevation and separates the original building from the plainer additions on the west side, which were erected in 1897. The two-storey lodge is designed in the same style as the main block.

[299] ST. SAVIOUR'S ALMSHOUSES (THE UNITED ST. SAVIOUR'S COLLEGE), HAMILTON ROAD

These almshouses were originally founded in the parish of St. Saviour's, Southwark, in the 16th, 17th and 18th centuries by Thomas Cure, Edward Alleyn, Henry Jackson, Henry Spratt and Henry Young.[137] After the purchase of their sites in Park Street by the Charing Cross Railway Company, all except Alleyn's were moved to Norwood. The earliest buildings there were completed in 1863 to the design of Edward Habershon; they comprised the chapel (fig. 61), flanked by 16 almshouses of the College or Hospital of the Poor. The west block, the western part of the north block, and the entrance lodge were built by 1866. Built into the wall of the west block are three inscribed stones:

1. THE GIFT OF HENRY SPRATT CARPENTER 1709
2. THE GUIFT OF MR. HENRY IACKSON BUILT IN THE YEARE 1685
3. THE GUIFT OF HENRY YOUNG IN THE YEARE 1690

In 1862 the inmates of Edward Alleyn's almshouses in Soap Yard, Southwark, were transferred to Gravel Lane, Southwark. Their new site was purchased by the South Eastern Railway Company in 1885, and the inmates were then moved to Hamilton Road.[137] They occupied the east block, which was opened in 1884; the architect was G. N. McIntyre North, and the builder W. Marriage. In 1908 an eastern extension was

added to the north block; this extension, and the recreation hall built in the north-west corner of the site in 1913, were designed by Henry Langston and Co. In 1931 the single-storey entrance lodge was replaced by a two-storey house designed by Arthur Cooksey and Partners. Five years later the south block flanking the chapel was rebuilt by the same architects and opened on October 16, 1937. The east block, destroyed by a flying bomb on July 22, 1944, was rebuilt by the same architects and opened on October 18, 1952.[138]

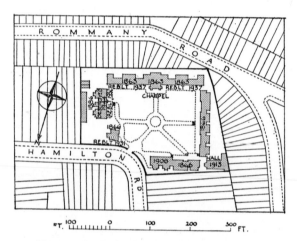

Fig. 61. St. Saviour's Almshouses, lay-out plan

The almshouses are all of two storeys and built of red brick with red tiled roofs. The older blocks on the north and west sides show Gothic influence in their narrow stone-mullioned windows and pointed-arched doorways. Their roofs are punctuated by small gables over each house. The chapel, which has heavily buttressed walls, is surmounted by an attenuated flèche. There are traceried windows over the altar and entrance. The modern ranges flanking the chapel and the east block are lighted by windows with horizontal steel sashes. Their façades are relieved by the setting forward of the entrances and staircases.

The commemorative tablets from the old buildings in Southwark recording the gifts of Henry Jackson, Henry Spratt, Henry Young and a number of ratepayers in the parish of St. Saviour are incorporated in the north and west blocks. The stone commemorating Edward Alleyn's gift is set up in the centre of the well-kept garden. Beneath Alleyn's arms and the date 1646 it is inscribed as follows

THE GIFT OF EDWARD
ALLEYN ESQVIER
CHVRCH WARDENS AT THE
SAME TYME
CLEMANT RICHARDSON
IOHN HARDWICKE
WILLIAM CROFTS
WILLIAM CHAPPELL
RICHARD DREWRY
& IOHN ALLSY

[300] BRITISH HOME AND HOSPITAL FOR INCURABLES, CROWN LANE

The British Home for Incurables was founded in 1861 and until 1894 occupied premises in Clapham Rise.[139] The buildings at Crown Lane were designed by Arthur Cawston, who died in a shooting accident in June 1894.[140] The hospital was opened by the Princess of Wales (later Queen Alexandra) on July 3, 1894;[141] a number of additions have been made later. The hospital consists of an asymmetrically arranged group of three-storey red brick and stone buildings which are plainly detailed in the Tudor and Jacobean styles. The quality of the design is domestic rather than institutional.

[301] WEST NORWOOD FREE PUBLIC LIBRARY, KNIGHT'S HILL

The site of this building was given by Frederick Nettlefold, who laid the foundation stone on November 26, 1887.[141] The architect was Sidney R. J. Smith, and the cost of the building was £4,050.[142] The library was the first to be provided by the Lambeth Public Libraries Commissioners, and was opened by Lord Northbrook and Sir Lyon (afterwards Lord) Playfair on July 21, 1888.[141] The contractors were F. and H. F. Higgs.[82] The building was extended southwards in 1936 to the designs of Osmond Cattlin, Lambeth Borough Engineer.[143]

The library is a three-storey building in Classical style showing Flemish influence, and is built of red brick with terracotta and Ham Hill stone dressings. It has a colonnaded entrance loggia with an enclosed balcony above. The balcony is fronted by tapering fluted piers bearing busts of famous men of letters. The piers are set forward at the centre and support a scrolled pediment. The wings flanking the entrance loggia are surmounted by broad overhanging dormer windows. The roof, which is of mansard type, is covered with red tiles.

UPPER NORWOOD PUBLIC LIBRARY, [302] WESTOW HILL

Designed by Edward Haslehurst in 1899 for the Libraries Commissioners of Lambeth and Croydon,[144] this is an uninteresting stone-dressed red brick building with effete Classical detail. It has two main storeys and is gabled on the main and side elevations.

DOMESTIC BUILDINGS

PEABODY BUILDINGS, ROSENDALE ROAD [303]

This estate (fig. 62) comprises nearly twenty acres, including the garden allotments on Knight's Hill, and is a late example of the work of the Peabody Trust, whose first buildings were erected in Spitalfields in 1864.[145] The blocks of flats fronting Rosendale Road were designed by William Cubitt and Co. and were erected in 1901[146] (Plate 73b). In 1905 82 cottages were added, and another 64 in 1907–8;[145] they were designed by W. E. Wallis.[146] The estate is further from the centre of London than most of the Peabody Trust's buildings, and some difficulty was at first experienced in obtaining tenants. The estate includes a communal hall built in 1913, an unusual feature of the Trust's work.[145]

NOS. 119 AND 121 NORWOOD ROAD [304]
Formerly Norwood Lane

The site of these two houses formed part of Brockwell Green Farm, which was purchased by Lord Thurlow in 1785, and which was a detached portion of the Manor of Leigham Court and of the parish of Streatham. In 1826 Lord Thurlow's trustees entered into a provisional agreement (which was subsequently approved by the Court of Chancery) to sell 27 acres of the farm to John Prince of Leadenhall Street,[147] slop-seller.[148] These two houses (fig. 63) were probably erected soon afterwards; they were certainly standing in 1836.[149] The interest of these paired houses lies in the unusual character of the front elevation, a Grecian design reflecting the influence of the late 18th century French architect Ledoux. The stucco-faced fronts combine to present a uniform composition of two storeys above a semi-basement, each storey having six rectangular windows widely spaced at equal intervals. Each

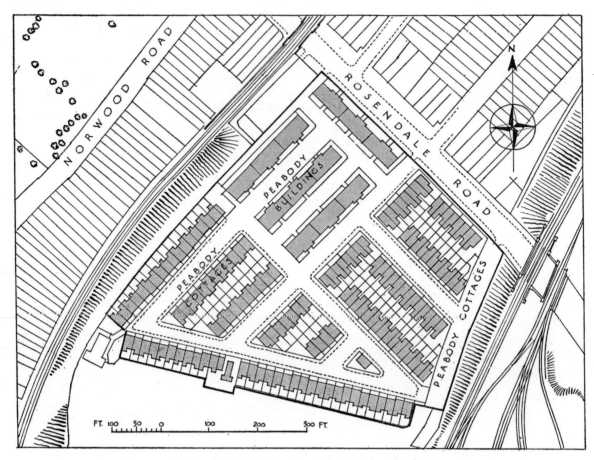

Fig. 62. Peabody Estate, Rosendale Road, lay-out plan

tier of windows is underlined by a plain sill-band, that to the ground floor being deeper than that to the first floor, which breaks forward below each window. Architraves are omitted but on the wall face over each ground-floor window is a flat pediment. The overhanging eaves of the low-pitched roof are carried on widely spaced wood mutules. Each house has a side extension to the ground floor, from which projects an enclosed porch with columns, originally with Ionic capitals, framed by a plain architrave and surmounted by a flat-pitched corniced pediment. No. 119 has, unfortunately, suffered considerable mutilation.

[305] Nos. 212 and 214 Knight's Hill

The site of these houses formed part of Norwood Common, and under the Inclosure Award of 1810 was allotted to Mary Nesbit. She surrendered this and other land to George Bacchus in 1820.[150] These houses were probably built

shortly before 1839.[151] They are a pair of plain stock brick houses, three storeys high with two storey wings, slightly recessed and containing the entrances. These have fluted quadrant reveals with dentilled caps, the dentils continuing across the transoms. No. 214 has original cast-iron window guards on the second floor and No. 212 has an entrance fanlight of circular pattern.

Nos. 3 and 5 Gipsy Road   [306]

The site of these houses formed part of Norwood Common, and under the Award of 1810 was allotted to Charles Field[152] of Lambeth Marsh, wax chandler. In 1811 he obtained licence to demise his property for 21 years,[153] but this was evidently too short a term for his purposes, for in 1834 he obtained another licence to demise this and adjoining land to John Loat of Balham Hill, builder, for 65 years from 1832.[154] These two houses were built under this licence and were

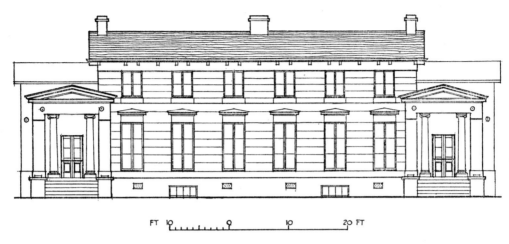

Fig. 63. Nos. 119 and 121 Norwood Road, 1826–36

described as "lately erected" in 1842.[155] They are paired houses of three storeys sharing a stock brick front of simple but good design which is adorned with a sill-band to the first-floor windows, and a crowning triangular pediment with a lunette window in its tympanum. This central feature stands slightly forward from the flanking wings of two storeys which contain the entrance door-ways.

[307] No. 109 Clive Road

Formerly Dudley House

This house was erected in 1882 and occupied by Ralph Gardiner, plasterer and builder.[156] The elaborate and rather bizarre plasterwork on the façade (Plate 58b) suggests that Gardiner intended it to advertise his skill.

POLICE STATION

[308] No. 10 Gipsy Hill

Formerly Gipsy Hill Police Station

This building was designed by Charles Reeves, Metropolitan Police Surveyor, and erected in 1854 at a cost of £2,461 (Plate 38a). It was converted for use as police flats in 1948.[157]

RAILWAY ARCHITECTURE

The first railway in Norwood was the West End of London and Crystal Palace Railway, which was opened in 1856; amongst its stations were those of West Norwood and Gipsy Hill. The lines built by the London, Chatham and Dover Company under its Metropolitan Extensions Act of 1860 ran slightly east of Norwood. The line built by the London, Brighton and South Coast Railway from Peckham to Streatham involved the construction of several iron bridges, including one over Rosendale Road (Plate 39d), [309] and a tunnel under Knight's Hill (Plate 39b). [310] R. J. Hood was the engineer for this line, which was opened in 1868. A brick bridge (Plate 39c) [311] across Rosendale Road carried the London, Chatham and Dover Company's line from Herne Hill to Tulse Hill, which was opened in 1869.[158]

NORWOOD PARK   [312]

The 33½ acres of land which form this Park were bought by the London County Council in 1909 from the Ecclesiastical Commissioners for £15,000,[159] of which Lambeth Borough Council contributed £5,000 and £2,500 were collected by local subscription.[160] The Park was opened on June 14, 1911.[161]

References

LIST OF ABBREVIATIONS

Allen — *The History and Antiquities of the Parish and Palace of Lambeth*, by T. Allen, 1826.

B.A. — Building Act Case, London County Council.

B.G. — Lambeth Board of Guardians Minutes.

B.M. — British Museum.

Brayley — *The History of Surrey*, by E. W. Brayley, 5 vols. extended to 11, 1841–

Cal. Charter Rolls. — Calendar of Charter Rolls.

Cal. L. and P. Henry VIII. — Calendar of Letters and Papers, Foreign and Domestic, Henry VIII.

Cal. Pat. Rolls. — Calendar of Patent Rolls.

Cal. S.P. Dom. — Calendar of State Papers Domestic.

C.C. — Church Commissioners.

C.E. — Church of England.

Ch.C. — Charity Commissioners, *Report on Endowed Charities (County of London), 1901–1903.*

C.L.C. — Chapter Library, Canterbury.

C.R.O. — City of London Record Office.

D.C. — Duchy of Cornwall.

D.N.B. — *Dictionary of National Biography.*

G.E.C. — *The Complete Peerage*, ed. G.E.C., 1910– in progress.

H.M.C. — Historical Manuscripts Commission.

L.B.C. — Lambeth Borough Council.

L.C.C. — London County Council.

L.C.C.R.O. — London County Council Record Office.

L.P.L. — Lambeth Palace Library.

L.S.B. — School Board for London.

Manning and Bray. — *The History and Antiquities of the County of Surrey*, by O. Manning and W. Bray, 3 vols, 1804–1814.

M.B.W. — Metropolitan Board of Works (records with London County Council).

M.P.L. — Minet Public Library.

N.S. — National Society Religious Education Office.

O.S. — Ordnance Survey.

P.C.C. — Prerogative Court of Canterbury.

P.O. — Post Office.

P.O.D. — *Post Office Directory.*

P.R.O. — Public Record Office.

Q.A.B. — Queen Anne's Bounty.

Q.S. — Quarter Sessions.

R.B. — Rate Books of St. Mary, Lambeth, in Lambeth Central Public Library.

R.I.B.A. — Royal Institute of British Architects.

S.A.C. — *Surrey Archæological Collections.*

S.C.C.R.O. — Surrey County Council Record Office, Kingston upon Thames.

T.E.B. — Technical Education Board.

T.P. — Town Planning Case, London County Council.

V.C.H. — *Victoria County History.*

V.M. — Lambeth Vestry Minutes, Lambeth Town Hall.

General Introduction

(pp. 1–17)

1. *Census of Great Britain*, 1801, vol. 1, p. 351. *Census of England and Wales*, 1901, County of London, p. 18.
2. Inclosure Map; printed copy in L.C.C. Members' Library. Original in custody of the Town Clerk of Lambeth Borough Council.
3. *Registrum Roffense*, ed. J. Thorpe, 1769, pp. 459–460.
4. 46 Geo. III c. 57, local.
5. *Cal. Charter Rolls*, vol. 4, p. 428.
6. *Red Book of the Exchequer*, vol. III, pp. 1020–1022.
7. *Cal. Pat. Rolls* 1361–1364, p. 254.
8. *London Gazette*, Aug. 8, 1862.
9. C.C., Deed 124456 f. 45.
10. *Cal. L. and P. Henry VIII*, vol. XIX, part 1, p. 38.
11. C.C., Deed 171235, quit-rent rolls 1669–1728, under "Lady Cambden's heires" in 1676 and 1682.
12. P.R.O., C142/443, No. 64.
13. *Ibid.*, E305/D8.
14. C.L.C., Register S, f. 306. C.C., Muniments Register, vol. 6, Deeds 86568–86613.
15. *Cal. Pat. Rolls* 1350–1354, p. 304.
16. *V.C.H. Surrey*, vol. IV, p. 96.
17. 50 Geo. III c. 19, local.

18. *Report and evidence of House of Commons Select Committee on Select and Other Vestries*, 1830. Evidence of Lambeth Vestry Clerk.
19. M.P.L., Surrey pamphlet 4266.
20. *With a spade on Stane Street*, by S. E. Winbolt, 1936, especially pp. 178 and 213.
21. *Roman Ways in the Weald*, by I. D. Margary, 1948, ch. 6.
22. Manning and Bray, vol. III, p. 381.
23. English Place-Name Society, vol. XI, *The Place-Names of Surrey*, p. 33.
24. 4 Geo. I c. 4, private.
25. For this road see 10 Geo. I c. 13, public.
26. 24 Geo. II c. 58, public.
27. 26 Geo. III c. 131, public.
28. 58 Geo. III c. 76, local.
29. Lambeth Manor Inclosure Award and Map; original in custody of the Town Clerk of Lambeth Borough Council.
   V.M. Oct. 7, 1823.
30. 49 Geo. III c. 175, local.
31. V.M. Dec. 14, 1821.
32. 16 and 17 Vict. c. 180, local and personal, West End of London and Crystal Palace Railway Act.
33. *The London, Chatham and Dover Railway*, by R. W. Kidner, 1952, pp. 4, 5.
34. 23 and 24 Vict. c. 177, local, L.C. and D. (Metropolitan Extensions) Act.
35. Information supplied by the Civil Engineer, British Railways (Southern Region).
36. *Third Report from the Select Committee of the House of Lords on Metropolitan Railway Communication*, Session 1863.
37. 26 and 27 Vict. c. 143, local, L.B. and S.C. Rly. (Extensions and Alterations) Act.
   27 and 28 Vict. c. 314, local, L.B. and S.C. Rly. (Additional Powers) Act.
   27 and 28 Vict. c. 195, local, L.C. and D. Rly. (New Lines) Act.
38. *The Builder*, 1864, p. 141.
39. 32 and 33 Vict. c. 99, local, Crystal Palace and South London Junction Railway Act.
40. 27 and 28 Vict. c. 195, local, L.C. and D. Rly. (New Lines) Act.
   Kidner, *op. cit.* (ref. 33), p. 10.
   The Builder, 1872, pp. 174, 533.
41. 26 and 27 Vict. c. 218, local, L.B. and S.C. Rly. (South London, Tooting, etc. Junction Railways) Act.
   27 and 28 Vict. c. 314, local, L.B. and S.C. Rly. (Additional Powers) Act.
   Dates of opening supplied by Civil Engineer, British Railways (Southern Region).
42. *The London Tramcar 1861–1951*, by R. W. Kidner, 1951, pp. 2–4.
   The Builder, 1862, p. 324.
43. Maps in the L.C.C. Members' Library.
44. *Address on the Streets and Traffic of London, delivered to the Society of Arts*, 1898, by Sir John Wolfe Barry, 1899, pp. 5 and 6 (copy in L.C.C. Members' Library).
45. *London's Underground*, by F. Henry Howson, 1951, pp. 31–35.
46. 16 Geo. III c. 58, private.
47. D.C., Minutes of the Prince's Council, Dec. 1, 1791.
48. 47 Geo. III (Sess. 2) c. 128, local.
49. 5 Geo. IV c. 37, private.
50. 6 Geo. IV c. 47, private.
51. P.R.O., C P 24 (10)/113/3.
52. V.M. Dec. 14, 1821.
53. *The Works of John Ruskin*, ed. E. T. Cook and A. Wedderburn, 1908, vol. XXXV: *Praeterita*, pp. 15, 20, 26.
54. *Ibid.*, pp. 35, 36 n.
55. *Ibid.*, p. 39.
56. *Ibid.*, pp. 130–131.
57. *Homes and Haunts of John Ruskin*, by E. T. Cook, 1912, p. 13.
58. *Praeterita*, p. 47.
59. 5 Geo. IV c. 5, private.
   P.R.O., C 110/21–22.
   L.C.C. R.O., C/85/550.
60. British Railways (Southern Region), Deeds.
61. 4 and 5 Vict. c. 35, public.
62. 6 Anne c. 31, public.
63. 7 and 8 Vict. c. 84, public.
64. 18 and 19 Vict. c. 122, public.
65. L.C.C. Records, District Surveyors' Returns.
66. *Higgs and Hill Limited, 1898–1948*: souvenir of the fiftieth anniversary of the Incorporation of the Company, 1948.
67. Information supplied by Mr. C. D. Hill.
68. *Life and Labour of the People in London*, by Charles Booth, 1902, 3rd series, vol. 4, p. 166.
69. D.C., Kennington Demesne Correspondence 71.
70. *Second Report of Royal Commission on Friendly and Benefit Building Societies*, 1872; vol. XXVI, sess. 1872.
71. 37 and 38 Vict. c. 42, public.
72. *Lambeth Building Society, 1852–1952*, p. 25 (copy in L.C.C. Members' Library).
73. L.C.C. R.O., C/85/550.
74. C.C., Deed 125761.
75. 27 and 28 Vict. c. 195, local, section 134.
76. L.C.C. Records: Housing development and workmen's fares, report by the Valuer to the Housing of the Working Classes Committee, 1912, appendix 5, p. 20.
77. V.M. March 5, 1819.
78. L.B.C., Churchwardens' Minutes, Jan. 29, 1850.
79. L.S.B. Minutes, March 15, 1876.
80. *The Builder*, 1875, p. 39.

CHAPTER I (pp. 19–56)

Kennington

1. P.R.O., E 36/168, pp. 95–101.
2. C.R.O., "A breife abstracte of the Survey of the manor of Kennington taken by John Norden 1615".
3. D.C., Harbord's survey of the demesne lands of the Manor of Kennington, 1636.
4. P.R.O., E 317/Surrey 33.
5. *Ibid.*, E 317/Surrey 34.
6. D.C., Survey of the Manor of Kennington, 1785–1786, by John Hodskinson and John Middleton.
7. M.P.L., History of the Manor of Kennington in the County of Surrey (MS.) by E. R. L. Clowes.
8. L.C.C. Architect's Dept., Street Naming Plan, No. 7837.
9. An exact survey of the cities of London, Westminster and boro' of Southwark and country near ten miles round, 1741–1745, by J. Rocque.
10. *Survey of London*, vol. XXIII, p. 67.
11. 24 Geo. II c. 58, public.
12. *Survey of London*, vol. XXV, pp. 41–43.
13. 21 Jas. I c. 29, public.
14. 16 Geo. III c. 58, private.
15. D.C., Kennington Demesne Enrolment Book 10, pp. 165–173.
16. *Ibid.*, Minutes of the Prince's Council, Dec. 1, 1791.
17. *Metropolitan Improvements or London in the Nineteenth Century*, by J. Elmes, 1827, p. 26.
18. C.C., Q.A.B., K 7109.
    M.P.L., Deed 12790.
19. 58 Geo. III c. 76, local.
20. D.C., Kennington Copyholds 95a, 105c and 105m, Correspondence.
21. *Ibid.*, Kennington Demesne 582, Correspondence.
22. *Ibid.*, Kennington Copyhold 106, Correspondence.
23. *Ibid.*, Kennington Copyhold 170c, Correspondence.
24. *Survey of London*, vol. XXIII, p. 8.
25. *Case between Sir William Clayton, Bart., and the Duchy of Cornwall*, 1834; opinion of T. G. Western, p. 9 (copy in L.C.C. Members' Library).
26. D.C., Kennington Demesne 562, Correspondence.
27. *Ibid.*, Kennington Demesne Enrolment Book D2, pp. 386–395.
28. *Ibid.*, Kennington Demesne Enrolment Book D3, pp. 388–394.
29. *Ibid.*, Kennington Demesne 581, Correspondence, Bundle 1.
30. *Surrey Cricket*, by Lord Alverston and C. W. Alcock, 1902, p. 355.
31. D.C., Kennington Demesne 581, Correspondence, Bundle 2.
32. *The History of Kennington and its Neighbourhood*, by H. H. Montgomery, 1889, pp. 169–175.
33. Alverston and Alcock, *op. cit.*, p. 62.
34. *Hundred Years of Surrey Cricket*, by H. D. G. Leveson Gower (centenary programme).
35. Montgomery, *op. cit.*, p. 173.
36. D.C., Kennington Demesne 581, Correspondence, Bundle 3.
37. Alverston and Alcock, *op. cit.*, p. 355.
38. D.C., Kennington Demesne 581, Correspondence, Bundle 4.
39. *Ibid.*, Kennington Leases Enrolment Book 59, pp. 152–160.
40. Alverston and Alcock, *op cit.*, p. 359.
41. *Ibid.*, p. 360.
42. *Ibid.*, p. 367.
43. C.C., Q.A.B., K7109.
44. R.B.
45. P.C.C., 615 Ely.
46. L.C.C., Kennington Park Papers (deposited by H.M. Office of Works with the Metropolitan Board of Works).
47. Except where other reference is given, this account is derived from a volume of Committee Minutes from 1823 onwards, preserved at St. Mark's School. Apart from Minutes, various documents, both printed and manuscript covering the period from 1817 onwards, have been bound into the volume.
48. St. Mark's School, Deeds.
49. V.M. June 4, 1825.
50. D.C., Kennington Demesne, Kennington Oval National Schools, Correspondence.
51. *Ibid.*, Kennington Demesne Enrolment Book D2, pp. 166–175.
52. *Ibid.*, Kennington Demesne Enrolment Book, Sales and Purchases, vol. XXXVII, pp. 355–364.
53. L.C.C. Minutes, May 30, 1905.
54. M.P.L., Deed 3457.
55. Newington Sessions House, Land Tax Books of St. Mary, Lambeth.
56. C.C., File 48165.
57. Allen, p. 383.
58. D.C., Kennington Demesne 69, Correspondence.
59. *Ibid.*, Kennington Demesne 582 (Old Vestry Hall), Correspondence.
60. V.M. April 20, 1849.
61. 13 and 14 Vict. c. 57, public.
62. M.P.L., Surrey pamphlet No. 4266.
63. V.M. March 25, 1852.

64. D.C., Kennington Demesne Enrolment Book, vol. VI, pp. 261–268.
65. V.M. March 17, 1853.
66. Minutes of the Churchwardens and Overseers of St. Mary, Lambeth, March 4, 1852 (Lambeth Town Hall).
67. *Ibid.*, July 13, 1852.
68. *Living in Lambeth*, by A. D. Nash, 1951, p. 56.
69. L.B.C. Minutes, April 2, 1908.
70. *Ibid.*, April 1, 1909.
71. *Everybody's Children: The Story of the Church of England Children's Society*, by M. de M. Rudolf, 1950, pp. 1–5.
72. *Annual Charities Register and Digest*, 1954, p. 133.
73. D.C., Kennington Court Rolls, Oct. 24, 1660.
74. *The Builder*, 1866, p. 437.
75. D.C., Gallows Common Correspondence.
76. *The Times*, April 11, 1848.
77. 15 & 16 Vict. c. 29, public.
78. 58 Geo. III c. 45, public.
79. *Survey of London*, vol. XXIII, p. 32.
80. C.C., File 18135.
81. 5 Geo. IV c. 103, public.
82. *Georgian London*, by J. Summerson, 1945, p. 208.
83. C.C., Church Building Commissioners' Minutes, Sept. 24, 1822.
84. *The Gentleman's Magazine*, 1827, part 1, pp. 10 and 11.
85. *Lambeth Official Guide*, 7th ed. (N.D., c. 1939), p. 86.
86. *The Builder*, 1849, p. 44.
87. 50 & 51 Vict. c. 34, public.
88. M.B.W Minutes, Jan. 13, 1888.
89. L.C.C. Minutes, July 18, 1922.
90. D.C., Kennington Park Extension 1920–22, Correspondence.
91. *The Builder*, 1862, p. 206.
92. *The Builder*, Jan. 2, 1953: "Henry Roberts, 1802–1876" by A. M. Foyle.
93. *The Brick Builder*, 1951, pp. 122–124.
94. *Official Descriptive Illustrated Catalogue of the Great Exhibition*, 1851, vol. II, pp. 774–775.
95. L.C.C. Minutes, May 24, 1898.
96. *D.N.B.*
97. P.C.C., 144 Pinfold.
98. *Ibid.*, 18 Glazier.
99. D.C., Kennington Court Rolls, June 4, 1754.
100. *Ibid.*, Jan. 22, 1767.
101. P.C.C., 494 Walpole.
102. 45 Geo. III c. 112, local.
103. Deeds held by Messrs. Parsons Lee.
104. D.C., Kennington Court Rolls, Sept. 16, 1819.
105. Deeds held by Messrs. Arnold, Fooks, Chadwick & Co.
106. *Heavenly Mansions*, by J. Summerson, 1949, p. 118.
107. *The Exhibition of the Royal Academy*, 1825 (catalogue), No. 884.
108. Roman Catholic Diocese of Southwark, Records, Appeal for the new Vauxhall Church, 1900.
109. Roman Catholic Diocese of Southwark, Records.
110. *Final Report of the Church Building Committee*, 1908 (copy with parish priest).
111. *The Builder*, Oct. 31, 1903, p. 439.
112. D.C., Kennington Copyholds 93a & 95b, Correspondence.
113. Deeds held by Messrs. Pritchard, Englefield.
114. D.C., Kennington Copyhold 95g, Correspondence.
115. *Ibid.*, Kennington Court Rolls, Oct. 29, 1824.
116. *Ibid.*, Kennington Court Rolls, Lib. G. f. 133.
117. *Kent's Directory*, 1776, 1779, 1780.
118. D.C., Kennington Court Rolls, May 16, 1882.
119. *Ibid.*, June 19, 1828.
120. *Ibid.*, Kennington Copyholds 88a/4.2, 88a/5.2 & 94e, Correspondence.
121. *Ibid.*, Kennington Court Rolls, July 27, 1819.
122. *Ibid.*, Kennington Copyholds 100 p. 1, 100 p. 2, 100 p. 3 & 100 p. 4, Correspondence.
123. Deeds held by Hayward Bros.
124. 45 Geo. III c. 119, local.
125. D.C., Kennington Court Rolls, Oct. 28, 1808.
126. *London Water Supply*, by Sir Francis Bolton, revised by P. A. Scratchley, 1888, pp. 82–85.
127. *Hydraulia; An Historical and Descriptive Account of The Water Works of London . . .*, by W. Matthews, 1835, p. 126.
128. L.C.C. R.O., Surrey and Kent Commissioners of Sewers, Court Minutes, March 22, 1833.
129. 4 & 5 Will. IV c. 78, local.
130. *Survey of London*, vol. XXIII, p. 51.
131. 8 & 9 Vict. c. 69, local.
132. Deeds held by the Navy, Army and Air Force Institutes.
133. D.C., Kennington Copyholds 100a and 100t, Correspondence.
134. *Metropolitan Improvements or London in the Nineteenth Century*, by J. Elmes, 1827, p. 157.
135. *The Morning Herald*, Jan. 22, 1836.
136. *A Biographical Dictionary of English Architects 1660–1840*, by H. M. Colvin, 1954, p. 514.
137. *Architectural Magazine*, vol. 3, 1836, p. 140.
138. D.C., Kennington Court Rolls, April 3, 1813.
139. *Ibid.*, April 29, 1800.
140. *Ibid.*, Oct. 28, 1806.
141. *Ibid.*, Kennington Copyholds 100d and 100h, Correspondence.
142. Deeds held by Mr. T. H. Gardner.
143. *Survey of London*, vol. XXV, p. 99.
144. 4 Geo. I c. 4, private.
145. D.C., Kennington Court Rolls, *passim*.
146. *Ibid.*, Nov. 27, 1764.
147. *Ibid.*, Oct. 3, 1813.

148. Allen, p. 384.
149. Montgomery, *op. cit.* (ref. 32), p. 50.
150. Brayley, vol. 3, part 2, p. 361.
151. L.S.B. Minutes, Dec. 19, 1895; Jan. 30, 1896; Oct. 7, 1897.
152. *Survey of London*, vol. XXIII, p. 32.
153. Deeds held by Messrs. E. G. and J. W. Chester.
154. M.B.W. Case 8564.
155. D.C., Kennington Court Rolls, Oct. 27, 1797.
156. M.P.L., Deed 3457.
157. D.C., Kennington Copyholds 107b and 107c, Correspondence.
158. M.P.L., Deed 3506.
159. D.C., Kennington Court Rolls, Sept. 14, 1815.
160. M.P.L., Deed 3520.
161. *Ibid.*, Deeds 3520, 3528, 3529 & 3530.
162. *Ibid.*, Deed 3527.
163. *Ibid.*, Deed 3522.
164. *Ibid.*, Deed 3521.
165. D.C., Kennington Court Rolls, Aug. 23, 1793.
166. *The Metropolitan*, Sept. 8, 1888.
167. *The Builder*, Aug. 11, 1888, p. 106.
168. M.P.L., Deed 3525.
169. *Ibid.*, Deed 3532.
170. *Ibid.*, Deed 3538.
171. D.C., Kennington Copyhold 107, Correspondence.
172. *Ibid.*, Bowden's Copyhold—Plans and Specifications.
173. M.P.L., Deed 3510.
174. *Ibid.*, Deed 3511.
175. *Ibid.*, Deed 3512.
176. *Ibid.*, Deed 3513.
177. *Ibid.*, Deed 3514.
178. *Ibid.*, Deed 3515.
179. *Ibid.*, Deed 3516.
180. *City and Guilds of London Institute* (pamphlet), 1952.
181. *The City and Guilds of London Art School*, prospectus 1954–1955, p. 4.
182. City and Guilds of London Institute, Records.
183. D.C., Kennington Court Rolls, Oct. 20, 1742.
184. *Ibid.*, May 13, 1763.
185. P.R.O., E 320/R 20.
186. D.C., Kennington Court Rolls, Oct. 21, 1726.
187. *Ibid.*, Oct. 28, 1779.
188. *Ibid.*, Aug. 8, 1829.
189. *Ibid.*, Oct. 30, 1815.
190. *Ibid.*, Oct. 28, 1817.

CHAPTER II (pp. 57–80)

Vauxhall and South Lambeth

1. The map is reproduced in *Survey of London*, vol. XXIII, Plate 123.
2. P.R.O., E 178/7073.
3. Rate Book, 1703; rate levied for new Vauxhall Bridge (in Town Clerk's custody, Lambeth Town Hall).
4. P.R.O., SC 2/205/11.
5. C.L.C., Miscellaneous Accounts, vol. 31, f. 39v.
6. P.R.O., E 178/4609.
7. *Calendar of Inquisitions*, vol. 1, 50, 564. *Cal. Charter Rolls* 1261–1264, p. 178. *Cal. Pat. Rolls* 1247–1248, p. 88, etc.
8. G.E.C., vol. IV, pp. 311–323.
9. P.R.O., C 132/29.
10. *Cal. Charter Rolls* 1231–1234, p. 323.
11. *Red Book of the Exchequer*, vol. III. Introduction and pp. 1014–1023.
12. P.R.O., SC 2/205/10–12. C.C., Deed 124453, *et. seq.*
13. *Survey of London*, vol. XXIII, p. 11.
14. *Chartulary of the Hospital of St. Thomas the Martyr* (Stowe MS. 942), 1932, p. 119.
15. *Cal. L. and P. Henry VIII*, vol. 16, No. 878/59.
16. *Cal. L. and P. Henry VIII*, vol. 17, No. 443/15.
17. "Chalcroft" which was part of the Archbishop of Canterbury's Manor of Lambeth in the 18th century (*Survey of London*, vol. XXIII, p. 31) was in the 15th century let by the Prior and Convent to the Archbishop under the name of "Calkescroft" (C.L.C., Miscellaneous Accounts, vol. 10, f. 26). The Prior and Convent also let land in the "Wild Marsh" to the Archbishop at the beginning of the 16th century. (C.L.C., Miscellaneous Accounts, vol. 31, f. 39v.)
18. *London Gazette*, Aug. 8, 1862, Order in Council No. 1371.
19. C.C., Deed 124453, ff. 4–62.
20. C.L.C., Miscellaneous Accounts, vol. 15, f. 107 v.
21. *Ibid.*, vol. 10, f. 26; vol. 31, f. 39 v.; vol. 15, f. 10.
22. *Ibid.* The volumes of accounts already cited record payments made by tenants for various closes.
23. C.L.C., Cartae Antiquae F 53.
24. *Ibid.*, F 54.
25. C.L.C., Register N, f. 239b.
26. C.C., Deed 70432.
27. C.L.C., Register W, f. 33.
28. *Ibid.*, Cartae Antiquae L 141.
29. L.C.C. Members' Library, Map JLA 2387, 1824.
30. *Ibid.*, MS. copy of lectures delivered by Dr. James F. Young, 1856–1857, on the history of Lambeth; first lecture, p. 72.
31. Victoria and Albert Museum, Print Collection, D 134.
32. C.L.C., Bedells Rolls, Fauxhall, Mich. 15–Mich. 16 Edward IV.
33. C.C., Deed 70308, f. 23.

34. *Ibid.*, Deed 73736.
35. L.B.C., Vauxhall Park Deeds.
36. C.L.C., Box 16, Mawbey Papers.
37. Brayley, vol. III, part II, p. 363.
38. L.C.C. Members' Library, Map FN 474, 1840.
39. Foundation stones.
40. P.R.O., C54/14001, No. 8.
41. *The Story of Congregationalism in Surrey*, by E. E. Cleal and T. G. Crippen, 1908, pp. 276–283.
42. L.S.B. Minutes, Oct. 23, 1878, p. 526.
43. C.C., Deed, 70436a.
44. *Ibid.*, Deed 124456, f. 76.
45. *Ibid.*, Deed 124457, pp. 252–254.
46. *Ibid.*, Deed 124458, pp. 278–285.
47. *Ibid.*, Deed 124453, ff. 157–158.
48. *Ibid.*, Deed 124455, ff. 73–74.
49. *Ibid.*, Deed 124456, ff. 83–84.
50. 6 & 7 Vict. c. 20, private.
51. C.C., Deed 124457, pp. 285–394.
52. *Ibid.*, Deed 124457, pp. 333–335.
53. *Ibid.*, File 12992.
54. *Ibid.*, File 24451.
55. *The Builder*, 1860, p. 688.
56. C.C., File 24831.
57. N.S. File.
58. C.C., Deed 124455, ff. 23–25.
59. *Ibid.*, Deed 124455, ff. 145–146.
60. *Ibid.*, Deed 124459, pp. 28–38.
61. *Ibid.*, Deeds 124457, pp. 208–354; 124458, pp. 14–40.
62. *The Builder*, 1850, p. 320.
63. C.C., File 18135.
64. L.C.C. R.O., St. Barnabas Church Records.
65. Information supplied by the vicar.
66. C.C., File 33062.
67. R.I.B.A. Library, H. S. Goodhart-Rendel's card index of churches.
68. C.C., File 28843. Plan dated 1862 and correspondence.
69. *Ibid.*, Deed 124453, f. 71.
70. *Ibid.*, Deed 124453, f. 170.
71. *Ibid.*, Deed 124459, pp. 85–87.
72. *Ibid.*, Deed 124456, f. 109.
73. *Ibid.*, Deed 124455, ff. 139–140.
74. *Ibid.*, Deed 124455, ff. 144–145, f. 163.
75. *Ibid.*, Deed 124456, ff. 118–120.
76. *Ibid.*, Deed 124458, pp. 240–246.
77. *Ibid.*, Deed 124455, f. 144.
78. R.B.
79. C.C., Deed 124457, p. 14. Nos. 1–12 New Dorset Place are here said to be in the tenure of Thomas Coope. "Coope" may be the Thomas Corpe who built similar houses elsewhere in Lambeth.
80. *Biographie Nationale publiée par L'Academie Royale . . . de Belgique*, 1872, tom. III.
81. P.R.O., C 54/1729.
82. *Ibid.*, C 66/1603.
83. C.L.C., Cartae Antiquae F 63.
84. *S.A.C.* vol. VII, part 2, p. 133.
85. *Survey of London*, vol. XXIII, p. 7.
86. *Cal. S.P. Dom.* 1623–1625, p. 401.
87. *Ibid.*, p. 458.
88. P.C.C., 74 Barrington.
89. C.C., Deed 70434.
90. *Acts of the Privy Council*, June–Dec. 1626, p. 369; *Ibid.*, Jan.–Aug. 1627, pp. 316–317.
91. P.R.O., PC 2/42, p. 142.
92. *S.A.C.*, vol. III, *The Manor of Kennington*, by W. H. Hunt, p. 32.
93. *H.M.C.*, *7th Report*, Appendix I, p. 159.
94. *Cal. S.P. Dom.* 1648–1649, p. 351.
95. *Ibid.*, 1660–1661, p. 337.
96. *Ibid.*, 1665–1666, p. 361.
97. P.R.O., C54/4216.
98. *Complete Baronetage*, ed. G.E.C.
99. *Cal. S.P. Dom.* April–Oct. 1667, p. 496.
100. P.C.C., 88 Hale.
101. Ch.C., vol. IV, pp. 504–507, 532–534.
102. M.P.L., Deed 234.
103. *D.N.B.*
104. M.P.L., Deed 216.
105. C.C., Deed 124456, ff. 4–5.
106. L.B.C., Vauxhall Park Deeds. *P.O.D.* *D.N.B.*
107. *Memorials of the Family of Beaufoy*, p. 36 (private collection of Mr. H. M. Beaufoy).
108. M.B.W. Case 35980.
109. *33rd Annual Report of the Proceedings of Lambeth Vestry, 1889*, p. 27.
110. 51 and 52 Vict. c. 178, local.
111. *London Parks and Gardens*, by Evelyn Cecil, 1907, p. 161, *et seq.*
112. *The Times*, July 7 and 8, 1890.
113. *Octavia Hill*, by E. Moberly Bell, 1942, p. 225.
114. *Return of Outdoor Memorials in London*, L.C.C., 1910, p. 23.
115. *Bibliotheca Topographica Britannica No. XXXIX, The History and Antiquities of the Parish of Lambeth*, . . . published by J. Nichols, 1786, p. 124.
116. South Eastern Gas Board, Deeds of Phoenix Gas Light and Coke Company.
117. Information supplied by Clerk of Lambeth Endowed Charities.
118. *Report of Commissioners inquiring into Charities and Education of the Poor*, 1815–1839, City of Westminster, pp. 677–678.
119. Ch.C., vol. V, pp. 355–360.
120. 16 and 17 Vict. c. 176, local and personal.
121. *P.O.D.*

O

122. Deeds and information of William Bloore and Son, Ltd.
123. *Survey of London*, vol. XXIII, p. 26.
124. L.C.C. Members' Library, Beaufoy Collection.
125. M.P.L., Deed P 219.
126. C.C., Deed 124453, f. 141.
127. P.C.C., 110 Fagg.
128. House of Lords, Acts of Parliament, No. 118, 18 Geo. III.
129. Maps of the 1840s show the gardens in the areas to be well set out.
130. M.P.L., Deed M 163.
131. M.P.L., Deeds B, D, 165.
     L.C.C. Legal and Parliamentary Dept., Deeds of South Lambeth Road School.
     See also p. 67.
132. C.C., File 22250.
133. *The Builder*, 1856, p. 667.
134. Mackeson's *London Church Guide*, 1894–1895.
135. *The Builder*, 1876, p. 571.
136. L.S.B. Minutes, Sept. 29, 1875; Nov. 17, 1875.
137. *The Times*, Dec. 3, 1888.
     Tate Central Library, local collection.
138. Deeds of Capital and County Laundries Ltd.
139. P.R.O., C 54/16644 No. 10.
140. *Survey of London*, vol. XXIII, p. 142 and Plate 111b.
141. C.L.C., Register Z f. 63.
142. 50 Geo. III, sess. 1810 c. 176, local and personal.
143. *Survey of London*, vol. XXV, pp. 82–83.
144. P.C.C., 63 Lee.
145. P.C.C., 72 Laud.
146. J. Nichols, *op. cit.* (ref. 115), Nos. XXIV and XXV.
147. P.C.C., 54 Reeve.
148. P.C.C., 97 Fane.
149. M.P.L., Deed N 219.
150. C.C., Deed 70434.
     M.P.L. Deeds S 219, V 219.
151. C.C., File 29221.
152. *Ibid.*, File 28519.
153. *Ibid.*, Deed 69507.
154. *Ibid.*, Deeds 69503, 69505 and 69507.
155. *Ibid.*, Deed 69510.
156. *Ibid.*, Deed 69504.
157. *Ibid.*, Deed 69503.
158. *Ibid.*, Deed 69505.
159. *Ibid.*, Deed 69529.
160. *Ibid.*, Deed 69525.
161. *Ibid.*, Deed 69526.
162. B.A. Case 64492.
163. C.C., Deed 69512.
164. *Ibid.*, Deed 69519.
165. C.L.C., Box 16. Bundle of papers, etc., Vauxhall Escheat.

166. British Railways (Southern Region), Deeds of Metropolitan Extension.
167. 45 Geo. III sess. 1805 c. 112, local and personal.
168. *Survey of London*, vol. XXIII, pp. 122, 123, 130.
169. Unless otherwise stated all the information about this house is gathered from British Railways (Southern Region), Deeds of Nine Elms Enlargement.
170. Burke's *Peerage*.
171. *Encyclopaedia Britannica*.
172. *Heavenly Mansions*, by J. Summerson, 1949 p. 118.
173. *Opening of Vauxhall Bridge*, L.C.C. Ceremonial Pamphlet, 1906.
174. 49 Geo. III c. 142, local and personal.
175. *Vauxhall Bridge*, by W. C. Copperthwaite, 1907.
176. *The Times*, Aug. 13, 1816.
177. 52 Geo. III c. 147, local and personal.
178. *The Life of Brigadier-General Sir Samuel Bentham, K.S.G.*, by M. S. Bentham, 1862, pp. 287, 295.
179. L.C.C. Members' Library, Metropolis Toll Bridges Act, 1877. In Arbitration. The Vauxhall Bridge Company *v.* The Metropolitan Board of Works. The Evidence of F. C. Stileman, July 24, 1878.
180. Allen, p. 378.
181. Minutes of evidence taken before Select Committee on Metropolitan Bridges, 1854, para. 1174.
182. L.C.C. Members' Library, Metropolis Toll Bridges Act, 1877, etc. (see ref. 179). The Evidence of Edgar Doggett.
183. Select Committee on Metropolitan Bridges, 1854, para. 799.
184. 21 & 22 Vict. c. 32, local.
185. 40 & 41 Vict. c. 99, local and personal.
186. *The Builder*, Oct. 5, 1907, p. 361.

CHAPTER III (pp. 81–105)

Stockwell

1. B.M., Harl. Chart. 52, E 18 (1294).
   P.R.O., C 134/97/1 (1326).
2. P.R.O., C 134/97/1.
3. C.L.C., Miscellaneous Accounts, vol. 15, f. 107 v.
4. C.C., Deed 124454, f. 1.
5. *Ibid.*, Deed 124456, f. 45.
6. M.P.L., Deed P 139.
7. P.R.O., SC2/205/12.
   C.C., Deeds 124453–124454.
8. *V.C.H. Surrey*, vol. 4, pp. 56–57.
9. P.C.C., 15 Bodfelde.

10. *Bibliotheca Topographica Britannica, No. XXXIX, The History and Antiquities of the Parish of Lambeth . . .* , published by J Nichols, 1786, Appendix, p. 55.

11. *Cal. L. and P. Henry VIII*, vol. XIX, part i, p. 38.

12. *Cal. Pat. Rolls* P & M., vol. II, p. 314.

13. G.E.C.

14. P.R.O., C 54/1602.

15. M.P.L., Deed V 139.

16 M P.L., Deed T 141 (John Norton). P.R.O., C 54/1602 (Thomas Norton).

17. M.P.L., Deed T 141.

18. P.R.O., C 142/374/97.

19. *The Knights of England*, by W. A. Shaw, 1906, p. 146.

20. P.C.C., 90 Fairfax.

21. M.P.L., Deed S 128. P.C.C., 2 Hare.

22. Deeds in the custody of the Trustees of the Angell Estate.

23. M.P.L., Deed G 130.

24. Newington Sessions House, title deeds of House of Correction, Brixton.

25. Deeds in the possession of C. Hammerton and Co.

26. Deeds relating to the Jackson Estate, in the custody of Messrs. Fisher, Dowson and Wasbrough. Deeds belonging to the Trustees of Spurgeon's Homes.

27. Manning and Bray, vol. III, pp. 498–499. M.P.L., Deed N 122. Tithe Map of Brixton District of Lambeth.

28. *P.O.D.*

29. Deeds in the possession of Mr. P. B. Diplock.

30. L.S.B. Minutes, July 10, 1884.

31. L.C.C. Architect's plans.

32. *L.C.C. Elementary Day Schools.* Report of the Education Committee, 1905.

33. Foundation stone.

34. L.C.C.R.O., Records of All Saints' Church, Allen Edwards Road.

35. *The Story of Congregationalism in Surrey*, by E. E. Cleal and T. G. Crippen, 1908, p. 230.

36. Deeds in the possession of the Trustees of Spurgeon's Homes.

37. P.R.O., C 54/6640.

38. R.B.

39. Deeds in the custody of Mr. G. Edmund Hodgkinson, and deeds in the possession of the National United Temperance Council.

40. Deeds relating to the Jackson Estate in the custody of Messrs. Fisher, Dowson and Wasbrough.

41. *Spurgeon's Homes*, by Graham W. Hughes [N.D.]

42. *The Metropolitan Tabernacle: its History and Work*, by C. H. Spurgeon, 1876, p. 104.

43. *The Life and Labors of Charles H. Spurgeon*, by G. C. Needham, 1881 [catalogue 1883], p. 207.

44. Title deeds of Spurgeon's Homes, Stockwell.

45. C. H. Spurgeon, *op. cit.*, p. 106.

46. *The Times*, Sept. 10, 1867.

47. Information supplied by the Secretary of Spurgeon's Homes.

48. Unless otherwise stated the information about the houses is based on the inscriptions on the foundation stones.

49. G. C. Needham, *op. cit.*, p. 208.

50. *Ibid.*, p. 210.

51. *Story of Spurgeon's Homes, 1867–1927.*

52. *Building News*, April 12, 1895, p. 511.

53. All the information about these houses was obtained from deeds in the custody of the Trustees of the estate of W. P. Goosey, deceased, and Rate Books.

54. Deed in the possession of Mr. H. J. Haswell.

55. Map evidence.

56. *The Friendly Almshouses*, by Hilda Martindale, C.B.E. [1939].

57. Annual Reports of the Society, 1940–1954.

58. C.C., File 17746.

59. 58 Geo. III c. 45, public.

60. Records of St. Michael's, Stockwell, faculty and plan.

61. *A Companion from London to Brighthelmston . . .*, by J. Edwards, 1801, part II, p. 7.

62. M.P.L., Deed T 141.

63. Manning & Bray, vol. III, p. 499.

64. Nichols, *op. cit.*, p. 123.

65. Date incised on façade.

66. London Museum, Print Collection, A 22047.

67. *The Encyclopaedia and Dictionary of Education*, edited by Professor Foster Watson, 1922, vol. IV, pp. 1595–1596. *The Builder*, 1871, p. 1004. Information supplied by the Principal.

68. P.R.O., C 103/Blunt 148.

69. *Historical Particulars of Lambeth Parish . . .*, by Rev. S. Denne, 1795, p. 436 n.

70. C.C., Deed 171202, pp. 170–175.

71. Denne, *op. cit.*, pp. 431–432.

72. M.P.L., Deed 1206.

73. Allen, p. 415.

74. M.B.W., Case 31214.

75. Deeds in the possession of the Trustees of John Benn Boys' Hostels Association.

76. L.C.C.R.O., Deed C 85/1250.

77. *Country Life*, vol. XLVII, 1920, pp. 214, 315–316.

78. Information supplied by the Secretary.

79. L.S.B. Minutes, Feb. 9, 1876.

80. Deeds in the possession of Mr. F. W. Surridge.

81. 9 Anne c. 22, public.
82. L.P.L., Records of Commissioners for building 50 new Churches, Lambeth Papers.
83. *Ibid.*, Minute Book I, Nov. 16, 1711.
84. *Ibid.*, Nov. 28, 1711.
85. P.R.O., C 54/6845 No. 7.
86. C.C., File 43576.
87. *S. Andrew, Stockwell, Diamond Jubilee, 1868–1928*, pp. 9–10. (copy in possession of the vicar.)
88. O.S., 1870.
89. *The Builder*, 1866, p. 173.
90. Information on tablet under tower.
91. Stockwell Congregational Church Records, notes in account book, 1865–1897.
92. Cleal, *op. cit.*, pp. 225–233.
93. Stockwell Congregational Church Records, Minute book, Dec. 3, 1849.
94. *Ibid.*, Sept. 9, 1850.
95. Stockwell Congregational Church Records, Church Magazine, *The Story of Stockwell Congregational Church*, by R. A. Gollop.
96. Edwards, *op. cit.*, part II, p. 6.
97. Newspaper cutting in office of C. Hammerton & Co.
98. Deeds in the possession of Mr. J. A. Farmer, and C. Hammerton & Co.
99. *The Builder*, 1876, p. 1203.
100. Tablets in entrance halls.
101. N.S. File.
102. Ch.C., vol. IV, p. 590.
103. Memorial stone.
104. *S. Andrew, Stockwell, Diamond Jubilee, 1868–1928*, p. 8 (copy in possession of the vicar).
105. *The Institution of the London Almshouses, in lieu of an illumination, to commemorate Reform in Parliament*, 1834 (Guildhall Library).
106. Corporation of London, Comptroller's Deeds, 927/39.
107. *The Corporation of London*, 1950, p. 230.
108. 10 Geo. IV c. 43, private.
109. 13 & 14 Vict. c. 10, private.
110. *The Builder*, 1854, pp. 173 and 209.
111. *The Corporation of London*, 1950, p. 197.
112. C.C., File 55356.
     The Builder, 1872, p. 69.
113. *The Life of the late George Peabody, Merchant and Philanthropist*, by J. S. Bryant, 1914, p. 21.
114. *The Builder*, 1872, pp. 69, 469.
115. C.C., File 55356.
116. *The Builder*, Sept. 10, 1881, p. 341.
117. L.S.B. Minutes, May 12, 1898.
118. *Ibid.*, July 26, Nov. 1, Nov. 22, 1900; Feb. 6, 1902, May 28, 1903.
119. *Ibid.*, Feb. 6, 1902.
120. *Higgs and Hill Limited, 1898–1948*. Souvenir of the fiftieth anniversary of the Incorporation of the Company, 1948.
121. *Kenyon Baptist Church: The Jubilee Story, 1884–1934* (copy in Baptist Church House Library).
     The Baptist Churches of Surrey, ed. A. H. Stockwell [1916], pp. 34–35.
122. *S. Andrew, Stockwell, Diamond Jubilee, 1868–1928*, pp. 27–28 (copy in possession of the vicar).
123. C.C., File 74118.
124. B. A. Case 35713.
125. Deeds in the possession of the Trustees of the Eighth Church of Christ, Scientist.
126. L.C.C. Legal and Parliamentary Dept., Deeds of Santley Street Site.
127. B.A. Case 48073.
128. Information supplied by the Trustees.
129. Information supplied by Mr. O. P. Milne.
130. Evidence of measurements taken from plan of 1773 and O.S. 1870.
131. L.C.C. Legal & Parliamentary Dept., Deeds of Santley Street Site.
132. M.P.L., Pamphlet S 1658/2; Deed of Endowment, Trinity Asylum.
133. Trinity Asylum Minute Books, Oct. 15, 1830.
134. *Ibid.*, April 15, 1828.
135. *Ibid.*, Oct. 15, 1839.
136. *Ibid.*, May 16, 1860.
137. *Ibid.*, June 6, 1860.
138. Deeds in the possession of the Church Army.
139. Deeds of the owners in the custody of Messrs. Richardson and Sadler.
140. L.B.C. Minutes, June 16, 1904.
141. *The Builder*, May 6, 1905, p. 487.
142. L.B.C. Minutes, Jan. 18, 1906.
143. *Ibid.*, Sept. 13, 1906.
144. *Ibid.*, April 29, 1908.
145. *Ibid.*, Dec. 10, 1908.
146. T.P. Case 8561.
147. *Westminster Cathedral and its Architect*, by Winefride de L'Hôpital, N.D., vol. 2, pp. 407–419.
148. Information supplied by the Rev. Bernard Kelly, F.R.Hist.S.
149. *The Universe*, July 17, 1886.
150. B.A. Case 23277.
151. de L'Hôpital, *op. cit.*, vol. 2, p. 541.
152. de L'Hôpital, *op. cit.*, vol. 2, p. 419.
153. C.C., File 48729, printed prospectus.
154. L.S.B. Minutes, July 11, 1877.
155. O.S. 1870.
156. Deeds in the custody of Messrs. Scott and Son.
157. Information supplied by the Trustees of the property.
158. *Survey of London*, vol. XXIII, p. 51.
159. 4 & 5 Will. IV c. 7, local and personal.

160. S.C.C.R.O., Q.S. Order Books, April 7, 1818.
161. *Ibid.*, July 14, 1818.
162. *Ibid.*, April 11, 1820.
163. *Ibid.*, Jan. 12, 1819.
164. *Ibid.*, Dec. 6, 1819.
165. *Ibid.*, July 11, 1820.
166. *Ibid.*, Oct. 17, 1820.
167. *The Criminal Prisons of London* . . . , by Henry Mayhew and John Binny, 1862, pp. 174, 113.
168. *Ibid.*, p. 183, footnote.
169. P.R.O., HO12/5054.
170. *English Prisons Under Local Government*, by Sidney and Beatrice Webb, 1922, p. 97.
171. S.C.C.R.O., Q.S. Order Books, Sept. 22, 1820.
172. *Ibid.*, Mar. 29, 1821.
173. *The Gentleman's Magazine*, July, 1822, Plate 1 and pp. 9–10.
174. Allen, p. 405.
175. Mayhew and Binny, *op. cit.*, pp. 493–494.
176. S.C.C.R.O., Q.S. Order Books, Oct. 19, 1852.
177. *D.N.B.*
178. 16 and 17 Vict., c. 99, public.
179. Report of the Surveyor General of Prisons . . . , by Lt. Col. Jebb, 1853, xxxiii, p. 61.
180. Deeds of owners in the custody of Messrs. Lewis W. Taylor and Co.

CHAPTER IV (pp. 106–40)

Brixton

1. L.C.C.R.O., transcript of Guildhall MS. 170: Surrey and Kent Commissioners of Sewers Court Roll, 1640.
2. Deeds of Sewell Estate held by Messrs. Purdy and Holley, Aylsham.
3. Deeds held by Primoff Properties Ltd.
4. The Belgrave Hospital for Children, 81st Annual Report, 1947.
5. Deeds of Belgrave Hospital, King's College Hospital Group.
6. *The Times*, June 28, 1900.
7. *Ibid.*, July 21, 1903.
8. *The British Architect*, June 22, 1900. Information supplied through Mr. John Summerson by Mr. Charles Holden.
9. *The Builder*, May 9, 1903, p. 488.
10. Deeds of Sewell Estate held by Messrs. Purdy and Holley.
    Deeds held by Primoff Properties Ltd.
11. *Survey of London*, vol. XXIII, p. 3.
12. *Cal. Pat. Rolls* 1266–1272, p. 605.
13. *Chartulary of the Hospital of St. Thomas the Martyr, Southwark* (Stowe MS. 942), 1932, Nos. 570–578.
14. C.C., Deeds 171184 $\frac{4}{4}$, Court Roll for Lambeth Wick Manor.
15. L.P.L., Court Rolls: Farmers' Accounts, Nos. 578–590; Reeves and Serjeants' Accounts, Nos. 545–547.
16. C.L.C. Register S, f. 306.
17. C.C., Deeds: Archbishopric of Canterbury, Registers of Leases.
18. *Ibid.*, Muniments Register vol. 6, Deed 86583 (the original deed is missing).
19. G.E.C.
20. The sister of the fourth Baron Holland, whose second son inherited the Surrey estates, was Baroness Lilford.
21. L.P.L., Parliamentary Surveys, Lambeth Manor, f. 71.
22. C.C., Deed 276006.
23. 47 Geo. III sess. 2, c. 128, local.
24. 58 Geo. III c. 76, local.
25. C.C., Deeds 276001–276005, 276007–276011, 276013–276017.
26. *Ibid.*, Deeds 276450, 276474, etc.
27. *Ibid.*, Deed 276018.
28. *Ibid.*, Deed 276018, endorsement.
29. L.C.C.R.O., Surrey and Kent Commissioners of Sewers plans, vol. 3/87.
30. R.I.B.A. *Journal*, Jan. 12, 1901, p. 113. *The Builder*, Dec. 1, 1900, p. 495.
31. C.C., Deed 276128, enclosed correspondence.
32. *D.N.B.*
33. C.C., Deed 276146. Copy of plan at Minet Public Library.
34. *The Huntingdon Peerage*, by H. N. Bell, 1820, pp. 127–128.
35. C.C., Deed 90510, book of contracts for leases.
36. House of Lords Act No. 16, 16 and 17 Car. II.
37. P.C.C. 62 Can.
38. Brayley, vol. III, part II, p. 365.
39. M.P.L., S 166.
40. *Ibid.*, S 3654.
41. L.C.C. Members' Library. MS. copy of lectures delivered by Dr. James F. Young, 1856–1857, on the history of Lambeth, p. 87.
42. C.C., Deed 276164.
43. *Ibid.*, Deed 276460.
44. *Ibid.*, Deed 276461.
45. *Ibid.*, Deed 276165.
46. *Ibid.*, Deed 276462.
47. *Ibid.*, Deed 276166.
48. *Ibid.*, Deed 276450.
49. *Ibid.*, Deed 276167.
50. *Ibid.*, Deed 276406.
51. *Ibid.*, Deeds 276472 and 276474.
52. *Ibid.*, Deeds 276096–276101.
53. *Ibid.*, Deed 276102.
54. *Ibid.*, Deed 276103.

55. C.C., Deed 276446.
56. *Ibid.*, Deeds 276105–276107.
57. *Ibid.*, Deed 276109.
58. *Ibid.*, Deed 276112.
59. *Ibid.*, Deed 276113.
60. *Ibid.*, Deed 276449.
61. *Ibid.*, Deed 276117.
62. *Ibid.*, Deed 276118.
63. *Ibid.*, Deed 276127.
64. *Ibid.*, Deed 276128.
65. *Ibid.*, Deed 276129.
66. *Ibid.*, Deed 276135.
67. *Ibid.*, Deeds 276134 and 276136.
68. *Ibid.*, Deed 276137.
69. *Ibid.*, Deeds 276138 and 276139.
70. *Ibid.*, Deed 276149.
71. L.C.C. Members' Library, File 962.
72. C.C., Deed 276210.
73. *Ibid.*, Deeds 276444, 276475–276477.
74. *Ibid.*, Deeds 276459, 276481, 276482.
75. *Ibid.*, Deed 276432.
76. *Ibid.*, Deed 276438.
77. *Ibid.*, Deed 276439.
78. *Ibid.*, Deed 276440.
79. *Ibid.*, Deed 276453.
80. *Ibid.*, Deed 276418.
81. *Ibid.*, Deed 276191.
82. *Ibid.*, Deed 276423.
83. *Ibid.*, Deed 276242.
84. *Ibid.*, Deed 276425.
85. *Ibid.*, Deed 276426.
86. *Ibid.*, Deed 276427.
87. *Ibid.*, Deed 276428.
88. *Ibid.*, Deed 276429.
89. *Ibid.*, Deed 276192.
90. *Ibid.*, Deed 276193.
91. *Ibid.*, Deed 276194 (missing, information taken from Register).
92. *Ibid.*, Deed 276037.
93. *Ibid.*, Deed 276451.
94. *Ibid.*, Deed 276158.
95. *Ibid.*, Deed 276159.
96. *Ibid.*, Deeds 276452 and 276160.
97. *Ibid.*, Deeds 276152–276154.
98. *Ibid.*, Deed 276454.
99. *Ibid.*, Deeds 276178–276180.
100. *Ibid.*, Deed 276413.
101. *Ibid.*, Deeds 276255, 276260–276262, 276266.
102. *P.O.D.*
103. C.C., Muniments Register.
104. *Ibid.*, Deed 276284.
105. *Ibid.*, File 20452.
106. *The Story of Congregationalism in Surrey*, by E. E. Cleal and T. G. Crippen, 1908, pp. 276–277.
107. Brayley, vol. III, part II, p. 364.
108. *The Builder*, Nov. 22, 1902, p. 476.
109. *Christ Church, North Brixton, Birthday Book*, 1910 (copy in possession of the vicar).
110. *Recent English Ecclesiastical Architecture*, by Sir Charles Nicholson and Charles Spooner, N.D., 2nd ed. [1911], p. 77.
111. *Fifty years at St. John the Divine, Kennington, 1874–1924*, ed. by the Rev. Canon Down, N.D., pp. 5–7 (copy in possession of the vicar).
112. C.C., File 36517.
113. *St. John the Divine, Kennington (Earliest Years, 1866–1871)*, by the Rev. D. T. W. Elsdale, 1921, p. 12 (copy in possession of the vicar).
114. Down, *op. cit.*, pp. 8–10.
115. *Ibid.*, pp. 13–14.
116. *The Builder*, 1874, p. 954.
117. Down, *op. cit.*, pp. 12, 14.
118. *Ibid.*, pp. 16–17.
119. Ch.C., vol. IV, p. 598.
120. L.C.C., Architect's list of Voluntary Schools of Architectural Interest, 1953.
121. L.S.B. Minutes, Oct. 8, 1885.
122. L.C.C. Architect's plans.
123. *L.C.C. Elementary Day Schools.* Report of the Education Committee, 1905.
124. L.S.B. Minutes, July 7, 1887.
125. *Ibid.*, April 7, 1892; Feb. 2, 1893.
126. *Ibid.*, Nov. 27, 1893.
127. Information supplied by Colonel E. D. Jackson, D.S.O., O.B.E.
128. C.C., Deed 171199, pp. 196–197.
129. *Ibid.*, Deed 171199, pp. 253–258.
130. *Ibid.*, Deed 171205, p. 137 (plan).
131. B.A. Case 55534.
132. C.C., Deed 171204, pp. 408–443.
133. *Ibid.*, Deed 171205, pp. 122–123.
134. *Ibid.*, File 17746, letter dated June 20, 1840. Deeds in the custody of Messrs. Fisher, Dowson and Wasbrough, plan on deed dated Nov. 7, 1840.
135. Deeds in the custody of Messrs. Fisher, Dowson and Wasbrough.
136. *A Few Particulars of the Name Slade*, by W. Slade, 1932 (privately printed).
137. C.C., Deed 171204, pp. 180–190 (entry omitted in proper place, i.e. June 15, 1805, and copied in here).
138. *Ibid.*, Deed 171198, pp. 166–169.
139. Ch.C., vol. IV, p. 599. The tithe map for St. Mark's District of Lambeth marks the school.
140. Memorial stone.
141. *Southwark Catholic Directory*, 1952.
142. T.P. Case 22813.
143. C.C., Deed 171194, pp. 14–16.
144. *Ibid.*, Deed 171196, pp. 167–172.
145. Foundation stone.
146. *Historical Particulars of Lambeth Parish ..*, by the Rev. S. Denne, 1795, p. 436.

147. Pedigree among the deeds in the custody of the Angell Estate Trustees.
148. P.C.C., 166 King.
149. C.C., Deed 171194, pp. 66–67.
150. M. P. L., 4812.
151. *Ibid.*, Deed Z59.
152. C.C., Deed 171194, pp. 9–12.
153. *Ibid.*, Deed 171198, pp. 166–169.
154. *Ibid.*, Deed 171195, pp. 107–108.
155. *Ibid.*, Deed 171195, pp. 157–158.
      Ibid., Deed 171196, p. 359.
156. P.R.O., C 103/Blunt 148.
      M.P.L., 4812.
      See also Chapter III, p. 91.
157. P.R.O., C 103/ Blunt 148.
158. C.C., Deed 171197, ff. 125–126.
159. *Ibid.*, Deed 171196, pp. 129–136.
160. *Ibid.*, Deed 171197, f. 255.
161. S. Denne, *op. cit.*, p. 430.
162. *Ibid.*, p. 441.
163. C.C., Deed 171198, p. 162.
164. *Ibid.*, Deed 171198, pp. 237–240.
165. S. Denne, *op. cit.*, p. 431.
166. C.C., Deed 171199, pp. 167–168.
167. *Ibid.*, Deed 171201, pp. 333–336.
168. L.P.L., Lambeth Inclosure Commissioners' Papers, Claims Files.
169. Lambeth Inclosure Map (copy in the custody of the Town Clerk).
170. C.C., Deed 171202, pp. 433–438.
171. *Ibid.*, Deed 171202, pp. 455–458.
172. M.P.L., Deed 37.
173. *Ibid.*, Deed 64.
174. R. B.
175. C.C., Deed 171206, p. 462.
176. Deeds in the custody of the Angell Estate Trustees.
177. C.C., File 20455.
178. *The Builder*, 1853, p. 296.
179. C.C., File 17749.
180. M.B.W. Case 31345.
181. T.P. Case 44119.
182. *The Builder*, 1853, p. 360.
183. Information supplied by the Chief Architect and Surveyor to the Metropolitan Police.
184. C.C., Deed 171200, pp. 484–485.
185. *Ibid.*, Deed 171202, pp. 170–175.
186. P.R.O., C54/17070, No. 8.
187. B.A. Case 48155, 1921 year book.
188. Information supplied by the priest-in-charge.
189. T.P. Case 46460.
190. 46 Geo. III c. 57, local.
191. 29 Geo. II c. 88, public.
192. Section 17.
193. Copy in custody of the Town Clerk of L.B.C.
194. 1 and 2 Geo. IV c. 55, local.
195. Report to the L.C.C. Town Planning and Building Regulation Committee, 1937.
196. M.B.W. Case 14451, and M.B.W. Cases 34634 and 34482 (both destroyed), quoted in Report of 1937.
197. M.B.W. Case 28699.
198. B.A. Case 15884.
199. B.A. Case 3005.
200. L.C.C. (General Powers) Act, 14 and 15 Geo. V c. 57, private, section 62.
201. L.C.C. (General Powers) Act, 1 and 2 Geo. VI c. 38, private, section 8.
202. L.C.C. (General Powers) Act, 2 and 3 Geo. VI c. 100, private, section 72.
203. L.C.C. (General Powers) Act, 10 and 11 Geo. VI, private, c. 46.
204. V.M. June 24, 1822.
205. C.C., File 18135.
206. Inclosure Map (copy in the custody of the Town Clerk).
207. *The Gentleman's Magazine*, 1829, part 1, pp. 577–579.
208. C.C., File 18135. *The Gentleman's Magazine* gives the architect's estimate as £15,340.
209. Allen, p. 414.
210. All the information for the history of these houses is derived from deeds in the custody of the Southwark Diocesan Registrar.
211. N.S. File.
212. Ch.C., vol. IV, p. 594.
213. *The Builder*, 1870, p. 934.
214. *The Times*, March 6, 1893.
215. Local history collection in Tate Central Library.
216. P.R.O., C 142/443, No. 64.
217. *Ibid.*, C 142/194/1.
218. *Cal. S.P. Dom.*, 1591–1594, p. 505.
219. M.P.L., Deed 11.
220. P.C.C., 166 King.
      C.C., Deeds 171194, pp. 14–16; 171196, p. 359; 171199, pp. 167–168.
221. P.R.O., C 110/22, part 1.
222. 5 Geo. IV, c. 5, private.
223. P.R.O., C 110/21.
224. L.C.C.R.O., C 85/550.
225. P.R.O., C 54/ 12690, No. 10.
226. Ch.C., vol. IV, p. 597.
227. C.C., Deed 90802.
228. *Ibid.*, and C.C., Deeds Bundle 540/86700, etc.
229. C.C., Deed Bundle 540/86706.
230. *Ibid.*, Deed 86725.
231. *The Builder*, 1867, p. 231.
232. C.C., File 37916.
233. C.C., Deed 125761.
234. *The Times*, March 31, 1869. This reference was first noted by H. J. Dyos in his unpublished London University Ph.D. thesis, entitled "The Suburban Development of Greater London South of the Thames, 1836–1914."
235. *The Builder*, 1872, p. 814.

236. *The Builder*, 1872, p. 536.
237. *Ibid.*, 1872, p. 743.
238. English Place-Name Society, vol. XI. *The Place-Names of Surrey*, p. 11.
239. Manning and Bray, vol. III, p. 493.
240. *Ibid.*, vol. I, p. liii.
241. P.C.C., 26 Jankin; see also *S.A.C.* vol. LII, pp. 37–38, where the will is quoted.
242. *The Story of Methodism in Brixton*, 1924 (copy at Epworth House library).
243. C.C., File 61422.

CHAPTER V (pp. 141–54)

Myattt's Fields Area, Denmark Hill and Herne Hill

1. *Pope Nicholas' Taxation* (Records Commission), p. 206.
2. Manning and Bray, vol. III, p. 416.
3. *Valor Ecclesiasticus* (Records Commission), II, p. 62.
4. *Cal. L. and P. Henry VIII*, vol XV, 1540, No. 942(49).
P.R.O., C66/694, No. 13.
5. *Cal. Pat. Rolls*, Edward VI, vol. 3, p. 424.
6. P.R.O., C142/306, No. 148.
7. *Catalogue of the Manuscripts and Muniments of Alleyn's College of God's Gift at Dulwich*, by G. F. Warner, 1881, Nos. 561–562.
8. P.R.O., C142/580, No. 100.
9. P.C.C., 168 Lee.
10. P.C.C., Admin. Act Book, 1660, f. 81.
11. P.C.C., 2 Duke.
12. P.R.O., C54/4740, No. 41.
13. *Ibid.*, CP43/359.
14. C.C., Deed 171235; quit-rent rolls 1669–1728, see under 'Lady Cambden's heires' in 1676 and 1682, and under 'Mr. Goodschall' in 1704 *et seq.*
15. P.R.O., CP24(10)/113/3.
16. L.P.L., Lambeth Inclosure Commissioners' Minutes, Feb. 27, 1807.
17. P.R.O., C54/4307.
18. P.C.C., 12 Tenison.
19. P.R.O., C54/5794, No. 16.
20. M.P.L., Deeds 152–153.
21. P.R.O., C54/6099.
M.P.L., Deed 157.
22. M.P.L., Deed 158.
23. *Ibid.*, Deed 169.
24. Manning and Bray, vol. III, p. 417.
25. *The Huguenot family of Minet*, by William Minet, [1892], pp. 24–52, 155–162.

26. Maps in the Minet Estate Office, and information supplied there by Mr. A. J. Carpenter, F.R.I.C.S.
27. C.C., File 43533.
28. Plans in possession of the vicar.
29. Deeds of Myatt's Fields, L.C.C. Legal and Parliamentary Dept.
L.C.C. Minutes, March 26, April 9, 1889.
30. Information supplied by Mr. Carpenter.
31. Lambeth Vestry Clerk's Report on the Minet Library, 1899 (copy in Minet Library).
32. 52 and 53 Vict., c. 9, public.
33. L.S.B. Minutes, March 19, 1896.
34. L.C.C. Architect's plans.
35. *L.C.C. Elementary Day Schools.* Report of the Education Committee, 1905.
36. *The Architect and Contract Reporter*, February 16, 1900, p. 112.
Fifty Years at St. John the Divine, Kennington, ed. Canon Down, N.D., p. 47.
37. R.B.
38. Rate Books of St. Giles, Camberwell, in custody of the Town Clerk of Camberwell Metropolitan Borough Council.
39. N.S. File.
40. *Fifty Years at St. John the Divine, Kennington*, ed. Canon Down, N.D., p. 43.
41. Ch.C., vol. IV, pp. 609–610.
42. *V.C.H. Surrey*, vol. IV, p. 25.
43. English Place-Name Society, vol. XI, *The Place-Names of Surrey*, p. 23.
44. P.C.C., 402 Pakenham.
45. *A Companion from London to Brighthelmston . . .*, by J. Edwards [1801], part 1, section XVII, p. 17.
46. Tithe Map of St. Matthew's District of Lambeth (copy with Tithe Redemption Commissioners).
47. Rate Books of St. Mary, Lambeth, and Land Tax assessments at Newington Sessions House.
48. P.C.C., 238 Lushington.
49. *Holden's Triennial Directory*, 1805–1807.
50. P.C.C., 462 Wynne. There may be a connection between this family and that of Charles Schreiber, husband of Lady Charlotte Schreiber, the collector of ceramics, but none has been found.
51. *A Biographical Dictionary of English Architects 1660–1840*, by H. M. Colvin, 1954, pp. 77–78.
52. *The Merchant and Tradesman's London Directory*, 1787.
53. *A London Directory*, printed for W. Lowndes, 1795, p. 87.
54. *Homes and Haunts of John Ruskin*, by E. T. Cook, 1912, pp. 12–21. Water-colour drawings of both houses are reproduced there.
55. C.C., File 17752.

56. *The History and Antiquities of Lambeth*, by John Tanswell, 1858, p. 121.

57. *Collection illustrative of the Geology, History, Antiquities and Association of Camberwell and the Neighbourhood*, by Douglas Allport, 1841, pp. 208–209.

58. *The Church under the Hill*, by W. Y. Fullerton, N.D., pp. 27, 30–32.

59. *Ibid.*, pp. 38, 49.

60. R.B., and deeds in possession of J. Lyons and Co., Cadby Hall.

61. C.C., File 30376.

62. R.I.B.A. Library, H. S. Goodhart-Rendel's card-index of churches.
Mackeson's *London Church Guide*, 1894–1895.

63. Foundation stone.

64. L.B.C. Minutes July 10, 1902.

65. Tablet in entrance hall.

66. L.B.C. Minutes, July 26, 1906.

67. Deeds of Ruskin Park, L.C.C. Legal and Parliamentary Dept.

68. L.C.C. Minutes, January 29, 1907.

69. *Ibid.*, February 8, 1910.

70. *The Builder*, November 22, 1912, p. 613 *et seq.*

71. *Ibid.*, October 4, 1912, p. 380.

72. *Ibid.*, March 3, 1911, p. 267.

73. Deeds of the hospital in custody of Withers and Co.

74. *The Builder*, August 1, 1913, p. 125.

75. *The Builder*, July 31, 1909, p. 130.

CHAPTER VI (pp. 155–66)

Tulse Hill and Brockwell Park

1. The descent of the Manor (the spelling of whose name varies considerably) has been traced in *V.C.H. Surrey*, vol. IV, p. 59, and is only summarized here.

2. The Lambeth Manor Inclosure Map of 1810, and the Tithe Maps for Brixton and Norwood are the best guides.

3. *Chartulary of the Hospital of St. Thomas the Martyr, Southwark* (Stowe MS. 942), 1932, Nos. 581–593.

4. *Cal. Pat. Rolls* 1350–1354, p. 304.

5. *Cal. Pat. Rolls* 1377–1381, p. 336.

6. St. Thomas' Hospital Deeds, S1/35.

7. *Cal. L. and P. Henry VIII*, 1545, part 2, p. 329.

8. P.R.O., C54/3017.

9. *G.E.C.*

10. P.C.C., 244 Tenison.

11. P.C.C., 179 Browne.

12. P.R.O., CP 43/774 membrane 183.
Ibid., CP 25(2)/1426, 18 Geo. III Mich.
Ibid., CP 25(2)/1476, 17 Geo. III Mich.

13. Lease and Release quoted in the schedule of L.C.C.R.O. Deed C85/1458.

14. Newington Sessions House, Land Tax Books of St. Mary, Lambeth.

15. C.C., Deed 171197, pp. 290–291, 333.

16. P.C.C., 564 Lushington.

17. Brayley, vol. III, part II, p. 379.

18. Amongst the L.C.C. deeds for Brockwell Park is a lease of 1823 which suggests that Blades had already bought part of Winter's land.

19. *Robson's London Commercial Directory*, 1826–27, p. 99.

20. V.M., Dec. 14, 1821; Dec. 20, 1822.

21. *D.N.B.*

22. C.C., File 20549.

23. *Ibid.*, Deed 171201, pp. 130–134.

24. L.C.C.R.O., Deeds C85/1378–1518.

25. Tithe Maps for Brixton and Norwood Districts of Lambeth; copies with Tithe Redemption Commissioners.

26. C.C., Deed 171206, pp. 273–276.

27. Deeds in possession of Messrs. Mole, Rosling and Vernon, London Road, Reigate.

28. Except where otherwise stated, the dates ascribed to houses are based on the Rate Books, Tithe Maps, and architectural evidence.

29. L.C.C.R.O., Deed C85/1497.

30. *Ibid.*, C85/1477.

31. *Ibid.*, C85/1457.

32. *Ibid.*, C85/1453.

33. *Robson's London Directory*, 1828.

34. L.C.C.R.O., Deed C85/1485.

35. *Ibid.*, C85/1486.
P.O.D., 1832, p. 168.

36. L.C.C.R.O., Deed C85/1453.
P.O.D., 1825, p. 258.

37. Deeds in possession of Mr. J. M. P. Price, A.R.I.B.A., 122, Upper Tulse Hill.
P.C.C., 485, 1849.

38. *The Builder*, 1865, p. 252.
P.O.D. 1858, p. 1050.
Ibid., 1861, pp. 861, 1939.

39. *P.O.D.*, 1850, p. 781; 1855, p. 186.

40. Article by John Summerson in *The Architectural Review*, Aug., 1948, p. 65.
The Builder, 1853, p. 444.

41. T.P. Case 38152.

42. L.C.C.R.O., Surveyors' Returns for Streatham and East Brixton, April, 1888, No. 63.

43. L.C.C.R.O., Deed C85/1385.

44. *Ibid.*, C85/1403–1405.
P.O.D., 1846, p. 324.

45. L.C.C.R.O., Deed C85/1401.

46. Deeds of Mr. G. C. Watkins, 166, Tulse Hill.
Robson's London Commercial Directory, 1830.

47. L.C.C.R.O., Deed C85/380.
Robson's Directory, 1838, p. 431.
48. *The Builder*, 1865, p. 108.
P.O. London Suburban Directory, 1868, pp. 700, 831.
49. *The Builder*, 1867, p. 791.
P.O.D., 1858, p. 1066.
Ibid., 1871, p. 941.
50. C.C., File 20470.
51. *Illustrated London News*, May 12, 1855, p. 460.
52. *The Gentleman's Magazine*, 1829, part 2, pp. 476, 653.
There is an illustrated account of Blades' glass-work in *The Repository of Art, Literature, Fashions etc.* by R. Ackerman, third series, vol. 1 (1823), pp. 210–213.
53. *Directories.*
54. *Topographical Surveys through Surrey, Sussex and Kent*, by James Edwards, 1818, p. 41 (copy in John Burns Collection, L.C.C. Members' Library).
55. *Dictionary of Architecture*, issued by The Architectural Publication Society, vol. VI, p. 38.
56. *John B. Papworth, architect to the King of Wurtemburg: a brief record of his life and works, etc.*, 1879, by Wyatt Papworth, p. 61 (copy in R.I.B.A. library).
57. Papworth drawings in R.I.B.A. library.
58. P.C.C., 676 Liverpool.
59. L.C.C. Minutes, Nov. 24, 1908.
60. 51 and 52 Vict., c. 174, local.
61. Brockwell Park Deeds, L.C.C. Legal and Parliamentary Dept.
62. *London Parks and Open Spaces*, 1924, p. 17.
63. L.C.C. pamphlet: *Opening of Brockwell Park Extension*, 1903.
64. L.C.C. Minutes, Nov. 5, 1907.
65. *Ibid.*, Dec. 19, 1919; Nov. 14, 1922.
66. R.B.
67. C.C., Copy Deed 8211.
68. *The Builder*, 1867, pp. 631–632.
69. *The Diamond Jubilee of St. Jude's, Herne Hill, 1868–1928*, ed. by Rev. Brian M. Osborne, p. 6 (copy in L.C.C. Members' Library).
70. *The Builder*, 1868, p. 192.
71. C.C., File 36035.
72. *The Builder*, 1868, p. 828.
73. C.C., File 40068.
74. Osborne, *op. cit.*, p. 11.

CHAPTER VII (pp. 167–87)

Norwood

1. *The life of Samuel Matthews, the Norwood Hermit, etc.*, N.D. (copy in Minet Public Library).
2. *Reminiscences of Norwood*, by Arthur A. Saward, 1907 (copy in Minet Public Library).
3. *Norwood in days of old*, by W. T. Phillips, 1912, pp. 7–11 (copy in Minet Public Library).
4. *Pepys' Diary*, Aug. 11, 1668.
5. *S.A.C.*, vol. XII, part 1, pp. 39–40.
6. In his *Natural History and Antiquities of the County of Surrey*, 1718, vol. 2, p. 33, John Aubrey speaks of the tree in the past tense.
7. *Surrey Record Society*, No. XLIII, p. 161.
8. Lambeth Manor Inclosure Map in custody of L.B.C. Town Clerk.
9. *V.C.H., Surrey*, vol. 4, pp. 96–97.
10. P.R.O., SC 4/bundle 7, no. 6.
11. *V.C.H., Surrey*, vol. 4, p. 58.
12. P.R.O., E318/708.
Ibid., E305/D8.
13. *Ibid.*, E315/105, f. 215.
14. *Ibid.*, E178/92.
15. *Ibid.*, C66/1017 m.2.
16. M.P.L., Deed 5176.
17. *Ibid.*, Deed 5177.
18. *Ibid.*, Deed 5181.
19. *Ibid.*, Deed 5186.
20. *Ibid.*, Deed 5187.
21. *Ibid.*, Deeds 5226, 5227.
22. British Railways (Southern Region) Deeds; abstract of title to land on north side of Sydenham Grove.
23. M.P.L., Deed 5178.
24. *Ibid.*, Deed 5183.
25. *Ibid.*, Deeds 5252, 5253.
26. *Ibid.*, Deeds 5280, 5281.
27. C.C., Deed 171196, pp. 116–118.
28. M.P.L., Deed 5287.
29. *Ibid.*, Deed 5435.
30. Manning and Bray, vol. 3, p. 385.
31. British Railways (Southern Region) Deeds; abstract of title of John Thompson to lands in Streatham.
32. C.C., Deed 171198, pp. 178–181.
33. Manning and Bray, *loc. cit.* The Lambeth Manor Inclosure Map of 1810 states that Lord Thurlow's Trustees held 498 acres of copyhold.
34. *D.N.B.*
35. *The Farington Diary*, ed. J. Greig, N.D., vol. 1, p. 5.
36. P.R.O., C119/97.
37. *The Great North Wood*, etc., by J. Corbet Anderson, 1898, p. 16.
38. P.C.C., 758 Pitt.
39. 49 Geo. III c. 175, local.
40. L.B.C., copy in custody of the Town Clerk.
41. C.C., Deed 171200, pp. 206–211.
P.R.O., C119/97.
42. P.R.O., C119/621.

43. C.C., Deed 171200, pp. 206–211.
44. 5 Geo. IV c. 37, private.
    6 Geo. IV c. 47, private.
45. Tithe Redemption Commissioners, Tithe Map of St. Luke's District of Lambeth.
46. B.M., Maps 137 b. 7(11).
47. C.C., Deed 171205, pp. 581–584.
48. *P.O.D.*, 1860, p. 665.
49. The Story of Norwood, by J. B. Wilson, p. 186 (typescript copy in L.C.C. Members' Library).
    P.O.D., 1860, p. 579.
50. Portobello House is described in B.M., Maps 137, b. 7(13).
51. A note in *Heavenly Mansions*, by John Summerson, 1949, p. 109, first drew attention to this side-light on 19th century building development.
52. *Census of 1861*, vol. I, p. 209.
53. *Census of 1901*, County of London, Table 12, p. 36.
54. *The Builder*, 1857, p. 411.
55. *P.O.D.*, 1828, p. 360.
56. 4 and 5 Vict. c. 35, public.
57. C.C., Deed 171206, pp. 101–107.
58. *Ibid.*, Deed 171206, pp. 153–157.
59. *P.O. London Suburban Directory*, 1868, pp. 619–620. Plasterers, brick-makers, etc., are included in this estimate.
60. *Annual Register*, 1862, pp. 462–472.
    Ibid., 1863, p. 266.
    The Electoral History of the Borough of Lambeth, by George Hill, 1879, pp. 128–156.
61. *The Builder*, 1867, p. 438.
62. *Ibid.*, 1871, p. 75.
63. C.C., Deed 171208, p. 287.
64. *The Builder*, 1865, p. 415.
65. C.C., File 18135.
66. V. M. March 5, 1819.
67. *Ibid.*, June 24, 1822.
68. C.C., Church Building Commissioners' Minutes, June 18, 1822.
69. *Ibid.*, April 8, 1823.
70. *Robson's London Commercial Directories*, 1821–1826.
71. *Survey of London*, vol. xxv, pp. 96 (note), 109.
72. C.C., Church Building Commissioners' Minutes, Dec. 14, 1824.
73. *Ibid.*, June 7, 1825.
74. C.C., File 39636.
75. *Ibid.*, File 31919.
76. *The Builder*, 1867, p. 455.
77. R.I.B.A. Library, H. S. Goodhart-Rendel's card-index of churches.
78. C.C., File 35399.
79. *The Builder*, July 17, 1886, p. 90.
80. Information supplied by the vicar.
81. C.C., File 46838.
82. Foundation stone.
83. Mackeson's *London Church Guide*, 1894–1895.
84. C.C., File 73686.
    M.B.W. Case 28635.
85. C.C., File 67849.
86. *Ibid.*, File 73613.
87. *Ibid.*, File 20470.
88. Information supplied by the Rev. Alfred Cole and Mr. D. Plaskett Marshall.
    T.P. Case 3353.
89. P.R.O., C54/10051 No. 4.
90. Wilson, *op. cit.*, pp. 188–190.
91. *The Story of Congregationalism in Surrey*, by E. E. Cleal and T. G. Crippen, 1908, pp. 297–298.
92. Information supplied by the Secretary for the Trustees.
93. Deed with London Baptist Property Board.
    The Baptist Churches of Surrey, ed. A. H. Stockwell, N.D., pp. 149–153.
    Baptist Handbook, 1902, p. 377.
94. *The Story of Methodism in Brixton*, 1924, p. 30 (copy at Epworth House Library).
95. *Wesleyan Methodism in the Brixton Hill Circuit*, 1898, pp. 38–39 (copy at Epworth House Library).
96. Deed with London Baptist Property Board.
    Stockwell, *op. cit.*, pp. 140–142.
97. B.A. Case 14438.
98. *House of Commons Papers. Reports from Commissioners*, vol. xxi, p. 577 *et seq.* Report on a general scheme of Extra-Mural Sepulture.
99. 6 and 7 William IV c. 129, local.
100. C.C., Deed 171205, pp. 49–51, 69–73.
101. Wilson, *op. cit.*, p. 34.
102. T.P. Case 10474.
103. Information supplied by the Secretary of the Company.
104. *The Greek Orthodox Church in London*, by Michael Constantinides, 1933, pp. 144–145.
    Information supplied by the Secretary of the Greek Cathedral, Moscow Road, W.2.
105. Information supplied by Professor Hector O. Corfiato, F.R.I.B.A., F.S.A.
106. *Memoir of George Edmund Street, R.A.*, by A. E. Street, 1888, p. 299.
107. Wilson, *op. cit.*, p. 36.
108. *Ibid.*, pp. 36–37.
109. 10 and 11 Vict. c. 65, public.
110. 13 and 14 Vict. c. 52, public.
111. 15 and 16 Vict. c. 85, public.
112. Ch.C., vol. IV, p. 590.
113. L.S.B. Minutes, Jan. 15, 1879.
114. L.C.C. Architect's plans.
115. *L.C.C. Elementary Day Schools.* Report of the Education Committee, 1905.
116. L.S.B. Minutes, Aug. 6, 1885.

117. *Ibid.*, July 18, 1895; Oct. 8, 1896.
118. *Ibid.*, Oct. 11, Dec. 13, 1894; March 17, 1895; Jan. 28, 1897; March 10, 1898.
119. L.C.C.R.O., B. G., June 19, 1849.
120. *Ibid.*, Norwood Nursery Committee Minutes, Aug. 21, 1810.
121. V. M., March 29, 1820; Oct. 29, 1824; April 10, 1828; Dec. 18, 1834.
122. L.C.C.R.O., B.G., Jan. 12, 1836.
123. *Ibid.*, Aug. 29, 1837.
124. *Ibid.*, Feb. 20, 1849.
125. *Ibid.*, May 29, 1849.
126. *Ibid.*, Aug. 16, 1882; Jan. 17, April 11, June 20, 1883.
127. P.R.O., C54/14369 No. 1.
128. B.A. Case 13240.
129. P.R.O., C54/16004 No. 13.
130. T.E.B. Minutes, Dec. 17, 1894; May 6, 1895; Oct. 28, 1901; July 21, 1902.
131. Information supplied by the Secretary.
132. P.R.O., C54/15384 No. 7. *Ibid.*, C54/15551 No. 16.
133. *The Builder*, 1862, pp. 514–515.
134. *Ibid.*, 1862, p. 450.
135. *Ibid.*, 1874, p. 20.
136. J. Corbet Anderson, *op. cit.*, pp. 19–20.
137. *The Corporation of Wardens of the Parish of St. Saviour, Southwark*, by R. T. Baines and L. M. Langston, 1912, pp. 15–16. (An account of some of the almshouses will be found in the *Survey of London*, vol. XXII, p. 83).
138. B.A. Case 31442.
139. J. Corbet Anderson, *op. cit.*, pp. 17–19.
140. *The Builder*, June 16, 1894, p. 467.
141. *Lambeth Official Guide*, N.D., p. 183.
142. Lambeth Public Library Local Collection.
143. B.A. Case 76361.
144. *Ibid.*, 13713.
145. Information supplied by the Secretary of the Peabody Donation Fund.
146. B.A., Case 17092.
147. P.R.O., C119/97/15.
148. C.C., Deed 171204, pp. 531–533.
149. *Ibid.*, Deed 171205, pp. 46–47.
150. *Ibid.*, Deed 171201, pp. 111–113.
151. *Ibid.*, Deed 171205, pp. 587–590.
152. *Ibid.*, Deed 171200, p. 114.
153. *Ibid.*, Deed 171200, p. 220.
154. *Ibid.*, Deed 171204, pp. 323–327.
155. *Ibid.*, Deed, 171205, pp. 604–607.
156. *Kelly's London Suburban Directory*, 1884, 1896.
157. Information supplied by the Chief Architect and Surveyor to the Metropolitan Police.
158. Information supplied by the Civil Engineer, British Railways (Southern Region).
159. Norwood Park Deeds, L.C.C. Legal and Parliamentary Dept.
160. L.C.C. Minutes, Nov. 24, 1908.
161. *London Parks and Open Spaces*, 1924, p. 60.

Index

NOTE

References to certain individuals or firms should be sought under the following main entries: (1) Architects, surveyors and engineers; (2) Artists and craftsmen; (3) Builders and allied tradesmen.

P*

PLATES

a. VAUXHALL BRIDGE, 1816. Sir Samuel Bentham and James Walker, engineers (p. 78)

b. VAUXHALL BRIDGE, 1906. Sir Alexander Binnie and Maurice Fitzmaurice, engineers. W. E. Riley, architect (p. 78)

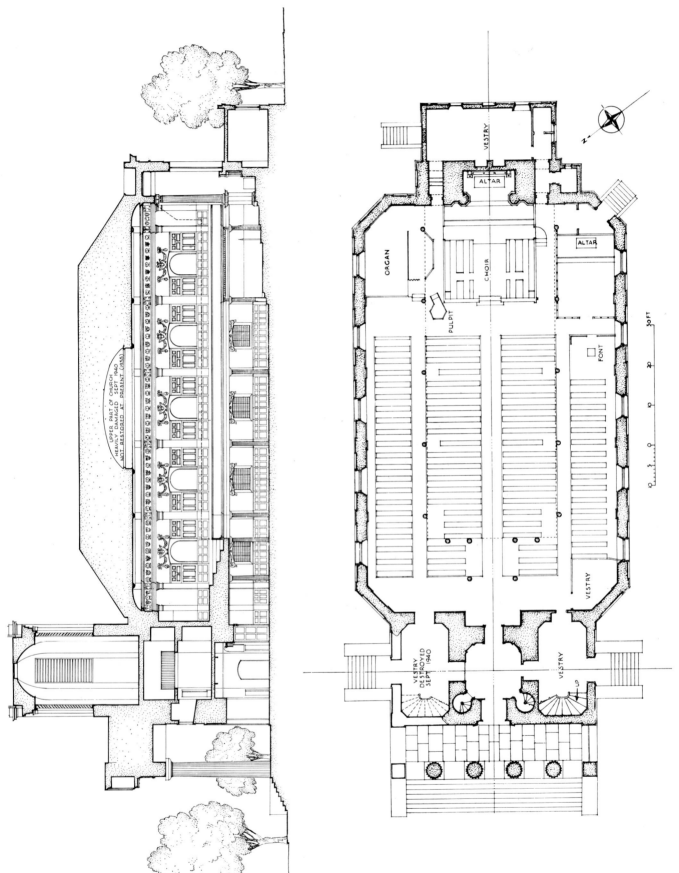

UPPER PART OF CHURCH
HEAVILY DAMAGED SEPT 1940
NOT RESTORED AT PRESENT (1955)

VESTRY

ALTAR

ORGAN

PULPIT

CHOIR

ALTAR

FONT

VESTRY

VESTRY
DESTROYED
SEPT 1940

VESTRY

UP

N

30 FT

St. Mark's, Kennington, 1822–4. D. R. Roper, architect (p. 31). Longitudinal section and ground floor plan

3

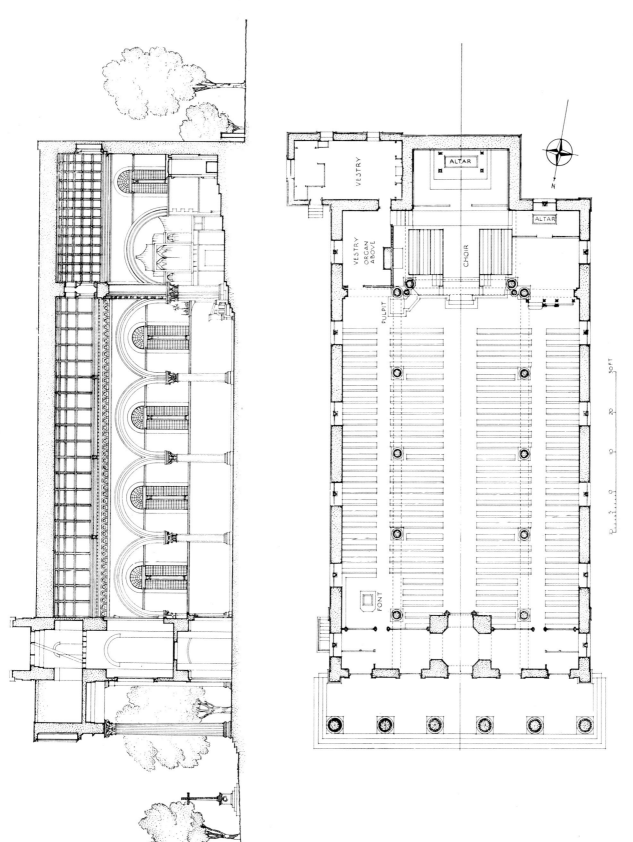

ST. LUKE'S, WEST NORWOOD, 1822–5. Francis Bedford, architect (p. 173). Longitudinal section and ground floor plan

Within the plan: VESTRY, ALTAR, VESTRY ORGAN ABOVE, ALTAR, CHOIR, PULPIT, FONT, N, 30FT

4

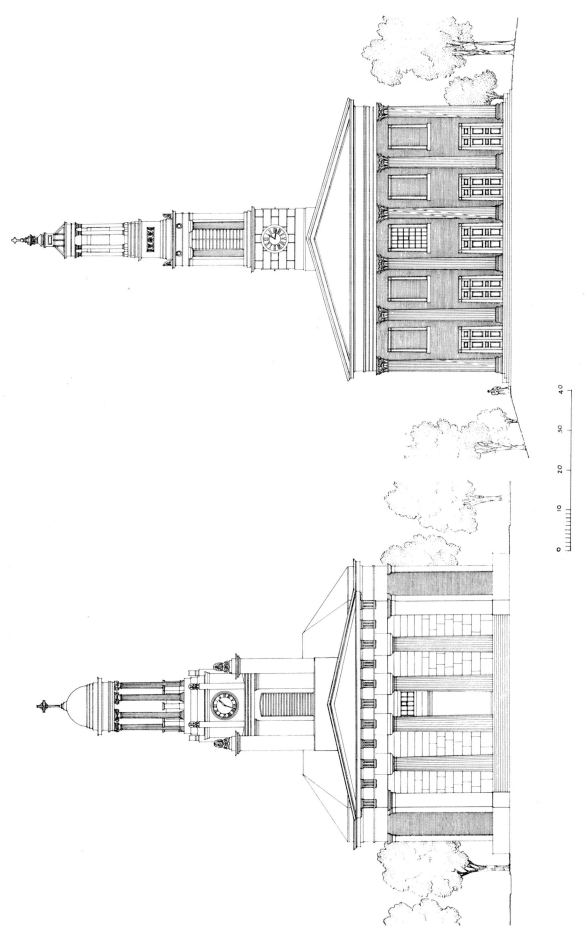

a. St. Mark's, Kennington, 1822–4. D. R. Roper, architect (p. 31).
North-west elevation

b. St. Luke's, West Norwood, 1822–5. Francis Bedford, architect (p. 173).
North elevation

5

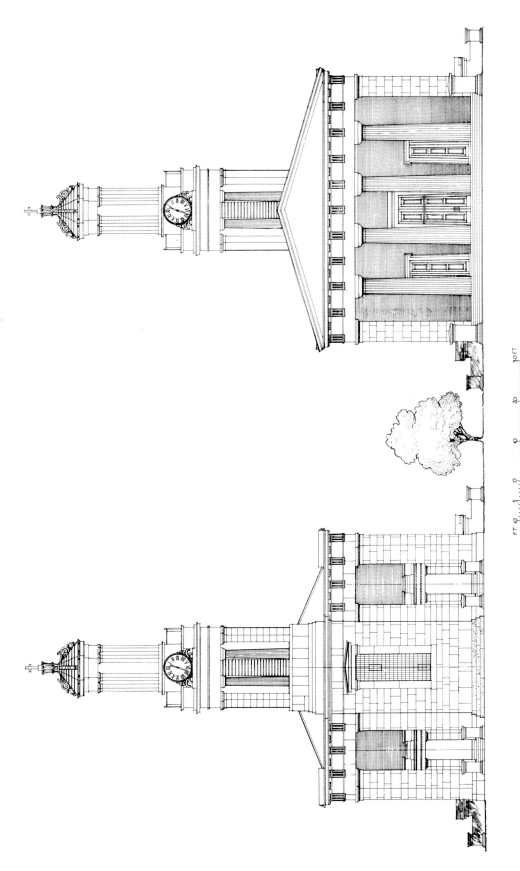

a. East elevation

b. West elevation

St. Matthew's, Brixton, 1822–4. C. F. Porden, architect (p. 132)

FT 0 5 10 20 30FT

6

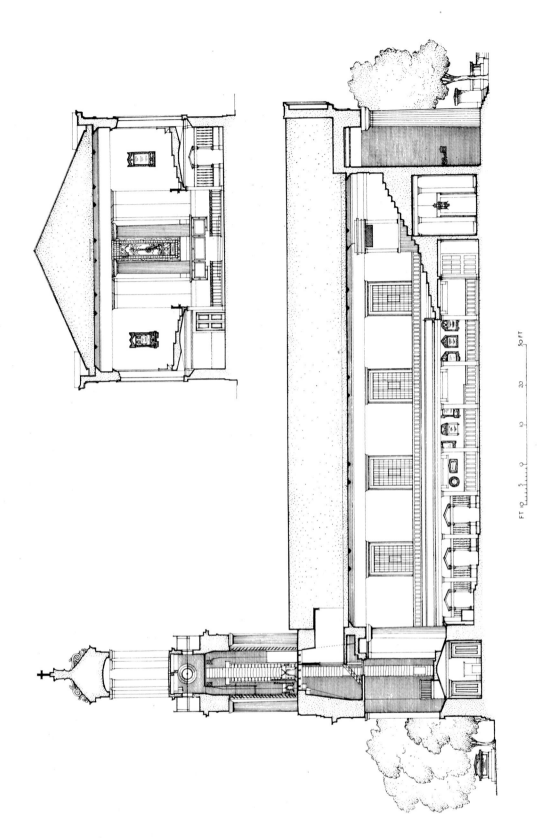

St. Matthew's, Brixton, 1822–4. C. F. Porden, architect (p. 132). Longitudinal section and cross section looking east

FT 10 5 0   10   20   30 FT

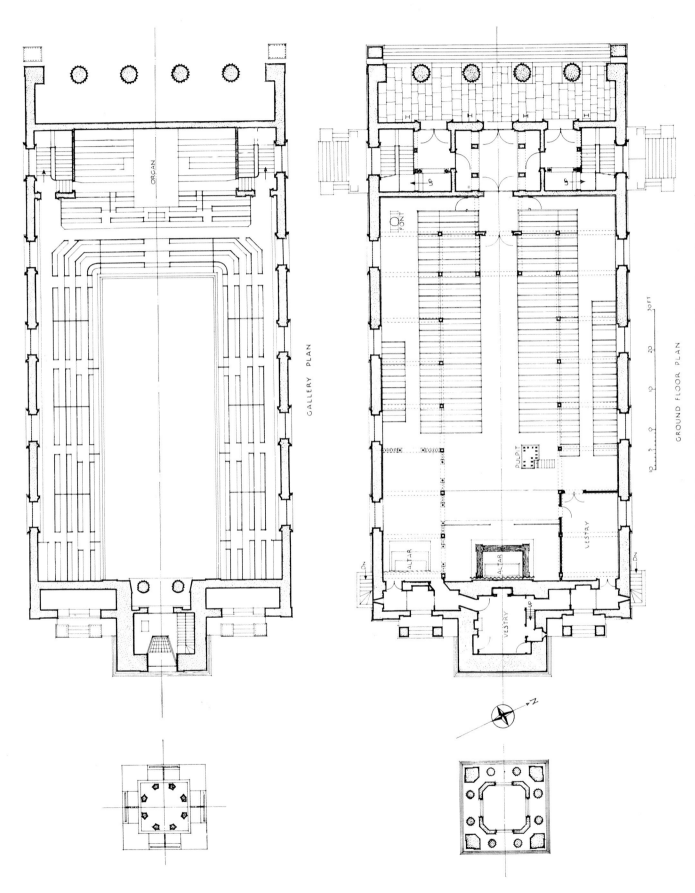

GALLERY PLAN

ORGAN

GROUND FLOOR PLAN

FONT

PULPIT

ALTAR

ALTAR

VESTRY

VESTRY

30 FT

20

St. Matthew's, Brixton, 1822–4. C. F. Porden, architect (p. 132). Ground floor plan and gallery plan

8

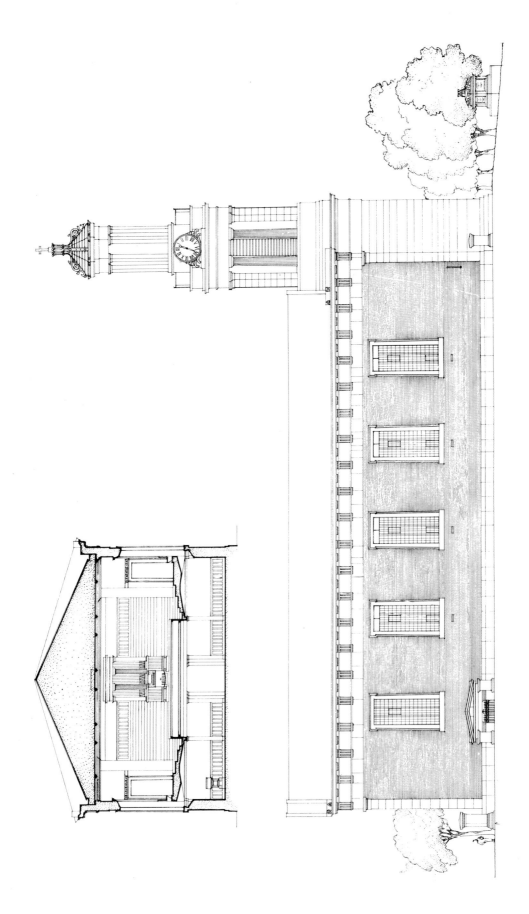

St. Matthew's, Brixton, 1822–4. C. F. Porden, architect (p. 132). South elevation and cross section looking west

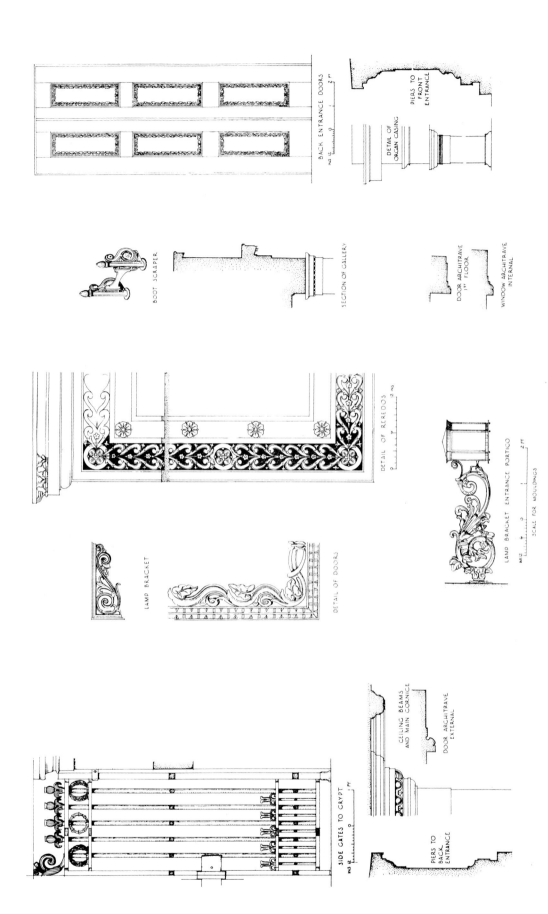

ST. MATTHEW'S, BRIXTON, 1822–4. C. F. Porden, architect (p. 132). Details

10

b. Interior, looking south

St. Luke's, West Norwood, 1822–5. Francis Bedford, architect (p. 173)

a. North front

11

b. St. Matthew's, Brixton, 1822–4. C. F. Porden, architect (p. 132)

South-east view

a. St. Mark's, Kennington, 1822–4. D. R. Roper, architect (p. 31)

North-west front

a. West front

b. Interior, looking east

St. Matthew's, Brixton, 1822–4. C. F. Porden, architect (p. 132)

a. Stockwell Chapel, erected *c.* 1767. Re-modelled 1867 (p. 93)

b. St. Andrew's, Stockwell Green. H. E. Coe, architect for re-modelling in 1867 (p. 93)

c. South Lambeth Chapel, erected 1793. Consecrated as St. Anne's, 1869 (p. 71)

d. St. Anne's, South Lambeth Road, rebuilt 1876. R. Parkinson, architect (p. 71)

a. St. Michael's, Stockwell Park Road, consecrated 1841. William Rogers, architect (p. 89)

b. St. Matthew's, Denmark Hill, consecrated 1848. A. D. Gough, architect (p. 151)

c. Holy Trinity, Trinity Rise, consecrated 1856. T. D. Barry, architect (p. 160)

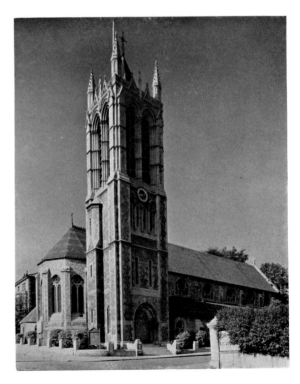

d. Christ Church, Gipsy Hill, consecrated 1867. John Giles, architect (p. 174)

15

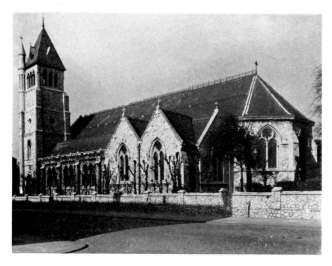

a. St. Saviour's, Herne Hill Road, consecrated 1867.
A. D. Gough, architect (p. 152)

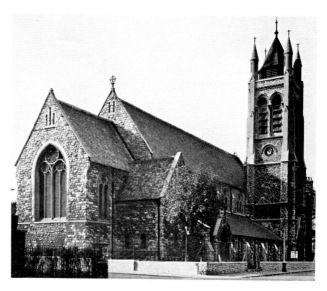

b. St. Saviour's, Lambert Road, consecrated 1875.
E. C. Robins, architect (p. 102)

c. St. Stephen's Church, St. Stephen's Terrace,
consecrated 1861. John Barnett, architect (p. 63)

d. St. John the Evangelist, Guernsey Grove, dedicated
1912. Leonard Martin, architect (p. 178)

16

St. John's, Angell Town, consecrated 1853. Benjamin Ferrey, architect (p. 129)

a. East front

b. Interior, looking west

Christ Church, Brixton Road, consecrated 1902. Beresford Pite, architect (p. 118)

18

a. North elevation

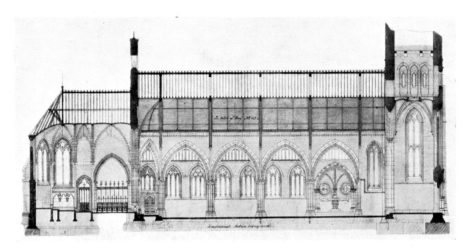

b. Longitudinal section

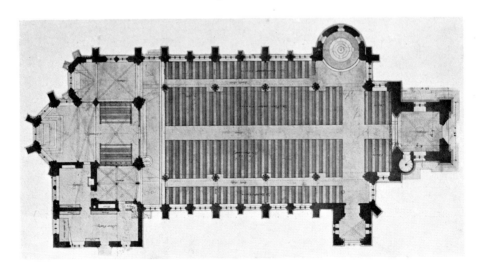

c. Ground floor plan

ST. JOHN THE DIVINE, VASSALL ROAD, 1871–4, tower and spire 1888–9.
G. E. Street, architect (p. 119)

b. Interior, looking east

a. Tower and spire from the south

St. John the Divine, Vassall Road, 1871–4, tower and spire 1888–9. G. E. Street, architect (p. 119)

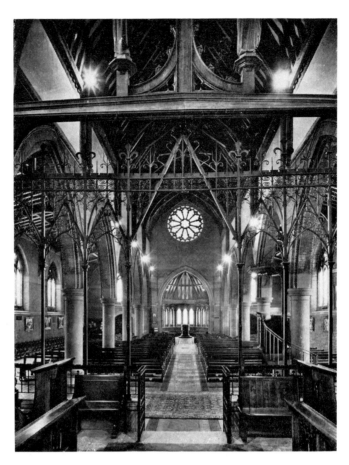

a. Interior, looking west

b. Baptistery and south side

St. Peter's, Leigham Court Road, east end 1870, Richard Drew, architect; west end 1886–7, G. H. Fellowes Prynne, architect (p. 175)

a. Interior, looking east

b. North-east view

ALL SAINTS', ROSENDALE ROAD, 1888–91. G. H. Fellowes Prynne, architect (p. 177)

b. Interior, looking east

a. South-east view

CORPUS CHRISTI ROMAN CATHOLIC CHURCH, Trent Road, 1886–7, transepts 1904. J. F. Bentley, architect (p. 100)

23

b. Reredos

a. North transept and aisle

CORPUS CHRISTI ROMAN CATHOLIC CHURCH, Trent Road, 1886–7, transepts 1904. J. F. Bentley, architect (p. 100)

24

b. Interior, looking south

a. Tower and north front

St. Anne's Roman Catholic Church, Kennington Lane, 1900–3, tower 1906–7. F. A. Walters, architect (p. 39)

b. CLAYLANDS CONGREGATIONAL CHURCH, Claylands Road, 1836 (p. 61)

a. TRINITY CONGREGATIONAL CHURCH, St. Matthew's Road, 1828 (p. 135)

a. CHAPEL ROAD CONGREGATIONAL CHURCH, 1819–21 (p. 179)

b. TRINITY PRESBYTERIAN CHURCH, Clapham Road, 1862. W. G. Habershon and
A. R. Pite, architects (p. 83)

a. M<small>OSTYN</small> R<small>OAD</small> M<small>ETHODIST</small> C<small>HURCH</small>, 1868.
John Tarring, architect (p. 125)

b. R<small>OUPELL</small> P<small>ARK</small> M<small>ETHODIST</small> C<small>HURCH</small>, Norwood Road,
1879–80. Charles Bell, architect (p. 180)

c. R<small>AILTON</small> R<small>OAD</small> M<small>ETHODIST</small> C<small>HURCH</small>, 1874.
R. Cable, architect (p. 137)

d. O<small>UR</small> L<small>ADY OF THE</small> R<small>OSARY</small> R<small>OMAN</small> C<small>ATHOLIC</small> C<small>HURCH</small>,
formerly Brixton Independent Church, 1870.
A. J. Phelps, architect (p. 130)

a. CHURCH OF ENGLAND MORTUARY CHAPEL, NORWOOD CEMETERY, *c.* 1837. William Tite, architect (p. 180)

b. GREEK MORTUARY CHAPEL, NORWOOD CEMETERY, *c.* 1872 (?)
John Oldrid Scott, architect (p. 181)

a. Family vault of George Dodd.
Thomas Allom, architect

b. Family vault of Henry Tate

c. Monument to J. W. Gilbart

d. Ralli family vault. G. E. Street, architect

MONUMENTS IN NORWOOD CEMETERY

a. Caron's Almshouses, Wandsworth Road, 1618. Demolished *c.* 1853 (p. 68)

b. Caron's Almshouses, Fentiman Road, 1854 (p. 68)

a. TRINITY HOMES, ACRE LANE, 1822. Bailey and Willshire, surveyors (p. 98)

b. GRESHAM'S ALMSHOUSES, FERNDALE ROAD, 1882. G. B. Williams, architect (p. 96)

a. JEWISH ORPHANAGE, WEST NORWOOD, 1861. Tillott and Chamberlain, architects (p. 183)

b. SPURGEON'S HOMES, CLAPHAM ROAD, general view (p. 85)

a. Licensed Victuallers' School, Kennington Lane, demolished *c*. 1836 (p. 43)

b. Imperial Court, formerly Licensed Victuallers' School, Kennington Lane, 1836.
Henry Rose, architect (p. 43)

a. St. Mark's Primary School, Harleyford Road, 1824–5. J. Bailey, architect (p. 25)

b. St. Luke's Primary School, Elder Road, 1825 (p. 181)

c. St. John's Primary School, Canterbury Crescent, 1853.
Benjamin Ferrey, architect (p. 129)

a. St. Jude's Primary School, Railton Road, 1834 (p. 137)

b. Kennington Manor Secondary School, Kennington Road, 1897 and 1900.
T. J. Bailey, architect (p. 48)

a. Vestry Hall, Kennington Road, 1853. Willshire and Parris, architects (p. 29)

b. Lambeth Town Hall, 1906–8. Septimus Warwick and
Herbert Austen Hall, architects (p. 100)

a. TREADMILL, BRIXTON HOUSE OF CORRECTION, 1821. William Cubitt, engineer (p. 104)

b. TOLL-HOUSE, KENNINGTON COMMON (p. 33)

38

b. Durning Free Public Library, Kennington Lane, 1889.
Sidney R. J. Smith, architect (p. 51)

a. No. 10 Gipsy Hill, formerly Gipsy Hill Police Station, 1854.
Charles Reeves, architect (p. 187)

39

a. Herne Hill Station, *c.* 1863 (p. 152)

c. Railway bridge, Rosendale Road, 1869 (p. 187)

b. Knight's Hill tunnel, 1868 (p. 187)

d. Railway bridge, Rosendale Road, 1868 (p. 187)

40

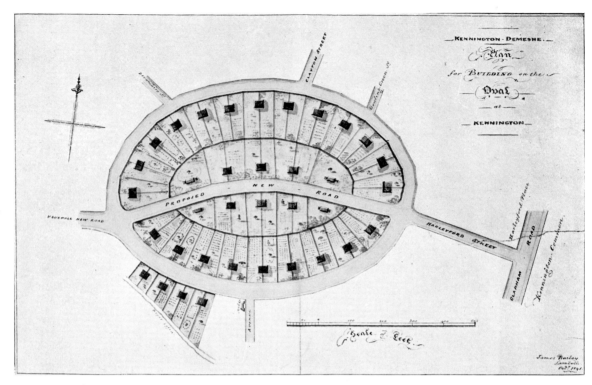

a. PLAN BY JAMES BAILEY FOR BUILDING ON KENNINGTON OVAL, 1841 (p. 22)

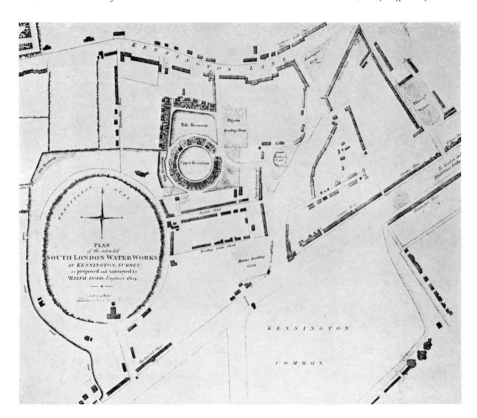

b. PLAN OF KENNINGTON OVAL AND PROPOSED SOUTH LONDON WATERWORKS, 1804 (p. 42)

a. Kennington Oval, 1858 (p. 23)

b. The Pavilion, Kennington Oval, 1895–7. Thomas Muirhead, architect (p. 24)

42

b. Caron Place

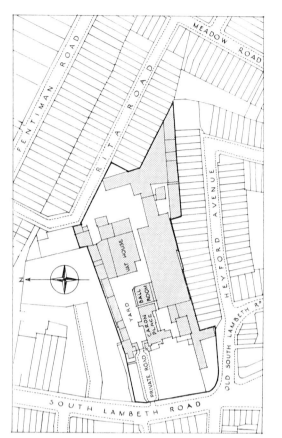

d. Site plan

a. Entrance gates, formerly at the Royal Exchange

c. Ball-room and vat house

No. 87 SOUTH LAMBETH ROAD (p. 69)

43

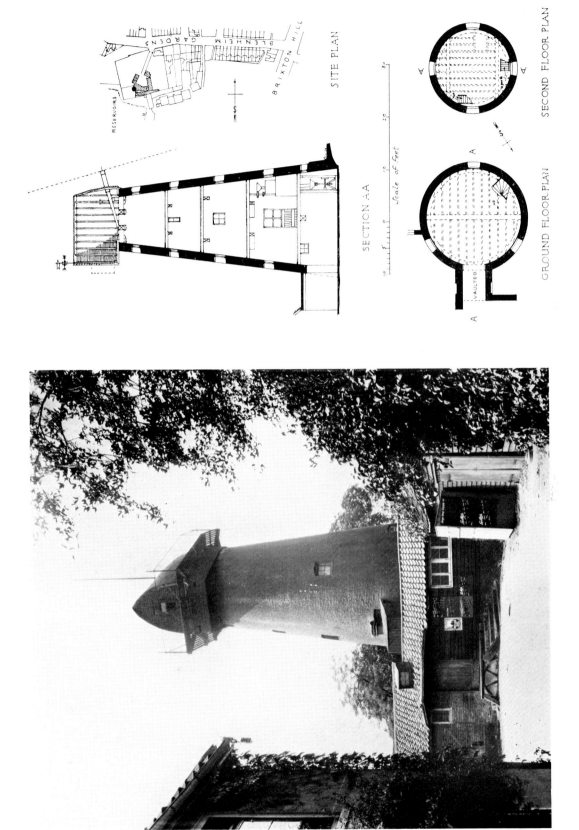

SITE PLAN

BLENHEIM GARDENS

BRIXTON HILL

RESERVOIRS

SECTION AA

Scale of feet

SECOND FLOOR PLAN

GROUND FLOOR PLAN

VAULTED

WINDMILL, BLENHEIM GARDENS, 1816–17 (p. 103)

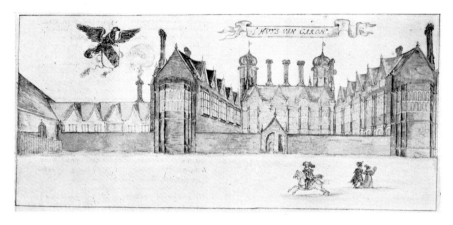

a. CARON HOUSE, demolished 1683–5 (p. 66)

b. THE TRADESCANTS' HOUSE (left) and ASHMOLE'S HOUSE (right).
Demolished *c*. 1880 (p. 74)

c. KNIGHT'S HILL, 1792–5. Henry Holland, architect, finished by Samuel Wyatt.
Demolished 1810 (p. 169)

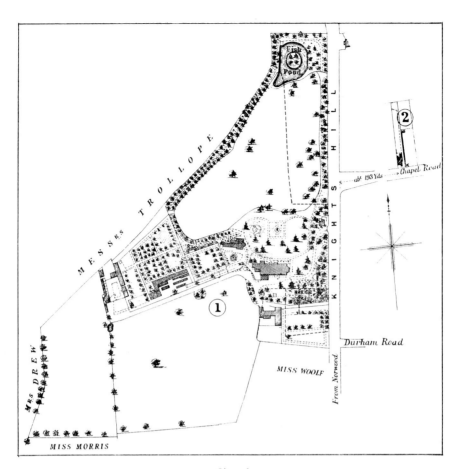

a. Site plan

b. Garden front

ST. JOHN'S LODGE, KNIGHT'S HILL, WEST NORWOOD, *c.* 1840, demolished *c.* 1884
(p. 170)

a. Nos. 26–41 Cleaver Square. Nos. 26–33 (right), 1844–53, William Rogers, architect (p. 51)

b. Nos. 284–300 South Lambeth Road, 1790–1. Built by William Head, builder, and Joseph Greated, carpenter (p. 76)

a. Grove Place, Brixton Road

b. Nos. 206–220 Brixton Road

Houses on the Jackson estate, Brixton Road (p. 122)

a. Nos. 9–21 COWLEY ROAD, 1824. Lessee, James Crundall, timber merchant
(p. 115)

b. Nos. 117–31 BRIXTON ROAD, 1823. Lessee, James Crundall, timber merchant
(p. 111)

c. Nos. 37–61 HILLYARD STREET, 1822. Lessee, James Crundall,
timber merchant (p. 111)

a. Nos. 152–60 Brixton Road, 1828. Lessees, Robert Stevens and William Thorowgood (p. 112)

b. Nos. 341–61 Brixton Road, 1855–68. Built by James Barker, builder (p. 129)

c. Methley Street, 1868. Alfred Lovejoy, architect (p. 49)

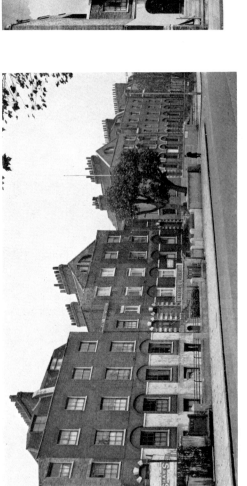

b. Nos. 91–103 Brixton Road, 1823. Lessee, Thomas Hill (p. 111)

d. Nos. 15–23 Albert Square, 1846. Lessee, John Glenn, builder (p. 62)

a. Nos. 116–32 Kennington Park Road, 1788. Lessees, William Ingle, builder, and associates (p. 52)

c. Nos. 194–8 Clapham Road, 1822. Lessee, Richard Howard, carpenter and builder (p. 75)

51

b. Nos. 32–8 Foxley Road, 1824. Lessee, N. P. Rothery (p. 113)

d. Nos. 1–8 Stockwell Terrace, *c.* 1843. Built by John Notley, builder (p. 62)

a. Nos. 309–13 Brixton Road, *c.* 1800 (p. 127)

c. Lansdowne Gardens, *c.* 1843. Lessee, John Snell, builder (p. 63)

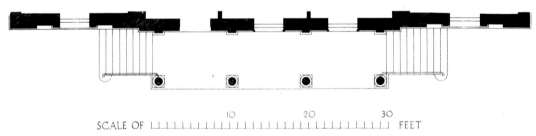

SCALE OF |⌐ı ¬| FEET

No. 154 DENMARK HILL, 1785–6. William Blackburn, architect (p. 146).
The south wing is now demolished

No. 154 Denmark Hill, 1785–6. William Blackburn, architect (p. 146)

54

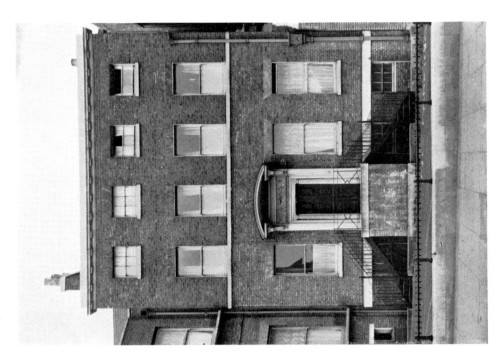

b. No. 150 Denmark Hill, 1785–6 (p. 146)

a. No 152 Denmark Hill, 1787–8 (p. 146)

55

a. Nos. 171–3 Clapham Road, 1802–3 (p. 84)

b. Nos. 205–7 Brixton Road, 1823. Lessees, W. and T. Cox, paper stainers (p. 112)

c. No. 112 Brixton Road, 1821. Lessee, William Bird, builder (p. 112)

d. No. 189 Camberwell New Road, 1833 (p. 145)

a. Nos. 27–33, 37–9 Lorn Road, *c*. 1840 (p. 124)

b. Nos. 2–8 Lorn Road, *c*. 1840 (p. 124)

a. No. 44 STOCKWELL PARK ROAD, 1840–1. Probably built by John Notley, builder (p. 88)

b. Nos. 2–4 STOCKWELL PARK CRESCENT, 1840–1. Probably built by John Notley, builder (p. 88)

58

b. No. 109 CLIVE ROAD, 1882. First occupier, Ralph Gardiner, plasterer (p. 187)

a. No. 45 GUILDFORD ROAD, *c.* 1844. Lessee, H. J. Lightly (p. 63)

59

b. No. 92 Upper Tulse Hill, 1822. Lessee, S. D. Guthrie (p. 157)

a. Nos. 155–63 Brixton Hill, 1820 (p. 139)

60

a. Nos. 58–62 Brixton Water Lane, 1816–23 (p. 165)

b. No. 108 Upper Tulse Hill, 1830. Lessee, D. W. Davidson, solicitor (p. 157)

a. No. 122 UPPER TULSE HILL, 1841. Lessee, W. White, hat manufacturer (p. 159)

b. No. 100 UPPER TULSE HILL, 1824. Lessee, W. Andrews (p. 157)

b. No. 155 TULSE HILL, 1856–7 (p. 159)

a. No. 148 TULSE HILL, 1843 (p. 160)

63

b. No. 157 Tulse Hill, 1888. W. Rowe, builder (p. 160)

a. No. 107 Tulse Hill, 1865. Charles Hambridge, architect (p. 159)

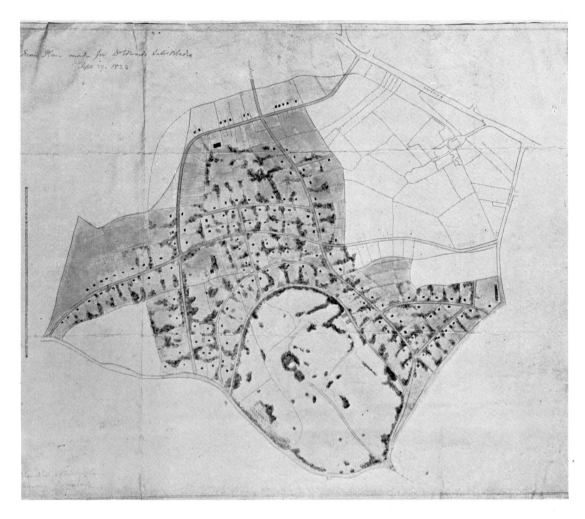

PROPOSED LAY-OUT FOR THE TULSE HILL AND BROCKWELL ESTATES, 1823 (p. 155)

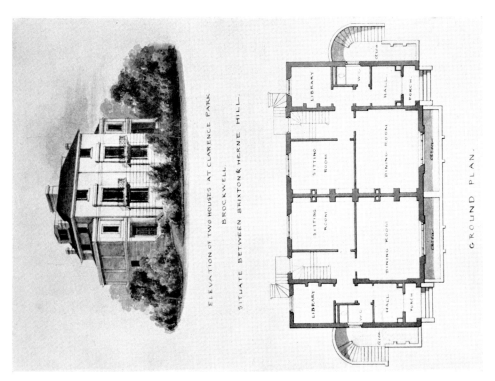

b. BROCKWELL TERRACE, 1828. J. B. Papworth, architect.
Demolished 1908 (p. 164)

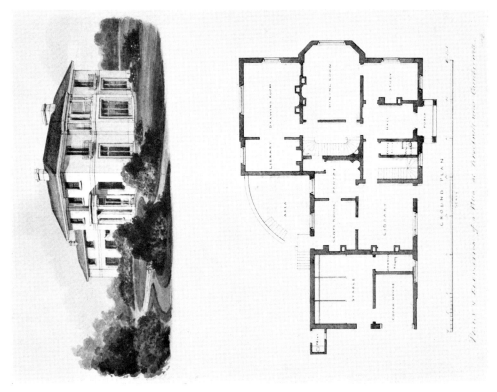

a. BROCKWELL (OR CLARENCE) LODGE, 1825–6. J. B. Papworth, architect.
Main block now demolished (p. 164)

a. South-east elevation

b. North-west elevation

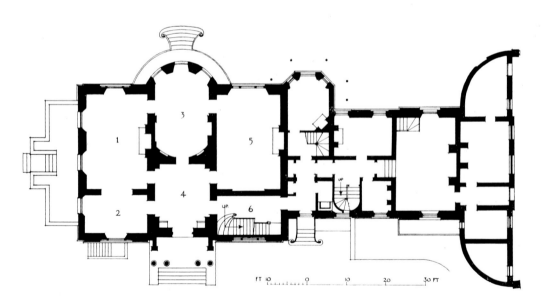

c. Plan. The numbers on the plan denote the position of the details in fig. 54

BROCKWELL HALL, 1811–13. D. R. Roper, architect (p. 161)

a. North view

b. South view

BROCKWELL HALL, 1811–13. D. R. Roper, architect (p. 161)

a. No. 350 Kennington Road, 1804–5 (p. 45)

b. No. 167 Clapham Road, *c.* 1807 (p. 84)

c. No. 179 Brixton Road, 1821 (p. 111)

d. No. 121 Brixton Road, 1823 (p. 111)

DOORCASES

69

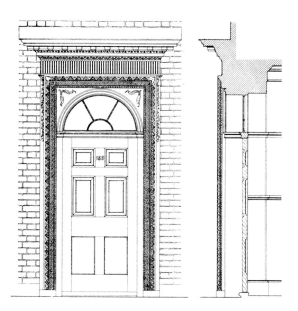

a. No. 155 Kennington Lane, 1776–80 (p. 27)

b. No. 150 Denmark Hill, 1785–6 (p. 146)

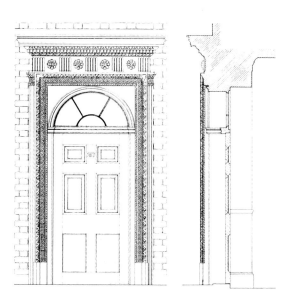

c. No. 157 Kennington Lane, 1776–80 (p. 27)

d. No. 30 Wandsworth Road, semi-circular porch (p. 78)

DOORCASES

70

c. No. 57 South Lambeth Road (p. 69)

f. No. 274 South Lambeth Road (p. 73)

b. No. 57 South Lambeth Road (p. 69)

e. No. 350 Kennington Road (p. 45)

a. No. 57 South Lambeth Road (p. 69)

d. No. 274 South Lambeth Road (p. 73)

KEYSTONES

71

b. Statue of Henry Fawcett, Vauxhall Park, 1893. Modelled by George Tinworth (p. 68)

a. Budd memorial, St. Matthew's churchyard, 1830. Designed by R. Day (p. 134)

a. Plan. The stippling denotes the area where building was proscribed by the Act of 1806

c. East side of Brixton Hill in 1938, showing encroachments

b. No. 95 Brixton Hill

RUSH COMMON AREA (p. 131)

a. Prince Consort's Model Lodge, Kennington Park, 1851–2.
Henry Roberts, architect (p. 34)

b. Peabody Buildings, Rosendale Road, 1901.
William Cubitt and Co., architects (p. 185)

c. Nos. 23–9 Dunbar Street, erected by the Lower Norwood
Co-operative Building Company, 1865 (p. 173)

d. Houses in Milkwood Road, 1869–72.
W. G. Habershon and A. R. Pite, architects (p. 138)

Working Class Housing

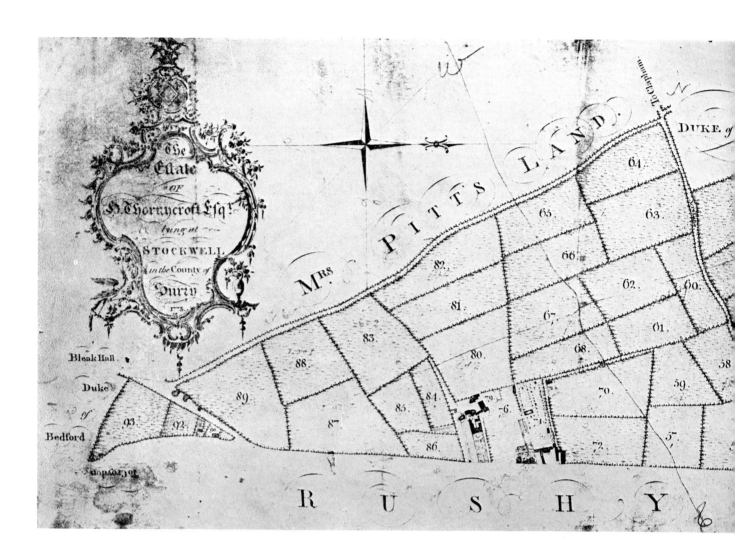

STOCKWELL MANOR IN 1773

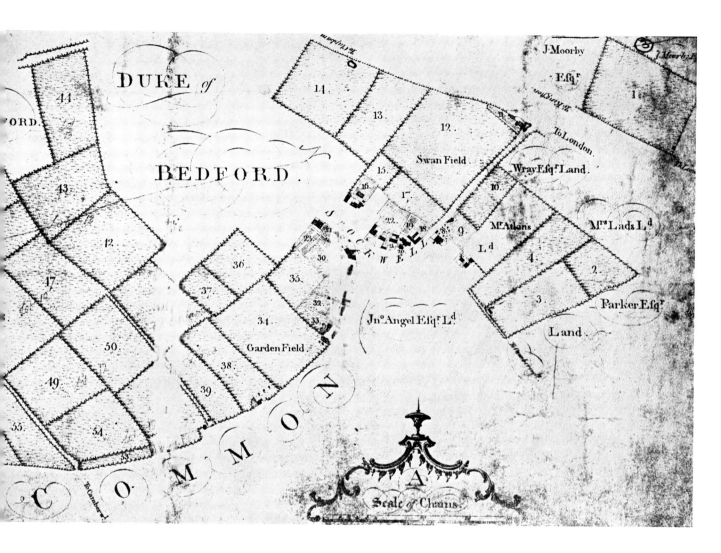

STOCKWELL MANOR IN 1773